ENGLISH
FOR EVERYONE
PRACTICE BOOK
LEVEL **3** INTERMEDIATE

FREE AUDIO
website and app
www.dkefe.com

Author

Barbara MacKay is an experienced English-language teacher and author. She has written for major English-language publishers including Oxford University Press and Macmillan Education.

Course consultant

Tim Bowen has taught English and trained teachers in more than 30 countries worldwide. He is the co-author of works on pronunciation teaching and language-teaching methodology, and author of numerous books for English-language teachers. He is currently a freelance materials writer, editor, and translator. He is a member of the Chartered Institute of Linguists.

Language consultant

Professor Susan Barduhn is an experienced English-language teacher, teacher trainer, and author, who has contributed to numerous publications. In addition to directing English-language courses in at least four different continents, she has been President of the International Association of Teachers of English as a Foreign Language, and an adviser to the British Council and the US State Department. She is currently a Professor at the School for International Training in Vermont, USA.

ENGLISH
FOR EVERYONE

PRACTICE BOOK
LEVEL ❸ INTERMEDIATE

SECOND EDITION
Senior Editor Ankita Awasthi Tröger
Editor Elizabeth Blakemore
Art Editor Amy Child
Managing Editor Carine Tracanelli
Managing Art Editor Sarah Corcoran
Production Editor Robert Dunn
Senior Production Controller Meskerem Berhane
Publisher Sarah Forbes
Managing Director Hilary Fine

DK INDIA
Senior Jacket Designer Suhita Dharamjit
Project Jacket Designer Juhi Sheth
Senior Jackets Coordinator Priyanka Sharma Saddi
DTP Designer Rakesh Kumar

FIRST EDITION
Editorial Assistants Jessica Cawthra, Sarah Edwards
Illustrators Edwood Burn, Denise Joos, Michael Parkin, Jemma Westing
Audio Producer Liz Hammond
Managing Editor Daniel Mills
Managing Art Editor Anna Hall
Project Manager Christine Stroyan
Producer, Pre-Production Luca Frassinetti
Producer Mary Slater
Jacket Designer Natalie Godwin
Jacket Editor Claire Gell
Jacket Design Development Manager Sophia MTT
Publisher Andrew Macintyre
Art Director Karen Self
Publishing Director Jonathan Metcalf

DK INDIA
Senior Editors Vineetha Mokkil, Anita Kakar
Senior Art Editor Chhaya Sajwan
Project Editor Antara Moitra
Editors Agnibesh Das, Nisha Shaw, Seetha Natesh
Art Editors Namita, Heena Sharma, Sukriti Sobti, Shipra Jain, Aanchal Singhal
Assistant Editors Ira Pundeer, Ateendriya Gupta, Sneha Sunder Benjamin, Ankita Yadav
Assistant Art Editors Roshni Kapur, Meenal Goel, Priyansha Tuli
Illustrators Ivy Roy, Arun Pottirayil, Bharti Karakoti, Rahul Kumar
Picture Researcher Deepak Negi
Managing Editor Pakshalika Jayaprakash
Managing Art Editor Arunesh Talapatra
Production Manager Pankaj Sharma
Pre-Production Manager Balwant Singh
Senior DTP Designers Vishal Bhatia, Neeraj Bhatia
DTP Designer Sachin Gupta
Jacket Designer Surabhi Wadhwa
Managing Jackets Editor Saloni Singh
Senior DTP Designer (Jackets) Harish Aggarwal

This edition published in 2025
First published in Great Britain in 2016 by Dorling Kindersley Limited
20 Vauxhall Bridge Road, London, SW1V 2SA

The authorised representative in the EEA is Dorling Kindersley Verlag GmbH.
Arnulfstr. 124, 80636 Munich, Germany

Copyright © 2016, 2025 Dorling Kindersley Limited
A Penguin Random House Company
10 9 8 7 6 5 4 3 2 1
001–348943–Jun/2025

A CIP catalogue record for this book is available from the British Library.
ISBN 978-0-2417-3478-0

Printed and bound in China

www.dk.com

MIX
Paper | Supporting
responsible forestry
FSC™ C018179

This book was made with Forest
Stewardship Council™ certified
paper – one small step in DK's
commitment to a sustainable future.
Learn more at
www.dk.com/uk/information/sustainability

Contents

How the course works

English for Everyone is designed for people who want to teach themselves the English language. Like all language courses, it covers the core skills: grammar, vocabulary, pronunciation, listening, speaking, reading, and writing. Unlike in other courses, the skills are taught and practiced as visually as possible, using images and graphics to help you understand and remember. The practice book is packed with exercises designed to reinforce the lessons you have learned in the course book. Work through the units in order, making full use of the audio available on the website and app.

COURSE BOOK

PRACTICE BOOK

Unit number The book is divided into units. Each practice book unit tests the language taught in the course book unit with the same number.

Practice points Every unit begins with a summary of the key practice points.

Modules Each unit is broken down into modules, which should be done in order. You can take a break from learning after completing any module.

26 Activities in progress

Use the present perfect continuous to talk about ongoing activities in the past. Use "for" and "since" to talk about the length or starting point of an activity.

New language Present perfect continuous
Aa Vocabulary Home improvements
New skill Talking about activities in the past

26.1 FILL IN THE GAPS BY PUTTING THE VERBS IN THE PRESENT PERFECT CONTINUOUS TENSE

Fatima ___has been shopping___ (shop) for clothes all day.

① Nathan _____ (read) a book in the back yard.

② I _____ (cook) breakfast in the kitchen.

③ Mike _____ (play) tennis with his friends.

④ Ted and John _____ (watch) TV all evening.

⑤ Mrs. Roberts _____ (paint) the house this weekend.

26.2 FILL IN THE GAPS USING "FOR" OR "SINCE"

I've been waiting ___for___ 20 minutes.

① He has been fishing _____ 3:30pm.

② We've been learning Spanish _____ six weeks.

③ Ruth has been cooking _____ a long time.

④ You've been decorating _____ March 8.

⑤ I've been driving _____ 11:45am.

⑥ He's been teaching science _____ 2012.

⑦ She's been watching TV _____ two hours.

⑧ I've been learning to dance _____ two weeks.

⑨ Alan has been tiling the floor _____ Monday.

⑩ It has been snowing _____ 10 days.

⑪ I've been working at home _____ last April.

26.3 READ THE EMAIL AND NUMBER T ORDER THEY ARE DESCRIBED

Ⓐ □ Ⓑ f Ⓒ □
Ⓓ □ Ⓔ □ Ⓕ □

26.4 LISTEN TO THE AUDIO AND WRIT HAS BEEN GOING ON

since last weekend

74

Vocabulary Throughout the book, vocabulary pages test your memory of key English words and phrases taught in the course book.

Visual practice Images and graphics offer visual cues to help fix the most useful and important English words in your memory.

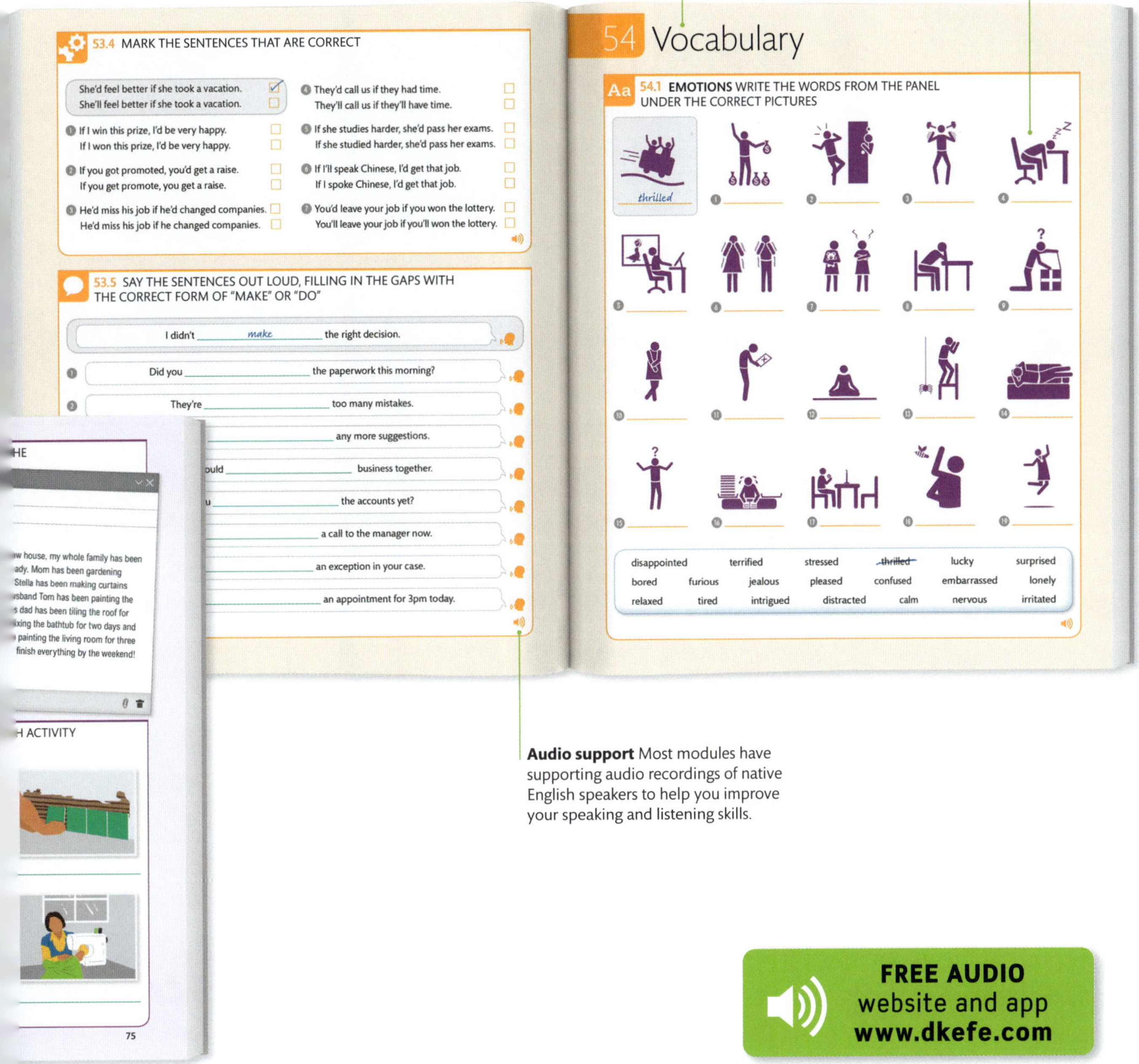

53.4 MARK THE SENTENCES THAT ARE CORRECT

She'd feel better if she took a vacation. ☑
She'll feel better if she took a vacation. ☐

① If I win this prize, I'd be very happy. ☐
If I won this prize, I'd be very happy. ☐

② If you got promoted, you'd get a raise. ☐
If you get promote, you get a raise. ☐

③ He'd miss his job if he'd changed companies. ☐
He'd miss his job if he changed companies. ☐

④ They'd call us if they had time. ☐
They'll call us if they'll have time. ☐

⑤ If she studies harder, she'd pass her exams. ☐
If she studied harder, she'd pass her exams. ☐

⑥ If I'll speak Chinese, I'd get that job. ☐
If I spoke Chinese, I'd get that job. ☐

⑦ You'd leave your job if you won the lottery. ☐
You'll leave your job if you'll won the lottery. ☐

53.5 SAY THE SENTENCES OUT LOUD, FILLING IN THE GAPS WITH THE CORRECT FORM OF "MAKE" OR "DO"

I didn't _make_ the right decision.

① Did you _____ the paperwork this morning?

② They're _____ too many mistakes.

_____ any more suggestions.

ould _____ business together.

u _____ the accounts yet?

_____ a call to the manager now.

_____ an exception in your case.

_____ an appointment for 3pm today.

54 Vocabulary

Aa **54.1 EMOTIONS** WRITE THE WORDS FROM THE PANEL UNDER THE CORRECT PICTURES

thrilled

disappointed	terrified	stressed	thrilled	lucky	surprised
bored	furious	jealous	pleased	confused	embarrassed	lonely
relaxed	tired	intrigued	distracted	calm	nervous	irritated

Audio support Most modules have supporting audio recordings of native English speakers to help you improve your speaking and listening skills.

w house, my whole family has been
ady. Mom has been gardening
Stella has been making curtains
sband Tom has been painting the
s dad has been tiling the roof for
xing the bathtub for two days and
painting the living room for three
finish everything by the weekend!

H ACTIVITY

75

FREE AUDIO
website and app
www.dkefe.com

Practice modules

Each exercise is carefully graded to drill and test the language taught in the corresponding course book units. Working through the exercises alongside the course book will help you remember what you have learned and become more fluent. Every exercise is introduced with a symbol to indicate which skill is being practiced.

 GRAMMAR Apply new language rules in different contexts.

 READING Examine target language in real-life English contexts.

 LISTENING Test your understanding of spoken English.

 VOCABULARY Cement your understanding of key vocabulary.

 SPEAKING Compare your spoken English to model audio recordings.

Module number Every module is identified with a unique number, so you can easily locate answers and related audio.

Exercise instruction Every exercise is introduced with a brief instruction, telling you what you need to do.

Sample answer The first question of each exercise is answered for you, to help make the task easy to understand.

Space for writing You are encouraged to write your answers in the book for future reference.

Supporting graphics Visual cues are given to help you understand the exercises.

Supporting audio This symbol shows that the answers to the exercise are available as audio tracks. Listen to them after completing the exercise.

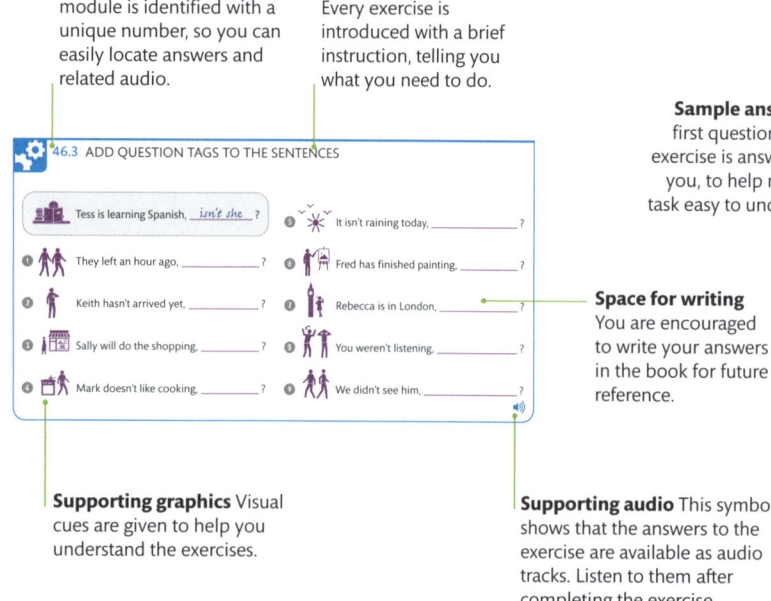

46.3 ADD QUESTION TAGS TO THE SENTENCES

Tess is learning Spanish, _isn't she_ ?

① They left an hour ago, _____ ?
② Keith hasn't arrived yet, _____ ?
③ Sally will do the shopping, _____ ?
④ Mark doesn't like cooking, _____ ?
⑤ It isn't raining today, _____ ?
⑥ Fred has finished painting, _____ ?
⑦ Rebecca is in London, _____ ?
⑧ You weren't listening, _____ ?
⑨ We didn't see him, _____ ?

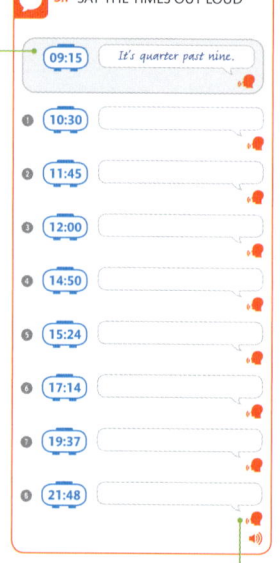

5.1 SAY THE TIMES OUT LOUD

09:15 — It's quarter past nine.
① 10:30
② 11:45
③ 12:00
④ 14:50
⑤ 15:24
⑥ 17:14
⑦ 19:37
⑧ 21:48

Speaking exercise This symbol indicates that you should say your answers out loud, then compare them to model recordings included in your audio files.

Listening exercise This symbol indicates that you should listen to an audio track in order to answer the questions in the exercise.

24.3 LISTEN TO THE AUDIO, THEN MARK WHETHER EACH PICTURE IS DESCRIBED IN THE PAST SIMPLE OR THE PRESENT PERFECT TENSE

Past simple ✓ Present perfect
① Past simple ☐ Present perfect ☐
② Past simple ☐ Present perfect ☐
③ Past simple ☐ Present perfect ☐
④ Past simple ☐ Present perfect ☐
⑤ Past simple ☐ Present perfect ☐

Audio

English for Everyone features extensive supporting audio materials. You are encouraged to use them as much as you can, to improve your understanding of spoken English, and to make your own accent and pronunciation more natural. Each file can be played, paused, and repeated as often as you like, until you are confident you understand what has been said.

LISTENING EXERCISES

This symbol indicates that you should listen to an audio track in order to answer the questions in the exercise.

SUPPORTING AUDIO

This symbol indicates that extra audio material is available for you to listen to after completing the module.

FREE AUDIO
website and app
www.dkefe.com

Answers

An answers section at the back of the book lists the correct answers for every exercise. Turn to these pages whenever you finish a module and compare your answers with the samples provided, to see how well you have understood each teaching point.

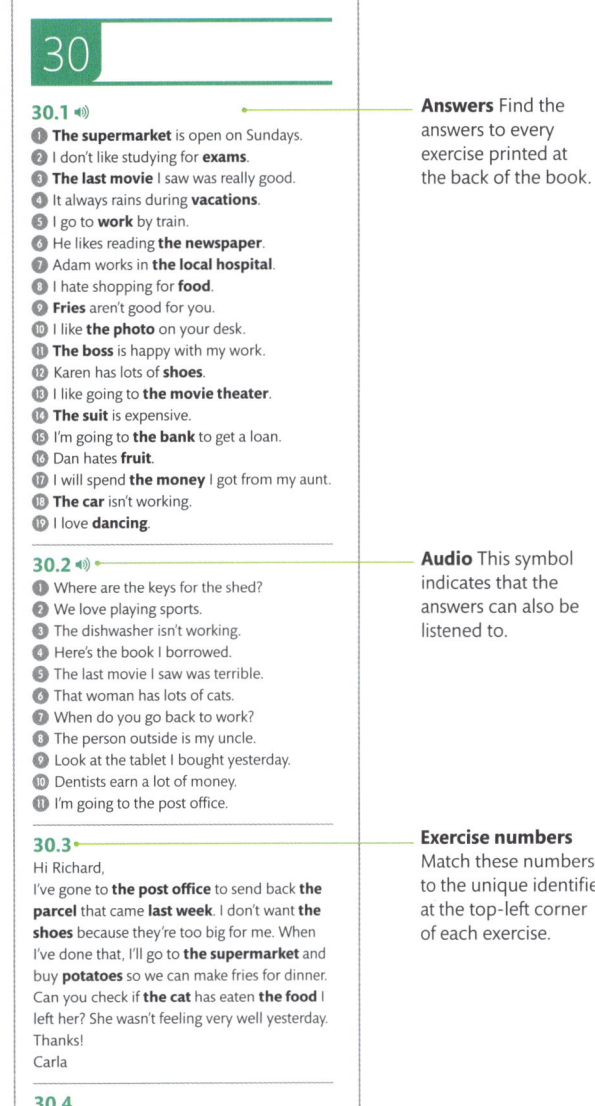

30

30.1 ◄))
1. **The supermarket** is open on Sundays.
2. I don't like studying for **exams**.
3. **The last movie** I saw was really good.
4. It always rains during **vacations**.
5. I go to **work** by train.
6. He likes reading **the newspaper**.
7. Adam works in **the local hospital**.
8. I hate shopping for **food**.
9. **Fries** aren't good for you.
10. I like **the photo** on your desk.
11. **The boss** is happy with my work.
12. Karen has lots of **shoes**.
13. I like going to **the movie theater**.
14. **The suit** is expensive.
15. I'm going to **the bank** to get a loan.
16. Dan hates **fruit**.
17. I will spend **the money** I got from my aunt.
18. **The car** isn't working.
19. I love **dancing**.

Answers Find the answers to every exercise printed at the back of the book.

30.2 ◄))
1. Where are the keys for the shed?
2. We love playing sports.
3. The dishwasher isn't working.
4. Here's the book I borrowed.
5. The last movie I saw was terrible.
6. That woman has lots of cats.
7. When do you go back to work?
8. The person outside is my uncle.
9. Look at the tablet I bought yesterday.
10. Dentists earn a lot of money.
11. I'm going to the post office.

Audio This symbol indicates that the answers can also be listened to.

30.3
Hi Richard,
I've gone to **the post office** to send back **the parcel** that came **last week**. I don't want **the shoes** because they're too big for me. When I've done that, I'll go to **the supermarket** and buy **potatoes** so we can make fries for dinner. Can you check if **the cat** has eaten **the food** I left her? She wasn't feeling very well yesterday. Thanks!
Carla

Exercise numbers Match these numbers to the unique identifier at the top-left corner of each exercise.

30.4
1. The campsite is in the south of France.
2. She has to clean the tents.
3. She hates doing the cleaning.
4. They play games and go to the beach.
5. She buys wine from the local vineyard.

01 Making conversation

In spoken English, you might hear small questions added to the ends of sentences. These are called question tags, and they are used to invite someone to agree with you.

⚙ **New language** Question tags
Aa Vocabulary Introductions and greetings
🧩 **New skill** Making conversation

1.1 MATCH THE BEGINNINGS OF THE SENTENCES TO THE CORRECT ENDINGS

John is a great friend, ──────→ isn't he?

1. Mom isn't at work today,   isn't it?
2. You're a flamenco dancer,   aren't they?
3. I'm not sitting in your chair,   aren't you?
4. This article is very interesting,   is she?
5. They're from Beijing,   am I?

🔊

1.2 MARK THE SENTENCES THAT ARE CORRECT

Her dress is beautiful, aren't I? ☐
Her dress is beautiful, isn't it? ☑

1. You're hungry, aren't you? ☐
   You're hungry, aren't I? ☐

2. She is Chris's boss, isn't he? ☐
   She is Chris's boss, isn't she? ☐

3. They're from Florida, aren't they? ☐
   They're from Florida, isn't they? ☐

4. It's warm today, is she? ☐
   It's warm today, isn't it? ☐

5. You're not tired, aren't I? ☐
   You're not tired, are you? ☐

6. We're from the same town, are they? ☐
   We're from the same town, aren't we? ☐

7. They're late, aren't they? ☐
   They're late, are you? ☐

8. Saira's sister is here, are they? ☐
   Saira's sister is here, isn't she? ☐

9. You're from the US, aren't you? ☐
   You're from the US, is it? ☐

🔊

1.3 SAY THE SENTENCES OUT LOUD, ADDING QUESTION TAGS

The food is delicious, _____ *isn't it?* _____

11 I'm in your class, _____

1 The music is very loud, _____

12 He isn't 30, _____

2 You're not from here, _____

13 You aren't waiting, _____

3 Tim is a great dancer, _____

14 This film is boring, _____

4 Fiona isn't here, _____

15 They're playing tennis, _____

5 The venue is lovely, _____

16 We aren't early, _____

6 I'm not late, _____

17 She's beautiful, _____

7 They are dancing, _____

18 You aren't from Boston, _____

8 The band is great, _____

19 He isn't outside, _____

9 You're having a good time, _____

20 They're watching TV, _____

10 It isn't warm today, _____

21 You aren't hurt, _____

1.4 FILL IN THE GAPS, ADDING QUESTION TAGS

It's very cold, _____isn't it_____ ?

1.  You're Sarah, _____ ?

2.  You're Sally's friend, _____ ?

3.  Fatima is funny, _____ ?

4.  The food is delicious, _____ ?

5.  Dev and Jai are twins, _____ ?

6.  You're not leaving now, _____ ?

7.  I'm not boring you, _____ ?

8.  The boss isn't here, _____ ?

9.  I'm late, _____ ?

10.  You've just woken up, _____ ?

11.  You can't see it, _____ ?

12.  He's getting old, _____ ?

13.  They're not studying, _____ ?

1.5 LISTEN TO THE AUDIO AND ANSWER THE QUESTIONS

Helena is at a party organized by her friend Danny's boss.

Danny and Helena are at a work party.
True ☑ False ☐

1. Danny introduces Helena to his boss.
True ☐ False ☐

2. Rachel and Chris are Danny's friends.
True ☐ False ☐

3. Rachel and Chris work in different offices.
True ☐ False ☐

4. Rachel knows nothing about Helena.
True ☐ False ☐

5. Helena likes the band.
True ☐ False ☐

6. Helena thinks the music is a bit loud.
True ☐ False ☐

7. Danny thinks the food looks delicious.
True ☐ False ☐

1.6 FILL IN THE GAPS USING THE PHRASES IN THE PANEL

Good evening, Mr. Fisher. _____*How are you*_____ ?

1 I'm very _____ .

2 This _____ .

3 _____ , Mrs. Reid. How are you?

4 Hi, Sally. How _____ ?

5 I'm _____ you, Ms. Chopra.

6 May _____ Frank Hill?

7 I'm very pleased _____ , Diana.

8 _____ meet you, Holly.

are you doing

is Tim

well, thank you

~~How are you~~

Great to

to meet you

delighted to meet

I introduce

Good morning

1.7 RESPOND TO THE GREETINGS, SPEAKING OUT LOUD

May I introduce Mr. Tom Grant?

I'm ____*delighted*____ to meet you.

3 This is Alexis.

_____ to meet you.

1 Hi, Vincent.

_____ , Maria.

4 Hi, Natasha. How are you doing?

_____ , thanks.

2 Hello, Mrs. Gardner. How are you?

I'm very well, _____ .

5 Darren! Lovely to see you!

Paul! _____ to see you, too.

Aa 2.1 COUNTRIES WRITE THE COUNTRY NAMES FROM THE PANEL UNDER THE CORRECT FLAGS

Cuba

1 _____

2 _____

3 _____

4 _____

5 _____

6 _____

7 _____

8 _____

9 _____

10 _____

11 _____

12 _____

13 _____

14 _____

15 _____

16 _____

17 _____

18 _____

19 _____

20 _____

21 _____

22 _____

23 _____

24 _____

Canada   Czech Republic   Poland   Germany   Turkey   Australia   Mexico   United Kingdom

Mongolia   Pakistan   United States of America   Argentina   South Korea   Spain   ~~Cuba~~

France   Peru   Bolivia   China   Portugal   Greece   Vietnam   Japan   Brazil   Kenya

03 | Where things are

English uses prepositions to talk about where things are. It is important to learn the correct prepositions for different phrases describing locations and directions.

New language Prepositions of place
Aa Vocabulary Countries and nationalities
New skill Talking about where things are

3.1 CROSS OUT THE INCORRECT WORDS IN EACH SENTENCE

Marge and Bert live in the Sunrise Apartments ~~on~~ / **in** / ~~opposite~~ the city center.

1 There is a tree **to the left of** / **on** / **around** the tall building in town.

2  We stayed in a small hotel just **in** / **around** / **by** the seaside.

3  The town library is **opposite** / **right next to** / **across** the movie theater.

4  Tom is planning on going for a walk **in** / **on** / **by** the country today.

5  Norway and Australia are on **around** / **opposite** / **off** sides of the world.

6  The Snow Slopes Ski Resort is **on** / **off** / **in** the mountains.

3.2 USE THE CHART TO CREATE 10 SENTENCES AND SAY THEM OUT LOUD

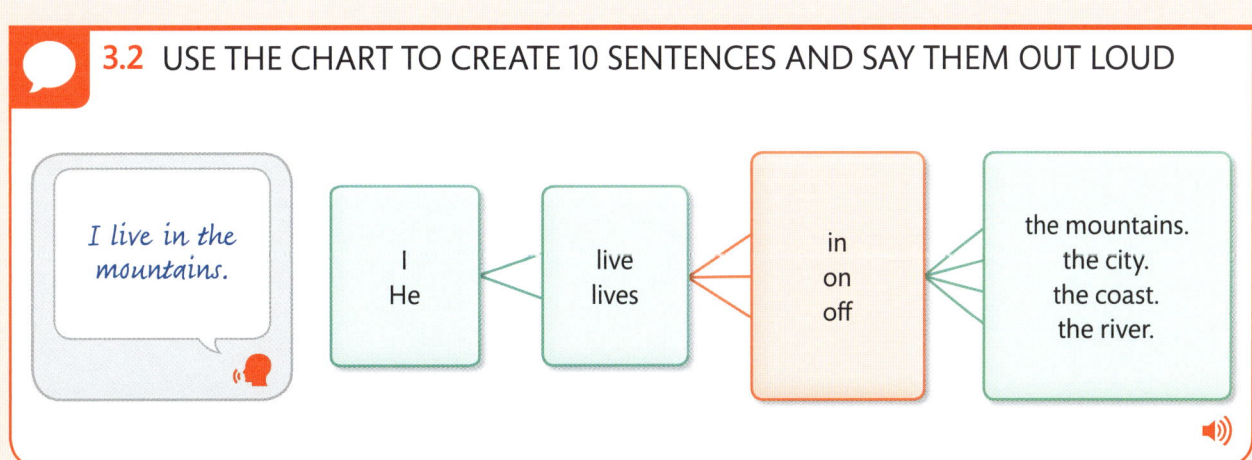

I live in the mountains.

| I / He | live / lives | in / on / off | the mountains. / the city. / the coast. / the river. |

3.3 LISTEN TO THE AUDIO AND ANSWER THE QUESTIONS

Jerry is a British student who recently moved to Spain.

Jerry is studying at Seville University.
True ☑ False ☐ Not given ☐

1 Jerry is from a busy city in England.
True ☐ False ☐ Not given ☐

2 In England he lived near the south coast.
True ☐ False ☐ Not given ☐

3 Seville is on the Guadalquivir river.
True ☐ False ☐ Not given ☐

4 Jerry is sharing an apartment with friends.
True ☐ False ☐ Not given ☐

5 His apartment is on the river.
True ☐ False ☐ Not given ☐

6 Next weekend he's touring Doñana National Park.
True ☐ False ☐ Not given ☐

7 The Doñana National Park is in the mountains.
True ☐ False ☐ Not given ☐

3.4 FILL IN THE GAPS USING THE WORDS IN THE PANEL

The lighthouse is ___*on*___ the east coast.

1 The castle is _____ the beach.

2 The island is just _____ the coast.

3 Visitors can take boat trips _____ the island.

4 They can eat at the restaurant _____ the island.

5 The statue is _____ the café and the church.

6 The restaurant is _____ opposite the café.

7 The lighthouse is diagonally _____ the church.

right next to	between	off	~~on~~
around	on	opposite	directly

3.5 MATCH THE BEGINNINGS OF THE SENTENCES TO THE CORRECT ENDINGS

They are traveling around — the world.

1. The lighthouse is just off — the sea.
2. The park is diagonally — opposite the lake.
3. We stayed in a chalet in — the mountains.
4. There's a café right — next to the theater.
5. Henry has a house by — the coast.
6. It's halfway between — the airport and the hotel.

Endings:
- opposite the lake.
- next to the theater.
- the sea.
- the world.
- the airport and the hotel.
- the coast.
- the mountains.

3.6 READ THE WEB PAGE AND ANSWER THE QUESTIONS

Travel Time

HOME | ENTRIES | ABOUT | CONTACT

POSTED FRIDAY, AUGUST 28

Visit Vancouver

Vancouver is a popular tourist destination in Canada. It's right on the Pacific coast, so why not take a boat trip around the harbor? The city is right next to miles of beautiful beaches but it is also close to beautiful mountains. Vancouver hosted the Winter Olympics in 2010 and now has excellent transportation links to Whistler ski resort. Whistler is 100km north of Vancouver. When you visit Vancouver, you can ski in the mountains in the morning and sail on the bay in the afternoon! If you prefer to stay in the city, you can take a tour around Stanley Park or learn something new in Science World.

Which country is Vancouver in?
America ☐ **Canada** ☑ **England** ☐

1. On which coast is Vancouver?
   Atlantic ☐ **Indian** ☐ **Pacific** ☐

2. How close is the city to beaches?
   Right next to ☐ **Far away** ☐ **Miles away** ☐

3. When did it host the Winter Olympics?
   2008 ☐ **2010** ☐ **2012** ☐

4. How far away is Whistler?
   10km ☐ **100km** ☐ **1,000km** ☐

5. What direction is Whistler from Vancouver?
   South ☐ **East** ☐ **North** ☐

6. Where can you sail?
   On the river ☐ **On the bay** ☐ **In the lake** ☐

04 Numbers and statistics

Fractions, decimals, and percentages are all pronounced differently in spoken English, following a few simple rules.

New language Numbers in spoken English
Aa Vocabulary Sports events
New skill Using numbers in conversation

4.1 SAY THE NUMBERS OUT LOUD

⅕ _one fifth_

1. 0.75
2. 42%
3. ⅙
4. 12.3
5. ¾

4.2 MATCH THE FIGURES TO THE CORRECT NUMBERS IN WORDS

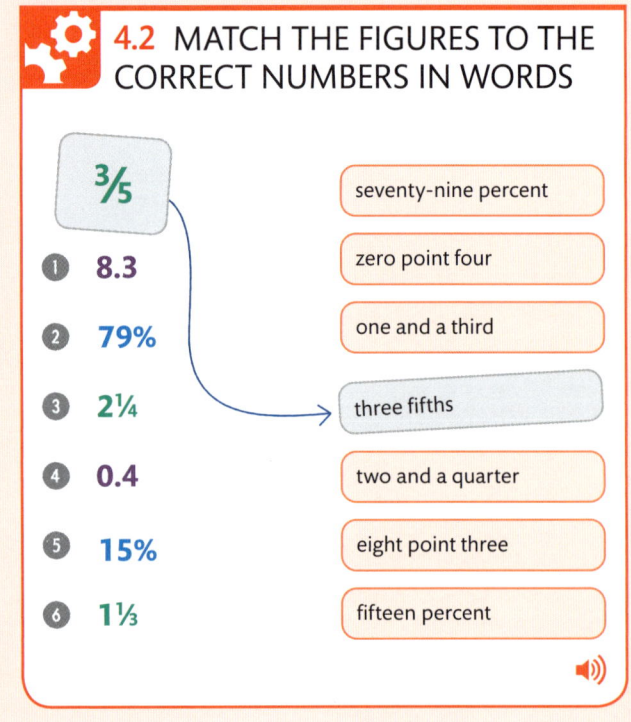

⅗

1. 8.3
2. 79%
3. 2¼
4. 0.4
5. 15%
6. 1⅓

- seventy-nine percent
- zero point four
- one and a third
- three fifths
- two and a quarter
- eight point three
- fifteen percent

4.3 LISTEN TO THE AUDIO AND WRITE ANSWERS TO THE QUESTIONS IN FULL SENTENCES

A sports commentator is providing the highlights of the Athletics Championship.

How full was the Stadium today?
The stadium was 90 percent full.

1. How high did Davis jump?

2. By how much did Mwange beat the record?

3. By how many seconds did Joslin win?

4. What fraction of all medals does Canada hold?

5. By how many centimeters did Edwards win?

4.4 LISTEN TO THE AUDIO AND WRITE ALL THE NUMBERS AND STATISTICS YOU HEAR

A news reporter summarizes the results from an athletics tournament.

2.07

2 _____   **4** _____   **6** _____

1 _____   **3** _____   **5** _____   **7** _____

4.5 MARK THE STRESSED SYLLABLES AND SAY THE NUMBERS OUT LOUD

fif<u>teen</u>

3 seventeen   **6** nineteen   **9** seventy

1 twenty   **4** eighty   **7** sixty   **10** eighteen

2 sixteen   **5** fifty   **8** fourteen   **11** thirty

4.6 CROSS OUT THE MISSPELLED WORD IN EACH SENTENCE

The high jump bar is over ~~too~~ / **two** meters high.

1 The Jamaican sprinter lost by **four fivths** / **four fifths** of a second.

2 Tracey Livingstone won the race by **three twelvths** / **three twelfths** of a second.

3 The Russian contestant won by an **eighth** / **eigth** of an inch.

4 There were a total of **fourty** / **forty** runners in the marathon this year.

5 The American won the 100 meters back stroke by **five sixs** / **five sixths** of a second.

6 Maxwell Peterson came in **nineth** / **ninth** place out of 48 contestants.

05 Times and dates

There are many ways of saying the time and the date in English. American and British English speakers often use different forms.

⚙ **New language** Precise times
Aa **Vocabulary** Dates in US and UK English
🧩 **New skill** Talking about times and dates

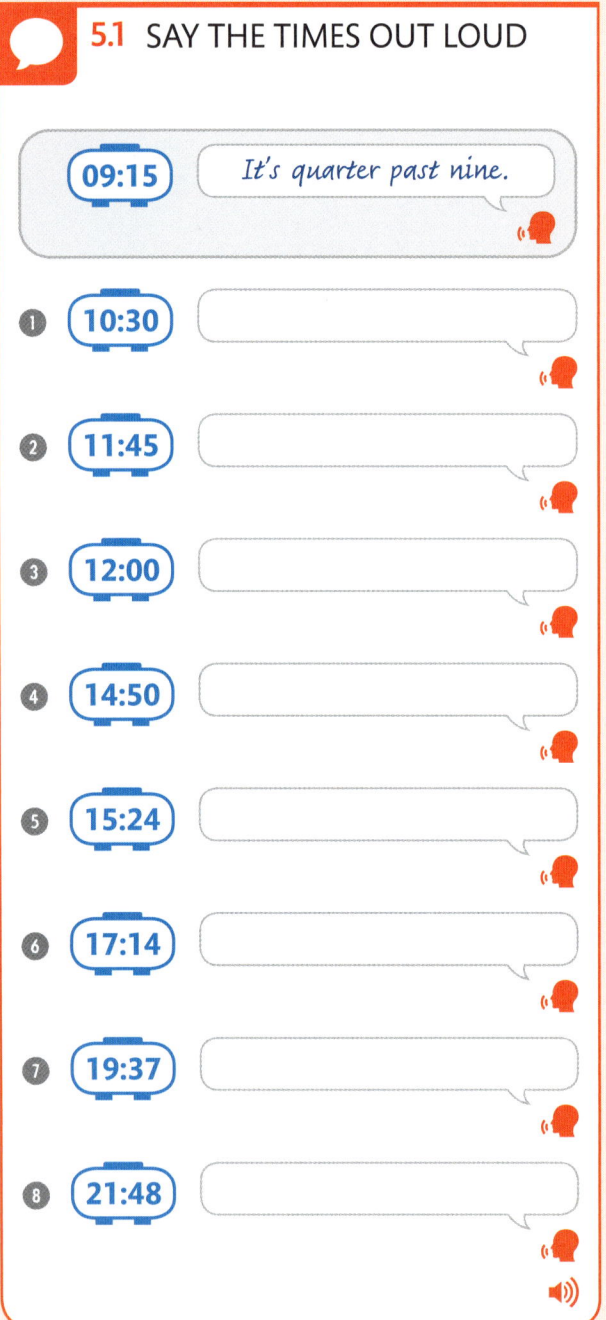

5.1 SAY THE TIMES OUT LOUD

09:15 — *It's quarter past nine.*

1. **10:30**
2. **11:45**
3. **12:00**
4. **14:50**
5. **15:24**
6. **17:14**
7. **19:37**
8. **21:48**

5.2 SAY THE DATES OUT LOUD

TIP
Remember the difference between UK and US dates.

09/05/01 (US) — *September fifth, two thousand and one*

1. **11/02/10 (UK)**
2. **03/04/12 (US)**
3. **09/23/06 (US)**
4. **31/12/14 (UK)**
5. **02/15/08 (US)**

5.3 MATCH THE TIMES TO THE STATEMENTS

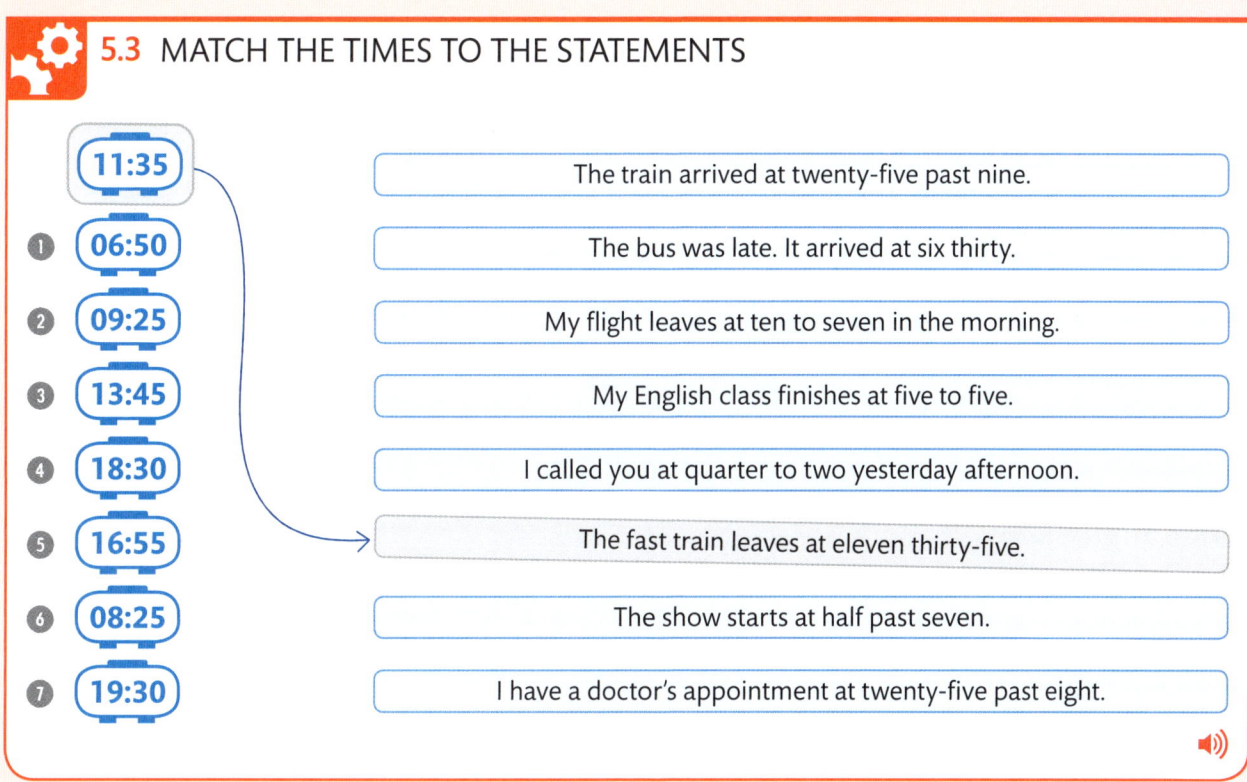

- **11:35**
- ❶ **06:50**
- ❷ **09:25**
- ❸ **13:45**
- ❹ **18:30**
- ❺ **16:55**
- ❻ **08:25**
- ❼ **19:30**

The train arrived at twenty-five past nine.

The bus was late. It arrived at six thirty.

My flight leaves at ten to seven in the morning.

My English class finishes at five to five.

I called you at quarter to two yesterday afternoon.

The fast train leaves at eleven thirty-five.

The show starts at half past seven.

I have a doctor's appointment at twenty-five past eight.

5.4 LISTEN TO THE AUDIO AND ANSWER THE QUESTIONS

People are talking about important dates and times in their lives.

Tim and Alison got married on...
- **February 10, 2004** ☐
- **August 6, 2009** ☑
- **November 30, 2015** ☐

❶ Simon's flight leaves at...
- 10:30 ☐
- 15:10 ☐
- 14:50 ☐

❷ Jamie graduated from college on...
- **June 30** ☐
- **June 13** ☐
- **July 30** ☐

❸ The fast train to Edinburgh leaves at...
- 07:24 ☐
- 11:24 ☐
- 10:45 ☐

❹ Harry's grandfather's 80th birthday was on...
- **October 27** ☐
- **November 27** ☐
- **November 17** ☐

❺ Jane and Paul's wedding is at...
- 2:30pm ☐
- 3:30pm ☐
- 4:30pm ☐

06 Contact details

Telephone numbers, street addresses, email addresses, and web addresses are expressed in slightly different ways in US and UK English.

⚙ **New language** Letters and numbers
Aa Vocabulary Contact details
New skill Exchanging personal information

6.1 LISTEN TO THE AUDIO AND WRITE THE PLACE NAMES THAT ARE SPELLED OUT

Shanghai

1 _____

2 _____

3 _____

4 _____

5 _____

6 _____

7 _____

8 _____

9 _____

10 _____

6.2 ANSWER THE QUESTIONS BY SPELLING THE WORDS OUT LOUD

How do you spell "Durban?"

D-U-R-B-A-N

1 How do you spell "California?"

2 How do you spell "Paddington?"

3 How do you spell "Bloomfield?"

4 How do you spell "Birmingham?"

5 How do you spell "Hong Kong?"

6 How do you spell "Cambridge?"

7 How do you spell "Sydney?"

8 How do you spell "New Delhi?"

6.3 LISTEN TO THE AUDIO AND WRITE DOWN THE PHONE NUMBERS YOU HEAR

033888701

1. ______________
2. ______________
3. ______________
4. ______________
5. ______________
6. ______________
7. ______________
8. ______________
9. ______________
10. ______________
11. ______________

6.4 LOOK AT THE ADDRESS BOOK ENTRY AND RESPOND TO THE AUDIO, SPEAKING OUT LOUD

Alice Watson
66 Queen's Walk
Melbourne
NSW 2024
Australia
00615508884
alice.watson@sunshine.au

Which country does Alice live in?
Australia

1. What is the name of her street?
2. What is the name of her city?
3. What's her zip code?
4. What's her email address?
5. What's her phone number?

6.5 LOOK AT THE BUSINESS CARD AND WRITE ANSWERS TO THE QUESTIONS AS FULL SENTENCES

Who does this business card belong to?

It belongs to Rachel Brodie.

1 What is her surname?

_____

2 What's her job?

_____

3 Which company does she work at?

_____

4 What's her phone number?

_____

RACHEL BRODIE
Sales Manager

Trademark Printers Ltd.

Mobile: 0785 9044678
Email: rachel.brodie@trademark.com

5 What's her email address?

_____

Aa **6.6** FIND NINE WORDS FOR CONTACT DETAILS IN THE GRID

P	G	N	C	D	S	T	R	E	E	T	N	S	D	R	A	O	W	O	N	S
H	S	A	X	O	I	N	G	T	S	E	F	T	I	T	L	E	Q	E	N	V
O	D	E	T	J	U	M	D	S	M	T	R	I	I	S	E	M	A	I	L	D
N	I	N	O	E	R	N	I	U	T	C	A	I	R	R	T	I	T	C	U	I
E	K	A	W	E	B	X	T	R	D	I	N	T	X	S	S	A	D	I	N	Z
N	D	I	N	R	Y	A	D	R	A	E	X	D	E	Y	T	N	X	E	N	I
U	Z	L	E	L	A	O	Z	I	Y	R	I	Z	L	A	O	N	O	R	I	P
M	A	V	H	S	N	V	O	N	S	T	N	D	S	N	V	O	A	X	N	C
B	C	D	J	T	N	D	E	G	J	A	G	I	T	N	D	E	J	M	M	O
E	H	I	E	A	R	I	A	I	E	O	S	S	A	R	I	A	E	O	E	D
R	E	C	B	H	O	U	S	E	N	U	M	B	E	R	K	I	B	G	Z	E

26

07 Talking about jobs

English uses the words "job" and "work" in a variety of contexts to talk about different professions, working conditions, and career paths.

⚙ **New language** "Job" and "work"
Aa Vocabulary Jobs and professions
🧩 **New skill** Talking about your career

Aa 7.1 FILL IN THE JOB TITLES USING THE WORDS IN THE PANEL

pilot

1 _____

2 _____

3 _____

4 _____

5 _____

6 _____

7 _____

architect   firefighter   journalist

butcher   plumber

~~pilot~~   surgeon   vet

🔊

Aa 7.2 MATCH THE DEFINITIONS TO THE CORRECT JOBS

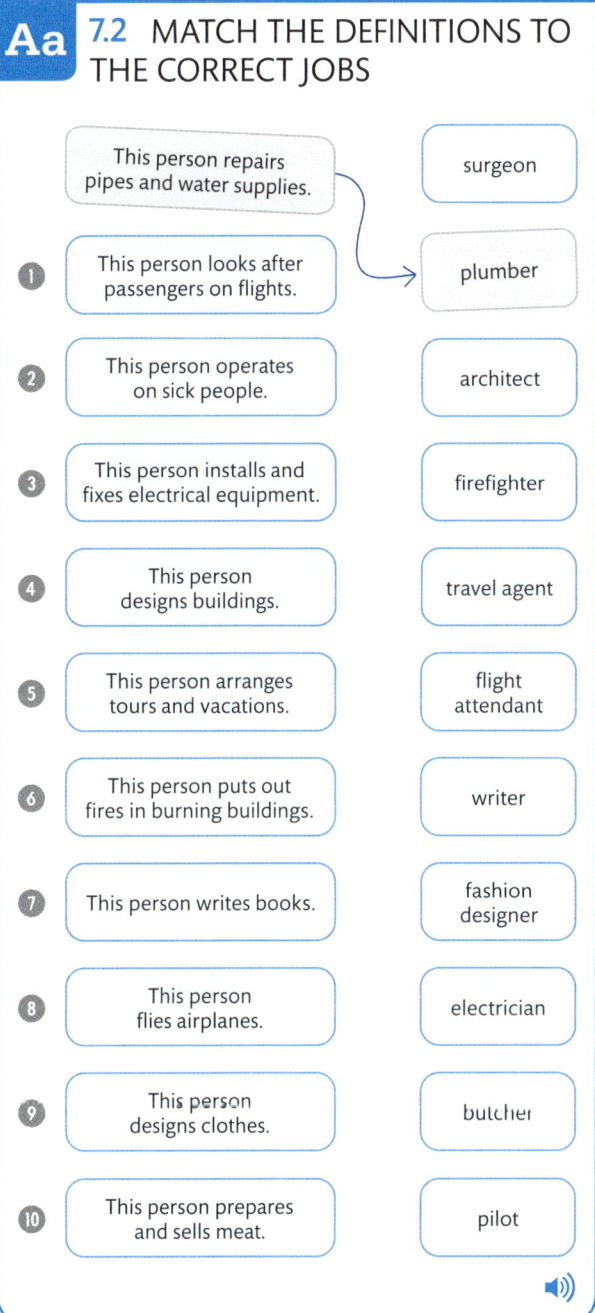

This person repairs pipes and water supplies. → plumber

surgeon

1 This person looks after passengers on flights.

2 This person operates on sick people.

architect

3 This person installs and fixes electrical equipment.

firefighter

4 This person designs buildings.

travel agent

5 This person arranges tours and vacations.

flight attendant

6 This person puts out fires in burning buildings.

writer

7 This person writes books.

fashion designer

8 This person flies airplanes.

electrician

9 This person designs clothes.

butcher

10 This person prepares and sells meat.

pilot

🔊

7.3 READ THE JOB ADVERTISEMENTS AND ANSWER THE QUESTIONS

City Law Firm is looking for an intern for one year.
True ✓ **False** ☐

❶ The intern at City Law Firm will get a small salary.
True ☐ **False** ☐

❷ Youth Orchestra candidates must be over 22.
True ☐ **False** ☐

❸ The Youth Orchestra is looking to hire technicians.
True ☐ **False** ☐

❹ The news journalist will have many days off.
True ☐ **False** ☐

❺ The trainee fashion designer will work long hours.
True ☐ **False** ☐

❻ The trainee fashion designer will get to travel.
True ☐ **False** ☐

❼ The travel agent's position is full-time.
True ☐ **False** ☐

26 **UPPERTON HERALD**

JOB LISTINGS

For the most comprehensive career listings

City Law Firm is looking for an intern for 12 months. No salary is offered, but the position may lead to a full-time job.

Musicians wanted for Youth Orchestra. Are you aged between 16 and 22? Apply online with your CV now.

News journalist needed. Good salary and generous vacation offered for the right candidate.

Trainee fashion designer wanted. This is a full-time post and will involve overtime and some travel.

Part-time travel agent wanted. We offer a competitive salary and good prospects for the right candidate.

7.4 FILL IN THE GAPS USING "JOB" OR "WORK"

Ivan loves his new _____*job*_____ at the bank.

❶ Annabelle starts _____ at 8:30am.

❷ Joe is looking for a new _____ .

❸ I've had to _____ all weekend.

❹ What time do you finish _____ ?

❺ Sam's cousin helped him get his first _____ .

❻ Laura has a well-paid _____ in finance.

❼ I _____ as a freelance consultant.
🔊

Emily is being interviewed for a position at a company.

What position does Emily want?
Trainee ☐ **Intern** ☑ **Part-time** ☐

❹ What opportunities will there be?
Vacation ☐ **Training** ☐ **Promotion** ☐

① What field does Emily want a career in?
Finance ☐ **Law** ☐ **Education** ☐

❺ What kind of salary can she earn after four years?
Average ☐ **Low** ☐ **High** ☐

② How long is this position for?
Six weeks ☐ **A year** ☐ **Six months** ☐

❻ How often will Emily have to work on weekends?
Always ☐ **Sometimes** ☐ **Often** ☐

③ What type of job may this position lead to?
Full-time ☐ **Part-time** ☐ **Freelance** ☐

❼ How often will Emily have to work shifts?
Often ☐ **Sometimes** ☐ **Never** ☐

Aa 7.6 FILL IN THE GAPS USING THE WORDS IN THE PANEL

Paul has just begun his _____*career*_____ in medicine.

① They got a pay _____ of 5 percent.

② Doctors can earn a great _____ .

③ I'll be late home tonight. I have to work _____ .

④ Peter was _____ for six months before he got a job.

⑤ This position may lead to a _____ job.

⑥ Eva might _____ because she hates her job.

⑦ Henry works for himself. He is a _____ reporter.

⑧ This job has four weeks' _____ .

rise	~~career~~
unemployed	
resign	salary
freelance	
full-time	vacation
overtime	

🔊

29

08 Routine and free time

You can use adverbs of frequency to talk accurately about your daily routine and how often you do work and leisure activities.

⚙ **New language** Adverbs of frequency
Aa Vocabulary Leisure activities
New skill Talking about routines

Aa 8.1 FIND SEVEN ADVERBS OF FREQUENCY IN THE GRID

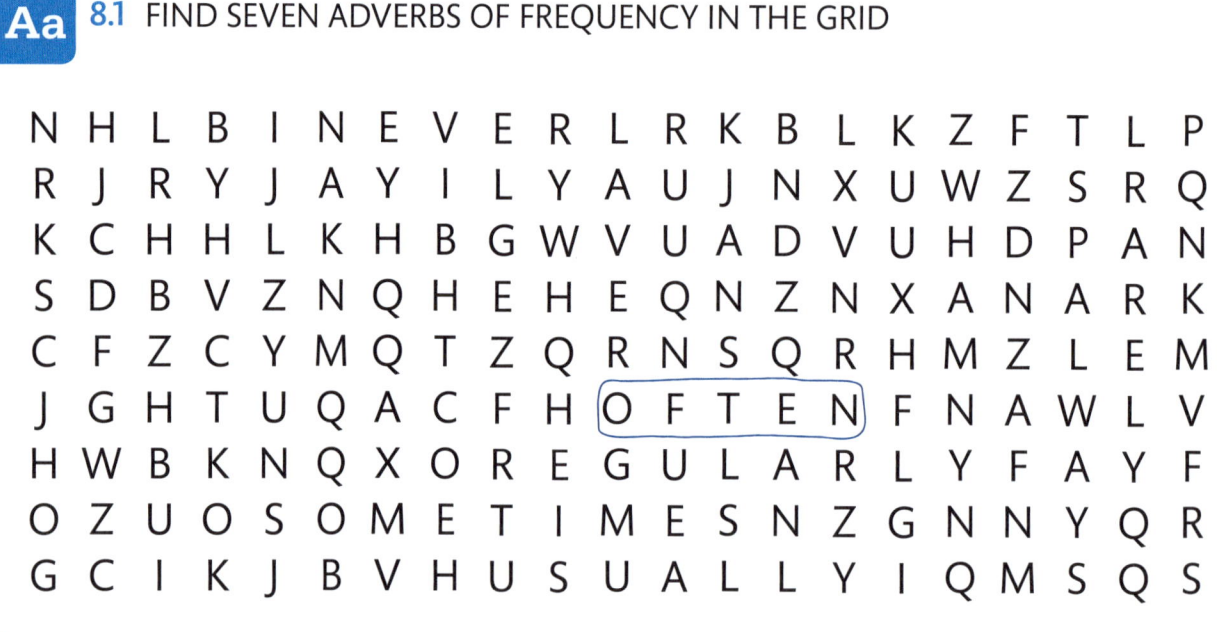

```
N H L B I N E V E R L R K B L K Z F T L P
R J R Y J A Y I L Y A U J N X U W Z S R Q
K C H H L K H B G W V U A D V U H D P A N
S D B V Z N Q H E H E Q N Z N X A N A R K
C F Z C Y M Q T Z Q R N S Q R H M Z L E M
J G H T U Q A C F H O F T E N F N A W L V
H W B K N Q X O R E G U L A R L Y F A Y F
O Z U O S O M E T I M E S N Z G N N Y Q R
G C I K J B V H U S U A L L Y I Q M S Q S
```

8.2 REWRITE THE SENTENCES, PUTTING THE WORDS IN THE CORRECT ORDER

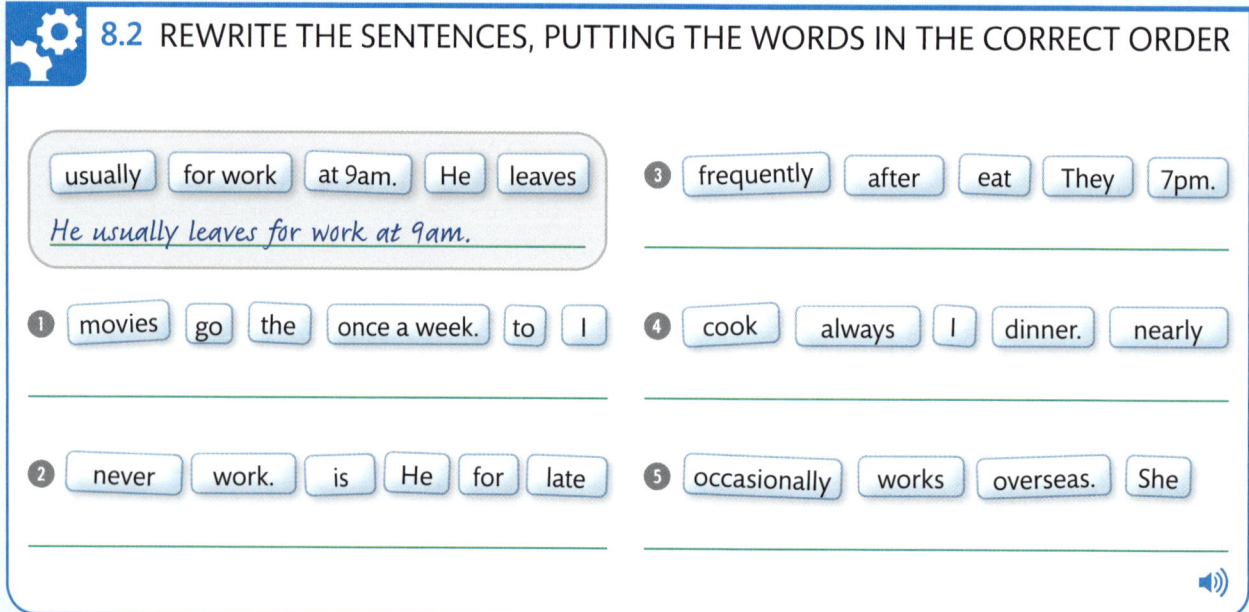

usually | for work | at 9am. | He | leaves

He usually leaves for work at 9am.

1 movies | go | the | once a week. | to | I

_____

2 never | work. | is | He | for | late

_____

3 frequently | after | eat | They | 7pm.

_____

4 cook | always | I | dinner. | nearly

_____

5 occasionally | works | overseas. | She

_____

8.3 MARK THE SENTENCES THAT ARE CORRECT

I wear hardly ever a suit and tie. ☐
I hardly ever wear a suit and tie. ☑

1. She gets home sometimes late. ☐
   She sometimes gets home late. ☐

2. He almost never goes to the gym. ☐
   He goes almost never to the gym. ☐

3. They very often are at home. ☐
   They are very often at home. ☐

4. He hardly ever takes a bath. ☐
   He has hardly takes a bath. ☐

5. He is always on time. ☐
   He always is on time. ☐

6. He rarely goes for a walk. ☐
   He goes rarely for a walk. ☐

7. You frequently stay out late. ☐
   You stay frequently out late. ☐

8. I nearly walk always to work. ☐
   I nearly always walk to work. ☐

9. We occasionally go out for lunch. ☐
   We go occasionally out for lunch. ☐

10. She plays regularly tennis. ☐
    She regularly plays tennis. ☐

11. They never go on vacation. ☐
    They go never on vacation. ☐

12. He goes very rarely to the doctor. ☐
    He very rarely goes to the doctor. ☐

13. You are hardly ever late. ☐
    You hardly are ever late. ☐

14. We regularly visit our uncle. ☐
    We visit regularly our uncle. ☐

15. She often goes to the park. ☐
    She goes often to the park. ☐

Aa 8.4 MATCH THE PHRASES WITH SIMILAR MEANINGS

all the time

1. none of the time
2. almost never
3. sometimes
4. most of the time
5. frequently

rarely
regularly
always
usually
never
occasionally

8.5 REWRITE THE SENTENCES, CORRECTING THE ERRORS

> I visit my cousin hardly ever.
> _I hardly ever visit my cousin._

1 I go almost never to the theater.

_____

2 He gets nearly always to work early.

_____

3 I watch occasionally a movie in the evening.

_____

4 She rarely is late for work.

_____

5 They have sometimes a party in December.

_____

6 She has very often a sandwich for lunch.

_____

7 They work rarely on the weekend.

_____

8 You often are tired when you get to work.

_____

9 I ask frequently my boss for help.

_____

10 She takes occasionally the train to work.

_____

11 I have almost never time to cook in the evening.

_____

🔊

8.6 LISTEN TO THE AUDIO AND ANSWER THE QUESTIONS

Lucy is talking to her friend about her new job.

> Lucy is happy to go to work every day.
> **True** ☑ **False** ☐

1 Lucy often asks her colleagues for help.
True ☐ **False** ☐

2 Lucy is sometimes late for work.
True ☐ **False** ☐

3 Lucy is often early for work.
True ☐ **False** ☐

4 Lucy regularly travels abroad for work.
True ☐ **False** ☐

5 Lucy sometimes takes clients to restaurants.
True ☐ **False** ☐

6 Lucy's office rarely pays for entertaining clients.
True ☐ **False** ☐

7 Lucy very often takes pastries to work.
True ☐ **False** ☐

8.7 SAY THE SENTENCES OUT LOUD, PUTTING THE ADVERBS OF FREQUENCY IN THE CORRECT PLACE

It rains in July. [often]

> *It often rains in July.*

① I go to the dentist. [hardly ever]

② He plays hockey with Ken. [occasionally]

③ They have breakfast at 7am. [usually]

④ I make the dinner. [almost never]

⑤ She is at work in the evening. [very often]

8.8 READ THE EMAIL AND ANSWER THE QUESTIONS

How often did Bobby see his friends in London?

Bobby hardly ever saw his friends in London.

① How often was Bobby tired?

_____

② What did he see while he was in London?

_____

③ How long has he been in Australia?

_____

④ How often does he have to work evenings or weekends?

_____

⑤ When does he usually finish work in Australia?

_____

⑥ How often does he email or video call family and friends?

_____

⑦ How often does his family visit him?

_____

✉   ∨ ✕

To: Ben Jones

Subject: Life down under

Hi Ben,
You asked me how I came to Australia. I used to be a nurse in London. Life was very stressful. I almost always worked evenings and weekends. I hardly ever saw my friends and I was always tired. Then I saw an advertisement for nurses to work in Australia.
I applied and I got the job. I was so excited! I have been here for six years and life is great. I now work in a children's hospital. I sometimes have to work evenings or weekends, but it's not all the time. Most days I finish at 8pm.
I miss my family and friends, so I regularly email or video call them. My family visits once a year and every two years I go back to Britain.
All the best,
Bobby

09 Everyday activities

English often uses phrasal verbs to talk about routine activities. Phrasal verbs are two-part verbs that are mostly used in informal, conversational English.

⚙ **New language** Phrasal verbs
Aa Vocabulary Work and leisure
🧩 **New skill** Talking about everyday activities

9.1 REWRITE THE SENTENCES, CORRECTING THE ERRORS

They **out eat** every weekend.
They eat out every weekend.

① She **wakes** usually **up** at 6:30am.

_____

② Max doesn't **get ups** early every day.

_____

③ I **up** sometimes **meet** with my co-workers.

_____

④ Do you **chill** often **out** with your friends?

_____

⑤ We don't **out work** on Thursdays.

_____

⑥ Mr. Wallis **checked** the **into** hotel on Saturday.

_____

⑦ Does Laura normally **turns up** on time?

_____

🔊

9.2 FILL IN THE GAPS USING THE PRESENT SIMPLE FORMS OF THE PHRASAL VERBS IN THE PANEL

This topic often ___*comes up*___ at meetings.

①  My brother _____ late for everything.

②  I _____ at the gym twice a week.

③  Katy never _____ early on Saturday mornings.

④  They sometimes _____ with friends on Friday.

turn up

meet up

wake up

work out

~~come up~~

🔊

9.3 REWRITE THE SENTENCES, PUTTING THE WORDS IN THE CORRECT ORDER

like early. getting doesn't Jake up

Jake doesn't like getting up early.

① meet We'll up work. after

_____

② his out room. chilling in He's

_____

③ name comes never up. Her

_____

④ quite out often. They work

_____

⑤ nights. stay I Friday in on

_____

⑥ late. The turned up bus

_____

⑦ out friends. our ate We with

_____

⑧ the checked hotel today. Jo into

_____

⑨ grew Oxford. up in Sam

_____

🔊

9.4 LISTEN TO THE AUDIO AND ANSWER THE QUESTIONS

Jack and Kate meet by the water cooler at work and talk about their weekend.

Kate met up with Jack on Friday night.
True ☐ **False** ☐ **Not given** ✔

① Kate got up late on Saturday.
True ☐ **False** ☐ **Not given** ☐

② She had lunch with her sister on Saturday.
True ☐ **False** ☐ **Not given** ☐

③ Jack always stays in on the weekend.
True ☐ **False** ☐ **Not given** ☐

④ Karl turned up late at the gym on Saturday.
True ☐ **False** ☐ **Not given** ☐

⑤ Jack and Karl sometimes go running on Sundays.
True ☐ **False** ☐ **Not given** ☐

⑥ Jack never chills out on the weekend.
True ☐ **False** ☐ **Not given** ☐

⑦ On Sunday evenings Jack usually watches a movie.
True ☐ **False** ☐ **Not given** ☐

9.5 FILL IN THE GAPS BY PUTTING THE PHRASAL VERBS IN THE CORRECT TENSE

His children, Tom and Alice, _____grew up_____ (grow up) in the United States.

1. I'm _____ (meet up) with some of my friends from college later.

2. He likes to _____ (chill out) in front of the TV on Friday evenings.

3. Rosa and her sister Anezka _____ (get up) late yesterday morning.

4. I'm tired. I think I _____ (stay in) tonight and read my book.

5. We aren't going to _____ (eat out) on Friday or Saturday.

6. Mr. and Mrs. Williams haven't _____ (check into) the hotel yet.

9.6 SAY THE SENTENCES OUT LOUD USING PHRASAL VERBS

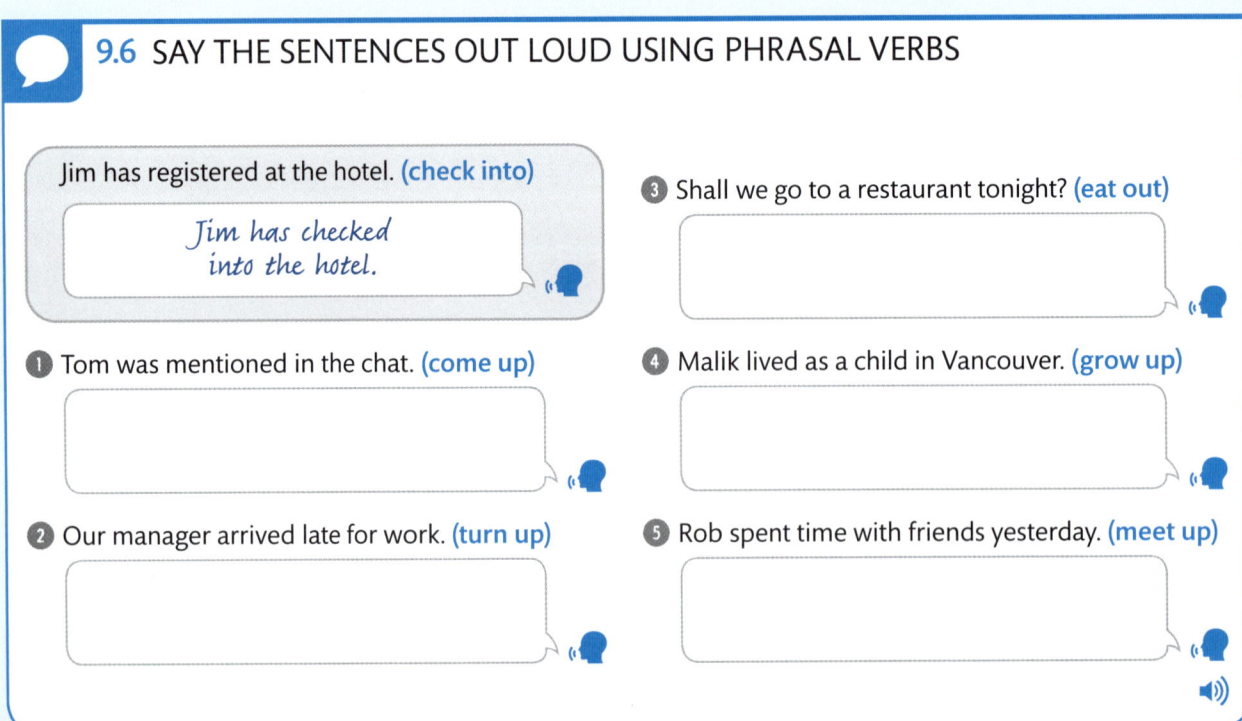

Jim has registered at the hotel. (check into)

> Jim has checked into the hotel.

1. Tom was mentioned in the chat. (come up)

2. Our manager arrived late for work. (turn up)

3. Shall we go to a restaurant tonight? (eat out)

4. Malik lived as a child in Vancouver. (grow up)

5. Rob spent time with friends yesterday. (meet up)

10 Vocabulary

Aa **10.1** **THE BODY** WRITE THE WORDS FROM THE PANEL UNDER THE CORRECT PICTURES

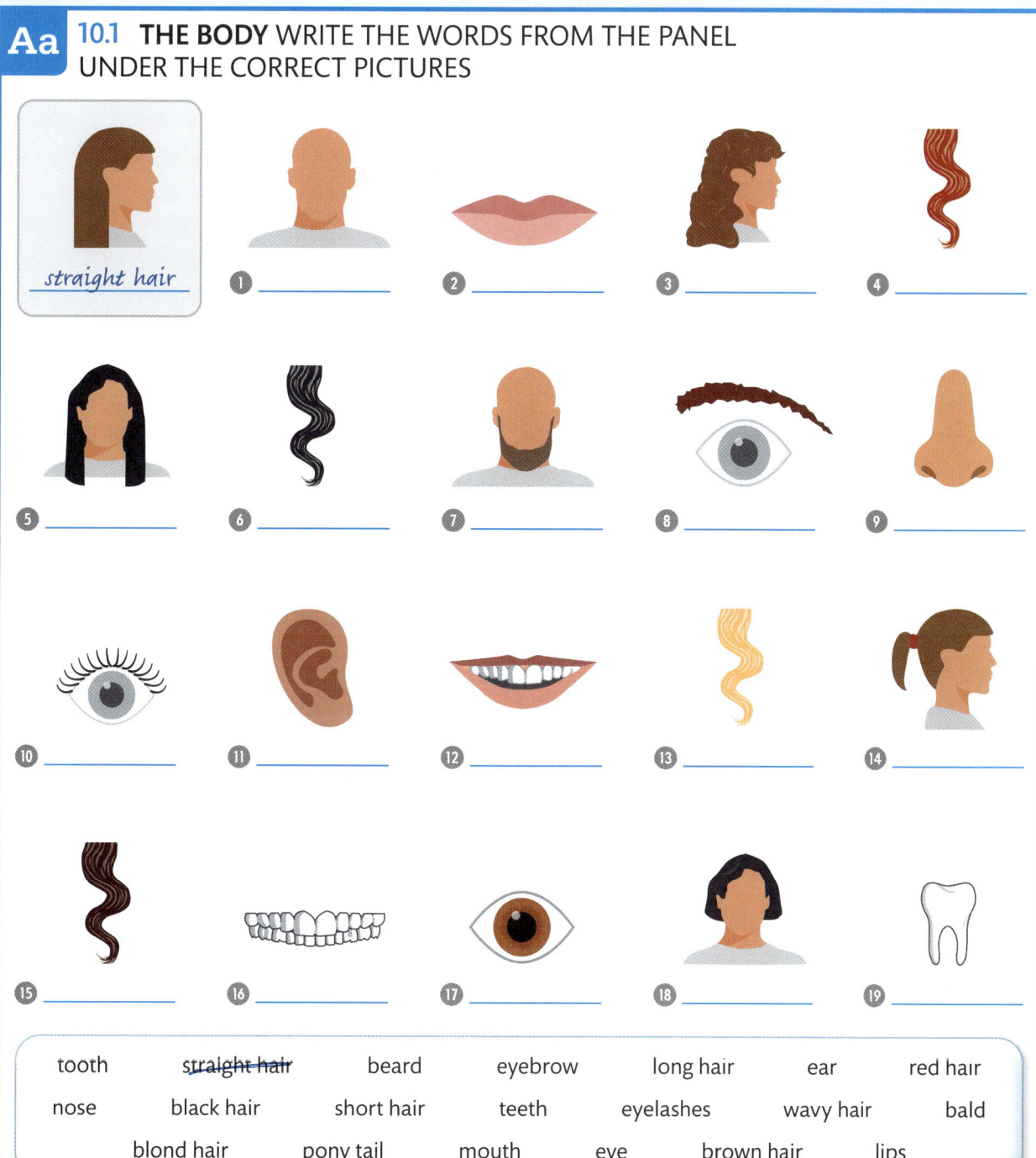

straight hair

1 _____

2 _____

3 _____

4 _____

5 _____

6 _____

7 _____

8 _____

9 _____

10 _____

11 _____

12 _____

13 _____

14 _____

15 _____

16 _____

17 _____

18 _____

19 _____

tooth	~~straight hair~~	beard	eyebrow	long hair	ear	red hair
nose	black hair	short hair	teeth	eyelashes	wavy hair	bald
	blond hair	pony tail	mouth	eye	brown hair	lips

11 Describing people

You often use more than one adjective in a row, for example when describing people. In English, adjectives must be written in a particular order, according to their meaning.

⚙ **New language** Adjective order
Aa Vocabulary Adjectives for describing people
🧩 **New skill** Describing people in detail

11.1 WRITE THE WORDS FROM THE PANEL IN THE CORRECT GROUPS

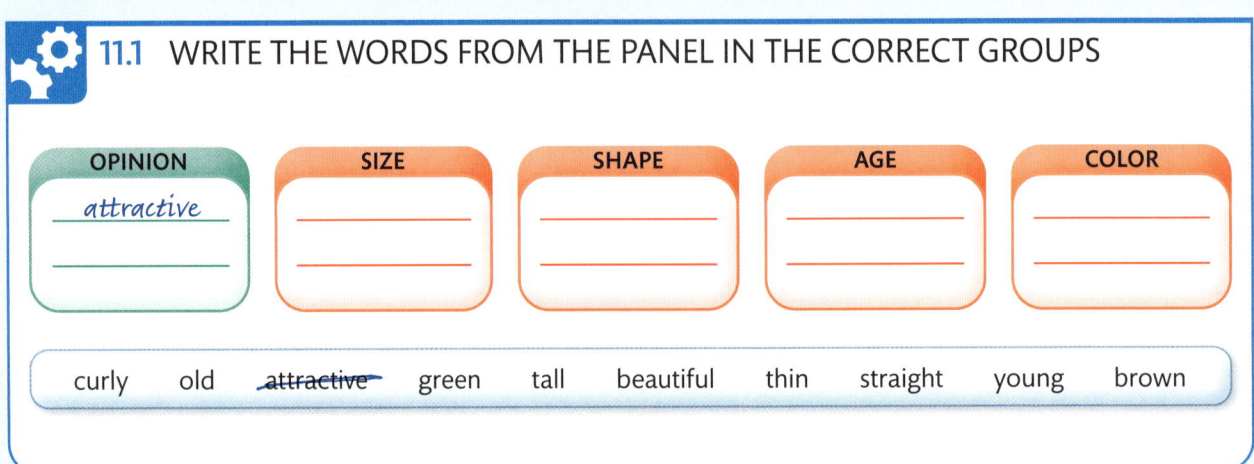

OPINION	SIZE	SHAPE	AGE	COLOR
attractive				

curly   old   ~~attractive~~   green   tall   beautiful   thin   straight   young   brown

---

11.2 REWRITE THE SENTENCES, PUTTING THE WORDS IN THE CORRECT ORDER

beautiful   eyes.   gray   has   big   She

She has beautiful, big gray eyes.

1. has   thin   He   a   mustache.   brown

2. thick   has   Susan   hair.   gorgeous,   blond   long,

3. thin   a   man.   James   tall,   young   is

4. has   hair.   shoulder-length,   curly   attractive,   black   She

🔊

11.3 READ THE ARTICLE AND ANSWER THE QUESTIONS

> The leader of the group is tall and thin.
> True ✓ False ☐ Not given ☐

1 The leader has straight blond hair.
True ☐ False ☐ Not given ☐

2 The driver is a tall young woman.
True ☐ False ☐ Not given ☐

3 The driver has short, curly red hair.
True ☐ False ☐ Not given ☐

4 The third person is a bald man.
True ☐ False ☐ Not given ☐

32 POLICE PATROL

ON THE RUN!
Supermarket robbers on the loose

Following a supermarket robbery in the early hours of yesterday morning, police are looking for three people believed to be involved in the crime. According to reports, the leader of the group was a tall, thin, middle-aged man with shoulder-length, straight blond hair.

The driver of the vehicle was a young woman aged between 20 and 25 years. She had short, curly red hair and she wore black glasses.

The third person at the scene of the crime was a thin young man aged between 25 and 30. He was average height with long, curly black hair and a short black mustache. If you have any information about the robbery please contact the police.

11.4 DESCRIBE THE PEOPLE USING THE WORDS IN THE PANEL, SPEAKING OUT LOUD

He is _bald_ and has a brown _mustache_ .

1
She has shoulder-length, _____ red hair.

2
He has _____ brown hair.

3
He has short _____ hair and a _____ .

4
She has attractive, _____ red hair.

curly   ~~bald~~

black   short

beard   straight

~~mustache~~

39

Aa 12.1 CLOTHES WRITE THE WORDS FROM THE PANEL UNDER THE CORRECT PICTURES

pajamas

1 _____

2 _____

3 _____

4 _____

5 _____

6 _____

7 _____

8 _____

9 _____

10 _____

11 _____

12 _____

13 _____

14 _____

15 _____

16 _____

17 _____

18 _____

19 _____

suit	jeans	shorts	jacket	belt	high-heels	striped
sandals	~~pajamas~~	socks	dress	t-shirt	leather bag	collar
checked	buttons	suede boots	silk scarf	tie	cardigan	

13 What I'm wearing

The present continuous is used to talk about ongoing actions that are happening now. It also describes the current state of things, such as what a person is wearing.

⚙ **New language** Present continuous
Aa **Vocabulary** Clothes and fashion
🧩 **New skill** Describing clothes

13.1 FILL IN THE GAPS BY PUTTING THE VERBS IN THE PRESENT CONTINUOUS

Samantha is _____ *wearing* _____ (wear) a new summer dress.

1. Martin is _____ (choose) some new boots.

2. I'm _____ (mend) my favorite wool cardigan.

3. Alison is _____ (shop) for some new jeans.

4. My little brother is _____ (try) on some pajamas.

13.2 LISTEN TO THE AUDIO AND ANSWER THE QUESTIONS

A commentator is describing a fashion show.

Who is this season's collection by?
Rosa May ☐ **Miller Brown** ☐ **Elena** ☑

1. What is Elena wearing?
An evening dress ☐ **Jeans** ☐ **A skirt** ☐

2. What color are the buttons?
Silver ☐ **Gold** ☐ **Black** ☐

3. What is Milly wearing?
A skirt ☐ **A coat** ☐ **A dress** ☐

4. What color is it?
Light blue ☐ **Dark blue** ☐ **Pale blue** ☐

5. What kind of cardigan is she wearing?
Cotton ☐ **Silk** ☐ **Suede** ☐

13.3 REWRITE THE SENTENCES, CORRECTING THE SPELLINGS

Anita is **makeing** a cake for her birthday.
Anita is making a cake for her birthday.

❶ I'm **puting** on a pair of new boots.

_____

❷ Brian is **liveing** in a house in London.

_____

❸ She's buying a pair of **causal shoos**.

_____

❹ Tanya is **shoping** for a new dress.

_____

❺ I've lost a **buton** from my cardigan.

_____

❻ He doesn't have a lot of expensive **cloths**.

_____

❼ They're **takeing** a lot of photos of the city.

_____

🔊

13.4 SAY THE SENTENCES OUT LOUD, FILLING IN THE GAPS WITH THE WORDS IN THE PANEL

He's wearing a
___**cardigan**___.

❸ She's wearing a pair of
_____.

❶ She's wearing a pair of
_____.

❹ He's wearing a
_____.

❷ He's wearing a
_____.

❺ She's wearing a leather
_____.

| belt | sandals | ~~cardigan~~ | shirt | boots | suit |

🔊

13.5 READ THE BLOG AND ANSWER THE QUESTIONS

Helen's Fashion Blog

HOME | ENTRIES | ABOUT | CONTACT

 POSTED SATURDAY, APRIL 3

About me

I'm a fashion writer and I'm working in Paris this summer. I write about the latest trends and what's new in fashion. I love my job because women's fashion is my passion! Today I'm browsing the stores on the Rue de Passy.

My style this season

It's summer, and the colors for this season are yellow, orange, and red. These are the colors that all the top designers are using this month. My favorite collection this season is by Donna Maxine. I'm wearing a short orange dress from her summer collection with a chic red belt by Rooster. She also has a fabulous range of skinny denim jeans in pale yellow, orange, and green. You can wear all of them with any of her stylish cropped cotton cardigans in a range of eight colors. This summer is all about color! I'm also looking at her gorgeous sandal collection in a range of pastel colors to complete the look!

Helen lives in Paris all the time.
True ☐ False ✔

❶ Helen writes about the latest trends in fashion.
True ☐ False ☐

❷ Helen is looking at some stores today.
True ☐ False ☐

❸ Helen loves men's fashion.
True ☐ False ☐

❹ This season's colors are yellow, orange, and red.
True ☐ False ☐

❺ Helen's favorite collection is by Rooster.
True ☐ False ☐

❻ Helen is wearing a Donna Maxine skirt.
True ☐ False ☐

❼ Helen is wearing a chic blue belt.
True ☐ False ☐

❽ The cardigans are available in eight colors.
True ☐ False ☐

❾ Helen is looking at a collection of boots.
True ☐ False ☐

Aa 14.1 ROOMS AND FURNITURE WRITE THE WORDS FROM THE PANEL UNDER THE CORRECT PICTURES

cushion

1 _____

2 _____

3 _____

4 _____

5 _____

6 _____

7 _____

8 _____

9 _____

10 _____

11 _____

12 _____

13 _____

14 _____

15 _____

16 _____

17 _____

18 _____

19 _____

lawn	cupboard	cushion	living room	washing machine	shower
bathroom	saucepan	bed	rug	dishwasher	towel	bedroom
plants	frying pan	light	kitchen	crockery	mirror	bedside table

15 Daily routines

Collocations are groups of words that are often used together in English. You can use them to make your spoken English sound more natural.

✿ **New language** Collocations
Aa Vocabulary Routines and chores
✿ **New skill** Talking about your day

15.1 REWRITE THE SENTENCES, PUTTING THE WORDS IN THE CORRECT ORDER

the | does | in | Nick | morning. | laundry | the

Nick does the laundry in the morning.

❸ floor | day. | Katy | the | every | sweeps

_____

❶ every | Tony | evening. | waters | the | plants

_____

❹ every | dishwasher | Mia | the | day. | loads

_____

❷ dog | Tom | the | after | walks | breakfast.

_____

❺ week. | Jamie | the | mows | lawn | every

_____

15.2 REWRITE THE NOTE, CORRECTING THE HIGHLIGHTED ERRORS

Hi Harry, Emma, and Paul,
While I'm visiting your grandma this weekend, please can you do the following chores? Harry, can you **make** the laundry on Saturday and **clear** the dog twice a day? Paul, can you **load** the cooking on Saturday? Then can you **sweep** the table and **do** the dishwasher? Emma, can you **fold** the beds, and **water** the towels in the bathroom, please? And don't forget to **mow** the plants in the house. Thanks!

Hi Harry, Emma, and Paul,
While I'm visiting your grandma this weekend, please can you do the following chores? Harry, can you do the laundry

15.3 CROSS OUT THE INCORRECT WORDS IN EACH SENTENCE

 Lottie usually **shops** / ~~is shopping~~ on her own, but today **she's shopping** / ~~she shops~~ with her sister.

1  I normally **am walking** / **walk** the dog in the evening, but this evening **I'm relaxing** / **I relax** at home.

2  **We're doing** / **We do** the laundry together today, but I usually **am doing** / **do** it myself.

3 Frank sometimes **goes** / **is going** to the gym after work, but today **he's working** / **he works** late.

4  Ben **does** / **is doing** the ironing today, but his dad usually **does** / **is doing** it.

5 **He's listening** / **He's listen** to music now, but he often **is watching** / **watches** TV in the evening.

6 **I mow** / **I'm mowing** the lawn today, but I normally **am mowing** / **mow** it on Saturdays.

15.4 LISTEN TO THE AUDIO AND ANSWER THE QUESTIONS

Where is Ben right now?
At the game ☐ **At home** ☑ **At school** ☐

1 What is Ben doing at the moment?
The laundry ☐ **The dishes** ☐ **The cooking** ☐

2 Which room is a mess?
Bedroom ☐ **Living room** ☐ **Kitchen** ☐

3 What does he need to do?
Clear the table ☐ **Relax** ☐ **Mow the lawn** ☐

4 When did he water the plants?
Yesterday ☐ **Last night** ☐ **This morning** ☐

5 Has he folded the towels?
Yes ☐ **No** ☐ **Not yet** ☐

6 Where were the towels?
On the chair ☐ **On the floor** ☐ **On the bed** ☐

7 Does Ben want some help?
Yes, now ☐ **Yes, later** ☐ **No** ☐

8 What is Ben going to do later?
Make the bed ☐ **Sleep** ☐ **Walk the dog** ☐

9 Does Ben usually cook lunch for his parents?
Yes, usually ☐ **No, never** ☐ **Sometimes** ☐

15.5 MATCH THE BEGINNINGS OF THE SENTENCES TO THE CORRECT ENDINGS

Thomas is going to load — the dishwasher this evening.

1. Laura is doing the cooking tonight,

2. I always sweep

3. James is walking the dog this evening,

4. Salman usually waters

5. Joan is doing the laundry now,

6. Jessica and Dan will clear

7. Donald usually mows

the plants at home.

but he usually walks him every morning.

but she often gardens in the afternoon.

the dishwasher this evening.

the lawn on Sunday morning.

the floor before I go to bed.

but she usually does the dishes.

the table after lunch.

15.6 READ THE INSTRUCTIONS AND ANSWER THE QUESTIONS

The chalet assistant will make breakfast.
True ✓ False ☐

1. After breakfast he/she will sweep the floors.
True ☐ False ☐

2. He/she will clean the bathrooms before noon.
True ☐ False ☐

3. In the afternoon he/she will do the laundry.
True ☐ False ☐

4. He/she must keep the chalet clean.
True ☐ False ☐

5. He/she doesn't have to cook dinner in the evening.
True ☐ False ☐

CHALET ASSISTANT
Daily tasks

Every morning, you will make breakfast for your guests. After breakfast, you will clear the table and load the dishwasher. Between 10am and noon you'll make the beds, clean the bathrooms, and sweep the floor. In the afternoon at 3pm, you should prepare an afternoon snack for the guests. You don't have to do the laundry, but you must load the dishwasher regularly and keep the chalet clean. In the evening, you'll cook dinner for 8pm, then clear the table and wash the dishes.

16 Separable phrasal verbs

All phrasal verbs consist of a verb and a particle. Some must have the verb and particle together, but with others, the object can appear in between.

⚙ **New language** Separable phrasal verbs
Aa Vocabulary Around town
🧩 **New skill** Describing a town in detail

16.1 REWRITE EACH SENTENCE, SEPARATING THE PHRASAL VERBS

> The workmen cut down some trees.
> _The workmen cut some trees down._

1 Tony has to fill in a form for work.

_____

2 I'm checking out the train timetable.

_____

3 Anna will pick up the shopping.

_____

4 They gave out some leaflets about the fair.

_____

5 We're putting on a dog show this summer.

_____

6 That little boy didn't pick up his litter.

_____

7 They're going to close down that store.

_____

8 John wants to show off his cell phone.

_____

9 Rita is putting on her coat.

_____

🔊

Aa 16.2 FILL IN THE GAPS USING THE WORDS IN THE PANEL

> We've decided to ___rent___ out our house.

1 Can you _____ out the menu?

2 Why don't you _____ up the word online?

3 They were _____ out free samples.

4 Did you _____ out the new cell phone?

5 I'll _____ up the children from school.

6 They _____ off the town parking lot.

7 He didn't _____ down the pine tree.

8 The school is _____ on a play.

9 Are you _____ up hockey in college?

10 They _____ down the old town hall.

11 What did you _____ out at the meeting?

> pick   giving   check
> ~~rent~~   find
> taking   cut
> look   try
> sold   putting   tore

🔊

48

16.3 REWRITE THE SENTENCES, PUTTING THE WORDS IN THE CORRECT ORDER

out. | will | find | them. | Sam
Sam will find them out.

1. took | it | I | back.

2. down. | it | They're | closing

3. up. | them | looked | Jess

4. up. | picked | We | it

5. Bob | up. | it | brightened

6. I | look | up. | it | will

7. tried | She | yesterday. | out | it

16.4 SAY THE SENTENCES OUT LOUD, REPLACING THE NOUNS WITH PRONOUNS

He's giving out some leaflets.
He's giving them out.

1. She's looking up a word.

2. They closed down the zoo.

3. They're renting out their house.

4. They sold off the site.

5. He cleaned up his apartment.

6. I'm checking out the trains.

7. They brightened up the office.

8. He took up basketball.

9. She found out the answers.

16.5 LISTEN TO THE AUDIO, THEN NUMBER THE PICTURES IN THE ORDER THEY ARE DESCRIBED

A ☐

B [1]

C ☐

D ☐

E ☐

F ☐

G ☐

H ☐

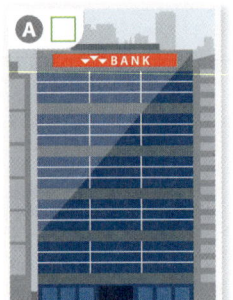
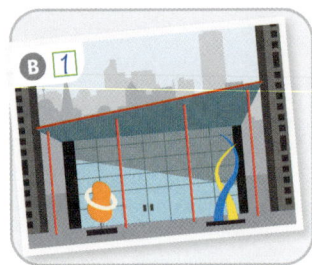

Aa 16.6 FILL IN THE GAPS USING THE WORDS IN THE PANEL

The city has a _____*lively*_____ nightlife.

1 Which paintings are in the _____?

2 Most people here are kind and _____.

3 The river is _____ with oil.

4 It's the tallest _____ building in the city.

5 The Royal Family live in the _____.

6 You can buy medicine at the _____.

7 The _____ streets are crowded with shoppers.

8 This place isn't safe. It's _____ at night.

9 The lawyer is meeting us at the _____.

10 His office isn't out of town. It's in the_____.

11 The country park is _____ and beautiful.

12 The streets are _____ and full of litter.

13 All the stores are in the _____.

palace	art gallery	unspoiled	shopping mall	pharmacy	friendly	dirty
lively	dangerous	law court	polluted	high-rise	city center	bustling

16.7 READ THE POSTCARD AND ANSWER THE QUESTIONS

Hi guys,
Hello from Copenhagen. We've been sightseeing for days and it's amazing. The tourist office organized a tour for us around the historic quarter in the city center. There are so many beautiful old buildings. Dan's favorite is the government building, but my favorite is the Amalienborg Palace. Amazing! Tomorrow is our last day. We're going to visit an art gallery and check out the shopping mall. I want to buy some souvenirs.
See you soon!
Love,
Bella

Bella and Dan are visiting Copenhagen.
True ✔ **False** ☐ **Not given** ☐

❶ They've been on a tour of the historic quarter.
True ☐ **False** ☐ **Not given** ☐

❷ Dan wants to see the law courts.
True ☐ **False** ☐ **Not given** ☐

❸ Dan's favorite building is the Amalienborg palace.
True ☐ **False** ☐ **Not given** ☐

❹ Bella wants to visit the shopping mall tomorrow.
True ☐ **False** ☐ **Not given** ☐

❺ Bella wants to buy clothes.
True ☐ **False** ☐ **Not given** ☐

Aa **16.8 WRITE THE WORDS FROM THE PANEL IN THE CORRECT GROUPS**

POSITIVE	NEGATIVE
friendly	

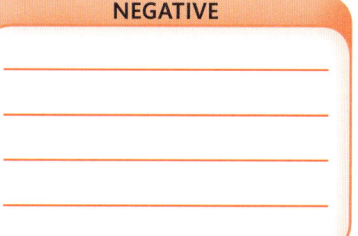

bustling   dirty   crowded

dangerous   unspoiled

lively   ~~friendly~~   polluted

17 Comparing places

You can use modifiers before comparatives and superlatives to compare places, such as geographical features, in more detail.

⚙ **New language** Modifiers
Aa Vocabulary Geographical terms
🧩 **New skill** Describing and comparing places

 17.1 LOOK AT THE PICTURES AND CROSS OUT THE INCORRECT WORDS IN EACH SENTENCE

The school is ~~slightly~~ / **much** bigger than the bank.

③ The café is **much** / **a bit** smaller than the factory.

❶ The hospital is **a lot** / **a bit** taller than the church.

④ The tower is **much** / **slightly** taller than the tree.

❷ The airport is **much** / **slightly** bigger than the station.

⑤ The hotel is **a bit** / **a lot** smaller than the castle.

17.2 SAY THE SENTENCES OUT LOUD, PUTTING THE ADJECTIVES IN THE COMPARATIVE FORM

The tree is much _____ *taller* _____ (tall) than the house.

1. The school is slightly _____ (big) than the church.

2. The hill is much _____ (tall) than the tree.

3. The house is much _____ (small) than the palace.

4. The car is much _____ (fast) than the bike.

5. The door is much _____ (wide) than the window.

17.3 REWRITE THE SENTENCES, PUTTING THE WORDS IN THE CORRECT ORDER

rivers | of | longest | the | one | The | is | Mekong | Asia. | in

The Mekong is one of the longest rivers in Asia.

1. tallest | The | city. | easily | the | building | office | in | is | the

_____

2. by | the | biggest | Pacific | is | ocean. | far | The

_____

3. countries | of | Sudan | hottest | one | the | is | of | all.

_____

4. Earth. | coldest | the | one | Antarctica | places | is | on | of

_____

53

17.4 LISTEN TO THE AUDIO, THEN NUMBER THE PICTURES IN THE ORDER THEY ARE DESCRIBED

A ☐

B 1

C ☐

D ☐

E ☐

F ☐

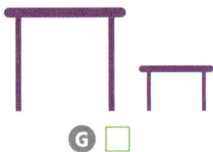

G ☐

17.5 REWRITE THE SENTENCES, CORRECTING THE ERRORS

The palace is much beautiful than the factory.

The palace is much more beautiful than the factory.

❶ The clock tower is much more old than the palace.

_____

❷ This is by far the better book I've ever read.

_____

❸ Your house is much biggest than mine.

_____

❹ The tower is a bit tall than the lighthouse.

_____

❺ The factory is slightly largest than the castle.

_____

17.6 READ THE ARTICLE AND WRITE ANSWERS TO THE QUESTIONS AS FULL SENTENCES

Record Breakers

From the largest deserts to the deepest lakes

- By far the largest desert in the world is the Sahara in Northern Africa. It's over 3,329,360 sq miles. The second largest is the Arabian Desert which is 899,618 sq miles. It's over 2.7 million sq miles smaller than the Sahara.

- The wettest place on Earth is Mawsynram in India. It's slightly wetter than Cherrapunji, which is 10 miles east.

- The Nile is by far the longest river in Africa. It's about 4,145 miles long and it flows through five countries. It's slightly longer than the Amazon, which is about 4,000 miles long.

- Mount Everest in the Himalayas is the highest mountain in the world. It's 29,035 feet high.

- Lake Baikal in Russia is easily the deepest lake in the world. It's 5,370 feet deep. It's also one of the largest lakes in the world. It's over 1,968 feet deeper than the Caspian Sea which is the second deepest lake.

Which is the largest desert in the world?
The Sahara is the largest desert in the world.

1 Which is the second largest desert in the world?

_____

2 In which country is the wettest place on Earth?

_____

3 Which place is slightly wetter than Cherrapunji?

_____

4 What is by far the longest river in Africa?

_____

5 How much longer is the Nile than the Amazon?

_____

6 What is the highest place in the world?

_____

7 How high is the highest place in the world?

_____

8 Which is easily the deepest lake in the world?

_____

9 What is one of the largest lakes in the world?

_____

10 How much deeper is Baikal than the Caspian Sea?

_____

11 Which is the second deepest lake in the world?

_____

18 Likes and dislikes

English uses adjectives ending in "-ing" and "-ed" to talk about likes and dislikes. This means that adjectives that look very similar can have different meanings.

⚙ **New language** Adjectives with "-ing" and "-ed"
Aa Vocabulary Feelings and emotions
🧩 **New skill** Talking about likes and dislikes

18.1 CROSS OUT THE INCORRECT WORD IN EACH SENTENCE

 The new John Keller movie was so ~~excited~~ / **exciting**.

①  Lily is bored / **boring** with her piano lessons.

②  I'm amazed / **amazing** that you want to try scuba diving.

③  The class on whales and dolphins was very interested / **interesting**.

④  Mr. Watkins was annoyed / **annoying** by all the traffic on the road.

🔊

18.2 FILL IN THE GAPS BY MAKING EITHER AN "-ED" OR "-ING" ADJECTIVE FROM THE VERBS IN BRACKETS

Tom was _____*exhausted*_____ (exhaust) after he ran a marathon.

① Were you _____ (surprise) when you opened your present?

② I found this recipe for paella really _____ (confuse).

③ Martha wasn't _____ (annoy) that I was late for her party.

④ The news about the airplane accident was _____ (shock).

⑤ Ethan is _____ (depress) because he failed his accounting exams.

⑥ I was _____ (amaze) when I heard about your new job.

🔊

18.3 LISTEN TO THE AUDIO AND ANSWER THE QUESTIONS

Ollie and Anna are discussing what Ollie is doing this weekend.

Ollie is excited about going to the theme park.
True ✔ **False** ☐

1 Ollie hasn't been to the theme park before.
True ☐ **False** ☐

2 Anna thinks theme parks are annoying.
True ☐ **False** ☐

3 Anna thought the roller coaster was frightening.
True ☐ **False** ☐

4 Anna thinks the Ghost Ride is exhausting.
True ☐ **False** ☐

5 Ollie didn't have to wait to go on the Ghost Ride.
True ☐ **False** ☐

6 Ollie was bored on the Ghost Ride.
True ☐ **False** ☐

7 Ollie doesn't want to try the roller coaster.
True ☐ **False** ☐

18.4 READ THE ARTICLE AND ANSWER THE QUESTIONS

What does James love about the summer?
The long days ✔ **His family** ☐ **Not given** ☐

1 How did they spend three days last summer?
Sightseeing ☐ **On a boat** ☐ **By the ocean** ☐

2 What did they enjoy in the afternoon?
Lunch ☐ **A picnic** ☐ **A barbecue** ☐

3 What does James absolutely love doing now?
Barbecuing ☐ **Sailing** ☐ **Driving** ☐

4 How did he feel about learning to pilot a boat?
Surprised ☐ **Excited** ☐ **Amazed** ☐

5 What did he really love doing?
Cooking ☐ **Living on a boat** ☐ **Gardening** ☐

6 Will he be doing it again next year?
Yes ☐ **No** ☐ **Not given** ☐

THE TRAVELER

Summer Story

James Young

The best thing about summer is the warm weather and the long days. There are so many interesting things to do.

As a family, we quite enjoy doing different things every year, and last summer we went on a three-day boat trip along the river. The weather was fabulous and we had an amazing time. One day we stopped at Stratford and explored the town. I was surprised how pretty it is. We really enjoyed exploring the charming old streets and taking photographs of the old houses. We all loved having picnics by the river in the afternoon. We had barbecues every day, too. I really don't like cooking, but I absolutely loved barbecuing. Luckily, it didn't rain once, which was very surprising. And I was amazed at how easily I learned to pilot a boat.

I really loved living on a boat and we'll definitely be doing it again next year. I'd recommend a boat trip to everyone.

Aa 18.5 MATCH THE BEGINNINGS OF THE SENTENCES TO THE CORRECT ENDINGS

She was annoyed when	the firework display.
1 Yesterday's biology class was	is very pretty and charming.
2 The news of Andy and Kay's	after their holiday in Mauritius.
3 Are you excited about your	she didn't get the job.
4 *Day of Terror* was a really	vacation in Australia?
5 Losing the game	very interesting.
6 Kevin was amazed by	when she won the lottery.
7 Are they tired after	was a bit confusing.
8 Chad and Dora were very relaxed	wedding wasn't surprising.
9 I think your new girlfriend	frightening horror movie.
10 Sandra was shocked	was disappointing for everyone.
11 The article about quantum physics	their long walk in the country?

18.6 CROSS OUT THE INCORRECT WORD IN EACH SENTENCE

He ~~absolutely~~ / **really** likes playing basketball.

1 We **quite** / **absolutely** enjoy sailing.

2 Jane **really** / **quite** loves cooking Italian food.

3 Tom **absolutely** / **quite** hates wearing shorts.

4 They **quite** / **really** don't like driving in traffic.

5 I **quite** / **absolutely** like running.

6 I **really** / **absolutely** enjoy walking my dog.

7 You **quite** / **absolutely** love cycling.

8 They **really** / **quite** don't like singing.

9 Alice **absolutely** / **quite** hates flying.

10 We **quite** / **really** love going to the cinema.

11 She **quite** / **absolutely** likes walking in the park.

19 Vocabulary

19.1 HENRY'S FAMILY WRITE THE WORDS FROM THE PANEL IN THE CORRECT PLACES ON HENRY'S FAMILY TREE

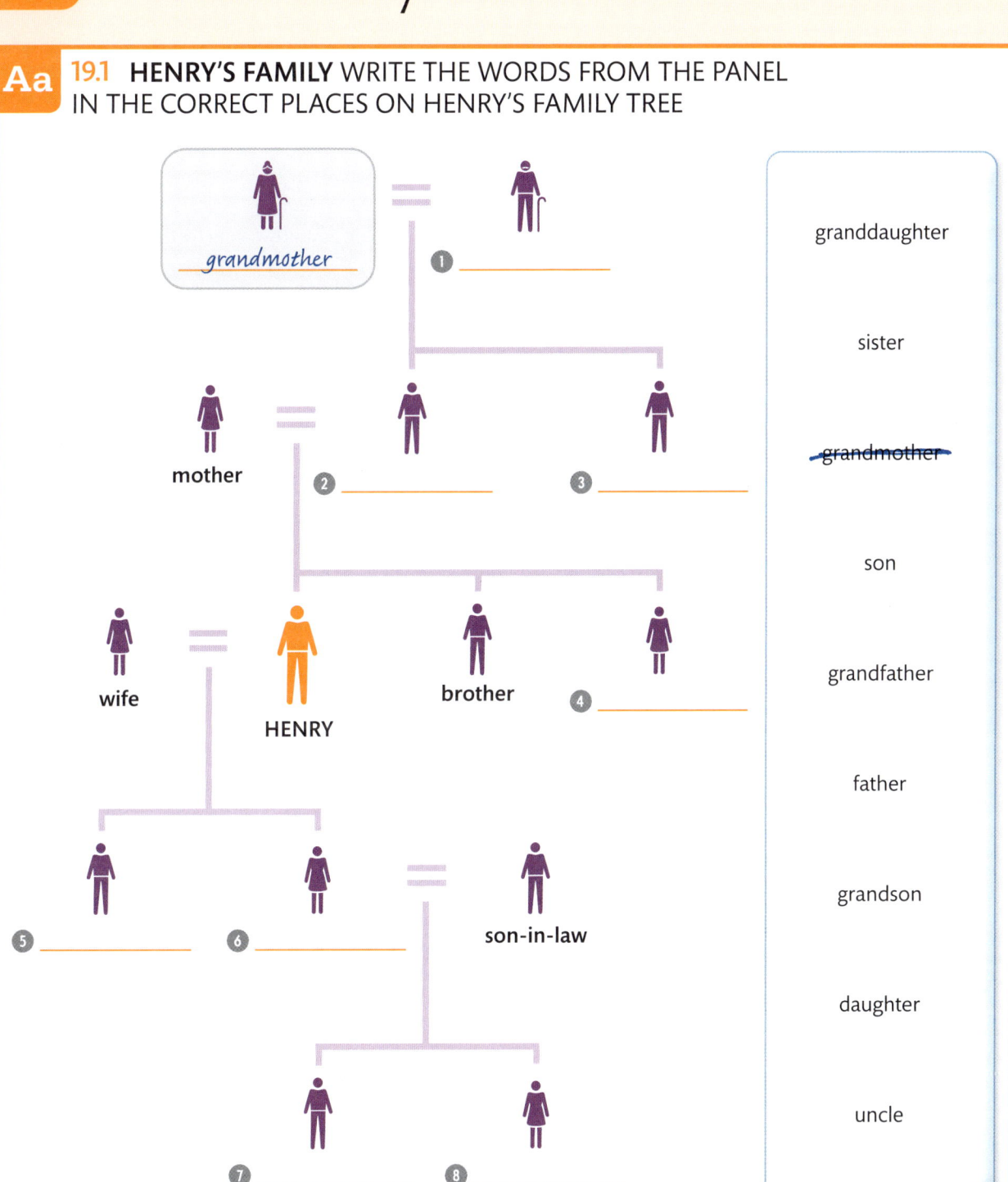

grandmother

① _____

mother

② _____

③ _____

wife

HENRY

brother

④ _____

⑤ _____

⑥ _____

son-in-law

⑦ _____

⑧ _____

granddaughter

sister

~~grandmother~~

son

grandfather

father

grandson

daughter

uncle

20 Early years

In English, the word "did" can be used for emphasis to assure someone that a past action really happened. It's useful for describing past events and memories.

⚙ **New language** "Did" for emphasis
Aa Vocabulary Baby equipment and parenting
🧩 **New skill** Describing your childhood

20.1 REWRITE THE SENTENCES USING THE PAST SIMPLE WITH "DID" FOR EMPHASIS

I called the cleaner yesterday. = *I did call the cleaner yesterday.*

1 She wrote a story for class. = _____

2 John bought her a present. = _____

3 They learned to read at school. = _____

4 I fed the cat this evening. = _____

5 We waited for you. = _____

🔊

20.2 UNDERLINE THE WORDS THAT SHOULD BE STRESSED, THEN SAY THE SENTENCES OUT LOUD

She <u>did</u> get to school on time.

1 He did call the babysitter.

2 Janet did sterilize the bottle.

3 I did enjoy school.

4 She did behave well in class.

5 He did bring the teacher a present.

6 They did work hard at school.

7 I did buy the baby's food.

🔊

Aa 20.3 MATCH THE PICTURES TO THE LABELS

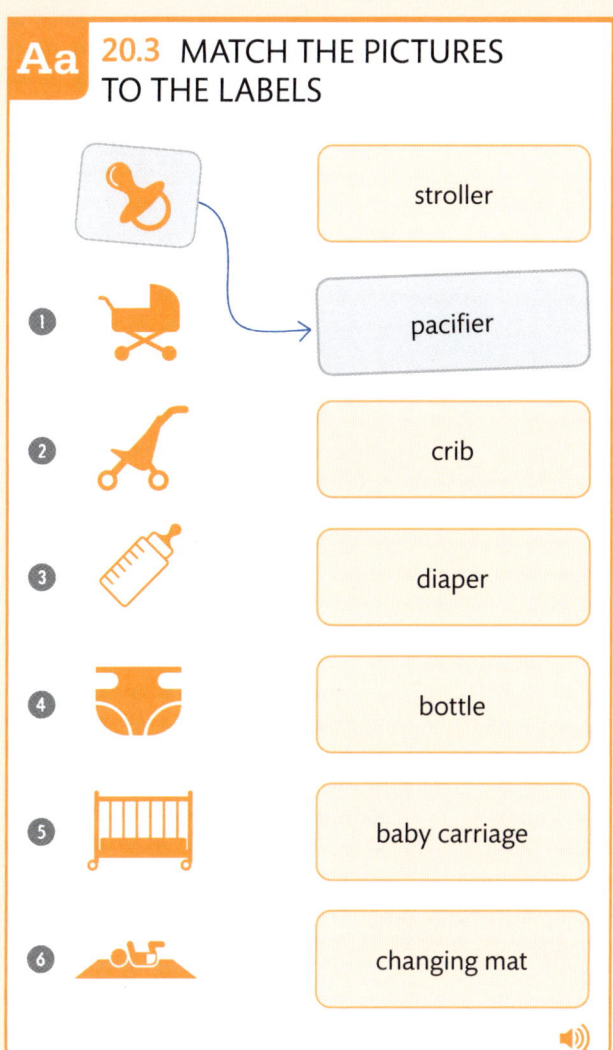

- stroller
1. pacifier
2. crib
3. diaper
4. bottle
5. baby carriage
6. changing mat

20.4 LISTEN TO THE AUDIO, THEN NUMBER THE PICTURES IN THE ORDER THEY ARE DESCRIBED

A ☐ B ☐ C 1 D ☐ E ☐

20.5 REWRITE THE SENTENCES, CORRECTING THE ERRORS

Martha **bite** the sandwich.
Martha bit the sandwich.

1. The toy duck **sinked** in the bath.
_____

2. Talin **drawed** on the wall of his bedroom.
_____

3. He **feeded** the baby an hour ago.
_____

4. The children **hided** under the table.
_____

5. His older sister **leaded** the way.
_____

20.6 READ THE BLOG AND ANSWER THE QUESTIONS

> The first things you'll need are a crib and a stroller.
> **True** ✓ **False** ☐ **Not given** ☐

① Strollers are more useful than baby carriages.
True ☐ **False** ☐ **Not given** ☐

② Baby's room should be clean and organized.
True ☐ **False** ☐ **Not given** ☐

③ Keep the changing mat in the bathroom.
True ☐ **False** ☐ **Not given** ☐

④ You won't need baby wipes.
True ☐ **False** ☐ **Not given** ☐

⑤ Pacifiers are usually expensive.
True ☐ **False** ☐ **Not given** ☐

⑥ All babies should have a teddy bear.
True ☐ **False** ☐ **Not given** ☐

HOME : ENTRIES : ABOUT : CONTACT

For new parents

When you have your first baby you have no idea how much stuff you will need. The first things to buy of course are a crib and a stroller. These will be your two most expensive items. You should keep your baby's room clean and organized so that you can find things easily. Put the changing mat on a table or dresser near the cot. And keep the diapers and baby wipes here, too. You'll need a lot of them! Not everyone wants to use a pacifier with their baby, but some parents find them useful. There's no right or wrong answer. But one thing I think is an absolute necessity, and that of course, is a teddy bear. Every baby needs a teddy bear!

 20.7 FILL IN THE GAPS USING THE WORDS IN THE PANEL

> Eddie _____led_____ the way to the garden.

① Jenny _____ a new changing mat for her baby girl.

② The little boy _____ behind a tree near the playground.

③ The baby _____ for two hours before waking up.

④ She _____ a picture of a bird in a tree.

⑤ The doll _____ in the bath rather than floating.

⑥ They _____ to the baby store together.

⑦ The baby _____ in his high chair and played quietly.

went
drew
hid
sat
~~led~~
sank
slept
bought

21 Vocabulary

Aa 21.1 EDUCATION WRITE THE WORDS FROM THE PANEL UNDER THE CORRECT PICTURES

essay

① _____

② _____

③ _____

④ _____

⑤ _____

⑥ _____

⑦ _____

⑧ _____

⑨ _____

⑩ _____

⑪ _____

⑫ _____

⑬ _____

⑭ _____

⑮ _____

⑯ _____

⑰ _____

⑱ _____

⑲ _____

exam   lecture   exercise book   teacher   degree   pencil   pass   student
~~essay~~   text book   English   ruler   science   pencil sharpener
library   psychology   fail   classroom   geography   grade

22 Changing meaning

Prefixes are small groups of letters that can be added to the beginnings of words to change their meaning. Suffixes are similar, but are added to the ends of words.

⚙ **New language** Prefixes and suffixes
Aa Vocabulary Studying
🧩 **New skill** Changing the meaning of words

22.1 FILL IN THE GAPS USING THE PREFIXES AND SUFFIXES IN THE PANEL

Those berries are ___*harmful*___ (harm). Don't eat them or you will get sick!

1. I'm late and it's _____ (likely) that I'll get my train in time to get home.

2. They found it too difficult to _____ (solve) the dispute about the best route.

3. She's so _____ (rest) she just can't relax at all.

4. His sore back was very _____ (pain). It hurt every time he took a step.

5. Do you have to _____ (write) your essay? That's a shame.

6. Be _____ (care) when you use this product. It's toxic and can make you sick.

7. His desk is so _____ (tidy) he can't find what he is looking for.

8. These earrings aren't gold. They're _____ (worth), I'm afraid.

9. Was the little girl crying because she was _____ (happy)?

re-	~~-ful~~	-less	un-	re-
un-	-ful	un-	-ful	-less

🔊

64

22.2 MARK THE SENTENCES THAT ARE CORRECT

I'm so tired. I had a very restless night. ✓
I'm so tired. I had a very restful night. ☐

1. They were hopeful for a positive result. ☐
   They were hopeless for a positive result. ☐

2. She's likely to play today if she's injured. ☐
   She's unlikely to play today if she's injured. ☐

3. It is pointful to argue with your manager. ☐
   It is pointless to argue with your manager. ☐

4. George wasn't able to rework his essay. ☐
   George wasn't able to unwork his essay. ☐

5. Her new hairstyle was really attractiveless. ☐
   Her new hairstyle was really unattractive. ☐

6. Their vacation was restful and relaxing. ☐
   Their vacation was restless and relaxing. ☐

7. It's careless to drive too fast. ☐
   It's careful to drive too fast. ☐

22.3 SAY THE SENTENCES OUT LOUD, USING PREFIXES AND SUFFIXES

He needs to write that letter again.

He needs to rewrite that letter.

1. Your bedroom isn't tidy.

2. It isn't painful.

3. I'm going to apply for that job again.

4. She isn't likely to be on time.

5. They aren't careful drivers.

6. I was full of hope for the future.

7. She solved the argument.

8. He's not likely to come to work.

9. The task was without point.

10. His mustache wasn't attractive.

11. He felt without power to argue.

65

Aa 23.1 TRAVEL WRITE THE WORDS FROM THE PANEL UNDER THE CORRECT PICTURES

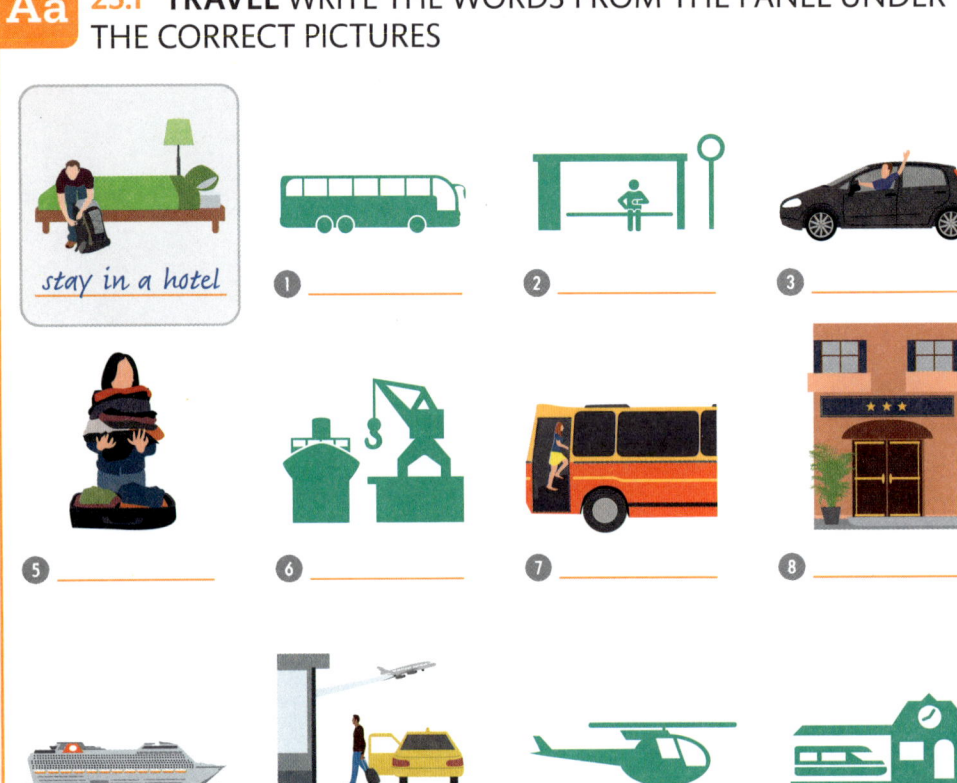

stay in a hotel

1 _____

2 _____

3 _____

4 _____

5 _____

6 _____

7 _____

8 _____

9 _____

10 _____

11 _____

12 _____

13 _____

14 _____

15 _____

16 _____

17 _____

18 _____

19 _____

arrive at the airport	bicycle	tram	bus stop	luggage	pack your bags
train ride	helicopter	taxi rank	drive a car	train station	reception	coach
get on a bus	cruise	hotel	airport	~~stay in a hotel~~	port	runway

24 Places I have been

In English, the present perfect is used to talk about recent or repeated past events. The past simple is used to say exactly when those events happened.

⚙ **New language** Present perfect
Aa Vocabulary Travel experiences
🧩 **New skill** Talking about the recent past

24.1 FILL IN THE GAPS BY PUTTING THE VERBS IN THE PRESENT PERFECT

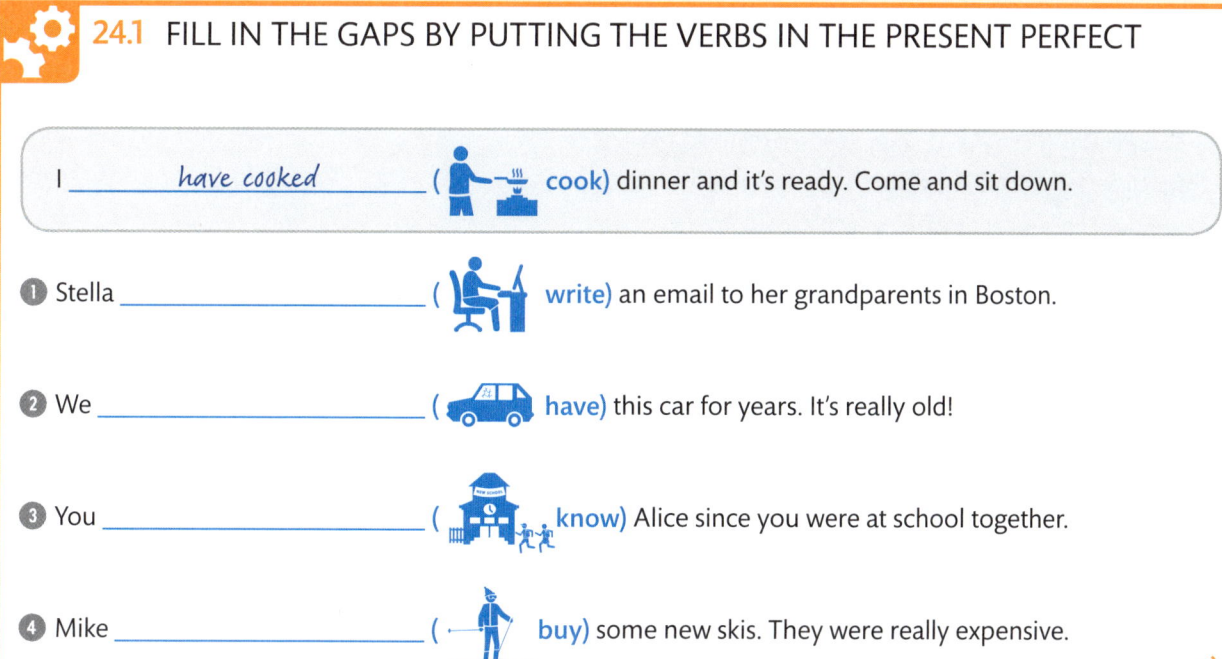

I _____*have cooked*_____ (cook) dinner and it's ready. Come and sit down.

1 Stella _____ (write) an email to her grandparents in Boston.

2 We _____ (have) this car for years. It's really old!

3 You _____ (know) Alice since you were at school together.

4 Mike _____ (buy) some new skis. They were really expensive.

24.2 CROSS OUT THE INCORRECT WORDS IN EACH SENTENCE

I **arrived** / ~~have arrived~~ at the station 20 minutes ago.

1 I **have visited** / **visited** France many times in my life. I love it.

2 Arabella **went** / **have been** swimming at 12:30pm.

3 We **have lived** / **lived** here for five years. It's our home.

4 Elsa **went** / **has been** out of the country for two months. We miss her.

5 Ravi **traveled** / **has traveled** to India in March.

6 He **spoke** / **has spoken** three languages since he was a child.

24.3 LISTEN TO THE AUDIO, THEN MARK WHETHER EACH PICTURE IS DESCRIBED IN THE PAST SIMPLE OR THE PRESENT PERFECT TENSE

Past simple ✓ Present perfect ☐

1 Past simple ☐ Present perfect ☐

2 Past simple ☐ Present perfect ☐

3 Past simple ☐ Present perfect ☐

4 Past simple ☐ Present perfect ☐

5 Past simple ☐ Present perfect ☐

 24.4 REWRITE THESE PRESENT PERFECT SENTENCES, CORRECTING THE ERRORS

We have went to China several times.
We have been to China several times.

1 I've paint a picture for you.

_____

2 Robert have cycled around the park.

_____

3 Janice has cooks paella lots of times.

_____

4 I have flew in a helicopter.

_____

5 They ridden a camel in Egypt.

_____

6 I has swum in the Great Barrier Reef.

_____

7 We have bring you a present.

_____

8 I've studies geography and science.

_____

9 The students have leave the building.

_____

24.5 SAY THE SENTENCES OUT LOUD, PUTTING THE VERBS IN THE PRESENT PERFECT

I _____have eaten_____ (eat) Indian food twice this week.

1. I _____ (learn) to speak a second language.

2. We _____ (buy) a new house.

3. Paula and Maria _____ (run) a marathon.

4. You _____ (see) an elephant.

5. David _____ (live) here for six months.

6. Elsa _____ (lose) her passport again.

7. They _____ (land) at the airport.

24.6 REWRITE THE SENTENCES IN THE PAST SIMPLE

I have lived in California for many years.
I lived in California for many years.

1. They've arrived at the hotel.

_____

2. John and Diane have eaten breakfast.

_____

3. He has been on vacation to Fiji.

_____

4. They've seen the Statue of Liberty.

_____

5. Our parents have flown to the US.

_____

6. I've studied history in college.

_____

7. They've bought some new clothes.

_____

8. She has been to Tokyo twice.

_____

9. You've finished that book.

_____

25 Things I have done

You can use the present perfect to talk about personal achievements. Modifying adverbs can help you to be precise about when the achievements happened.

⚙ **New language** Modifying adverbs
Aa Vocabulary Adventure sports
🧩 **New skill** Talking about your achievements

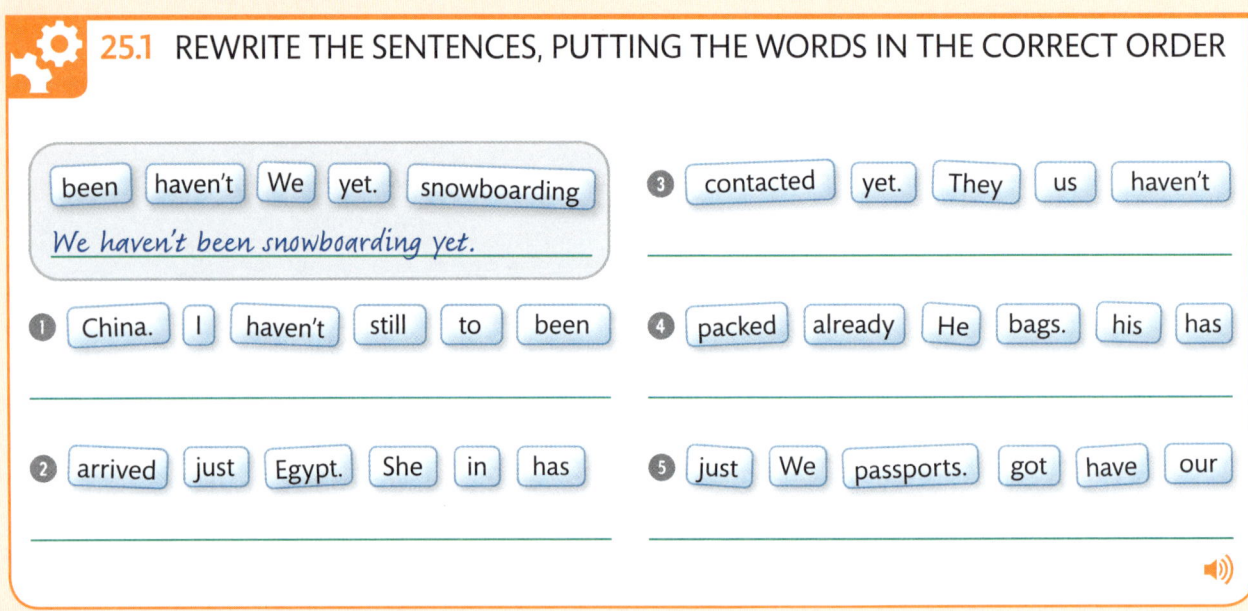

25.1 REWRITE THE SENTENCES, PUTTING THE WORDS IN THE CORRECT ORDER

been | haven't | We | yet. | snowboarding

We haven't been snowboarding yet.

① China. | I | haven't | still | to | been

_____

② arrived | just | Egypt. | She | in | has

_____

③ contacted | yet. | They | us | haven't

_____

④ packed | already | He | bags. | his | has

_____

⑤ just | We | passports. | got | have | our

_____

25.2 SAY THE SENTENCES OUT LOUD, PUTTING THE ADVERBS IN THE CORRECT PLACE

We've arrived at the hotel. **[just]**

We've just arrived at the hotel.

① She hasn't tried windsurfing. **[still]**

② The plane has landed. **[just]**

③ I've unpacked my bags. **[already]**

④ They haven't bought their tickets. **[yet]**

⑤ He hasn't swum in the ocean. **[still]**

25.3 CROSS OUT THE INCORRECT WORDS IN EACH SENTENCE

We ~~yet~~ / still / ~~already~~ haven't had time to call home.

1. I've yet / just / still seen the mountains for the first time.

2. Nick hasn't booked his flight to Nepal already / just / yet.

3. They've yet / just / still bought two new backpacks for their trip to South America.

4. We've already / still / yet learned some German on our last trip to Berlin.

5. Andrew has yet / just / still missed his flight to Stockholm.

6. We just / still / yet haven't tried scuba diving or snorkeling in the Indian Ocean.

7. Maria hasn't ordered a taxi to take her to the airport yet / already / just.

8. Joe and Paolo have yet / still / already tried bungee jumping off a bridge.

25.4 MATCH THE BEGINNINGS OF THE SENTENCES TO THE CORRECT ENDINGS

I haven't seen a kangaroo yet ──────→ and we've been in Australia for two weeks.

1. We've just booked the hotel — and they're waiting to get off.

2. She has already been to Peru — and now I can buy some souvenirs.

3. He still hasn't taken any photos — and he's coming home tomorrow.

4. The plane has just landed — and it will be here in 10 minutes.

5. We haven't seen a shark yet — and now she might miss her flight.

6. I've already called a taxi — and now we can book our flights.

7. She still hasn't reached the airport — but we've seen a dolphin.

8. I've just been to the bank — but she'd love to go again.

25.5 READ THE EMAIL AND ANSWER THE QUESTIONS

Alec has already written to Noah.
True ☐   **False** ☑   **Not given** ☐

1 Alec and Trudi have just arrived in Cape Town.
True ☐   **False** ☐   **Not given** ☐

2 They still haven't done much.
True ☐   **False** ☐   **Not given** ☐

3 Alec has just been hang gliding.
True ☐   **False** ☐   **Not given** ☐

4 Trudi has already been to Cape Town.
True ☐   **False** ☐   **Not given** ☐

5 They haven't been snorkeling yet.
True ☐   **False** ☐   **Not given** ☐

6 Trudi has already been scuba diving.
True ☐   **False** ☐   **Not given** ☐

7 They haven't been on safari yet.
True ☐   **False** ☐   **Not given** ☐

To: Noah

Subject: Fun times

Hi Noah,
Sorry I haven't written until now. We've been so busy. We arrived in Cape Town three days ago and it's really beautiful. We've done a lot already. I've just been hang gliding along the coast. It was absolutely awesome, but Trudi didn't want to try it. We've both been snorkeling. The water is so clear you can see everything. And we've booked some scuba diving lessons. Trudi has already been scuba diving in Egypt, but I haven't. I can't wait. We haven't been on safari yet, but we're going on Friday. I really hope we see some elephants. I'll send you a photo!
See you soon!
Alec and Trudi

25.6 MATCH THE DEFINITIONS TO THE ACTIVITIES

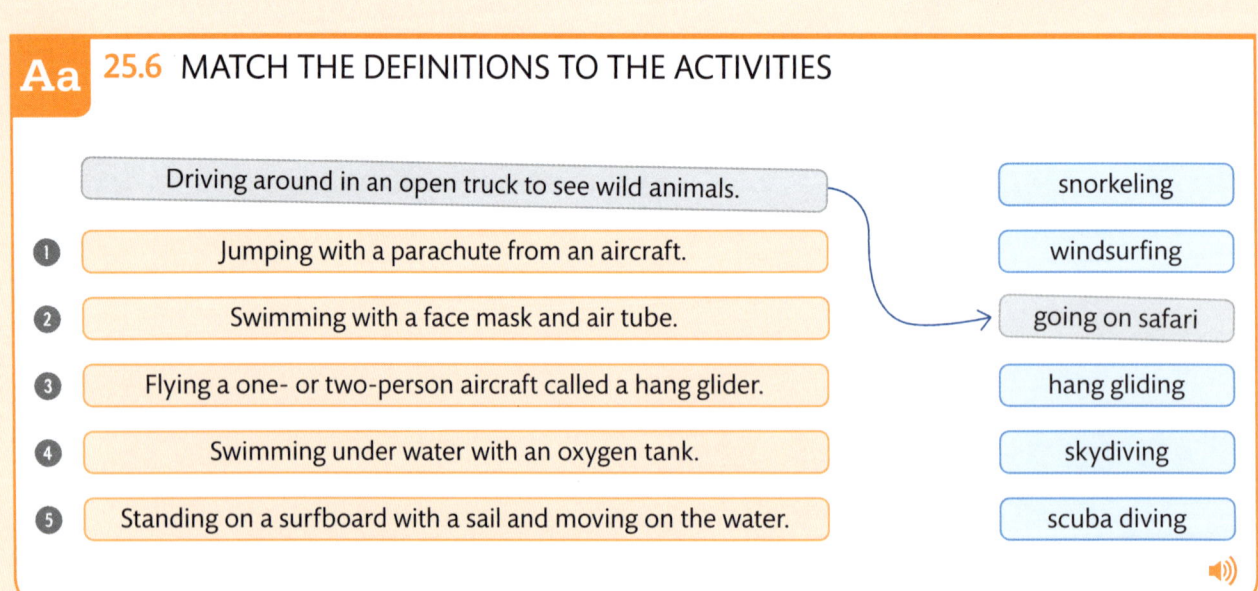

Driving around in an open truck to see wild animals. ——→ going on safari

1 Jumping with a parachute from an aircraft.

2 Swimming with a face mask and air tube.

3 Flying a one- or two-person aircraft called a hang glider.

4 Swimming under water with an oxygen tank.

5 Standing on a surfboard with a sail and moving on the water.

snorkeling

windsurfing

going on safari

hang gliding

skydiving

scuba diving

25.7 FILL IN THE GAPS USING THE WORDS IN THE PANEL

I haven't been to Los Angeles _____*yet*_____ .

1 We have _____ come back from the beach.

2 They haven't tried hang gliding _____ .

3 I _____ haven't been on safari.

4 Alexia has _____ been snorkeling before.

5 I haven't tried windsurfing _____ .

6 We have _____ arrived at the hotel 10 minutes ago.

7 He's _____ been skydiving before.

8 Tom has _____ called us a minute ago.

9 They haven't done much _____ .

10 I _____ haven't finished my work.

11 Kai has _____ booked the tour.

yet	already	yet	already	~~yet~~	just
just	still	just	still	already	yet

25.8 LISTEN TO THE AUDIO AND MARK WHETHER OR NOT ALEX HAS DONE THE ACTIVITY IN EACH PICTURE

Yes ☐   No ☑

1 Yes ☐   No ☐

2 Yes ☐   No ☐

3 Yes ☐   No ☐

4 Yes ☐   No ☐

5 Yes ☐   No ☐

26 Activities in progress

Use the present perfect continuous to talk about ongoing activities in the past. Use "for" and "since" to talk about the length or starting point of an activity.

⚙ **New language** Present perfect continuous
Aa **Vocabulary** Home improvements
🧩 **New skill** Talking about activities in the past

⚙ 26.1 FILL IN THE GAPS BY PUTTING THE VERBS IN THE PRESENT PERFECT CONTINUOUS TENSE

Fatima ___*has been shopping*___ (**shop**) for clothes all day.

1 Nathan _____ (**read**) a book in the back yard.

2 I _____ (**cook**) breakfast in the kitchen.

3 Mike _____ (**play**) tennis with his friends.

4 Ted and John _____ (**watch**) TV all evening.

5 Mrs. Roberts _____ (**paint**) the house this weekend.

🔊

⚙ 26.2 FILL IN THE GAPS USING "FOR" OR "SINCE"

I've been waiting ___*for*___ 20 minutes.

1 He has been fishing _____ 3:30pm.

2 We've been learning Spanish _____ six weeks.

3 Ruth has been cooking _____ a long time.

4 You've been decorating _____ March 8.

5 I've been driving _____ 11:45am.

6 He's been teaching science _____ 2012.

7 She's been watching TV _____ two hours.

8 I've been learning to dance _____ two weeks.

9 Alan has been tiling the floor _____ Monday.

10 It has been snowing _____ 10 days.

11 I've been working at home _____ last April.

🔊

26.3 READ THE EMAIL AND NUMBER THE PICTURES IN THE ORDER THEY ARE DESCRIBED

 A ☐

 B 1

 C ☐

 D ☐

 E ☐

 F ☐

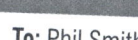

To: Phil Smith

Subject: Settling in

Hi Phil,

Since we bought our new house, my whole family has been helping us get things ready. Mom has been gardening every day, while Auntie Stella has been making curtains for all the rooms. My husband Tom has been painting the windows outside and his dad has been tiling the roof for 10 days now. I've been fixing the bathtub for two days and my sister Anna has been painting the living room for three days. We're hoping we'll finish everything by the weekend!
Love,
Jane

 26.4 LISTEN TO THE AUDIO AND WRITE HOW LONG EACH ACTIVITY HAS BEEN GOING ON

since last weekend

❶ _____

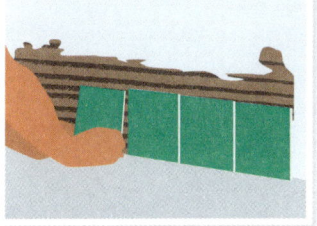

❷ _____

❸ _____

❹ _____

❺ _____

26.5 USE THE CHART TO CREATE 12 CORRECT SENTENCES AND SAY THEM OUT LOUD

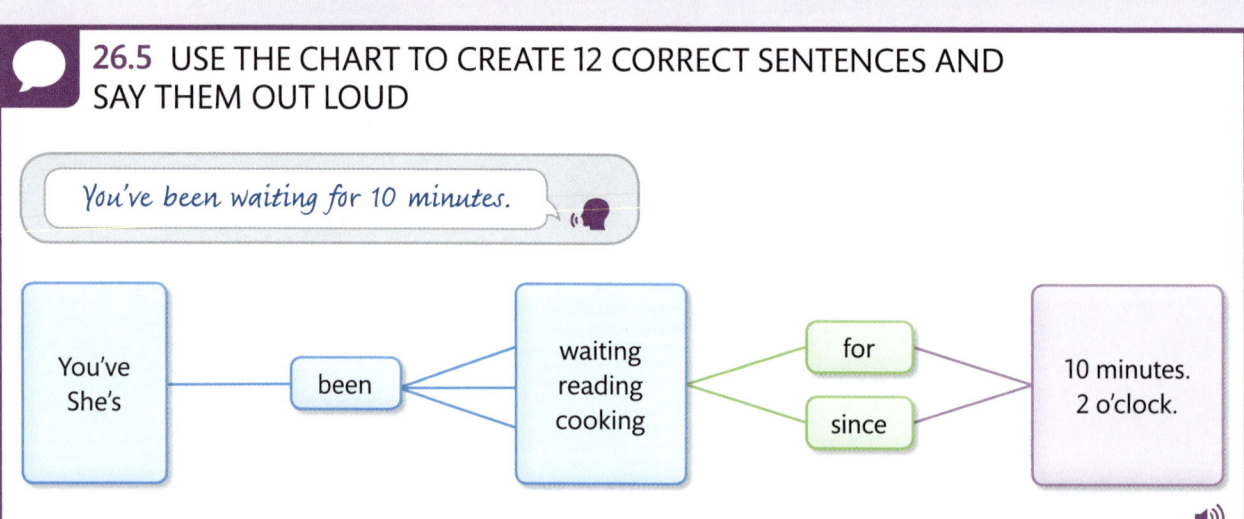

You've been waiting for 10 minutes.

| You've She's | → | been | → | waiting reading cooking | → | for | → | 10 minutes. 2 o'clock. |

since

26.6 REWRITE THE SENTENCES, CORRECTING THE ERRORS

She been making curtains for two weeks.
She's been making curtains for two weeks.

1 We've been put up shelves all day.

_____

2 Jane has been painting the bedroom for 10:30am.

_____

3 They has been fixing the bathtub for six hours.

_____

4 I've tiling the kitchen since last Monday.

_____

5 He's been fitting the carpet for yesterday morning.

_____

Aa 26.7 FIND SIX WORDS FOR HOUSEHOLD OBJECTS IN THE GRID

S	B	Y	M	E	N	M	O	B	W	O	C	S
N	S	H	E	L	F	Y	W	T	Q	E	A	V
N	D	E	M	J	S	M	D	S	B	A	R	D
R	I	B	A	T	H	T	U	B	E	C	P	I
S	K	R	T	E	B	I	A	R	D	I	E	G
E	D	I	S	R	Y	L	D	F	A	E	T	D
M	Z	L	O	L	A	E	Z	I	O	R	O	Z
P	A	V	E	S	N	S	O	N	S	E	V	D
T	C	U	R	T	A	I	N	S	J	A	R	I
E	H	I	J	A	R	Y	A	I	E	O	D	S

1. _____ *shelf*
2. _____
3. _____
4. _____
5. _____
6. _____

⚙ 26.8 REWRITE THE HIGHLIGHTED PHRASES, CORRECTING THE ERRORS

have been fitting

1. _____
2. _____
3. _____
4. _____
5. _____
6. _____
7. _____
8. _____
9. _____

Katie's Blog

HOME | ENTRIES | ABOUT | CONTACT

POSTED SUNDAY, MAY 14

MOVING IN

We moved into our new apartment last Thursday and it's slowly beginning to look like home. The workmen **have fitting** the carpet **since** three days now and Dad has been **help** me in the house. **He's be** painting the living room and **he been** tiling the kitchen. But he can only help in the evenings, so he hasn't finished yet. **I been** painting my bedroom **for** Friday evening. I can't wait to put the curtains up. Mom **has making** the curtains all week and I know they'll be great! **I've been cook for I got home** from work today because I'm making Mom and Dad a special meal to say thank you! They're arriving in 20 minutes so wish me luck!

27 My talents and skills

When you see evidence that something has happened, you can use the present perfect continuous to ask questions about it.

⚙ **New language** Present perfect continuous questions
Aa Vocabulary Hobbies and interests
🧩 **New skill** Asking about past events

⚙ 27.1 REWRITE THE SENTENCES AS QUESTIONS

You've been playing tennis.
Have you been playing tennis?

① Tina has been cooking lunch.

_____

② They've been visiting friends.

_____

③ You've been studying the piano.

_____

④ Dad has been gardening.

_____

⑤ They've been training for a race.

_____

🔊

⚙ 27.2 REWRITE THE SENTENCES, PUTTING THE WORDS IN THE CORRECT ORDER

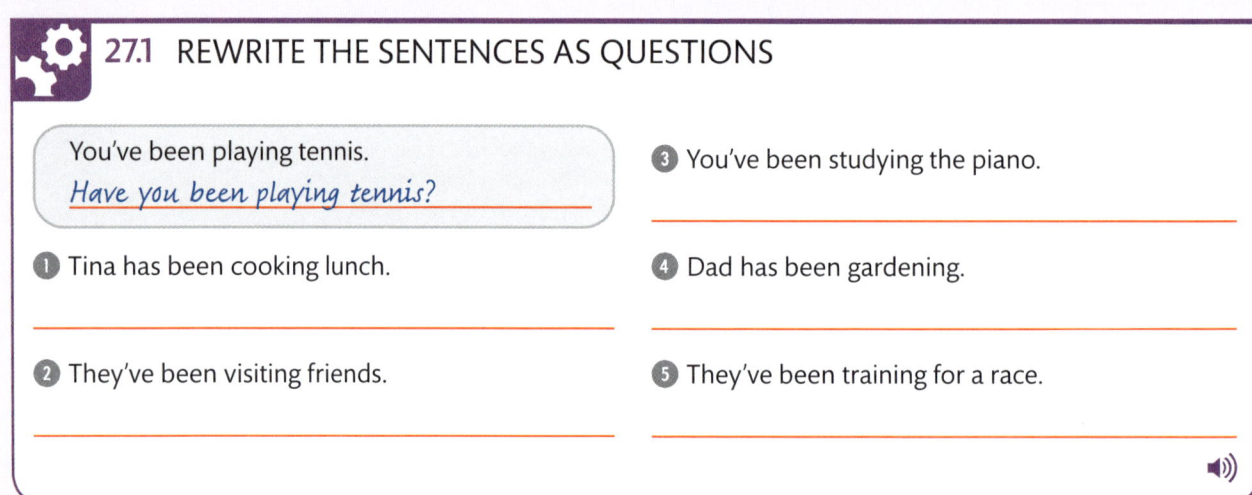

| been | Italian? | long | you | How | have | studying |

How long have you been studying Italian?

① | you | living | there? | been | How | have | long |

_____

② | the | at | working | bank? | How | you | have | long | been |

_____

③ | English? | been | How | Nina | has | long | teaching |

_____

④ | long | playing | How | been | hockey? | you | have |

_____

🔊

27.3 READ THE INTERVIEW AND ANSWER THE QUESTIONS

When did Akio start writing his blog?
Yesterday ☐   Three years ago ☑   Last summer ☐

1 What kind of food does he cook?
Chinese ☐   Japanese ☐   Indonesian ☐

2 How long has he been making cooking videos?
Since last summer ☐   For six weeks ☐   For a year ☐

3 When did he start cooking?
Last summer ☐   Years ago ☐   In high school ☐

4 Who taught him Japanese cooking?
A professional ☐   His parents ☐   His grandma ☐

5 How long has his grandma been cooking?
Since she was five ☐   For five years ☐   Since 2005 ☐

COOKING TIPS

Offbeat chef

Learn more about Japanese cooking from Chef Akio

How long have you been writing your blog, Akio?
For about three years. It's been really fun!

And your Japanese cooking tips are really popular. How long have you been making cooking videos?
Since last summer. I've been cooking since I was in high school. I had lots of great ideas and so I started making videos.

There are some great recipes on your blog. Have you been taking professional lessons?
No way. I've learned everything from my grandma. Cooking is such an important part of Japanese family life. My grandma has been cooking since she was five years old. She learned from her grandma.

That's amazing, Akio.
Thank you.

 27.4 REWRITE THE SENTENCES, CORRECTING THE ERRORS

How long you been practicing yoga?
How long have you been practicing yoga?

1 How long you have been studying Chinese?
_____

2 How long has he been cook Indian food?
_____

3 How long have they living in Sydney?
_____

4 How long she been mountain biking?
_____

5 How long have you be writing a novel?
_____

6 How long you have been playing the piano?
_____

7 How long have he been salsa dancing?
_____

8 How long have they working together?
_____

9 How long has she been paint with oils?
_____

🔊

27.5 SAY THE SENTENCES OUT LOUD, FILLING IN THE GAPS

How long ___*have*___ they been ___*living*___ (live) in that apartment?

1. How long _____ she been _____ (drive) that car?

2. How long _____ you been _____ (play) the guitar?

3. How long _____ he been _____ (sing) in the choir?

4. How long _____ he been _____ (cook) dinner?

5. How long _____ you been _____ (read) that magazine?

6. How long _____ she been _____ (study) French?

7. How long _____ they been _____ (work) in that office?

8. How long _____ you been _____ (learn) to drive?

27.6 MARK THE CORRECT REPLY TO EACH QUESTION

How long have they been writing songs? 
- For a long time. ✓
- Since a long time. ☐

1. How long have you been working in New York? 
- Since 2012. ☐
- For 2012. ☐

2. How long have you been writing your book? 
- For two years. ☐
- Since two years. ☐

3. How long have you been living in Paris? 
- For August. ☐
- Since August. ☐

4. How long have you been taking singing lessons? 
- Since last summer. ☐
- For last summer. ☐

5. How long have you been painting the house? 
- Since three days. ☐
- For three days. ☐

6. How long have you been learning to cook? 
- For six weeks. ☐
- Since six weeks. ☐

28 Activities and their results

English uses the present perfect continuous to talk about recent activities that are probably still ongoing. Use the present perfect simple to talk about finished activities.

⚙ **New language** Forms of the present perfect
Aa Vocabulary State and action verbs
🧩 **New skill** Talking about results of activities

🎧 **28.1** LISTEN TO THE AUDIO AND MARK WHICH TENSE DESCRIBES THE ACTIVITY IN EACH PICTURE

Ⓐ **PRESENT PERFECT CONTINUOUS**   Ⓑ **PRESENT PERFECT SIMPLE**

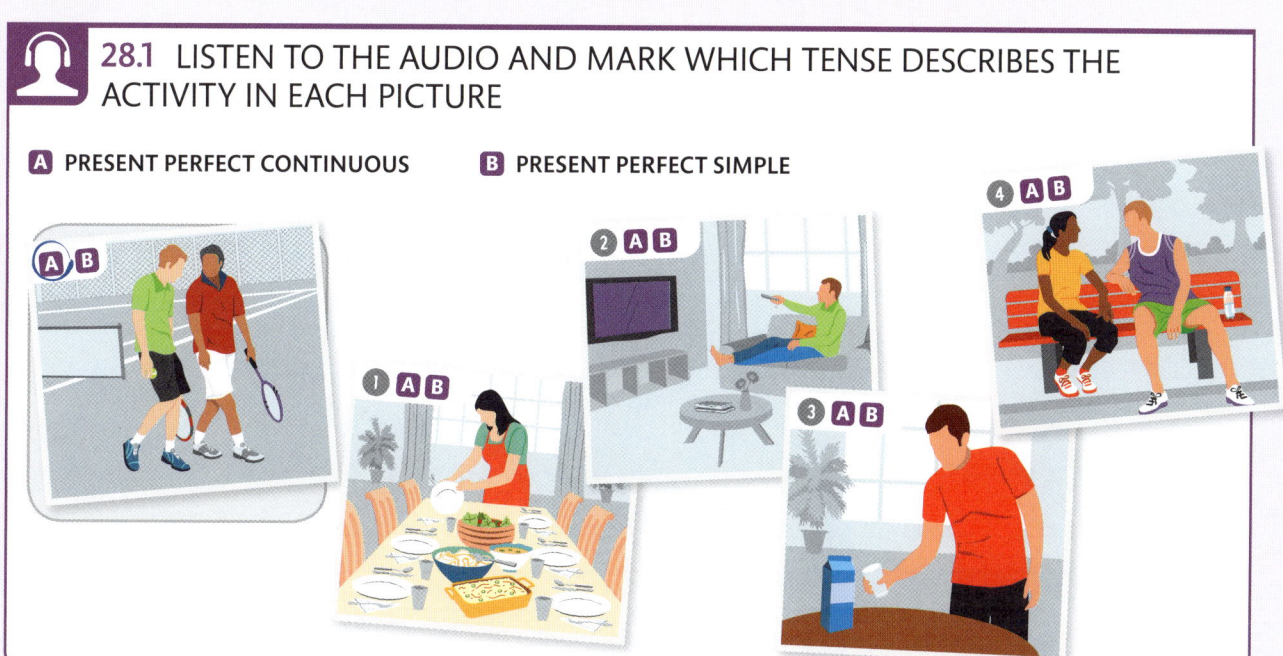

⚙ **28.2** MATCH THE PAIRS OF SENTENCES

Tom has been working in the garden. ────────────┐   Now I'm going to read a book.

① I've read my magazine.   Now she's cleaning the bathroom.

② Rosa has lost her house keys.   His eyes are red.

③ He has broken the window. ────────►   His hands are dirty.

④ Monica has been cleaning the kitchen.   The package is empty.

⑤ That little boy has been crying.   They're both tired.

⑥ Roger has eaten all the pretzels.   There's glass everywhere.

⑦ Alice and Jane have been playing tennis.   She can't get into her house.

🔊

28.3 DESCRIBE THE PICTURES OUT LOUD USING THE PRESENT PERFECT CONTINUOUS TENSE

John _has been walking_ (walk) the dog.

1. Rebecca _____ (swim).

2. Victor and Joe _____ (play) soccer.

3. Alexia _____ (sweep) the floor.

4. Thomas _____ (repair) the car.

5. Davina _____ (watch) TV.

28.4 CROSS OUT THE INCORRECT WORDS IN EACH SENTENCE

You ~~haven't been understanding~~ / **haven't understood** me.

1. I **have liked** / **have been liking** all of his plays.

2. Dan **has watched** / **has been watching** TV all afternoon.

3. The movie **has been starting** / **has started**.

4. I **have been reading** / **have read** my book. I haven't finished it yet.

28.5 READ THE BLOG AND ANSWER THE QUESTIONS

Gina has bought a house in Rome.
True ☐ **False** ☐ **Not given** ✓

1 She has made many new friends.
True ☐ **False** ☐ **Not given** ☐

2 She hasn't visited the Trevi Fountain yet.
True ☐ **False** ☐ **Not given** ☐

3 Her friends sometimes drive to the coast.
True ☐ **False** ☐ **Not given** ☐

4 She has been studying Italian.
True ☐ **False** ☐ **Not given** ☐

5 Gina's parents are coming to visit her.
True ☐ **False** ☐ **Not given** ☐

Gina's Blog

HOME | ENTRIES | ABOUT | CONTACT

POSTED FRIDAY, AUGUST 28

TWO WEEKS IN ROME

I've been living in Rome for two weeks now and I absolutely love it. I've been renting a small apartment with two friends from work, and we're going to stay for two more weeks. We've met some great people and I've made a lot of new friends. I've visited all the famous sites of course. My favorite is the Piazza Navona and the Trevi Fountain. I've been studying Italian in a private language school. I only go twice a week, but I've learned a lot already. One of my favorite things about Rome is the food. But the problem is that I've been eating so much pasta I've put on pounds! Anyway, I've been talking to my parents this morning and I said I'd post some photos online for them. So, here they are!

28.6 FILL IN THE GAPS BY PUTTING THE VERBS IN THE CORRECT TENSE

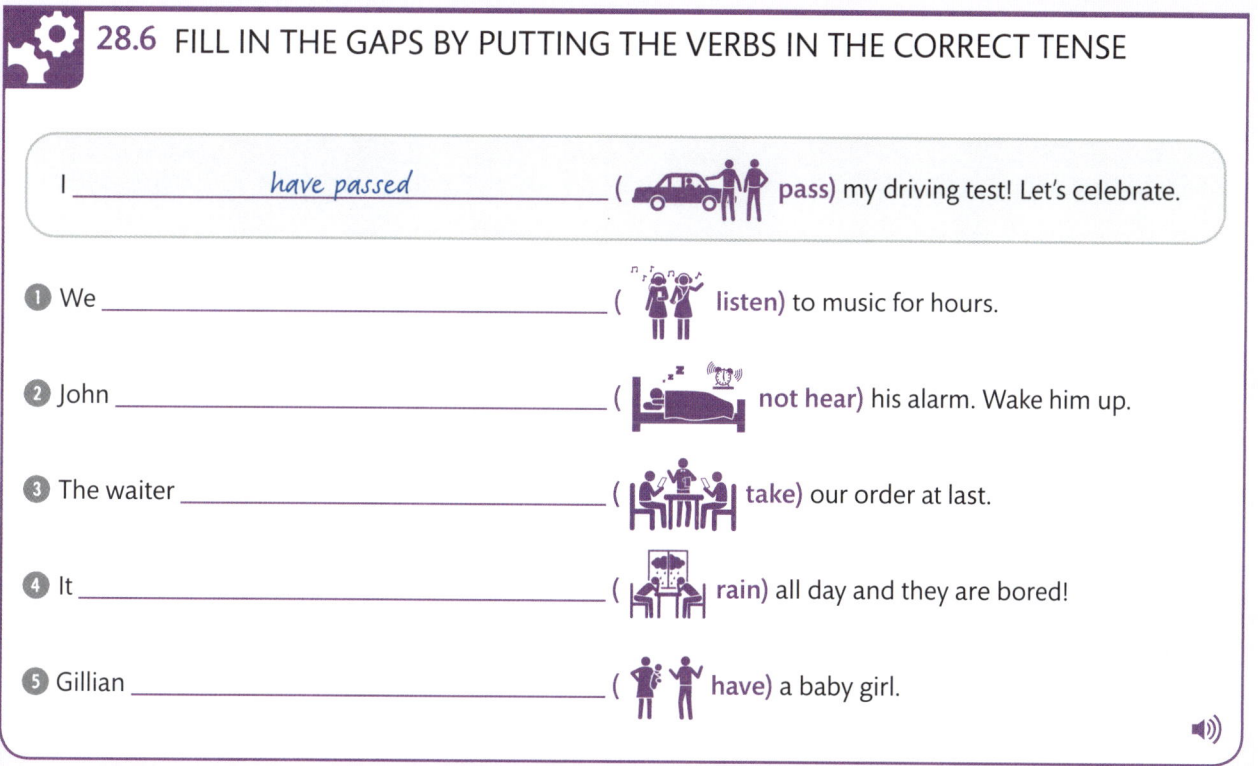

I _____*have passed*_____ (**pass**) my driving test! Let's celebrate.

1 We _____ (**listen**) to music for hours.

2 John _____ (**not hear**) his alarm. Wake him up.

3 The waiter _____ (**take**) our order at last.

4 It _____ (**rain**) all day and they are bored!

5 Gillian _____ (**have**) a baby girl.

29 Everyday problems

Prefixes that mean "not" are called negative prefixes. Many words that have negative prefixes are useful for talking about everyday workplace and urban problems.

⚙ **New language** Negative prefixes
Aa Vocabulary Urban problems
🧩 **New skill** Talking about everyday problems

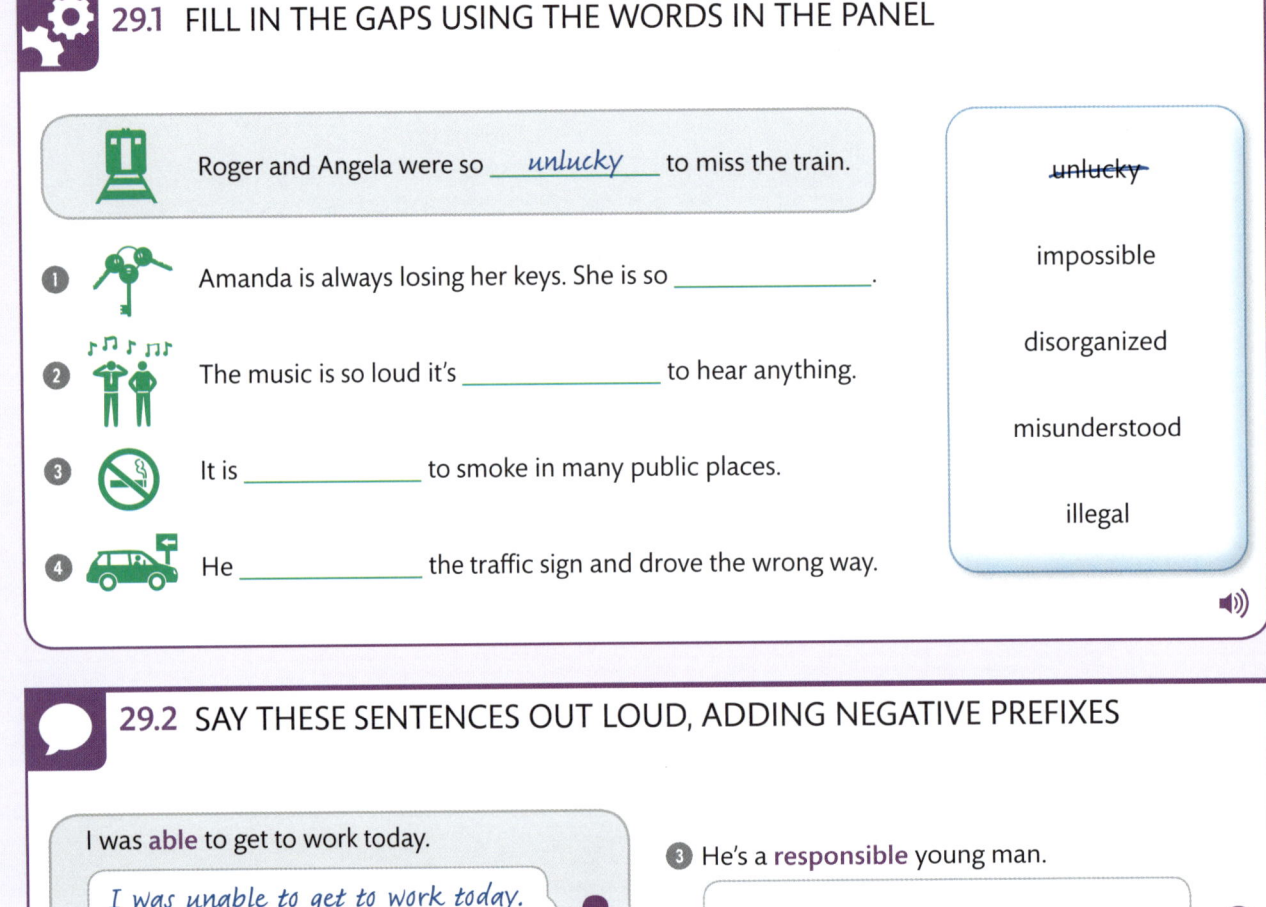

29.1 FILL IN THE GAPS USING THE WORDS IN THE PANEL

Roger and Angela were so ___*unlucky*___ to miss the train.

1. Amanda is always losing her keys. She is so _____.

2. The music is so loud it's _____ to hear anything.

3. It is _____ to smoke in many public places.

4. He _____ the traffic sign and drove the wrong way.

~~unlucky~~

impossible

disorganized

misunderstood

illegal

29.2 SAY THESE SENTENCES OUT LOUD, ADDING NEGATIVE PREFIXES

I was **able** to get to work today.

I was unable to get to work today.

1. Arriving late for work is **acceptable**.

2. Andy **agrees** with your decision.

3. He's a **responsible** young man.

4. Maria is always **patient** with people.

5. It's **possible** to park in the city.

29.3 REWRITE THE SENTENCES, PUTTING THE WORDS IN THE CORRECT ORDER

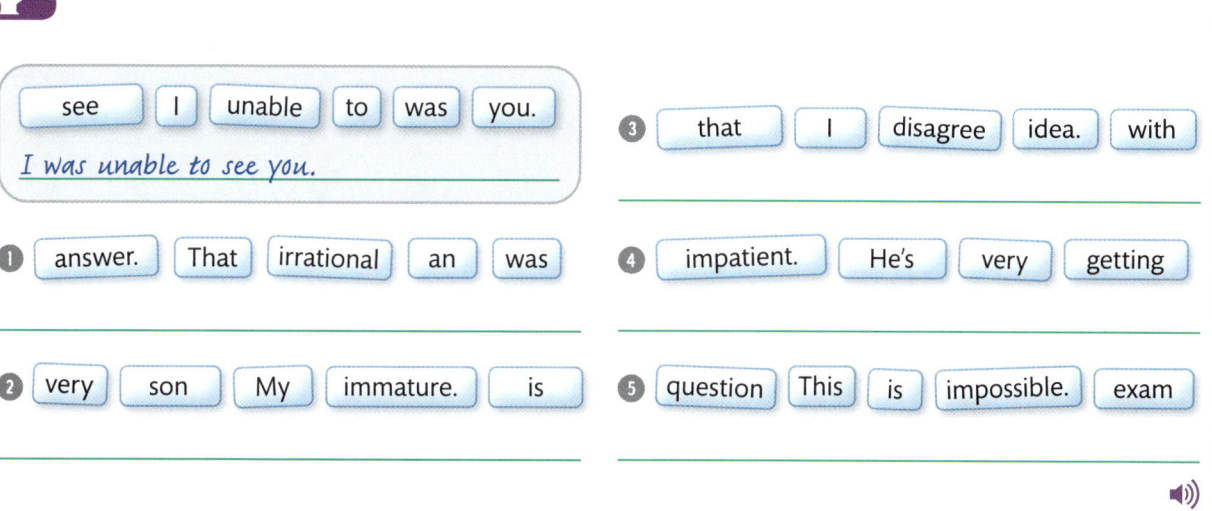

| see | I | unable | to | was | you. |

I was unable to see you.

1 | answer. | That | irrational | an | was |

_____

2 | very | son | My | immature. | is |

_____

3 | that | I | disagree | idea. | with |

_____

4 | impatient. | He's | very | getting |

_____

5 | question | This | is | impossible. | exam |

_____

 29.4 REWRITE THE SENTENCES, CORRECTING THE ERRORS

Tom is very **ilorganized**. He's always late.
Tom is very disorganized. He's always late.

1 Layla has a **disrational** fear of the dark.

_____

2 My son's friends can be quite **unmature**.

_____

3 It's **misrespectful** to laugh during a lecture.

_____

4 Your doctor's handwriting is **unpossible** to read.

_____

5 The art exhibition was **imusual**, but interesting.

_____

6 She **disunderstands** everything I say.

_____

7 I **unagree** with your suggestions.

_____

8 Jack can be **misresponsible** sometimes.

_____

9 My boss is often **unpatient** with me.

_____

10 Our hotel room was **ilacceptable**.

_____

11 He left his room in total **misorder**.

_____

12 It was an **disimportant** decision.

_____

13 The chocolate cookies were **misresistible**.

_____

Aa 29.5 MATCH THE DEFINITIONS TO THE WORDS

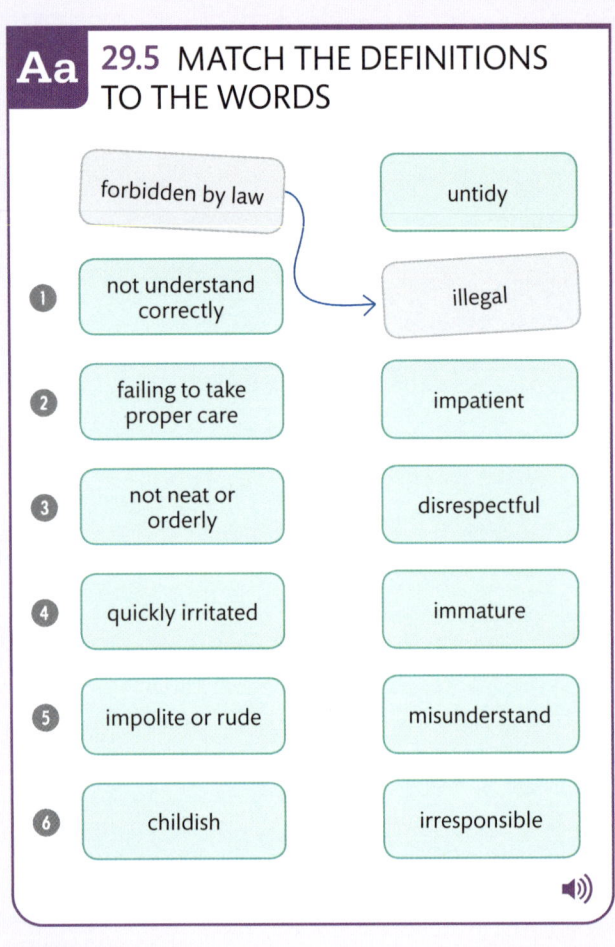

forbidden by law → illegal

untidy

1 not understand correctly

2 failing to take proper care

impatient

3 not neat or orderly

disrespectful

4 quickly irritated

immature

5 impolite or rude

misunderstand

6 childish

irresponsible

29.6 LISTEN TO THE AUDIO AND ANSWER THE QUESTIONS

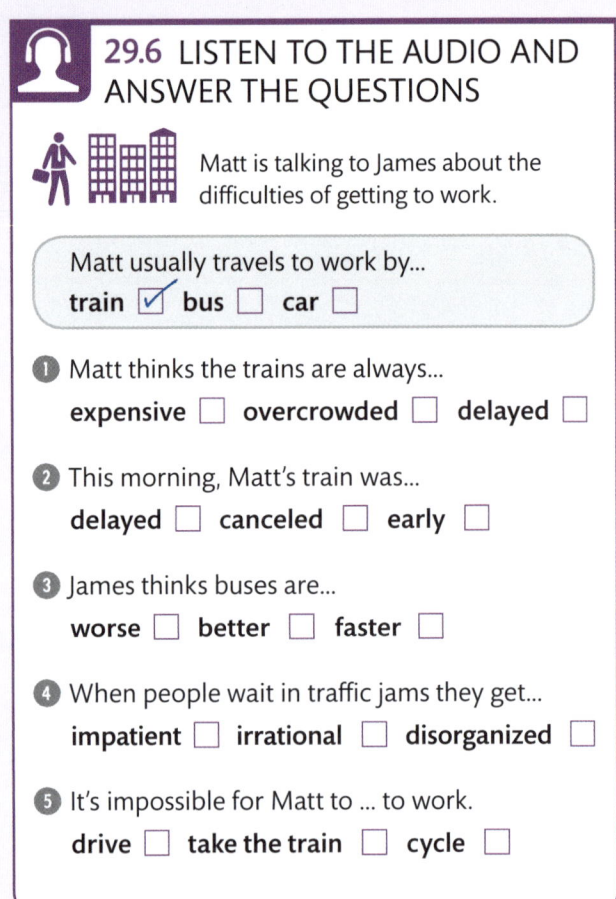

Matt is talking to James about the difficulties of getting to work.

Matt usually travels to work by...
train ☑ **bus** ☐ **car** ☐

1 Matt thinks the trains are always...
expensive ☐ **overcrowded** ☐ **delayed** ☐

2 This morning, Matt's train was...
delayed ☐ **canceled** ☐ **early** ☐

3 James thinks buses are...
worse ☐ **better** ☐ **faster** ☐

4 When people wait in traffic jams they get...
impatient ☐ **irrational** ☐ **disorganized** ☐

5 It's impossible for Matt to ... to work.
drive ☐ **take the train** ☐ **cycle** ☐

29.7 FILL IN THE GAPS USING THE WORDS IN THE PANEL

There will be long _____*lines*_____ on freeway 56 today.

1 There has also been an _____ on freeway 25.

2 There will be long _____ of 40–45 minutes because of the accident.

3 There are _____ trains on the eastern line because of the congestion on the roads.

4 Several trains on the western line have also been _____.

5 The situation has made travel to the suburbs _____.

| ~~lines~~ | overcrowded | delays | accident | impossible | canceled |

Aa 29.8 MATCH THE BEGINNINGS OF THE SENTENCES TO THE CORRECT ENDINGS

It's unusual to → meet someone who speaks Latin.

1. It's unacceptable that the — in this parking lot on weekends.

2. You were very irresponsible — the shop window looked irresistible.

3. There's a traffic jam and it will be — he misunderstood what I said.

4. The luxury chocolate cake in — impossible to get home in time.

5. The train passengers were — they're so disorganized all the time.

6. He wasn't concentrating so — trains are so overcrowded.

7. It's illegal to park your vehicle — unimpressed with the long delays.

8. They're always late because — to walk home alone after midnight.

29.9 READ THE EMAIL AND ANSWER THE QUESTIONS

Annie is having a bad morning.
True ☑ **False** ☐ **Not given** ☐

1. Annie couldn't get the train to work.
True ☐ **False** ☐ **Not given** ☐

2. She didn't want to wait for a taxi.
True ☐ **False** ☐ **Not given** ☐

3. There were long delays on her drive.
True ☐ **False** ☐ **Not given** ☐

4. She tried to park outside her office.
True ☐ **False** ☐ **Not given** ☐

5. She thinks it's unusual that there's nowhere to park.
True ☐ **False** ☐ **Not given** ☐

✉ ⌄ ✕

To: Becky

Subject: Having a bad day

Hi Becky,
I've had such a terrible morning. There was an accident at the train station so they canceled my train! I missed the 7:45 bus and I was too impatient to wait for the next one, so I decided to drive. But there was construction, which caused 30 minute delays. When I got into town, there was nowhere to park, and I was late for work! It's totally unacceptable that there is never anywhere to park in this city! I can't wait to get home!
How's your day so far?
Love,
Annie

30 General and specific things

Articles sit before the noun in English, and give more information about which item is being described. Use "the" to talk about specific items.

🔧 **New language** Definite and zero articles
Aa Vocabulary Possessions
🧩 **New skill** Talking about the things you own

30.1 REWRITE THE SENTENCES, CORRECTING THE ERRORS

I like eating the fruit.
I like eating fruit.

1. Supermarket is open on Sundays.

2. I don't like studying for the exams.

3. Last movie I saw was really good.

4. It always rains during the vacations.

5. I go to the work by train.

6. He likes reading newspaper.

7. Adam works in local hospital.

8. I hate shopping for the food.

9. The fries aren't good for you.

10. I like photo on your desk.

11. Boss is happy with my work.

12. Karen has lots of the shoes.

13. I like going to movie theater.

14. Suit is expensive.

15. I'm going to bank to get a loan.

16. Dan hates the fruit.

17. I will spend money I got from my aunt.

18. Car isn't working.

19. I love the dancing.

30.2 MARK THE SENTENCES THAT ARE CORRECT

Cherries are my favorite fruit. ✓
The cherries are my favorite fruit. ☐

1 Where are the keys for the shed? ☐
Where are keys for the shed? ☐

2 We love playing the sports. ☐
We love playing sports. ☐

3 The dishwasher isn't working. ☐
Dishwasher isn't working. ☐

4 Here's book I borrowed. ☐
Here's the book I borrowed. ☐

5 Last movie I saw was terrible. ☐
The last movie I saw was terrible. ☐

6 That woman has lots of cats. ☐
That woman has lots of the cats. ☐

7 When do you go back to work? ☐
When do you go back to the work? ☐

8 Person outside is my uncle. ☐
The person outside is my uncle. ☐

9 Look at the tablet I bought yesterday. ☐
Look at tablet I bought yesterday. ☐

10 The dentists earn a lot of money. ☐
Dentists earn a lot of money. ☐

11 I'm going to post office. ☐
I'm going to the post office. ☐

◀))

30.3 REWRITE THE NOTE, CORRECTING THE ERRORS

Hi Richard,
I've gone to post office to send back parcel that came the last week. I don't want shoes because they're too big for me. When I've done that, I'll go to supermarket and buy the potatoes so we can make fries for dinner. Can you check if cat has eaten food I left her? She wasn't feeling very well yesterday.
Thanks!
Carla

Hi Richard,

I've gone to the post office

30.4 READ THE BLOG POST AND ANSWER THE QUESTIONS

What is Alice doing for her summer job?
She is working at a campsite.

❶ Where is the campsite?

_____

❷ What does Alice have to clean?

_____

❸ What does Alice hate doing?

_____

❹ What do the children do at the kids' clubs?

_____

❺ Where does Alice buy wine from?

_____

❻ When will Alice go back to college?

_____

Alice's blog

HOME | ENTRIES | ABOUT | CONTACT

 POSTED MONDAY, AUGUST 14
My Job

Welcome to my blog about my summer job. This year I am working at a campsite in the south of France. I have to clean the tents and prepare them for new guests. People come from all over Europe to camp here. I hate doing the cleaning. But I like doing the kids' clubs for the children. We play games and go to the beach. I also like doing wine and cheese evenings for the parents. I buy wine from the local vineyard and French cheese from the store. I'm working here until the middle of September. Then I will go back to college.

 30.5 REWRITE EACH SENTENCE IN ITS OTHER FORM

I **have** a computer.
I have got a computer.

❶ Tom **has got** a dog.

_____

❷ Anna and Sally **have** a nice apartment.

_____

❸ I **have got** my own bedroom.

_____

❹ She **has** a difficult job.

_____

❺ They **have got** a new car.

_____

❻ I **have** good friends.

_____

30.6 USE THE CHART TO CREATE 16 CORRECT SENTENCES AND SAY THEM OUT LOUD

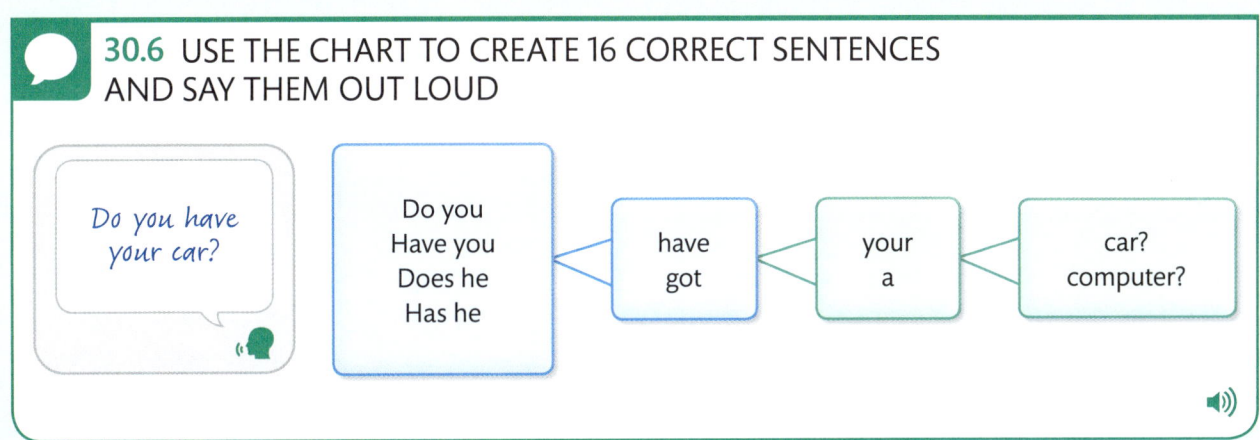

Do you have your car?

| Do you / Have you / Does he / Has he | have / got | your / a | car? / computer? |

30.7 LISTEN TO THE AUDIO AND NUMBER THE GADGETS IN THE ORDER YOU HEAR THEM

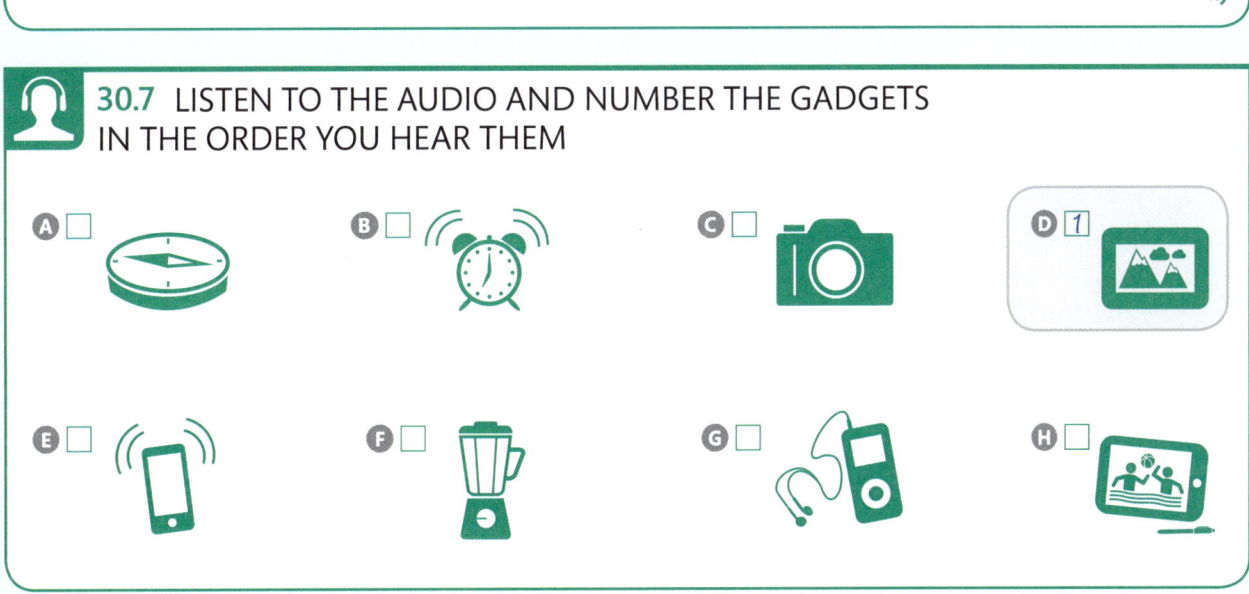

A ☐

B ☐

C ☐

D 1

E ☐

F ☐

G ☐

H ☐

30.8 LISTEN TO THE AUDIO AGAIN AND ANSWER THE QUESTIONS

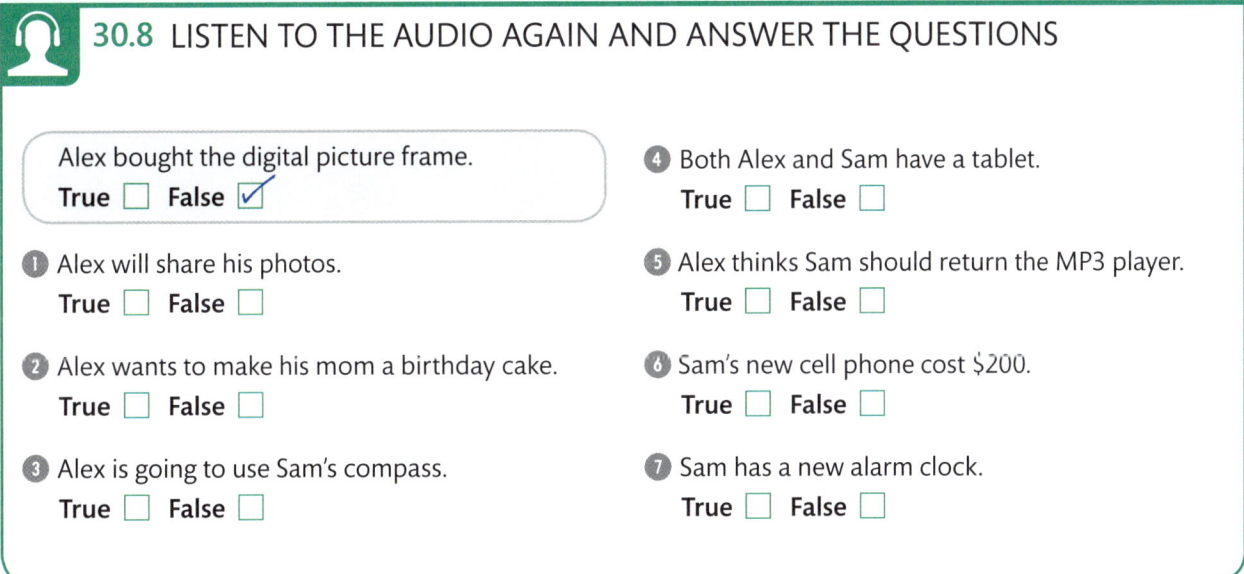

Alex bought the digital picture frame.
True ☐ **False** ✓

1 Alex will share his photos.
True ☐ **False** ☐

2 Alex wants to make his mom a birthday cake.
True ☐ **False** ☐

3 Alex is going to use Sam's compass.
True ☐ **False** ☐

4 Both Alex and Sam have a tablet.
True ☐ **False** ☐

5 Alex thinks Sam should return the MP3 player.
True ☐ **False** ☐

6 Sam's new cell phone cost $200.
True ☐ **False** ☐

7 Sam has a new alarm clock.
True ☐ **False** ☐

31 Vocabulary

Aa 31.1 FOOD AND DRINK WRITE THE WORDS FROM THE PANEL UNDER THE CORRECT PICTURES

tomato

① _____

② _____

③ _____

④ _____

⑤ _____

⑥ _____

⑦ _____

⑧ _____

⑨ _____

⑩ _____

⑪ _____

⑫ _____

⑬ _____

⑭ _____

⑮ _____

⑯ _____

⑰ _____

⑱ _____

⑲ _____

milk	lettuce	eggs	beef	cheese	onion	chocolate
garlic	potatoes	lemonade	burger	pasta	mango	ice cream
~~tomato~~	peach	avocado	tea	chicken	raspberries	

Myself, yourself

English uses reflexive pronouns when the subject of the verb is the same as the object. They show that the action affects the person who is carrying it out.

 New language Reflexive pronouns
Aa Vocabulary Measurements and flavors
New skill Talking about food and recipes

32.1 FILL IN THE GAPS USING THE CORRECT REFLEXIVE PRONOUN

I think Tom is enjoying _____ *himself* _____ listening to music.

① We've bought _____ a small apartment in the town.

② The children are amusing _____ in the park.

③ Your little sister has fallen over and hurt _____ .

④ You should both take photos of _____ for Granny.

⑤ Dad burned _____ while he was making dinner.

32.2 CROSS OUT THE INCORRECT WORD IN EACH SENTENCE

I've burned ~~me~~ / **myself** on the hot pan.

① Help **yourself** / you to some more coffee, Joe.

② Did the kids enjoy them / **themselves** at the park?

③ The teacher told **us** / ourselves to be quiet.

④ Has the computer turned it / **itself** off yet?

⑤ I'm helping **them** / themselves to cook lunch.

⑥ Take time off, or you'll make you / **yourself** sick.

⑦ Can you give myself / **me** that book, please?

⑧ Mom cut **herself** / her with the bread knife.

⑨ Luckily, I didn't hurt **myself** / me when I fell.

⑩ I've known himself / **him** since I was in college.

⑪ Everyone, please help you / **yourselves** to food.

32.3 WRITE EACH PRONOUN IN ITS OTHER FORM

| me | = | *myself* | | yourself | = | *you* |

① them = _____   ⑤ herself = _____

② us = _____   ⑥ yourselves = _____

③ him = _____   ⑦ itself = _____

④ it = _____   ⑧ myself = _____

32.4 READ THE LIST OF INGREDIENTS OUT LOUD

> *Eight ounces of butter.*

COFFEE CAKE

- 8 oz butter
- 6 oz sugar
- four eggs
- 8 oz flour
- 5 tsp instant coffee in 1 tbsp hot water
- 1/2 pt cream
- 0.3 oz walnuts

32.5 LISTEN TO THE AUDIO AND MARK WHETHER OR NOT EACH ITEM IS MENTIONED

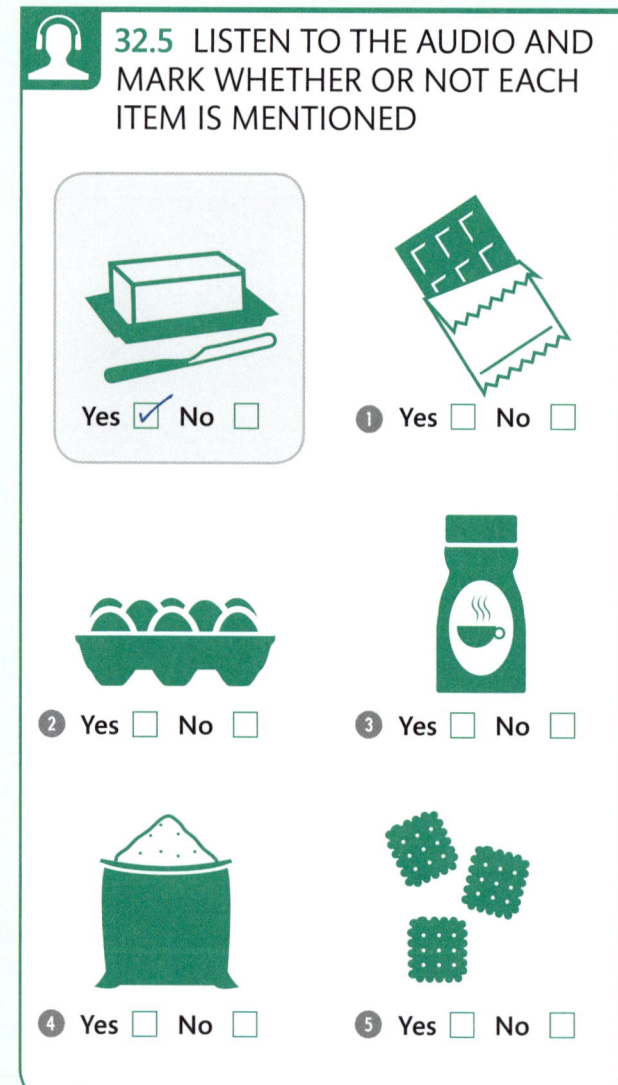

Yes ✓ No ☐   ① Yes ☐ No ☐

② Yes ☐ No ☐   ③ Yes ☐ No ☐

④ Yes ☐ No ☐   ⑤ Yes ☐ No ☐

32.6 LISTEN TO THE AUDIO AGAIN AND ANSWER THE QUESTIONS

How much butter will you need?   Two ounces ☐   One ounce ☐   Eight ounces ☑

1 How much sugar will you need?   Two ounces ☐   Six ounces ☐   Eight ounces ☐

2 How many eggs will you need?   Four ☐   Seven ☐   Ten ☐

3 How much coffee will you need?   One teaspoon ☐   Four teaspoons ☐   Three teaspoons ☐

4 How much hot water will you need?   Two tablespoons ☐   One teaspoon ☐   One tablespoon ☐

5 How much flour will you need?   Eight ounces ☐   Two ounces ☐   Four ounces ☐

6 How many ounces of walnuts will you need?   One ounce ☐   Four ounces ☐   Three ounces ☐

32.7 MARK THE SENTENCES THAT ARE CORRECT

I don't like sweet food at breakfast. I prefer savory things, like omelets. ☑
I don't like sweet food at breakfast. I prefer mixed things, like omelets. ☐

1 These strawberries are delicious! So sweet and juicy. ☐
These strawberries are delicious! So strong and juicy. ☐

2 That soup looks bitter. Can I try some? ☐
That soup looks tasty. Can I try some? ☐

3 The best thing to drink on a hot day is some nice salty orange juice. ☐
The best thing to drink on a hot day is some nice chilled orange juice. ☐

4 Oranges can be very bitter if they're not very ripe. ☐
Oranges can be very spicy if they're not very ripe. ☐

5 Those nuts were very fresh. They made me really thirsty. ☐
Those nuts were very salty. They made me really thirsty. ☐

6 I like my chilli nice and chilled, so it makes your mouth tingle. ☐
I like my chilli nice and spicy, so it makes your mouth tingle. ☐

33 What things are for

English uses gerunds and infinitives to talk about why people use things. This is useful for describing the purpose of everyday objects and household gadgets.

⚙ **New language** Gerunds and infinitives
Aa Vocabulary Household gadgets
New skill Talking about why you use things

⚙ 33.1 FILL IN THE GAPS USING THE WORDS IN THE PANEL

I use this gadget for ___*opening*___ cans.

1 Elsie uses that knife for _____ food.

2 I use the remote control to _____ the TV.

3 My sister uses her blender for _____ soup.

4 He uses this fan to _____ cool.

5 We use this machine for _____ clothes.

6 She uses her laptop to _____ emails.

7 They use the sound system to _____ to music.

8 He uses a camera for _____ photos.

9 She uses this cloth to _____ the dishes.

keep	turn on	write	making	wash
taking	~~opening~~	washing	chopping	listen

🔊

⚙ 33.2 MARK THE SENTENCES THAT ARE CORRECT

You use the microwave for heating food. ☑
You use the microwave for heat food. ☐

1 I use my phone to texting my friends. ☐
I use my phone for texting my friends. ☐

2 They use this for wash clothes. ☐
They use this for washing clothes. ☐

3 She uses that knife for chopping. ☐
She uses that knife for to chopping. ☐

4 Larry uses his laptop to sending emails. ☐
Larry uses his laptop to send emails. ☐

5 We use the refrigerator for keep fruit. ☐
We use the refrigerator for keeping fruit. ☐

6 I use the DVD player for watching movies. ☐
I use the DVD player to watching movies. ☐

7 She uses the sound system to play music. ☐
She uses the sound system to playing music. ☐

🔊

Aa 33.3 MATCH THE OBJECTS TO THEIR USES

You use it to keep cool.

①

You use it to do the laundry.

②

You use it to take photos.

③

You use it to send emails.

④

You use it to cut vegetables.

⑤

You use it to open cans.

⑥

You use it to turn on the TV.

⑦

You use it to wash the dishes.

⑧

You use it to dry your hair.

33.4 REWRITE THE SENTENCES, CORRECTING THE ERRORS

He used the remote control for turning on the TV.
He used the remote control to turn on the TV.

① He chose that knife for cutting up the carrots.

② We used the camera for taking photos of the puppy.

③ She picked up her phone for texting a friend.

④ I used the laptop for sending you an email.

⑤ Dan went to the refrigerator for getting some milk.

⑥ I turned on the DVD player for watching the movie.

⑦ Emma used the sound system for playing music.

⑧ He turned on the microwave for heating up a pizza.

⑨ I used the washing machine for washing my jeans.

⑩ He turned on the sound system for listening to music.

⑪ He used the remote control for rewinding the movie.

⑫ Jenny used the can opener for opening a can of fruit.

33.5 MATCH THE BEGINNINGS OF THE SENTENCES TO THE CORRECT ENDINGS

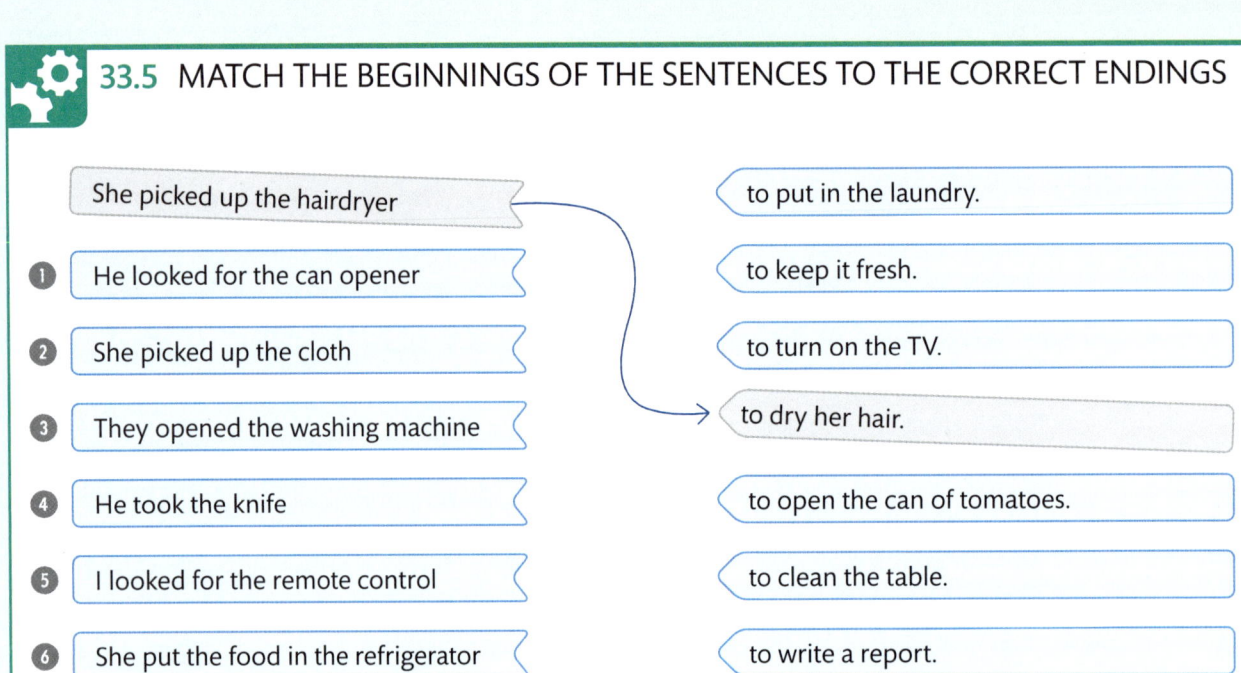

She picked up the hairdryer

1 He looked for the can opener

2 She picked up the cloth

3 They opened the washing machine

4 He took the knife

5 I looked for the remote control

6 She put the food in the refrigerator

7 He used his laptop

to put in the laundry.

to keep it fresh.

to turn on the TV.

to dry her hair.

to open the can of tomatoes.

to clean the table.

to write a report.

to cut up the fruit.

33.6 LISTEN TO THE AUDIO AND ANSWER THE QUESTIONS

Sharon and Olivia are discussing the various smart gadgets they own.

The remote control controls the heating.
True ✓ **False** ☐

1 Sharon uses it to turn on the TV.
True ☐ **False** ☐

2 She uses it to turn the stove on while she's out.
True ☐ **False** ☐

3 She uses the remote control nearly every day.
True ☐ **False** ☐

4 She uses it a lot on weekends.
True ☐ **False** ☐

5 Olivia has just bought a blender.
True ☐ **False** ☐

6 She uses her blender to make soup.
True ☐ **False** ☐

7 She can use her blender to peel vegetables.
True ☐ **False** ☐

8 She uses her blender to make juice.
True ☐ **False** ☐

9 She used her blender to make fresh orange juice.
True ☐ **False** ☐

33.7 CROSS OUT THE INCORRECT WORDS IN EACH SENTENCE

No one is watching the TV now. Let's turn it ~~in~~ / ~~out~~ / off.

1 My phone battery is very low. Can I plug it on / in / up somewhere?

2 There's an important email for you. Shall I print it on / out / up?

3 The TV is too loud. Can you turn it in / up / down, please?

4 There's a good movie on TV now. Let's turn it in / on / down.

5 We can't hear the radio. I'm going to turn it up / down / off.

6 I've typed the report for you, but I won't print it out / in / up yet.

7 Let's watch TV. Where's the remote control? I'll turn it down / in / on.

8 I've finished working on my laptop. I'll turn it on / off / down now.

33.8 READ THE ARTICLE AND ANSWER THE QUESTIONS

Where can you use the Rapid Cool High-performance Fan?
Vehicles ☐ **Buildings** ☐ **Outside** ✓

1 How big is the largest fan?

12 inches ☐ **24 inches** ☐ **18 inches** ☐

2 What can you use to operate the fan?

Plug and socket ☐ **Remote control** ☐ **Red button** ☐

3 Which button do you use to turn on the fan?

Red ☐ **Black** ☐ **Green** ☐

4 What is the fastest speed?

Cool ☐ **Super-cool** ☐ **Rapid-cool** ☐

5 What does the black button make the fan do?

Rotate ☐ **Go faster** ☐ **Go quiet** ☐

PRODUCT SPOTLIGHT

Fan Following

Introducing the latest Rapid Cool Fan

Your guide to the Rapid Cool High-performance Fan. This stylish fan is suitable for every space, from the office to the home. The fans come in three sizes, with the smallest at 12 inches diameter, then 14 inches, and the largest size at 18 inches. The most convenient way to operate the fan is by using the remote control. Use the red button to turn the fan on or off. Then use the green button to control the speed. There are three speeds: regular, cool, and super-cool. Use the black button to rotate the fan for extra effect. We think this fan is great value and will help you keep cool during those long, hot summers.

Aa 34.1 SPORTS WRITE THE WORDS FROM THE PANEL UNDER THE CORRECT PICTURES

rowing

1 _____
2 _____
3 _____
4 _____
5 _____
6 _____
7 _____
8 _____
9 _____
10 _____
11 _____
12 _____
13 _____
14 _____
15 _____
16 _____
17 _____
18 _____
19 _____

rugby   tennis racket   basketball   ice hockey   running track   diving   baseball

high jump   cycling   running a marathon   judo   motor racing   golf club   fishing

rowing   boxing   table tennis   archery   skis   swimming pool

35 Opinions and plans

When you give opinions on activities such as sports, you often use verbs with gerunds. When you talk about plans to do an activity, you use verbs with infinitives.

⚙ **New language** Simple verb patterns
Aa Vocabulary Sports and leisure
New skill Talking about opinions and plans

 35.1 REWRITE THE SENTENCES, CORRECTING THE ERRORS

She promised **doing** the laundry.
She promised to do the laundry.

1 She can't stand **to play** tennis.

2 Do you feel like **to watch** a movie?

3 We missed **to see** you at the party.

4 Andrew didn't agree **working** on Saturday.

5 Joe can't stand **to study** in the evening.

6 Nina enjoys **to swim** in the sea.

7 We hoped **passing** the exam easily.

8 They decided **going** out for dinner.

9 I don't enjoy **to scuba dive**.

10 Did she promise **helping** you later?

11 She doesn't feel like **to go** shopping.

◀))

 35.2 CROSS OUT THE INCORRECT WORDS IN EACH SENTENCE

Matt really enjoys ~~to read~~ / **reading** comics.

1 She arranged **to send** / **sending** the parcel today.

2 I can't stand **to listen** / **listening** to jazz.

3 Todd promised **to do** / **doing** his homework.

4 We missed **to see** / **seeing** the grandchildren.

5 You don't like **to ride** / **riding** a bike.

6 Eva didn't expect **to win** / **winning** a prize.

7 I wanted **to go** / **going** to bed early.

◀))

35.3 FILL IN THE GAPS WITH GERUNDS OR INFINITIVES

He really likes _____*playing*_____ (play) soccer with his friends.

1 She promised _____ (teach) us to swim.

2 Edward can't stand _____ (travel) by bus because it's boring.

3 Alice wanted _____ (ski) all day with her friends.

4 Do you enjoy _____ (work out) in the gym?

5 We don't like _____ (watch) TV during the day.

6 I often feel like _____ (meet) my friends after work.

7 Did you decide _____ (go) shopping after work?

8 Duncan can't cope with _____ (sit) at a desk all day.

9 She's waiting _____ (run) in her first marathon.

35.4 USE THE CHART TO CREATE 10 CORRECT SENTENCES AND SAY THEM OUT LOUD

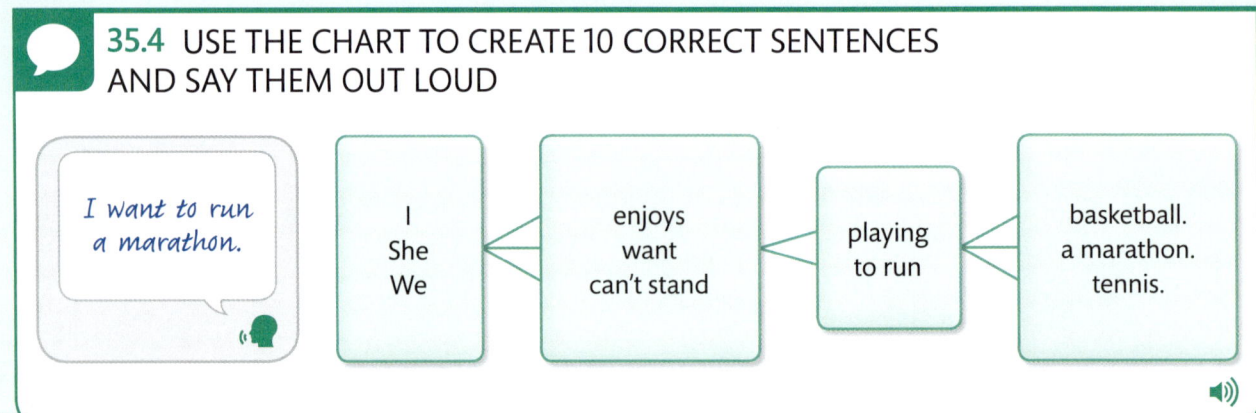

I want to run a marathon.

| I / She / We | enjoys / want / can't stand | playing / to run | basketball. / a marathon. / tennis. |

35.5 FILL IN THE GAPS BY PUTTING THE VERBS IN THE CORRECT FORM

She decided ___*to buy*___ (buy) tickets for the game on Saturday.

1 I didn't enjoy _____ (sit) in the stadium for hours.

2 He agreed _____ (play) on the team with his friends.

3 They don't mind _____ (train) three times a week.

4 Will you promise _____ (go) to the gym with me tomorrow?

5 You really love _____ (do) gymnastics, don't you?

6 Their team really didn't expect _____ (win) the game.

7 I miss _____ (run) in the park every day now that we've moved.

8 Ian can't stand _____ (watch) other people play sports.

9 We're waiting _____ (use) the squash court, but my friend is late.

35.6 LISTEN TO THE AUDIO AND NUMBER THE PICTURES IN THE ORDER THAT YOU HEAR THEM

A ☐

B 1

C ☐

D ☐

E ☐

F ☐

36 Future arrangements

In English, the present continuous can be used when talking about future arrangements that have already been planned for a specific time.

 New language Present continuous for plans

Aa Vocabulary Collocations with "take"

New skill Talking about future arrangements

36.1 FILL IN THE GAPS BY PUTTING THE VERBS IN THE PRESENT CONTINUOUS

Janet *'s playing* (play) tennis with Sally on Saturday at 2pm.

1. We _____ (catch) the bus at 10:30am and going to the stadium to watch the game.

2. Sarah _____ (meet) me next Sunday to go to the new exhibition at the art gallery.

3. They _____ (travel) to Italy by train. It's a long way, but it will be fun.

4. I _____ (try) a new dance class this evening. It's at the sports center at 7pm.

5. He _____ (go) to a concert this evening, so he'll be home late.

6. We _____ (buy) the tickets online because it's cheaper.

7. Clare and Hannah _____ (visit) their aunt in the hospital this afternoon.

8. I _____ (get) up early tomorrow as I have to be at the station at 6am.

9. He _____ (give) a presentation to the whole company this afternoon.

10. We _____ (fly) to Washington to meet our cousins this Christmas.

11. Daniel _____ (take) Rachel to the movie theater tonight to see a comedy.

36.2 LISTEN TO THE AUDIO AND ANSWER THE QUESTIONS

Kai and Claire are talking about their plans for the week and the weekend.

What is Kai doing next Saturday?

Playing tennis ☐
Going to a concert ✓
Visiting his parents ☐

2 What is Claire doing on Friday?

Visiting her parents ☐
Cooking dinner ☐
Meeting Kai ☐

1 What is Claire doing next Saturday?

Going to her sister's party ☐
Visiting her sister ☐
Going to Ben's party ☐

3 What are Kai and Claire doing tomorrow?

Playing tennis ☐
Watching tennis ☐
Going to a restaurant ☐

36.3 REWRITE THE SENTENCES, PUTTING THE WORDS IN THE CORRECT ORDER

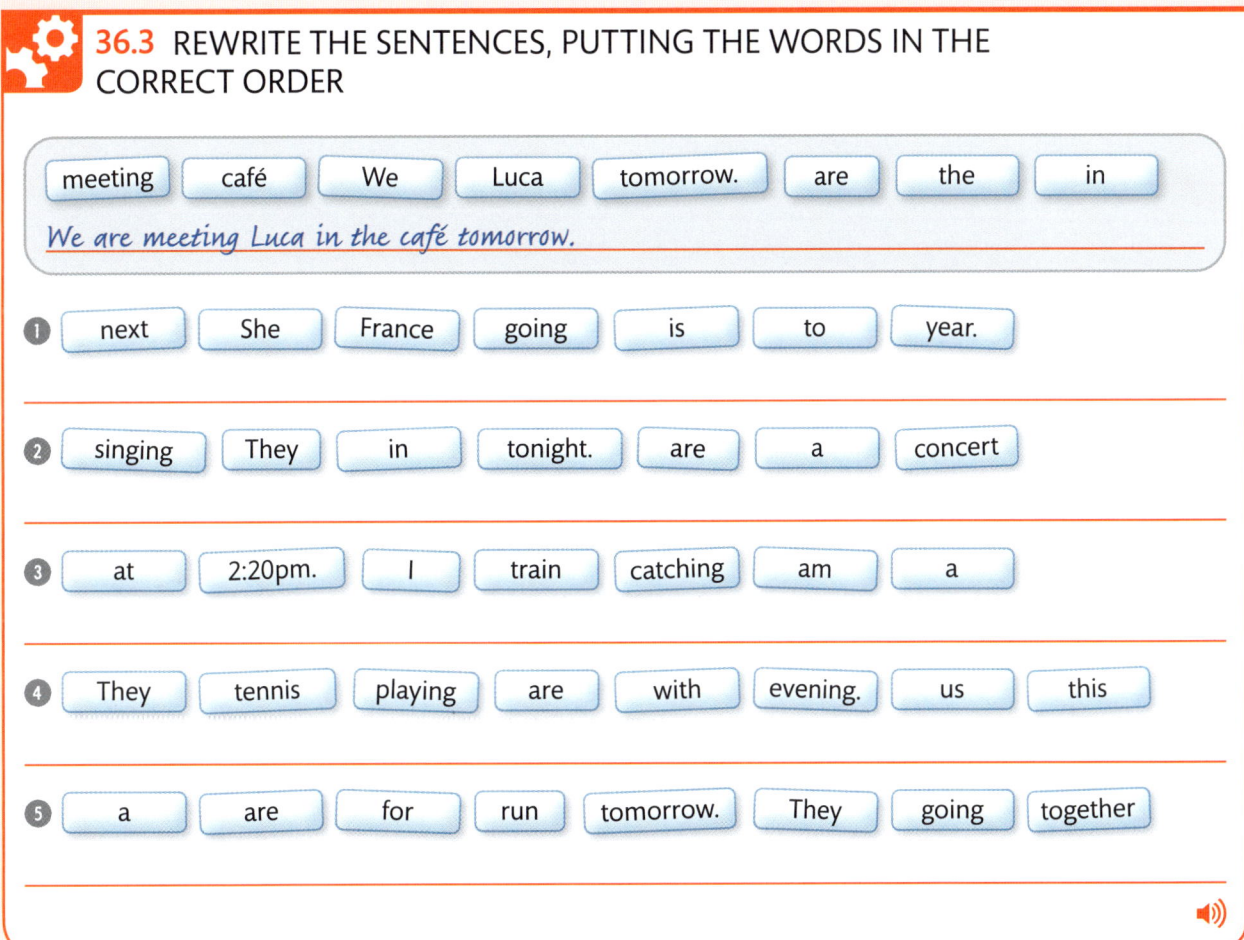

| meeting | café | We | Luca | tomorrow. | are | the | in |

We are meeting Luca in the café tomorrow.

1 | next | She | France | going | is | to | year. |

_____

2 | singing | They | in | tonight. | are | a | concert |

_____

3 | at | 2:20pm. | I | train | catching | am | a |

_____

4 | They | tennis | playing | are | with | evening. | us | this |

_____

5 | a | are | for | run | tomorrow. | They | going | together |

_____

Aa 36.4 MATCH THE BEGINNINGS OF THE SENTENCES TO THE CORRECT ENDINGS

They got on the train	to take good care of it.
1 You should take time out for lunch	this beautiful view.
2 We're taking a trip	to do some work on the house.
3 When you finish your performance,	and took their seats.
4 If you have a pet, it's important	to the mountains this weekend.
5 Should we go to the shopping center	or you'll get really stressed.
6 We're taking some time off in May	and take a look at the new store?
7 Let's take a picture of	remember to take a bow.

Aa 36.5 CROSS OUT THE INCORRECT WORD IN EACH SENTENCE

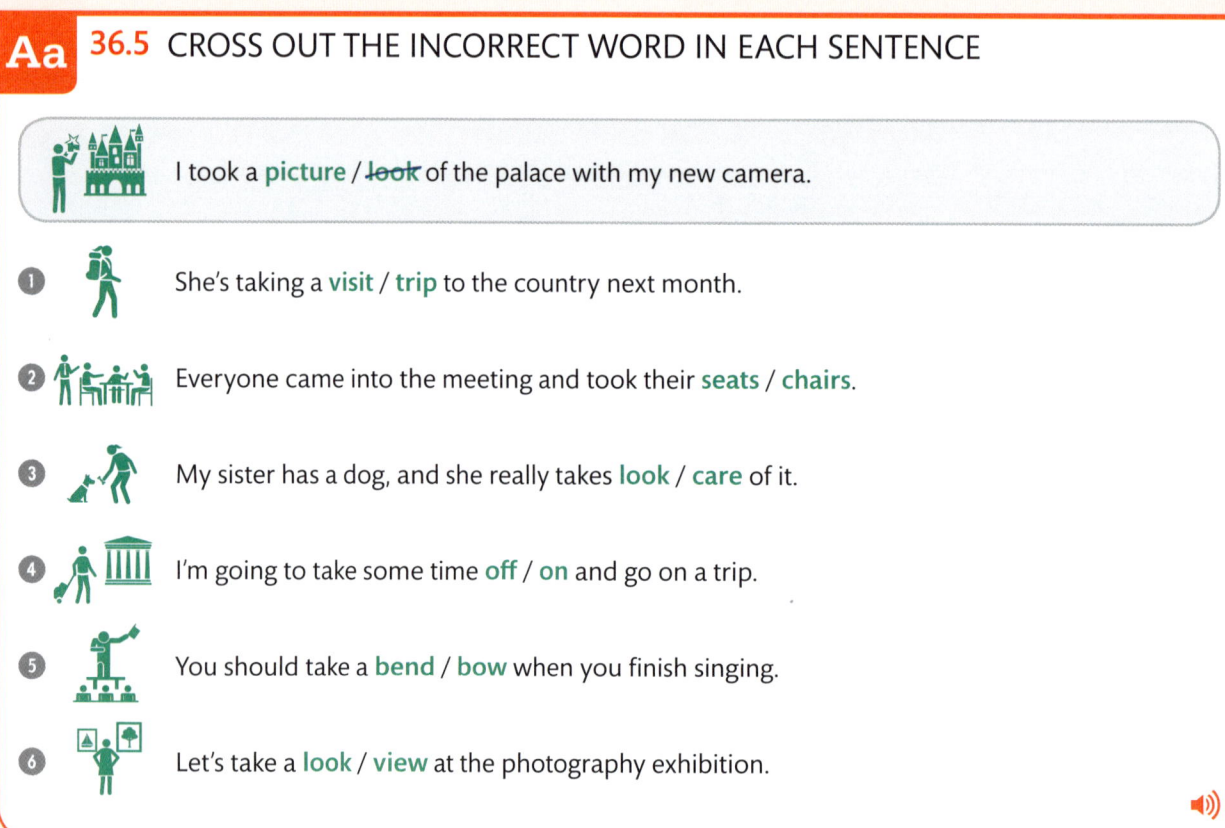

I took a **picture** / ~~look~~ of the palace with my new camera.

1 She's taking a **visit** / **trip** to the country next month.

2 Everyone came into the meeting and took their **seats** / **chairs**.

3 My sister has a dog, and she really takes **look** / **care** of it.

4 I'm going to take some time **off** / **on** and go on a trip.

5 You should take a **bend** / **bow** when you finish singing.

6 Let's take a **look** / **view** at the photography exhibition.

Aa 36.6 LOOK AT THE PICTURES AND COMPLETE THE SENTENCES USING COLLOCATIONS WITH "TAKE"

She's _____ *taking a trip* _____ to the beach this morning.

1. Josh likes _____ of old buildings.

2. Jack and Daisy always _____ of their pet rabbit.

3. Lee finished his performance and _____ .

4. Matt and Ben are _____ at the paintings in the art gallery.

5. Please, _____ .

6. My dad is _____ work and having a vacation.

36.7 SAY THE SENTENCES OUT LOUD, FILLING IN THE GAPS USING THE PHRASES IN THE PANEL

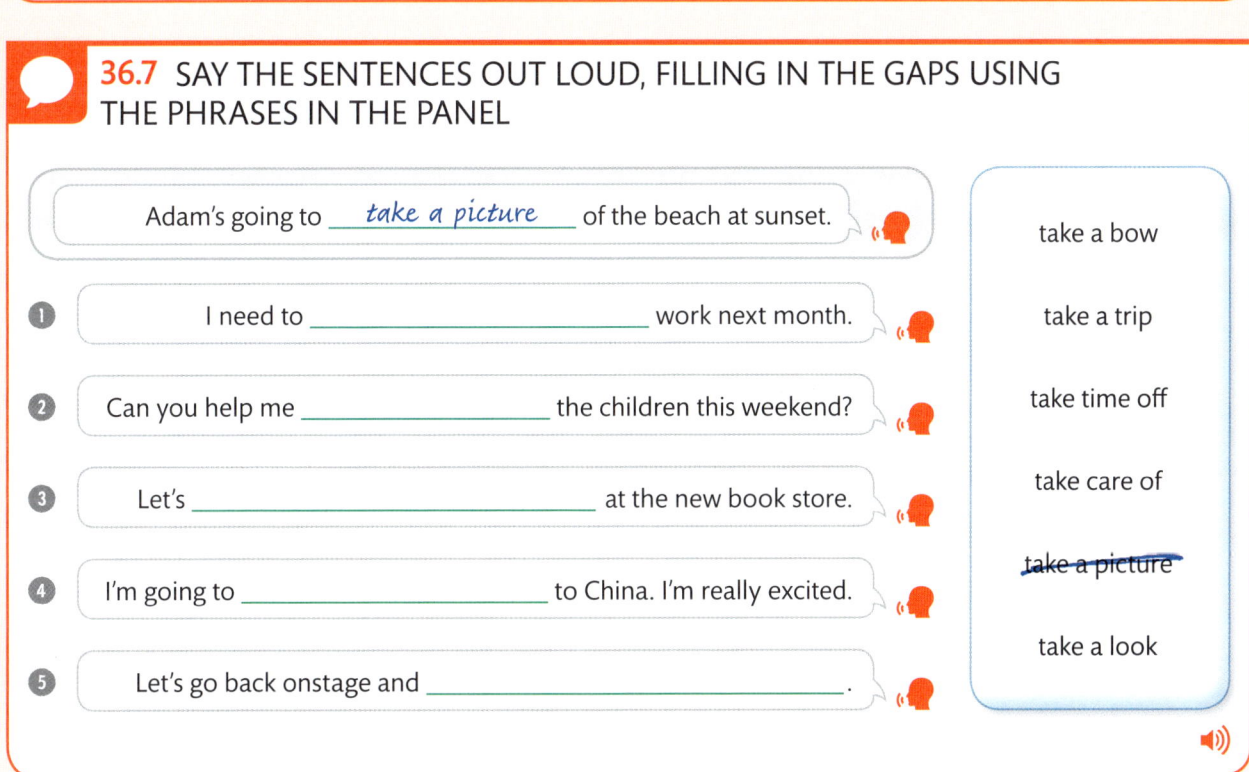

Adam's going to _____ *take a picture* _____ of the beach at sunset.

1. I need to _____ work next month.

2. Can you help me _____ the children this weekend?

3. Let's _____ at the new book store.

4. I'm going to _____ to China. I'm really excited.

5. Let's go back onstage and _____ .

take a bow

take a trip

take time off

take care of

~~take a picture~~

take a look

37 Planning the future

You can use "going to" when talking about something you've decided to do in the future, such as getting fit. This is useful for discussing intentions and predictions.

⚙ **New language** "Going to"
Aa Vocabulary Healthy living
🧩 **New skill** Talking about plans to keep fit

37.1 REWRITE THE SENTENCES, CORRECTING THE ERRORS

Pablo's going to **eating** fruit every morning.
Pablo's going to eat fruit every morning.

❶ Peter's going **learn** to swim this year.

_____

❷ Lauren's going to **trains** hard for the match.

_____

❸ Kate and Amy **is** going to run in the morning.

_____

❹ Cho **are** going to start a dance class.

_____

❺ Ali's going to **cycling** to work tomorrow.

_____

🔊

37.2 FILL IN THE GAPS TO COMPLETE THE SENTENCES ABOUT EACH PERSON'S RESOLUTIONS

Angie _____ *is going to play tennis* _____ every week.

❶ Joe _____ his dog in the park every evening after work.

❷ Matt _____ for half an hour a day.

❸ Liz _____ four miles every day.

❹ Millie and Josh _____ their bikes in the countryside more often.

❺ Debbie and Shinko _____ yoga every week.

🔊

37.3 READ THE NOTE AND ANSWER THE QUESTIONS

Susan wants to eat healthier foods.
True ✓ False ☐

1 Susan likes being unhealthy.
True ☐ False ☐

2 Susan doesn't like grains.
True ☐ False ☐

3 She's going to eat a lot of chocolate.
True ☐ False ☐

4 She wants to lose weight.
True ☐ False ☐

5 She doesn't like salad.
True ☐ False ☐

MY NEW YEAR'S RESOLUTIONS
I'm going to get fit and eat healthier foods this year. I don't like being unhealthy. First, I'm going to think about my diet. I'm going to eat food from all the food groups, even grains! I don't really like them. At the moment I eat a lot of chocolate, which isn't very nutritious, so I must cut down on that.
I want to lose a bit of weight, so I'm going to eat low carbohydrate foods, like chicken and fish. I love salad, too, so I'm going to eat more of that, and fewer high-calorie meals. No more fries or burgers!

 37.4 MATCH THE BEGINNINGS OF THE SENTENCES TO THE CORRECT ENDINGS

I'm very out of shape,

because they need to lose weight.

1 I'm going to have a better diet

because she wants to be more relaxed.

2 Matt is going to jog to work

because I want to learn something new.

3 Annie is going to start yoga

so I'm going to do exercise every day.

4 Lily is going to swim every day,

because they aren't healthy.

5 Si and Tom are going to join a gym

because I want to be healthier.

6 I'm going to make a salad for lunch

as she wants to get really fit.

7 Shahid is going to stop eating burgers

because it's good exercise, and it's free.

8 I'm going to join a pilates class

because it's low in fat and nutritious.

37.5 FILL IN THE GAPS BY PUTTING THE VERBS IN THE FUTURE TENSE WITH "GOING TO"

Look at that black cloud. It _____is going to rain_____ (rain) very soon.

1. We _____ (go) to the theater. I've already bought the tickets.

2. I _____ (join) a local basketball team.

3. Dan _____ (train) very hard because he has a tennis competition next week.

4. Helen _____ (be) in great shape because she cycles to work every day.

5. We _____ (leave) at 11:30pm to catch the train.

6. Tomorrow evening, they _____ (train) for the game.

7. It's very hot, so it _____ (be) difficult to run today.

8. You _____ (feel) a lot healthier because you're eating better food.

9. I _____ (go) for a long run with Charlotte in the morning.

10. The other team looks very fit. It _____ (be) a difficult match.

11. Wear a coat. It _____ (snow) this afternoon.

12. Sam _____ (lose) weight because he's stopped eating burgers.

13. Jake _____ (get) fitter because he's exercising every day.

37.6 MARK THE SENTENCES THAT ARE CORRECT

James thinks he is going to get fit this year. ☑
James probably he's going to get fit this year. ☐

1. I'm definitely going to start tennis lessons. ☐
   I'm going definitely to start tennis lessons. ☐

2. Sally hopes she's going lose weight. ☐
   Sally hopes she's going to lose weight. ☐

3. Ali's certainly going to do more exercise. ☐
   Certainly Ali going to do more exercise. ☐

4. Beth probably going to start training for the marathon. ☐
   Beth's probably going to start training for the marathon. ☐

5. My sister thinks she's going to start dance lessons. ☐
   My sister thinks she going to start dance lessons. ☐

6. Jack doubts he's going to join a gym. ☐
   Jack's doubts he going to join a gym. ☐

7. I'm definitely going to eat healthier foods. ☐
   I'm going definitely to eat healthier foods. ☐

8. Probably we're going to cycle to work every day. ☐
   We're probably going to cycle to work every day. ☐

37.7 USE THE CHART TO CREATE 16 CORRECT SENTENCES AND SAY THEM OUT LOUD

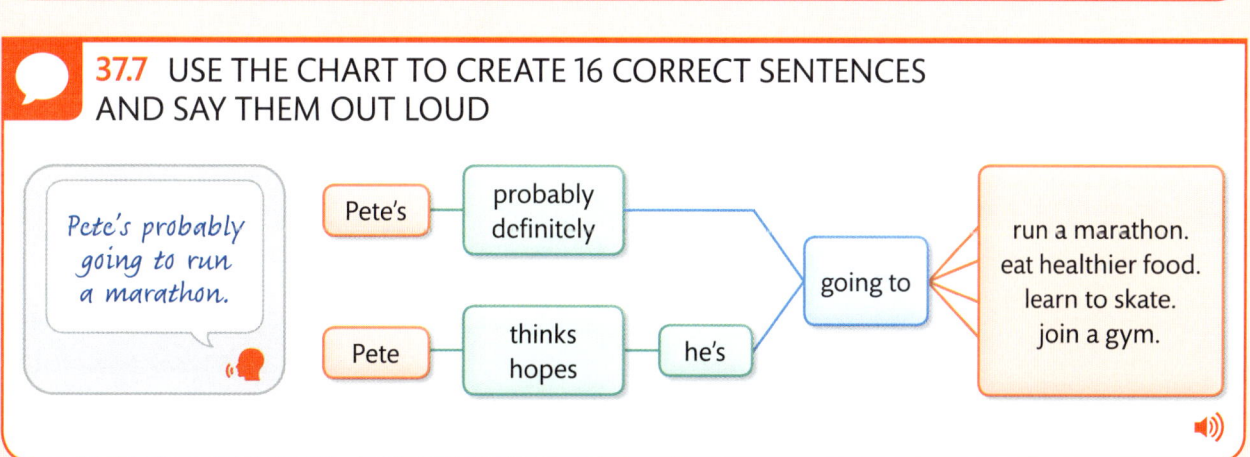

Pete's probably going to run a marathon.

Pete's — probably / definitely ⟶ going to ⟶ run a marathon. / eat healthier food. / learn to skate. / join a gym.

Pete — thinks / hopes — he's ⟶ going to

111

38 Vocabulary

Aa 38.1 **WEATHER AND CLIMATE** WRITE THE WORDS FROM THE PANEL UNDER THE CORRECT PICTURES

heatwave

① _____

② _____

③ _____

④ _____

⑤ _____

⑥ _____

⑦ _____

⑧ _____

⑨ _____

⑩ _____

⑪ _____

⑫ _____

⑬ _____

⑭ _____

⑮ _____

⑯ _____

⑰ _____

⑱ _____

⑲ _____

boiling	blue sky	chilly	blustery	mild	smog	snowflake
raindrop	temperature	drought	puddle	freezing	tornado	hot
hailstone	flood	lightning	~~heatwave~~	clear sky	rainbow	

39 Predictions and promises

You can talk about future events in English using the verb "will." This construction has several meanings, which are all different from the future using "going to."

⚙ **New language** Future tense with "will"

Aa Vocabulary Weather

🧩 **New skill** Making predictions and promises

 39.1 FILL IN THE GAPS USING "WILL" OR "GOING TO"

Tess is _____ *going to* _____ play tennis with Cathy after lunch.

1 Eric and John are _____ go to the movies on Saturday.

2 I _____ help you do the dishes, Dad. Go and sit down.

3 We are _____ go skiing for our next winter vacation.

4 He thinks it _____ rain all day today and tomorrow.

5 I am _____ go swimming with two friends this afternoon.

6 Jack is _____ take the dog for a long walk after dinner.

7 You look hungry. I _____ make you a chicken sandwich.

8 Jenny is _____ study music in college when she leaves school.

9 I think Argentina _____ win the next World Cup.

10 Maxine is _____ have her first baby at the end of August.

11 Tomorrow there _____ be heavy rain and risk of flooding.

12 In the year 2020, people _____ be healthier than they are now.

13 She is _____ stay with her cousins in Florida next week.

14 Don't worry. We _____ get there in plenty of time.

15 They are _____ get married on a Caribbean island in October.

16 Don't forget to put on some sun cream or you _____ get sunburned.

17 I promise we _____ be outside the theater before 8:30pm.

🔊

39.2 READ THE EMAIL AND MARK WHETHER EACH SENTENCE IS A PREDICTION, OFFER, PROMISE, OR DECISION

I'll pick up your coat for you today.
Prediction ☐ **Offer** ☑ **Promise** ☐ **Decision** ☐

1 I'm going to go to the supermarket, too.
Prediction ☐ **Offer** ☐ **Promise** ☐ **Decision** ☐

2 I'll cook tonight.
Prediction ☐ **Offer** ☐ **Promise** ☐ **Decision** ☐

3 I think I'll leave the office 15 minutes early.
Prediction ☐ **Offer** ☐ **Promise** ☐ **Decision** ☐

4 The traffic will be terrible.
Prediction ☐ **Offer** ☐ **Promise** ☐ **Decision** ☐

5 I'll be home by six o'clock.
Prediction ☐ **Offer** ☐ **Promise** ☐ **Decision** ☐

6 You'll get caught in the traffic.
Prediction ☐ **Offer** ☐ **Promise** ☐ **Decision** ☐

✉

To: Jeff

Subject: Plan for the day

Hi Jeff,
I just wanted you to know that I'll pick up your coat for you from the dry cleaner today. I'm going to go to the supermarket, too. I'll cook tonight. I think I'll make Moroccan lamb for dinner. Would you like that?
I think I'll leave the office 15 minutes early because there's road construction in town, so the traffic will be terrible. I'll be home by 6pm. I promise! Don't leave work late or you'll get caught in the traffic. See you later.
Emma

39.3 USE THE WORDS IN THE PANEL TO MAKE PREDICTIONS ABOUT THE WEATHER, SPEAKING OUT LOUD

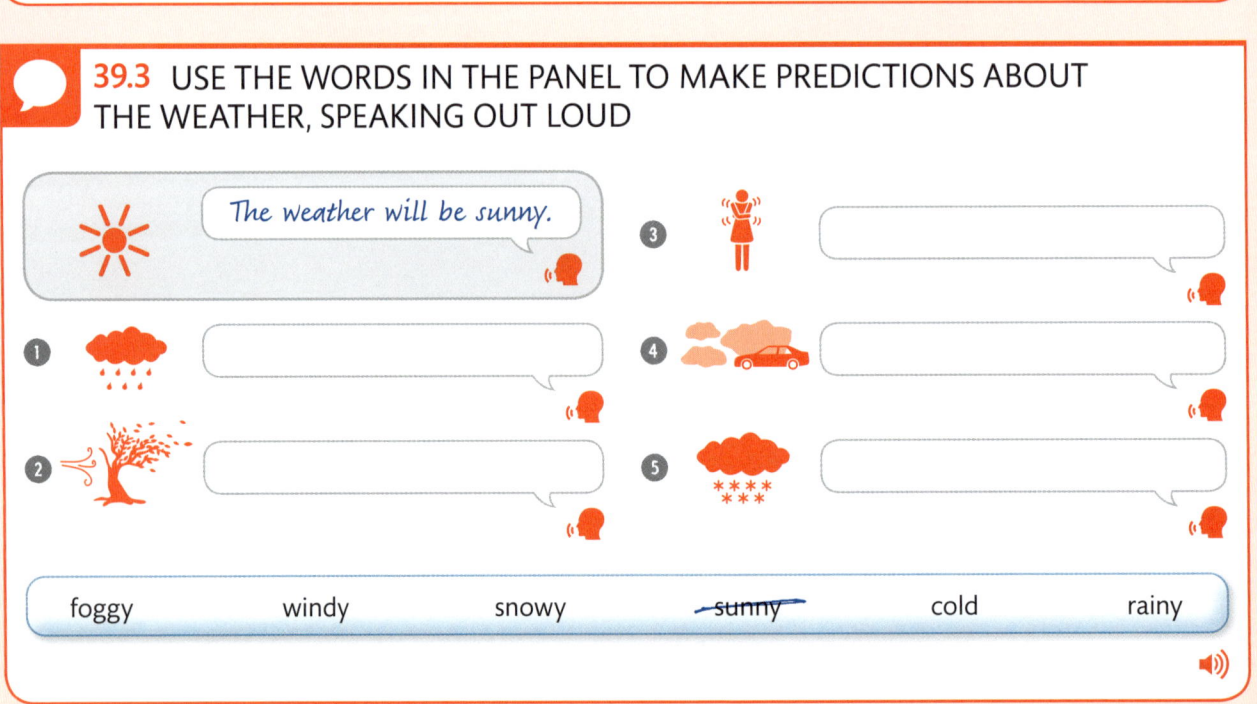

The weather will be sunny.

1

2

3

4

5

| foggy | windy | snowy | ~~sunny~~ | cold | rainy |

LISTEN TO THE AUDIO AND WRITE ANSWERS TO THE QUESTIONS IN FULL SENTENCES

Elena is making some predictions.

What does Elena think the weather will be like tomorrow?

Elena thinks the weather will probably be cold and windy tomorrow.

❶ What does Elena think will happen this weekend?

_____

❷ What is Elena going to do on vacation this year?

_____

❸ What does Elena think she'll do tonight?

_____

39.5 REWRITE THE SENTENCES, PUTTING THE WORDS IN THE CORRECT ORDER

it's   to   go   will   sunny.   They   probably   beach   if   the

They will probably go to the beach if it's sunny.

❶ will   the   competition.   know   win   he   I

_____

❷ coat   I   definitely   warm   wear   it's   cold.   if   a   will

_____

❸ will   an   new   certainly   The   improvement.   be   office

_____

❹ doubt   lose   match.   she   I   tennis   will   the

_____

40 Possibility

The modal verb "might" is used to talk about things that are possible but not certain. It is often used when talking about the weather.

⚙ **New language** "Might" to show possibility
Aa Vocabulary Weather and landscape
🧩 **New skill** Discussing possibilities

40.1 MARK THE SENTENCES THAT ARE CORRECT

I don't recognize this place. We might be lost. ☑
I don't recognize this place. We might have been lost. ☐

1. I might take some photos later this afternoon. ☐
   I might have taken some photos later this afternoon. ☐

2. She might not go out. She isn't in her room. ☐
   She might have gone out. She isn't in her room. ☐

3. I think it might rain soon. Look at those black clouds. ☐
   I think it might have rained soon. Look at those black clouds. ☐

4. If the traffic doesn't clear soon, we might be late. ☐
   If the traffic doesn't clear soon, we might have been late. ☐

40.2 MATCH THE PAIRS OF SENTENCES

There's snow on the mountains. ⟶ We might go skiing this weekend.

1. I can't find my house keys.   She might have caught a cold.

2. Samantha has a sore throat.   There might be a storm soon.

3. Look at the sky! It's black.   I might have left them at work.

4. Where's Dan? He isn't at his desk.   I think they might be yours.

5. These aren't my glasses.   He might not have come to work today.

40.3 CROSS OUT THE INCORRECT WORDS IN EACH SENTENCE

 I don't feel like going out. I ~~might be~~ / ~~might have stayed~~ / **might stay** at home.

❶  The clouds are clearing. It **might not** / **might be** / **might not have** snow after all.

❷ There was a robbery last night. Someone **might see** / **might be** / **might have seen** something.

❸  I don't want to cook tonight. I **might be** / **might have got** / **might get** a takeout.

❹  Who is in that limousine? It **might be** / **might have been** / **might** someone famous.

❺  Did you hear that? I think I **might** / **might have dropped** / **might drop** some money.

40.4 READ THE EMAIL AND ANSWER THE QUESTIONS

Laura sent her mom a necklace for her birthday.
True ☐ **False** ☐ **Not given** ☑

❶ Her mom's present might not have arrived.
True ☐ **False** ☐ **Not given** ☐

❷ Laura has sent John a present.
True ☐ **False** ☐ **Not given** ☐

❸ John has visited Laura in the mountains.
True ☐ **False** ☐ **Not given** ☐

❹ Laura thinks it might snow later.
True ☐ **False** ☐ **Not given** ☐

❺ Laura's mom might have read her blog.
True ☐ **False** ☐ **Not given** ☐

To: Cindy Smith

Subject: Belated Happy Birthday!

Hi Mom,

How was your birthday? Did you get your present? It might not have arrived yet because I sent it late. Sorry! I sent a postcard to John, but I might have written the wrong address. I couldn't remember his zip code. Well, it's beautiful here in the mountains. You'd love it. The sky changes all the time and I think it might snow later. I've taken loads of photos. I might upload them onto my blog. Have you read my blog yet? John says you've read it, but you haven't said anything to me. Let me know what you think.

Lots of love,

Laura

40.5 SAY THE SENTENCES OUT LOUD, CONTRACTING "HAVE"

They might not have known each other.

They might not've known each other.

1 Ben might have booked a table for us.

2 I might not have loaded the dishwasher.

3 They might have already seen that movie.

4 She might not have been here before.

5 He might have caught a cold.

6 I might not have locked the door.

7 She might have left the theater.

40.6 LISTEN TO THE AUDIO, THEN NUMBER THE SENTENCES IN THE ORDER YOU HEAR THEM

Doug and Alan are lost in the mountains.

A They might be in big trouble. ☐

B Doug might be able to use the GPS on his phone. ☐

C Doug and Alan might be lost because they don't recognize the path. ☐ 1

D They might find a different way down the mountain. ☐

E They might have taken the wrong turn. ☐

F It might snow soon. ☐

G Alan might have dropped his compass. ☐

41 Vocabulary

Aa 41.1 SICKNESS AND HEALTH WRITE THE WORDS FROM THE PANEL UNDER THE CORRECT PICTURES

sore throat

1 _____

2 _____

3 _____

4 _____

5 _____

6 _____

7 _____

8 _____

9 _____

10 _____

11 _____

12 _____

13 _____

14 _____

15 _____

16 _____

17 _____

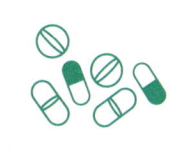

18 _____

19 _____

stomach ache   thermometer   tonsillitis   food poisioning   medicine / medication   x-ray

exercise   pills / tablets   rest   to vomit   runny nose   backache   broken bone

~~sore throat~~   drink water   headache   recovery   stitches   cough   test results

42 Obligations

In English, you can use "have to" or "must" when talking about obligations or things that are necessary. You may hear it in important instructions such as medical advice.

⚙ **New language** "Must" and "have to"
Aa Vocabulary Health and sickness
🧩 **New skill** Expressing obligation

Aa 42.1 MATCH THE PHRASES THAT MEAN THE SAME

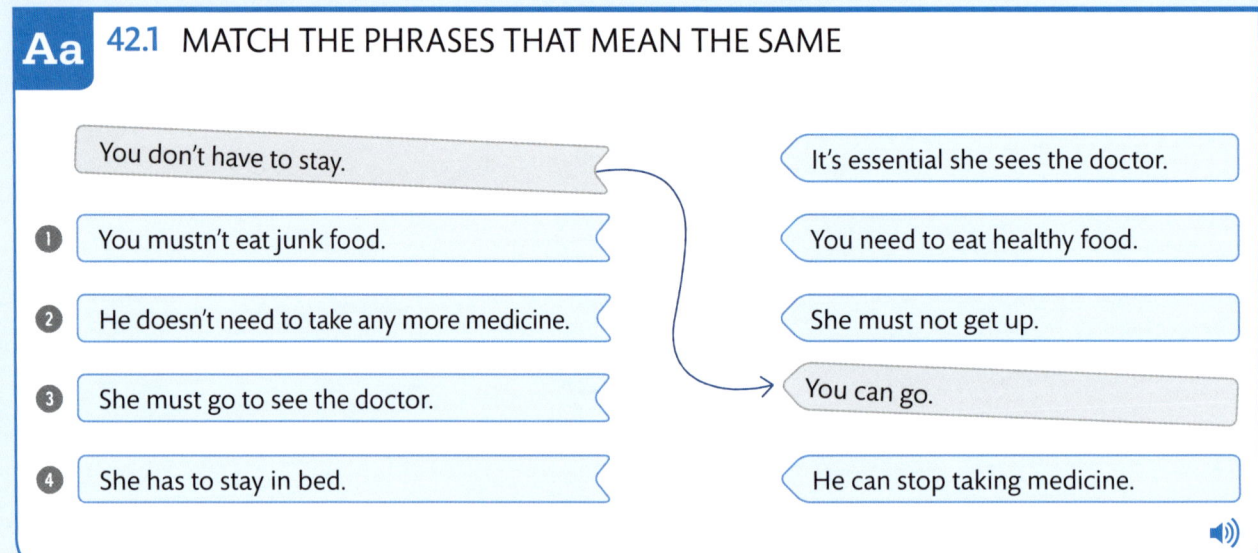

You don't have to stay. ────────→ You can go.

❶ You mustn't eat junk food. — It's essential she sees the doctor.

❷ He doesn't need to take any more medicine. — You need to eat healthy food.

❸ She must go to see the doctor. — She must not get up.

❹ She has to stay in bed. — He can stop taking medicine.

🔊

⚙ 42.2 CROSS OUT THE INCORRECT WORDS IN EACH SENTENCE

You ~~must~~ / ~~haven't to~~ / must not go to work. You're ill and you need to stay at home.

❶ You **must not** / **don't have to** / **must** make an appointment at the clinic. I'll do it for you.

❷ She **must** / **doesn't have to** / **must not** drink a lot of water. It will help her sore throat.

❸ I **must** / **don't have to** / **have to** take any painkillers. I don't need them because I feel better.

❹ We all **must not** / **don't have to** / **must** look after ourselves and take care of our health.

❺ You **have to** / **don't have to** / **must not** walk on your broken ankle. It needs time to heal.

❻ It's the first day of Tanya's vacation today. She **has to** / **doesn't have to** / **must not** go to work.

❼ Jill **doesn't have to** / **must not** / **has to** go to hospital for an operation, but it isn't serious.

❽ I really **must** / **must not** / **don't have to** diet and do more exercise. I want to lose weight.

🔊

42.3 LISTEN TO THE AUDIO AND ANSWER THE QUESTIONS

Mr. Carlton is asking his doctor for advice.

	True	False
Mr. Carlton has a fever and he is feeling tired.	☑	☐
❶ The doctor says he should rest and must not go to work.	☐	☐
❷ Mr. Carlton planned to go to London on business tomorrow.	☐	☐
❸ Mr. Carlton must not stay at home or sleep too much.	☐	☐
❹ He doesn't have to stay in bed, but could lie down on a sofa.	☐	☐
❺ He has to drink a lot of water and eat healthy food.	☐	☐
❻ He has to take some medicine to get rid of the illness.	☐	☐

42.4 READ THE DOCTOR'S NOTE AND WRITE ANSWERS TO THE QUESTIONS AS FULL SENTENCES

Can Mrs. Jones go back to work after the operation?
No, she must not go to work for six weeks.

❶ Does she have to stay in bed?

_____

❷ Can she drive after the operation?

_____

❸ What does she have to take for two weeks?

_____

❹ How much water must she drink a day?

_____

❺ What must she do if she feels unwell?

_____

MRS. JONES'S
POST-OPERATION NOTES:

• She must not go to work for six weeks after her operation.

• She doesn't have to stay in bed, but she must rest.

• She must not drive for four weeks.

• She has to take painkillers for two weeks.

• She must drink at least 1.5 liters of water a day.

• She must call the hospital immediately if she feels unwell.

43 Making deductions

In English, you can add an extra verb (called a "modal verb") to show if a statement is likely or unlikely. You may hear modal verbs when people talk about sickness.

 New language "Might" and "could"

Aa Vocabulary Health and sickness

New skill Talking about possibility

43.1 REWRITE THE SENTENCES, CORRECTING THE ERRORS

I might change not tomorrow's appointment with the doctor.
I might not change tomorrow's appointment with the doctor.

1 Sam mights go to the movie theater with Jim after work this evening.
_____

2 Tina has red spots all over her body. She coulds have chicken pox.
_____

3 Frank hasn't replied to my email yet. He might bes not at work yet.
_____

4 Harriet had a sore throat and a fever yesterday. She mights be off sick today.
_____

5 Dawn could being at the dentist's. She said she had a toothache.
_____

6 Tom should see someone about the pain in his stomach. It might being appendicitis.
_____

7 The doctor doesn't think you have broken your arm, but it could to be a sprain.
_____

8 That rash might not been serious, but you should get it checked out.
_____

9 I don't feel very well. I've got a headache and a temperature. I could to have the flu.
_____

10 John isn't at work yet, which is unusual. He might been stuck in traffic.
_____

43.2 LISTEN TO THE AUDIO AND NUMBER THE PICTURES IN THE ORDER YOU HEAR THEM

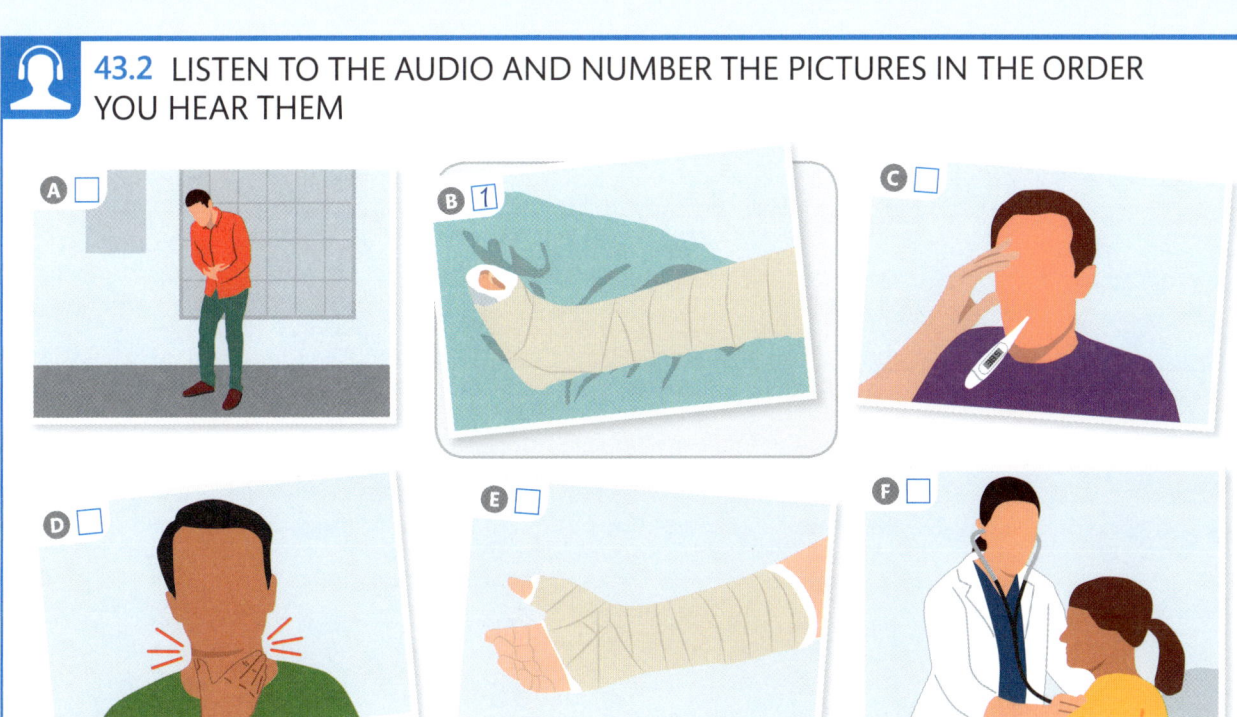

A ☐   B ☐1   C ☐

D ☐   E ☐   F ☐

43.3 MATCH THE SYMPTOMS TO THE LIKELY CAUSES

John has a sore ankle. ────────┐

① Paula has a high temperature.

② Ryu has a stomach ache.

③ Jo has a sore throat, but she can swallow.

④ John can't stop coughing.

⑤ Belinda can't lose weight.

⑥ Sam is covered in red, itchy spots.

⑦ Tina has a sore wrist.

⑧ Alan can't stop sneezing.

It might be sprained.

He could have bronchitis.

He thinks it could be hay fever.

It might be broken. ◄────────

It might not be tonsillitis.

It could be appendicitis.

She might be eating the wrong sort of food.

She could have an infection.

He could have chicken pox.

123

43.4 REWRITE THE SENTENCES, PUTTING THE WORDS IN THE CORRECT ORDER

| need | to | today. | doctor | to | John | go | the | might |

John might need to go to the doctor today.

1. pain | arm | The | in | could | an | be | infection. | by | your | caused

2. to | sister | today. | go | My | enough | might | to | be | well | not | work

3. so | could | ill. | bed | Karim | not | was | get | he | of | because | out

4. because | fever. | You | flu | can't | a | have | don't | you | have

5. allergic. | It | be | hay | cannot | fever | I'm | because | not

43.5 CROSS OUT THE INCORRECT WORDS IN EACH SENTENCE

She had a terrible headache yesterday, so she ~~could~~ / **couldn't** go to work.

1. Don't worry, you **might** / **could** not be allergic to cats. It could be something else.

2. I'm afraid Jonathan's ankle is very swollen. It **could** / **couldn't** be broken.

3. Priyanka **might** / **can't** have the flu. I saw her last night and she was fine.

4. I'm feeling a bit better today, so the doctor **might not** / **might** say I can go home tomorrow.

5. My leg is so much better now that I **might** / **can** walk about on my own.

6. If someone cancels an appointment, the doctor **can** / **might** have time to see you.

43.6 USE THE CHART TO CREATE 15 CORRECT SENTENCES AND SAY THEM OUT LOUD

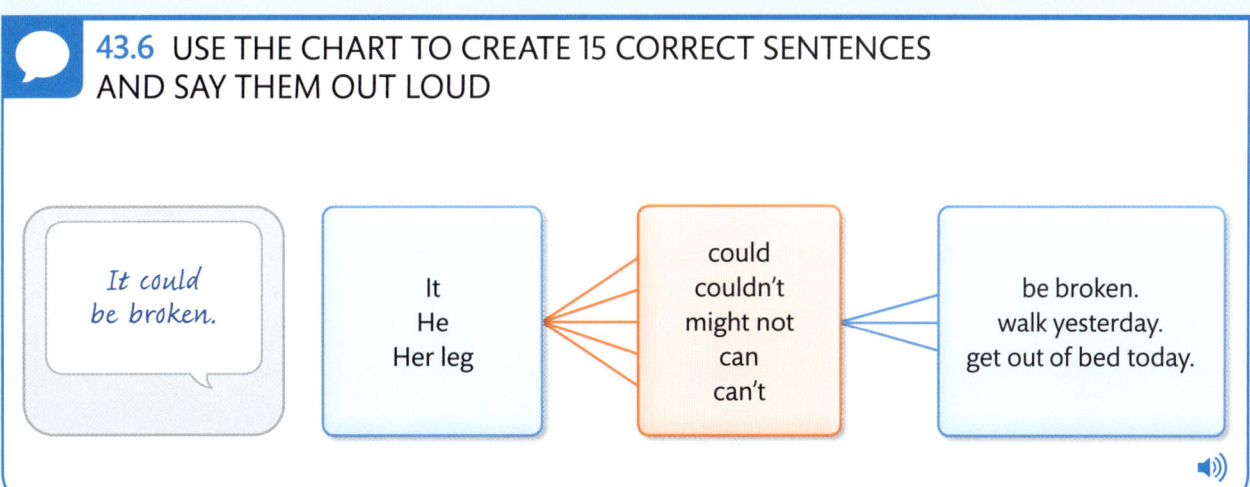

It could be broken.

It		could		be broken.
He		couldn't		walk yesterday.
Her leg		might not		get out of bed today.
		can		
		can't		

43.7 READ THE EMAIL AND ANSWER THE QUESTIONS

To: Vicky

Subject: Injured arm

Hi Vicky,

I hope you are well. I am writing this email with my left hand because my right arm hurts. I went to the doctor this morning and he thinks my right wrist might be broken. I fell on my arm when I was playing tennis yesterday and could have broken it then.

I have to go to the hospital this afternoon for an x-ray. I might have to wait because it is a big hospital. My friend had to wait two hours last year when he broke his arm. My sister is going to give me a ride to the hospital.

I would write more, but it is really slow using only one hand.

John

The doctor thinks John's wrist could be broken. **True** ☑ **False** ☐ **Not given** ☐

1 John thinks it might have happened when he was playing tennis. **True** ☐ **False** ☐ **Not given** ☐

2 John won't have to wait long for an X-ray at the hospital. **True** ☐ **False** ☐ **Not given** ☐

3 John's sister has done first-aid training. **True** ☐ **False** ☐ **Not given** ☐

4 John wants to write more, but he can't. **True** ☐ **False** ☐ **Not given** ☐

44 Polite requests

Use "can," "could," and "may" to ask permission to do something, or to ask someone to do something for you. Some constructions are more formal than others.

⚙ **New language** "Can," "could," and "may"
Aa Vocabulary Good manners
🧩 **New skill** Asking permission

44.1 REWRITE THE SENTENCES, PUTTING THE WORDS IN THE CORRECT ORDER

| more | have | please? | some | Could | risotto | I |

Could I have some more risotto please?

① | I | you | question? | Excuse | could | a | me, | ask |

② | water? | glass | have | I | May | of | a |

③ | borrow | I | pen? | Hi | your | Monica, | can |

④ | sit | table | me, | we | at | please? | this | could | Excuse |

⑤ | tonight? | Excuse | I | may | me, | reserve | table | for | a |

⑥ | meeting | our | Could | for | we | tomorrow? | rearrange |

⑦ | I | cup | coffee? | a | May | you | of | offer |

⑧ | your | could | you | chair? | me, | Excuse | move |

🔊

44.2 MARK THE BEST REPLY TO EACH QUESTION

Excuse me, could you help me please?

Yes, of course. ✓

No, I can't. ☐

---

1. Shirley, can I have another piece of cake?

I'm afraid you may not. ☐

No, you can't. That piece is for Avi. ☐

---

2. Excuse me, may I sit here?

Yes, thank you. ☐

Yes, of course. ☐

---

3. Could we meet on Tuesday?

I'm afraid I'm busy on Tuesday. ☐

No, we can't. ☐

---

4. Can you drive me to work tomorrow?

I'm sorry, but that won't be possible. ☐

Yes, sure! ☐

---

5. May I buy two tickets for tonight's show?

I'm afraid all the tickets have been sold. ☐

Sorry, you can't! ☐

🔊

44.3 RESPOND OUT LOUD TO THE AUDIO, USING THE WORDS IN THE PANEL

Excuse me, could I have a glass of water?

Yes, _of course_ .

---

1. Can I have another cookie?

_____ . Here you go.

---

2. May I offer you a cup of tea?

No, _____ .

---

3. Can I watch the sports channel?

No, _____ .

---

4. Good morning. May I check into the hotel?

_____ we're fully booked.

---

5. Good evening. May I take you to your table?

Yes, _____ . Thank you.

| you can't | Sure | please | thank you | ~~of course~~ | I'm afraid |

🔊

127

45 More phrasal verbs

Some phrasal verbs contain three words rather than two. Like two-word phrasal verbs, they are often used in informal spoken English.

 New language Three-word phrasal verbs
Aa Vocabulary Personal relationships
New skill Understanding informal English

45.1 REWRITE THE SENTENCES, CORRECTING THE ERRORS

We've run in of coffee.
We've run out of coffee.

1 Elaine gets along by her dad.

2 We're look forward to seeing the movie.

3 I came down with a solution to the problem.

4 The players look up at their coach.

5 Kathy puts up for her husband's cooking.

6 Ollie look down on most people.

7 I've run out on time. I'm going to be late.

45.2 LISTEN TO THE AUDIO AND NUMBER THE PICTURES IN THE ORDER THEY ARE DESCRIBED

45.3 READ THE EMAIL AND ANSWER THE QUESTIONS

To: Luke Johnson

Subject: My job

Hey Luke,

Can you help? I really love my job and I used to look forward to coming to work, but I don't now. I get along well with all my colleagues except for Pippa. She's a nightmare. She's always late, she's messy, and she doesn't do her job properly. She looks down on everyone and she's rude, too. I don't know why everyone puts up with her. I know I'm going to lose my temper with her one day, but that will only make things worse. I want to leave my job and I need to come up with a plan. I really look up to you, Luke, so I wanted to ask your advice. What should I do?

Love,
Rose

Rose doesn't enjoy coming to work now.
True ☑ **False** ☐ **Not given** ☐

① She has a good relationship with Pippa.
True ☐ **False** ☐ **Not given** ☐

② Pippa really admires everyone at work.
True ☐ **False** ☐ **Not given** ☐

③ Pippa gets a better salary than Rose.
True ☐ **False** ☐ **Not given** ☐

④ Pippa's colleagues tolerate her.
True ☐ **False** ☐ **Not given** ☐

⑤ Rose has found a new job.
True ☐ **False** ☐ **Not given** ☐

45.4 REWRITE THE SENTENCES, PUTTING THE WORDS IN THE CORRECT ORDER

forward | spring. | I'm | looking | to

I'm looking forward to spring.

① out | ran | of | We | time.

④ along | you. | I | with | get

⑤ answer. | with | Mark | came | an | up

② to | looks | Elena | Jo. | up

⑥ along | with | Sue | Ian. | well | gets

③ puts | his | job. | up | with | Tom

⑦ down | looks | people. | He | on

46 Asking for agreement

Use question tags in spoken English to encourage another person to agree with you, or to check that information is correct.

⚙ **New language** Question tags
Aa **Vocabulary** Travel and leisure plans
🧩 **New skill** Checking information

46.1 MARK THE SENTENCES THAT ARE CORRECT

Ellie lives near the coast, isn't it? ☐
Ellie lives near the coast, doesn't she? ☑

1 You haven't made any coffee, have you? ☐
You haven't made coffee, haven't you? ☐

2 Peter visited his parents, isn't he? ☐
Peter visited his parents, didn't he? ☐

3 Jane won't wait for us, will she? ☐
Jane won't wait for us, wait she? ☐

4 They've moved to Boston, didn't they? ☐
They've moved to Boston, haven't they? ☐

5 He's really handsome, he is? ☐
He's really handsome, isn't he? ☐

6 He hasn't met your sister, has he? ☐
He hasn't met your sister, had he? ☐

7 That wasn't your dog, was it? ☐
That wasn't your dog, isn't it? ☐

8 Oh, no. We're late again, not we? ☐
Oh, no. We're late again, aren't we? ☐

9 Max lived in New York, didn't he? ☐
Max lived in New York, lived he? ☐

10 It's beautiful here, doesn't it? ☐
It's beautiful here, isn't it? ☐

🔊

46.2 REWRITE THE SENTENCES, CORRECTING THE ERRORS

Jack has two older brothers, don't he?
Jack has two older brothers, doesn't he?

1 They didn't buy anything, buy they?

_____

2 You've seen this film, have you?

_____

3 We very happy about this, aren't we?

_____

4 Trish hasn't been here long, be she?

_____

5 Your friends know Mary, aren't they?

_____

6 They'll buy something, don't they?

_____

7 This is a busy street, it is?

_____

8 You haven't find my purse, have you?

_____

9 They didn't look happy, look they?

_____

🔊

46.3 ADD QUESTION TAGS TO THE SENTENCES

Tess is learning Spanish, _isn't she_ ?

① They left an hour ago, _____ ?

② Keith hasn't arrived yet, _____ ?

③ Sally will do the shopping, _____ ?

④ Mark doesn't like cooking, _____ ?

⑤ It isn't raining today, _____ ?

⑥ Fred has finished painting, _____ ?

⑦ Rebecca is in London, _____ ?

⑧ You weren't listening, _____ ?

⑨ We didn't see him, _____ ?

46.4 READ THE EMAIL AND ANSWER THE QUESTIONS

Tom thinks the meeting was difficult.
True ☑ False ☐ Not given ☐

① Tom didn't like Leo's presentation.
True ☐ False ☐ Not given ☐

② Geoff agreed to their suggestions.
True ☐ False ☐ Not given ☐

③ Geoff is a quiet man.
True ☐ False ☐ Not given ☐

④ Jean wants to sell products in the US.
True ☐ False ☐ Not given ☐

⑤ Tom thinks Leo has met Jean before.
True ☐ False ☐ Not given ☐

⑥ Tom wants to meet up with Leo.
True ☐ False ☐ Not given ☐

To: Leo Johnson

Subject: The sales figures presentation

Hi Leo,

Thanks for coming to the meeting last night. It was difficult, wasn't it? But I thought you made a great presentation of the sales figures. Geoff wasn't going to agree to anything, was he? That's OK. He hasn't been boss for long so he's probably being careful. Jean had some great ideas for selling our products in the United States, didn't she? You haven't met her before, have you? She used to work in production, but now she's in sales. It would be good to meet up after work one day, wouldn't it? Let me know your plans for next week and then maybe we can arrange a day to get together.

See you soon,

Tom

46.5 MATCH THE BEGINNINGS OF THE SENTENCES TO THE CORRECT ENDINGS

We could live here,

① You shouldn't do that,

② Daniel would love to go,

③ I could meet you later,

④ Sue and Aki wouldn't enjoy this,

⑤ Callum should be here now,

⑥ Rachel couldn't finish the exam,

⑦ She could take the train,

⑧ They would love this film,

wouldn't he?

would they?

shouldn't he?

couldn't we?

should you?

could she?

couldn't I?

wouldn't they?

couldn't she?

46.6 ADD QUESTION TAGS WITH MODAL VERBS TO THESE SENTENCES

I should get a new car, _____shouldn't I_____ ?

① We couldn't go to the party, _____ ?

② Ivan would love to meet you, _____ ?

③ She wouldn't say anything, _____ ?

④ I could get a taxi, _____ ?

⑤ He shouldn't be angry, _____ ?

⑥ You wouldn't do that, _____ ?

⑦ Katy couldn't make a cake, _____ ?

⑧ You should be happy, _____ ?

⑨ We could shop there, _____ ?

⑩ Rita shouldn't worry, _____ ?

⑪ We would help, _____ ?

132

46.7 LISTEN TO THE AUDIO AND ANSWER THE QUESTIONS

Noah, Thomas, and Rosie are discussing Thomas's plans for the evening.

Thomas is going out tonight.
True ✓ False ☐ Not given ☐

1 Thomas is going to a concert with Elsa.
True ☐ False ☐ Not given ☐

2 Noah hasn't seen the show.
True ☐ False ☐ Not given ☐

3 Rosie saw the show with her friends.
True ☐ False ☐ Not given ☐

4 Thomas hasn't booked tickets.
True ☐ False ☐ Not given ☐

5 Thomas thinks the tickets are expensive.
True ☐ False ☐ Not given ☐

6 Thomas won't be able to get tickets now.
True ☐ False ☐ Not given ☐

7 Elsa will think this is really funny.
True ☐ False ☐ Not given ☐

8 Rosie thinks Thomas should apologize to Elsa.
True ☐ False ☐ Not given ☐

9 Thomas will take Elsa to a restaurant instead.
True ☐ False ☐ Not given ☐

46.8 SAY THE SENTENCES OUT LOUD, FILLING IN THE GAPS

She's starting a new job, _isn't she_ ?

1 You shouldn't call now, _____ ?

2 Alice didn't call, _____ ?

3 Jake isn't tired, _____ ?

4 I could help you, _____ ?

5 He wouldn't enjoy it, _____ ?

6 Sarah told you to come, _____ ?

7 Nick won't tell anyone, _____ ?

8 You couldn't hold this, _____ ?

9 We haven't met, _____ ?

10 It's noisy here, _____ ?

11 Ann would like this, _____ ?

Aa 47.1 SCIENCE WRITE THE WORDS FROM THE PANEL UNDER THE CORRECT PICTURES

liquid

1 _____

2 _____

3 _____

4 _____

5 _____

6 _____

7 _____

8 _____

9 _____

10 _____

11 _____

12 _____

13 _____

14 _____

15 _____

16 _____

17 _____

18 _____

19 _____

to melt	to boil	to float	thermometer	~~liquid~~	safety goggles	crystals
electric shock	to mix	to sink	magnet	static electricity	to attract
to freeze	microscope	reaction	gas	to repel	battery	to pour

48 Things that are always true

English uses the zero conditional to talk about actions that always have the same results. This is useful for talking about scientific facts.

⚙ New language Zero conditional
Aa Vocabulary Scientific facts
✚ New skill Talking about general truths

⚙ 48.1 MATCH THE BEGINNINGS OF THE SENTENCES TO THE CORRECT ENDINGS

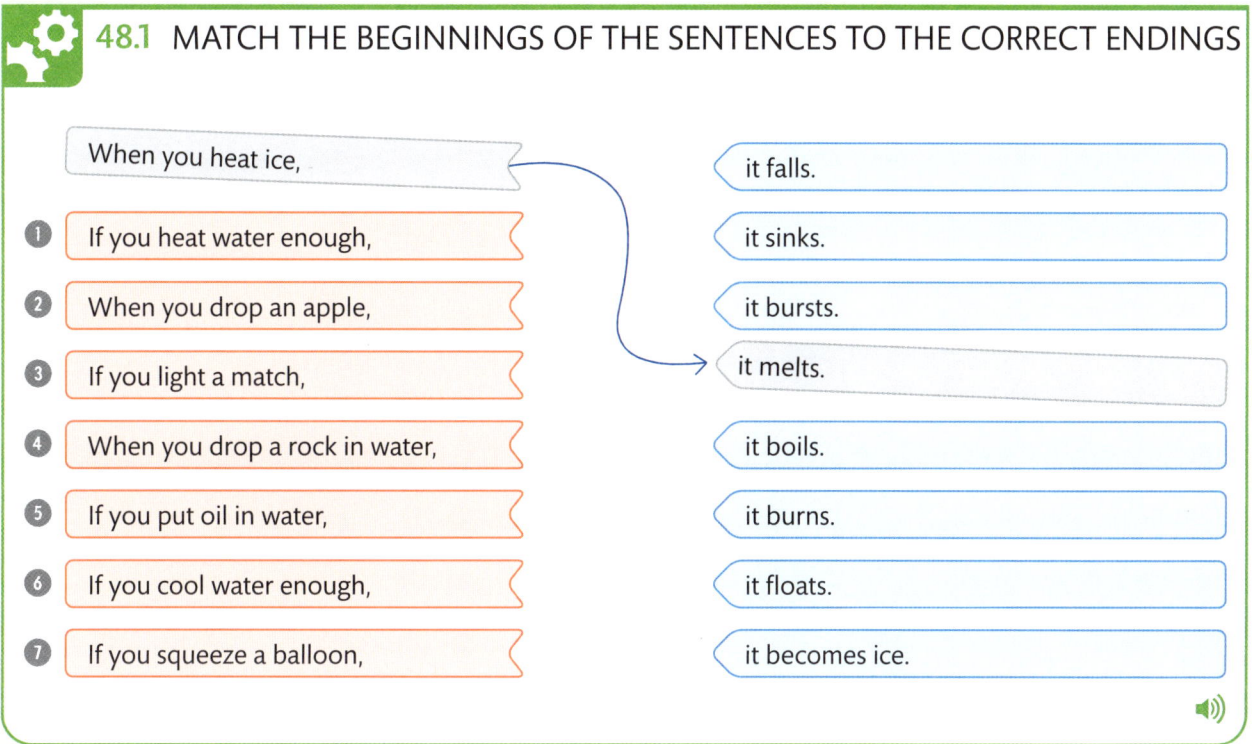

When you heat ice,

1 If you heat water enough,

2 When you drop an apple,

3 If you light a match,

4 When you drop a rock in water,

5 If you put oil in water,

6 If you cool water enough,

7 If you squeeze a balloon,

it falls.

it sinks.

it bursts.

it melts.

it boils.

it burns.

it floats.

it becomes ice.

🔊

Aa 48.2 FILL IN THE GAPS USING THE WORDS IN THE PANEL

If you put a coin in water, it _____*sinks*_____ .

1 When you _____ chocolate, it melts.

2 When you _____ water, it becomes ice.

3 When you add salt to water, it _____ .

4 If you _____ an orange, it falls.

5 When you drop a glass, it _____ .

heat

dissolves

freeze

drop

breaks

~~sinks~~

🔊

48.3 SAY THE SENTENCES OUT LOUD, PUTTING THE VERBS IN THE CORRECT FORMS

When you _____*freeze*_____ (freeze) water, it _____*turns*_____ (turn) to ice.

1 If you _____ (put) a cork in water, it _____ (float).

2 When you _____ (heat) metal, it _____ (expand).

3 When you _____ (drop) a rock, it _____ (fall).

4 When you _____ (light) paper, it _____ (burn).

48.4 REWRITE THE SENTENCES SO THAT THEY START WITH THE RESULT

When you cool steam, you get water.
You get water when you cool steam.

1 If you freeze water, you make ice.
_____

2 If there is no sunlight, plants don't grow.
_____

3 If you mix yellow and blue paint, you get green.
_____

4 When it rains, the grass gets wet.
_____

5 When you burn wood, you get smoke.
_____

48.5 REWRITE THE SENTENCES, CORRECTING THE ERRORS

> If you heated milk, it boils.
> *If you heat milk, it boils.*

1 If you lit wood, it burns.

_____

2 When you don't water plants, they are dying.

_____

3 If you boil water, it is making steam.

_____

4 If you rubbed a balloon, it makes static electricity.

_____

5 When you heat ice cream, it melted.

_____

6 If you cooled metal, it contracts.

_____

7 If you drop a basketball, it is falling.

_____

🔊

 48.6 READ THE NOTE AND ANSWER THE QUESTIONS

> When you put an apple in water, it floats.
> **True** ✓ **False** ☐ **Not given** ☐

1 If you put an orange in water, it sinks.
True ☐ **False** ☐ **Not given** ☐

2 An orange without peel sinks in water.
True ☐ **False** ☐ **Not given** ☐

3 If you put half an orange without peel in water, it floats.
True ☐ **False** ☐ **Not given** ☐

4 If you put an apple without peel in water, it sinks.
True ☐ **False** ☐ **Not given** ☐

5 An orange is heavier than an apple.
True ☐ **False** ☐ **Not given** ☐

6 Orange peel contains air.
True ☐ **False** ☐ **Not given** ☐

LECTURE NOTES
- If you put an apple in water, it floats.
- When you put an orange in the water, it floats.
- Now, remove the orange peel and see what happens.
- If you put the orange in the water now, it sinks.
- Now try the same with the apple.
- If you put the apple in the water without its peel, it still floats.
- Why does the orange without peel sink? It sinks because the peel is full of tiny air bubbles, which help the orange to float.

49 Describing a process

When the thing receiving the action is more important than the person or thing doing the action, you can emphasize it using the present simple passive.

⚙ **New language** Present simple passive
Aa Vocabulary Science experiments
New skill Describing a process

49.1 MARK THE SENTENCES THAT ARE IN THE PASSIVE VOICE

He pours the water into the tube. ☐
The water is poured into the tube. ☑

1 They heat the water until it boils. ☐
The water is heated until it boils. ☐

2 The thermometer is hung above the water. ☐
I hang the thermometer above the water. ☐

3 I record the results on the chart. ☐
The results are recorded on the chart. ☐

4 After two minutes, the temperature is taken. ☐
After two minutes, I take the temperature. ☐

5 She freezes water to make ice. ☐
The water is frozen to make ice. ☐

6 The mixture is allowed to cool. ☐
He allows the mixture to cool. ☐

7 The reaction releases gases. ☐
Gases are released by the reaction. ☐

◀))

49.2 REWRITE THE SENTENCES USING THE PRESENT SIMPLE PASSIVE

We freeze the water for 30 minutes.
The water is frozen for 30 minutes.

1 They take the temperature after 10 minutes.
_____

2 He heats the oil until it boils.
_____

3 They record the results on the chart.
_____

4 We boil the liquid for 20 seconds.
_____

5 We compress the solids.
_____

6 They hang a thermometer above the liquid.
_____

7 He pours the chemicals into a measuring cup.
_____

8 We measure the gas three times.
_____

9 They put a thermometer into the jar.
_____

◀))

49.3 FILL IN THE GAPS BY PUTTING THE VERBS IN THE PRESENT SIMPLE PASSIVE

In the experiment, the liquid _____*is stirred*_____ (stir) for 15 minutes.

1 The results _____ (record) on the chart.

2 The water _____ (pour) into the tube.

3  The gas _____ (collect) in a flask.

4  The temperature _____ (take) after 30 minutes.

5 The water _____ (heat) for 10 minutes until it boils.

6 The jars _____ (wash) in the laboratory.

7 The liquid _____ (boil) in a flask for 20 minutes.

8  Electricity _____ (produce) during the experiment.

9  Many different calculations _____ (make) each day.

10  The solids _____ (compress) for 10 minutes.

11  After the experiment, the data _____ (examine) carefully.

12  The thermometer _____ (hang) above the jar for 15 minutes.

13 The cells _____ (observe) using the latest microscope.

Aa 49.4 MATCH THE PICTURES TO THE CORRECT SENTENCES

The temperature is taken with a thermometer.

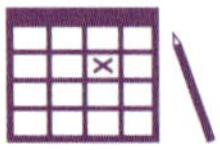

5 | The jars are washed and dried.

1 | The water is poured into the tube.

6 | The solids are melted in a jar.

2 | The results are recorded every 10 minutes.

7 | The data is examined on the computer.

3 | The water is heated until it boils.

8 | The chemicals are poured into a measuring cup.

4 | The gas is collected in a gas flask.

9 | The liquid is stirred until the salt dissolves.

49.5 LISTEN TO THE AUDIO, THEN NUMBER THE SENTENCES IN THE ORDER YOU HEAR THEM

A professor is giving instructions for a simple science experiment.

A The temperature at which the acid starts to solidify is recorded. ☐

B The temperature at which the acid melts is recorded. ☐

C Some stearic acid is put into a test tube. [1]

D Next, the test tube is put into a beaker of water. ☐

E The results are recorded on a graph. ☐

F A thermometer is put into the test tube. ☐

G The water is heated until it boils. ☐

H Then the mixture is allowed to cool. ☐

49.6 READ THE ARTICLE AND ANSWER THE QUESTIONS

The experiment uses clear vinegar.
True ☑ False ☐ Not given ☐

1 The experiment uses a teaspoon of baking soda.
True ☐ False ☐ Not given ☐

2 Baking soda is put into the balloon.
True ☐ False ☐ Not given ☐

3 The balloon is not attached to the bottle.
True ☐ False ☐ Not given ☐

4 The baking soda is poured into the vinegar.
True ☐ False ☐ Not given ☐

5 A chemical reaction causes the balloon to inflate.
True ☐ False ☐ Not given ☐

CHEMISTRY TODAY

Fun with chemicals

Inflate a balloon without blowing into it

P ut 300ml of clear vinegar into a plastic bottle. Put two tablespoons of baking soda into a small balloon, using a funnel or a teaspoon. Attach the balloon to the top of the bottle. Pour the baking soda from the balloon into the vinegar. A chemical reaction releases gas into the bottle. Watch as the rising gas inflates the balloon!

49.7 SAY THE SENTENCES OUT LOUD, CORRECTING THE ERRORS

The liquid is pour into the tube.

The liquid is poured into the tube.

1 The results recorded on the chart.

2 The chemicals are pour into a measuring cup.

3 The water is heat until it boils.

4 The gases released.

5 The liquid is collects in a jar.

6 The solids compress for 5 minutes.

7 The data is examine on the computer.

8 The thermometer puts into the liquid.

9 The temperature taken after 10 minutes.

141

50 Things that might happen

English uses conditional verbs to describe the future results of a proposed action. This is useful for suggesting plans and giving advice.

⚙ **New language** First conditional
Aa Vocabulary Tools and making things
New skill Giving advice and instructions

50.1 FILL IN THE GAPS BY PUTTING THE VERBS IN THE CORRECT TENSES

If you _____cook_____ (cook) dinner, I _____will load_____ (load) the dishwasher.

1. If I _____ (go) on vacation, I _____ (bring) you back a present.

2. If I _____ (find) your keys, I _____ (call) you.

3. If they _____ (visit) Paris, they _____ (travel) on the metro.

4. If it _____ (not rain), we _____ (have) a picnic.

50.2 MATCH THE BEGINNINGS OF THE SENTENCES TO THE CORRECT ENDINGS

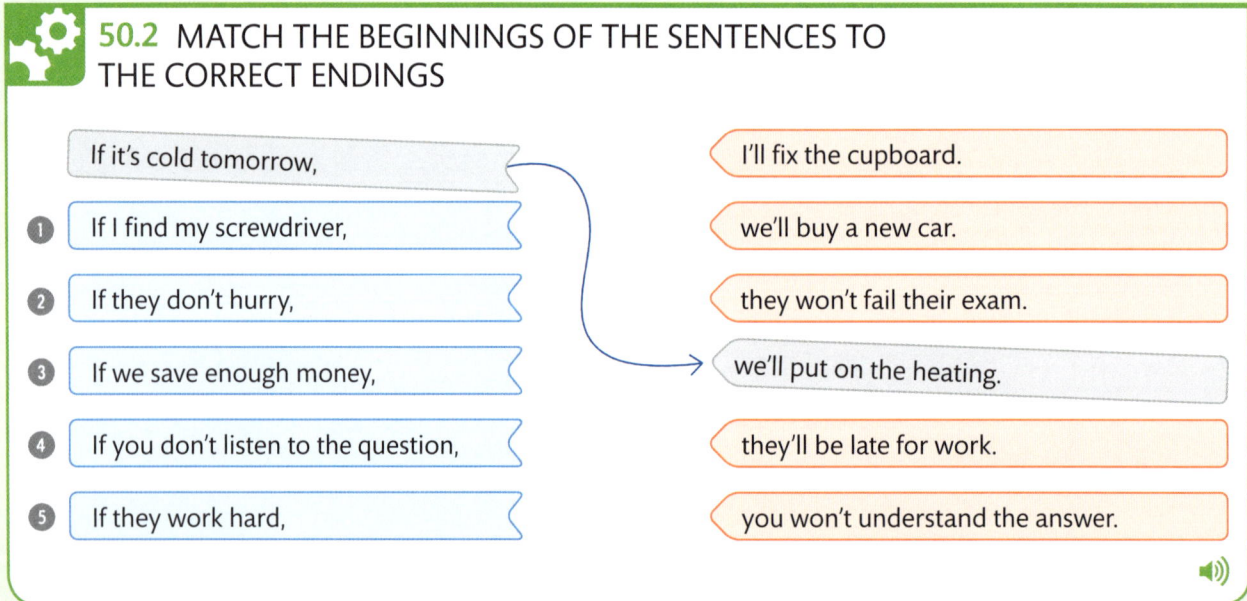

If it's cold tomorrow,

1. If I find my screwdriver,
2. If they don't hurry,
3. If we save enough money,
4. If you don't listen to the question,
5. If they work hard,

I'll fix the cupboard.

we'll buy a new car.

they won't fail their exam.

we'll put on the heating.

they'll be late for work.

you won't understand the answer.

50.3 MARK THE SENTENCES THAT ARE CORRECT

If it will snow this weekend, we go skiing. ☐
If it snows this weekend, we'll go skiing. ☑

1 If I will have time, I read the paper. ☐
If I have time, I'll read the paper. ☐

2 If you don't eat healthily, you'll be ill. ☐
If you don't eat healthily, you are ill. ☐

3 Will you come with me if I walk the dog? ☐
Will you come with me if I'll walk the dog? ☐

4 If it rains, we'll stay at home. ☐
If it will rain, we'll stay at home. ☐

5 If we go to the beach, we'll sunbathe. ☐
If we'll go to the beach, we'll sunbathe. ☐

6 If I'll see Martha in town, I say hello. ☐
If I see Martha in town, I'll say hello. ☐

7 If my son will fall over, he doesn't cry. ☐
If my son falls over, he won't cry. ☐

8 If she loses weight, she'll buy new clothes. ☐
If she'll lose weight, she'll buy new clothes. ☐

9 If I'll sweep the floor, will you do the dishes? ☐
If I sweep the floor, will you do the dishes? ☐

🔊

50.4 SAY THE SENTENCES OUT LOUD, REVERSING THE ORDER OF THE PHRASES

If you visit, you'll have a great time.

You'll have a great time if you visit. 🗣

1 If she gets that job, she'll move to Vancouver.

🗣

2 If your wife calls, I'll tell you.

🗣

3 If you stop eating bread, you'll lose weight.

🗣

4 If he buys a new car, he'll have no money.

🗣

5 If she's late for work again, she'll lose her job.

🗣

6 If you buy some eggs, I will make a cake.

🗣

7 If you tell me the truth, I won't be angry.

🗣

8 If he explains, I'll understand.

🗣

9 If they fix the oven, I'll be so happy.

🗣

🔊

50.5 REWRITE THE SENTENCES USING "UNLESS"

If we leave now, we won't be late.
Unless we leave now, we'll be late.

1 You won't get promoted if you don't work harder.

_____

2 If it doesn't rain, I'll go for a walk tomorrow.

_____

3 If the traffic doesn't improve, we'll miss our flight.

_____

4 They won't help you if you don't ask them.

_____

5 You'll get wet if you don't bring an umbrella.

_____

6 I won't go to the party if you don't come, too.

_____

7 You'll be hungry later if you don't eat breakfast.

_____

8 If he doesn't slow down, he'll crash the car.

_____

9 I'll see you tomorrow if I don't have to work late.

_____

50.6 FILL IN THE GAPS WITH "IF" OR "UNLESS"

_____ *If* _____ we save enough money, we'll go on vacation.

1 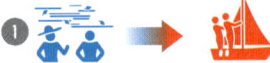 They won't go sailing _____ there's enough wind.

2  _____ Mike goes to New York, he'll see the Statue of Liberty.

3  Tara won't get home on time _____ the traffic gets better.

4  _____ I go shopping after work, I'll cook us lasagne.

5  _____ it snows next week, we'll go skiing.

6  Vicky won't be able to make the bed _____ the sheets are clean.

50.7 FILL IN THE GAPS USING THE PHRASES IN THE PANEL

If _____*it rains*_____, we'll take an umbrella.

1. If _____, he'll pass his exam.

2. If it's sunny, _____ .

3. If she's hungry, _____ .

4. Unless _____, he won't wear a coat.

5. If you're sick, _____ .

6. If _____, he won't stay up late.

7. If the kitchen is dirty, _____ .

8. If _____, we'll watch TV.

9. If I'm thirsty, _____ .

10. If the cat isn't frightened, _____ .

11. If you listen carefully, _____ .

I'll drink some water   I'll wear sunglasses   I'll call the doctor   we're bored   he works hard

~~it rains~~   she'll eat an apple   he's tired   he'll clean it   it won't run away   I'll explain   it's cold

🔊

50.8 LISTEN TO THE AUDIO, THEN NUMBER THE PICTURES IN THE ORDER THEY ARE DESCRIBED

A ☐

B [1]

C ☐

D ☐

E ☐

F ☐

G ☐

H ☐

51 Solving problems

You can use the first conditional with an imperative to give people practical instructions or advice, such as how to solve problems or improve their lifestyle.

⚙ **New language** First conditional with imperative
Aa Vocabulary Health and wellbeing
🧩 **New skill** Giving advice and instructions

51.1 MATCH THE BEGINNINGS OF THE SENTENCES TO THE CORRECT ENDINGS

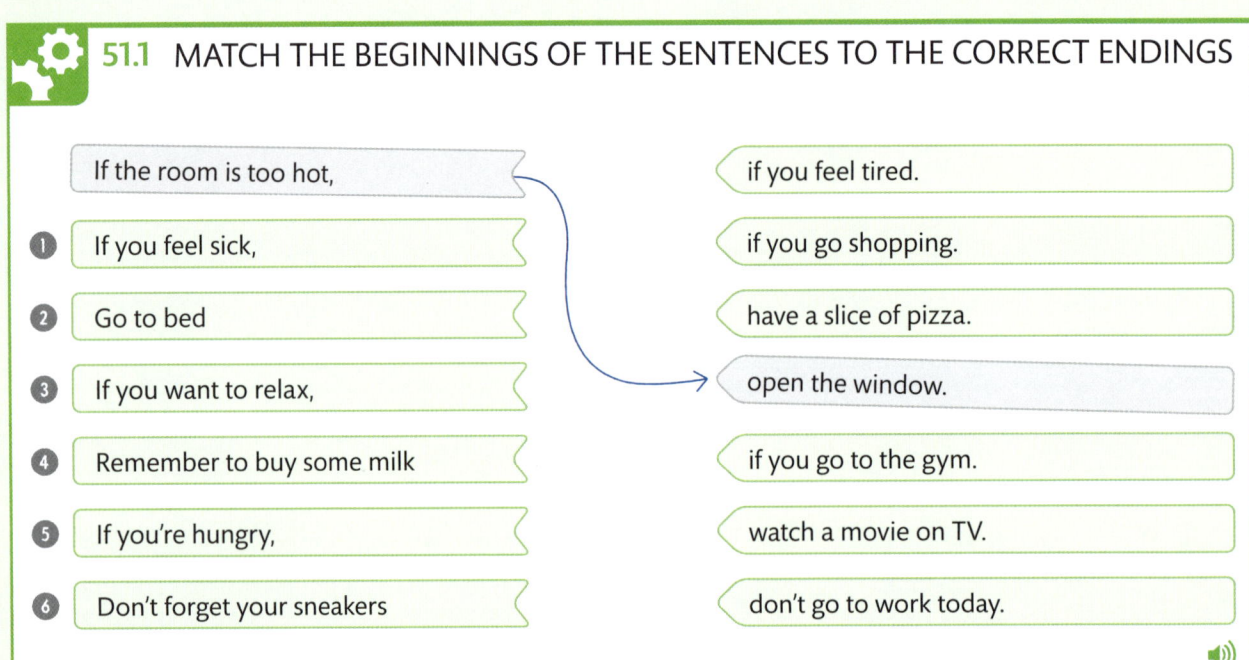

If the room is too hot, → open the window.

if you feel tired.

1 If you feel sick,

if you go shopping.

2 Go to bed

have a slice of pizza.

3 If you want to relax,

open the window.

4 Remember to buy some milk

if you go to the gym.

5 If you're hungry,

watch a movie on TV.

6 Don't forget your sneakers

don't go to work today.

51.2 REWRITE THE SENTENCES, CORRECTING THE ERRORS

If you will be thirsty, drink some water.
If you're thirsty, drink some water.

1 If you want a new car, you buy one.

_____

2 Don't stay up late if you tired.

_____

3 If you to see James, tell him to call me.

_____

4 Don't eat junk food if you want lose weight.

_____

5 Remember to shut the door when you left.

_____

6 If you like that jacket, to buy it.

_____

7 If you're hungry, you're making a sandwich.

_____

51.3 FILL IN THE GAPS USING THE WORDS IN THE PANEL

If you are overstressed, _____*take*_____ a lunch break.

① If you never have any money, don't _____ .

② If you don't like your job, _____ for a new one.

③ Learn to relax more if you want to feel _____ .

④ _____ your phone if you can't sleep at night.

~~take~~	look	calmer	overspend	Turn off

51.4 READ THE ARTICLE AND ANSWER THE QUESTIONS

Make sure you spend less than you earn.
True ✔ False ☐ Not given ☐

① Buy new things online.
True ☐ False ☐ Not given ☐

② Wait for 10 days before you buy something new.
True ☐ False ☐ Not given ☐

③ If you go out to work, don't eat lunch.
True ☐ False ☐ Not given ☐

④ Your friends will love having dinner with you.
True ☐ False ☐ Not given ☐

⑤ At home, turn off the lights when you leave rooms.
True ☐ False ☐ Not given ☐

SAVE MONEY
Here are five easy ways to save money

First, make a list of what you earn and your costs. You need to know exactly how much money you can spend, and you need to spend less than you earn! If you want to save money, don't buy everything new. Buy used things online. It's much cheaper and it can be fun. If you really want to buy something new, wait for 10 days. If you still want it at the end of 10 days, then buy it. After 10 days you probably won't remember what it was you wanted. If you go out to work, take your lunch. Don't buy it

in town. It's an easy way to save a lot of money. If you want to see your friends, invite them to your house for dinner. It's cheaper than going to a restaurant and you can ask your friends to bring the dessert. And when you are at home, think about your fuel bills. When you leave a room, turn off the lights!

SAY THE SENTENCES OUT LOUD, FILLING IN THE GAPS USING THE WORDS IN THE PANEL

If you want to get in better shape, _____ *go* _____ to the gym.

1. If you don't like your job, _____ a new one.

2. If you like those jeans, _____ them.

3. If your tooth hurts, _____ the dentist.

4. If you have too many possessions, _____ them.

5. If you work too hard, _____ some time off.

| find | buy | ~~go~~ | sell | take | see |

51.6 MATCH THE PICTURES TO THE SENTENCES

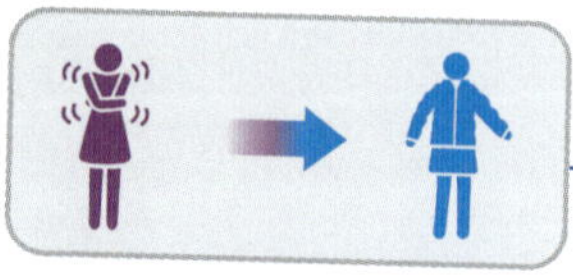

1

2

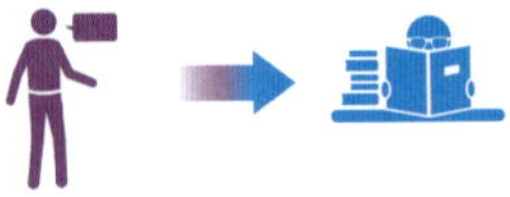

3

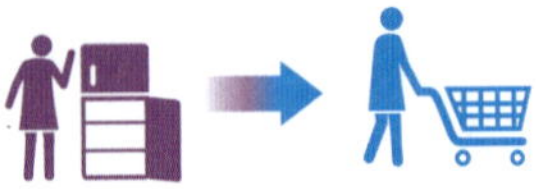

4

If you feel tired, take a vacation.

If you want to speak Spanish, start a class.

If you're cold, put on a warm coat.

If you want to get in better shape, do some exercise.

If you need some food, go shopping.

51.7 REWRITE THE SENTENCES, PUTTING THE WORDS IN THE CORRECT ORDER

home | want | go | If | a | you | taxi. | to | now, | take

If you want to go home now, take a taxi.

① tired | bed | in | you're | the | If | go | earlier. | morning, | to

_____

② you | those | leather | buy | them. | boots, | want | If

_____

③ yourself | feel | cheese | If | you | a | sandwich. | make | hungry,

_____

④ don't | money, | have | you | If | never | any | overspend.

_____

⑤ swim, | learn | to | take | want | some | lessons. | If | you | to

_____

51.8 LISTEN TO THE AUDIO AND MARK WHETHER THE PICTURES SHOW PROBLEMS OR SOLUTIONS

Problem ☐ Solution ☑

① Problem ☐ Solution ☐

② Problem ☐ Solution ☐

③ Problem ☐ Solution ☐

④ Problem ☐ Solution ☐

52 Planning activities

You can use subordinate time clauses to talk about sequences of events, where one thing must happen before another thing can happen.

⚙ **New language** Subordinate time clauses
Aa Vocabulary Building works
🧩 **New skill** Describing sequences of events

52.1 FILL IN THE GAPS BY PUTTING THE VERBS IN THE PRESENT SIMPLE OR FUTURE WITH "WILL"

As soon as it _stops_ (stop) raining, I _will do_ (do) some gardening.

① When they _____ (arrive) at the station, I _____ (get) them.

② As soon as I _____ (get) your message, I _____ (call) you.

③ When the bus _____ (stop), we _____ (get) off.

④ When the movie _____ (end), I _____ (make) us some coffee.

⑤ As soon as the paint _____ (dry), I _____ (put) the curtains up.

🔊

52.2 MARK THE SENTENCES THAT ARE CORRECT

When it will get dark, I'll put the lights on. ☐
When it gets dark, I'll put the lights on. ☑

① When I finish breakfast, I'll go running. ☐
When I'll finish breakfast, I'll go running. ☐

② As soon as he'll get home, he has lunch. ☐
As soon as he gets home, he'll have lunch. ☐

③ When we'll get to the theater, I'll buy tickets. ☐
When we get to the theater, I'll buy tickets. ☐

④ When I find a table, I'll order food. ☐
When I'll find a table, I'll order food. ☐

⑤ As soon as I will have the money, I buy a car. ☐
As soon as I have the money, I'll buy a car. ☐

🔊

52.3 READ THE EMAIL AND ANSWER THE QUESTIONS

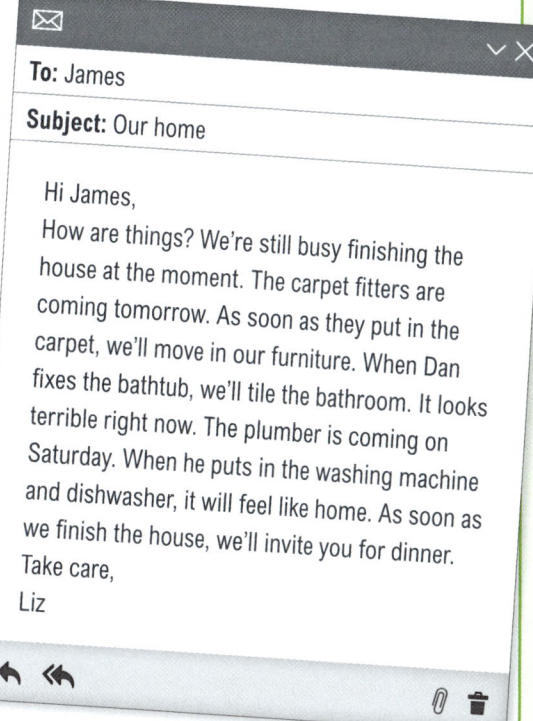

To: James

Subject: Our home

Hi James,

How are things? We're still busy finishing the house at the moment. The carpet fitters are coming tomorrow. As soon as they put in the carpet, we'll move in our furniture. When Dan fixes the bathtub, we'll tile the bathroom. It looks terrible right now. The plumber is coming on Saturday. When he puts in the washing machine and dishwasher, it will feel like home. As soon as we finish the house, we'll invite you for dinner.

Take care,

Liz

The carpet fitters have started putting in the carpet.

True ☐ **False** ☑

1 Liz and Dan will move in the furniture when the carpet is in.

True ☐ **False** ☐

2 Dan hasn't fixed the bathtub yet.

True ☐ **False** ☐

3 The bathroom will be tiled before the bathtub is fixed.

True ☐ **False** ☐

4 Liz will put in the dishwasher.

True ☐ **False** ☐

5 They'll invite James for dinner when they finish the house.

True ☐ **False** ☐

52.4 REWRITE THE SENTENCES, REVERSING THE ORDER OF THE CLAUSES

As soon as he buys the car, he'll go for a drive.
He'll go for a drive as soon as he buys the car.

1 When she sees this house, she'll want to live here.

_____

2 As soon as your cousins arrive, I'll call you.

_____

3 You'll laugh a lot when you see this movie.

_____

4 When the music starts, we'll get up and dance.

_____

5 I'll make a pizza as soon as Tom buys the cheese.

_____

6 As soon as you're ready, I'll order a taxi.

_____

7 I'll turn off the TV when the news finishes.

_____

8 We'll go home as soon as the train arrives.

_____

9 When it gets really cold, he'll light the fire.

_____

52.5 USE THE CHART TO CREATE EIGHT CORRECT SENTENCES AND SAY THEM OUT LOUD

When she arrives, we'll have dinner.

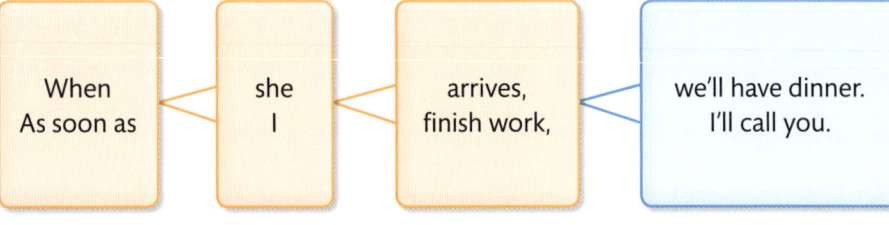

| When / As soon as | she / I | arrives, / finish work, | we'll have dinner. / I'll call you. |

52.6 REWRITE THE SENTENCES USING THE PRESENT PERFECT TENSE

As soon as the meeting starts, we'll look at the figures.
As soon as the meeting has started, we'll look at the figures.

1 When they call our flight number, we'll board the plane.

_____

2 As soon as they finish tiling the kitchen, I'll put up some shelves.

_____

3 When the baby goes to sleep, we'll cook a nice meal.

_____

4 As soon as we book our vacation, I'll buy some new clothes.

_____

52.7 LISTEN TO THE AUDIO, THEN NUMBER THE PICTURES IN THE ORDER THE EVENTS WILL TAKE PLACE

A ☐  B ☐  C ☐  D 1  E ☐

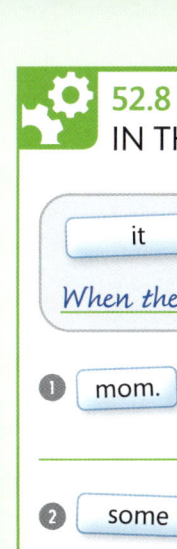

52.8 REWRITE THE SENTENCES, PUTTING THE WORDS IN THE CORRECT ORDER

it | we'll | arrives, | When | mail | read | together. | the

When the mail arrives, we'll read it together.

1. mom. | I'll | soon | as | we | As | get | home, | your | call

2. some | shopping. | When | work, | she'll | do | she's | finished

3. I've | that | dishes, | movie. | When | done | the | we'll | watch

4. soon | the | go | as | beach, | she'll | sees | swimming. | As | she

5. as | you've | As | sent | go | email, | home. | that | soon | we'll

52.9 MATCH THE BEGINNINGS OF THE SENTENCES TO THE CORRECT ENDINGS

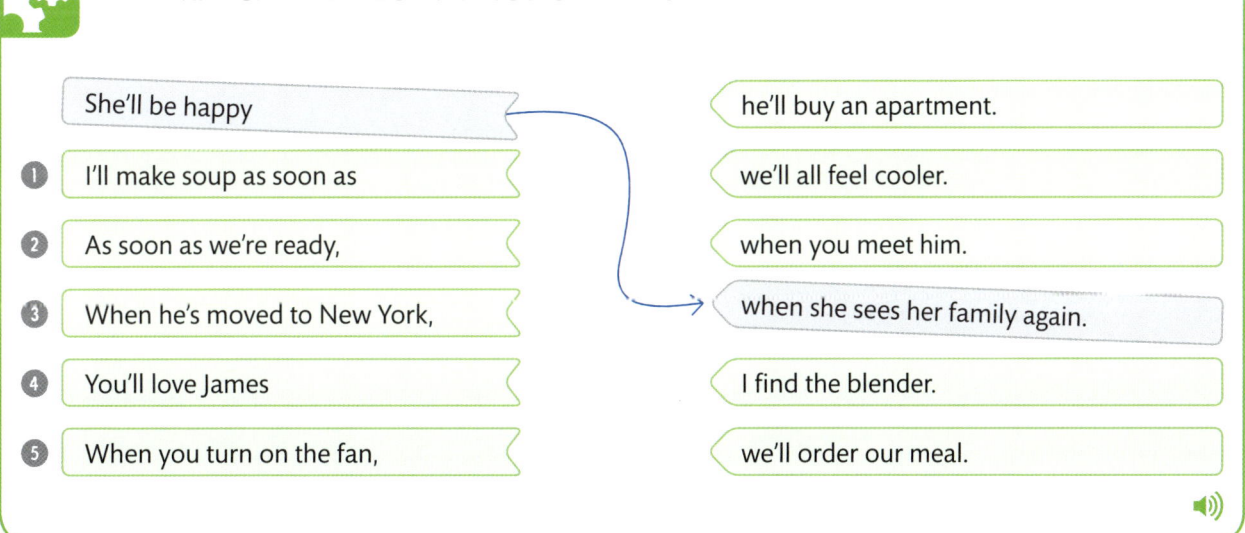

She'll be happy → when she sees her family again.

1. I'll make soup as soon as
2. As soon as we're ready,
3. When he's moved to New York,
4. You'll love James
5. When you turn on the fan,

- he'll buy an apartment.
- we'll all feel cooler.
- when you meet him.
- when she sees her family again.
- I find the blender.
- we'll order our meal.

53 Unlikely situations

English uses the second conditional to describe the result of an unlikely or impossible event. Because the event is unlikely, the result is also unlikely.

⚙ **New language** Second conditional
Aa Vocabulary Collocations with "make" and "do"
🧩 **New skill** Talking about future dreams

⚙ **53.1 FILL IN THE GAPS TO FORM SECOND CONDITIONAL SENTENCES USING THE VERBS IN BRACKETS**

If he _____got_____ (get) more exercise, he _____would feel_____ (feel) fitter.

① If he _____ (be) richer, he _____ (buy) an expensive car.

② She _____ (leave) her job if she _____ (win) the lottery.

③ If he _____ (do) more training, he _____ (get) a better job.

④ If we _____ (sell) our apartment, we _____ (buy) a house in Athens.

⑤ They _____ (help) you if you _____ (ask) them.

⑥ We _____ (increase) our sales figures if we _____ (advertise).

⑦ If her job _____ (be) easier, she _____ (be) happier.

⑧ If I _____ (go) traveling, I _____ (go) to Thailand.

⑨ If we _____ (have) the money, we _____ (start) a business.

⑩ He _____ (be) very bored if he _____ (sit) at a desk all day.

⑪ If they _____ (offer) him a raise, he _____ (take) it.

🔊

53.2 REWRITE THE SENTENCES, PUTTING THE WORDS IN THE CORRECT ORDER

won | big | If | the | house. | I | buy | a | I'd | lottery,

If I won the lottery, I'd buy a big house.

① find | time, | had | job. | another | If | he | he'd

_____

② knew | if | She'd | number. | she | call | him | his

_____

③ Japan. | I'd | could | If | I | go | anywhere, | go | to

_____

④ address, | them. | knew | we | If | visit | their | we'd

_____

53.3 LISTEN TO THE AUDIO AND ANSWER THE QUESTIONS

Andy is talking to his friend Ellen about opening a pet store.

Andy wants to start his own business.
True ✔ **False** ☐ **Not given** ☐

① Andy would need to borrow $5,000.
True ☐ **False** ☐ **Not given** ☐

② He wants to sell things online.
True ☐ **False** ☐ **Not given** ☐

③ He wouldn't sell rabbits or goldfish.
True ☐ **False** ☐ **Not given** ☐

④ Andy thinks a pet store is a great idea.
True ☐ **False** ☐ **Not given** ☐

⑤ Andy sits in an office all day.
True ☐ **False** ☐ **Not given** ☐

⑥ Ellen thinks Andy should do some training.
True ☐ **False** ☐ **Not given** ☐

⑦ If Andy had more money, he'd visit Hawaii.
True ☐ **False** ☐ **Not given** ☐

53.4 MARK THE SENTENCES THAT ARE CORRECT

She'd feel better if she took a vacation. ✔
She'll feel better if she took a vacation. ☐

1. If I win this prize, I'd be very happy. ☐
   If I won this prize, I'd be very happy. ☐

2. If you got promoted, you'd get a raise. ☐
   If you get promote, you get a raise. ☐

3. He'd miss his job if he'd changed companies. ☐
   He'd miss his job if he changed companies. ☐

4. They'd call us if they had time. ☐
   They'll call us if they'll have time. ☐

5. If she studies harder, she'd pass her exams. ☐
   If she studied harder, she'd pass her exams. ☐

6. If I'll speak Chinese, I'd get that job. ☐
   If I spoke Chinese, I'd get that job. ☐

7. You'd leave your job if you won the lottery. ☐
   You'll leave your job if you'll won the lottery. ☐

53.5 SAY THE SENTENCES OUT LOUD, FILLING IN THE GAPS WITH THE CORRECT FORM OF "MAKE" OR "DO"

I didn't _____make_____ the right decision.

1. Did you _____ the paperwork this morning?

2. They're _____ too many mistakes.

3. Please don't _____ any more suggestions.

4. I think we should _____ business together.

5. Have you _____ the accounts yet?

6. She's just _____ a call to the manager now.

7. We've _____ an exception in your case.

8. He was able to _____ an appointment for 3pm today.

54 Vocabulary

thrilled

1 _____

2 _____

3 _____

4 _____

5 _____

6 _____

7 _____

8 _____

9 _____

10 _____

11 _____

12 _____

13 _____

14 _____

15 _____

16 _____

17 _____

18 _____

19 _____

disappointed	terrified	stressed	~~thrilled~~	lucky	surprised
bored	furious	jealous	pleased	confused	embarrassed	lonely
relaxed	tired	intrigued	distracted	calm	nervous	irritated

55 Giving advice

The phrase "If I were you" is often used to give advice in English. By saying it, you imagine that you are in the same position as the person you are talking to.

🕸 **New language** "If I were you"
Aa Vocabulary Phrases for giving advice
🧩 **New skill** Making suggestions

55.1 MARK THE SENTENCES THAT ARE CORRECT

If I am you, I'd accept that job. ☐
If I were you, I'd accept that job. ☑

1. If I were you, I'd go trekking. ☐
   If I were you, I'll go trekking. ☐

2. If I were you, I take that job. ☐
   If I were you, I would take that job. ☐

3. I wouldn't go to that café if I were you. ☐
   I don't go to that café if I were you. ☐

4. I would to go on vacation if I were you. ☐
   I would go on vacation if I were you. ☐

5. I'd invest my money if I'd were you. ☐
   I'd invest my money if I were you. ☐

🔊

55.2 REWRITE THE SENTENCES, PUTTING THE WORDS IN THE CORRECT ORDER

early. | the | get | were | If | I | you, | I'd | to | theater

If I were you, I'd get to the theater early.

1. were | you, | for | job. | better | If | I | I'd | look | a

2. buy | wouldn't | if | I | you. | were | suit | that | I

3. business | city. | own | start | you, | I'd | the | If | in | were | I | my

4. you. | go | were | around | if | I | I'd | the | traveling | world

🔊

158

55.3 FILL IN THE GAPS USING THE WORDS IN THE PANEL TO GIVE ADVICE, SPEAKING OUT LOUD

I never have time to clean my house.

If I were you, I'd _get a cleaner_.

1 I need some new clothes.

If I were you, I'd _____.

2 It's raining outside.

If I were you, I'd _____.

3 I don't like my boss.

If I were you, I'd _____.

4 I want to get my hair cut.

If I were you, I'd _____.

5 It's my father's birthday on Saturday.

If I were you, I'd _____.

6 I feel sick.

If I were you, I'd _____.

7 My laptop is old and slow.

If I were you, I'd _____.

take an umbrella   go shopping   cut my hair myself   look for another job

buy him a present   ~~get a cleaner~~   buy a new one   go to the doctor

55.4 LISTEN TO THE AUDIO AND MARK WHETHER THE SPEAKER IN EACH PICTURE IS GIVING OR ASKING FOR ADVICE

Giving ☑   Asking ☐

1 Giving ☐   Asking ☐

2 Giving ☐   Asking ☐

3 Giving ☐   Asking ☐

4 Giving ☐   Asking ☐

5 Giving ☐   Asking ☐

55.5 REWRITE EACH SENTENCE AS A SUGGESTION, USING QUESTION PHRASES WITH GERUNDS

Have a chat over dinner with close friends.
How about *having a chat over dinner with close friends?*

1 Buy a new laptop and printer for our son's birthday.

What about _____

2 Learn how to cook healthy Indian food.

Have you tried _____

3 Take a vacation on the Italian Riviera this summer.

What about _____

4 Discuss the sales figures with the team after the meeting.

How about _____

5 Get a new desk and chair for the office.

Have you thought of _____

6 Apply for a new job in sales and marketing.

Have you tried _____

7 Try the new Italian restaurant for dinner tonight.

What about _____

55.6 FILL IN THE GAPS USING THE WORDS IN THE PANEL

Have you thought of ___ *learning* ___ Arabic?

1 What about _____ home early?

2 How about _____ a new car?

3 What about _____ us later?

4 Have you tried _____ about it?

5 How about _____ a meeting?

6 Have you thought of _____ your money?

7 Have you tried _____ less coffee?

investing   talking   ~~learning~~   buying   going   drinking   visiting   organizing

55.7 MATCH THE PAIRS OF SENTENCES

The traffic is terrible.

1. My car is 10 years old.
2. I want to leave my job.
3. It's cold and wet outside.
4. My home looks old-fashioned.
5. It's my boss's birthday.
6. I'm meeting an important client.
7. I never have enough money.
8. My boyfriend and I had an argument.
9. This fish tastes bad.

How about buying her a card?

If I were you, I'd take an umbrella.

Have you tried calling him?

If I were you, I wouldn't drive to work.

If I were you, I'd dress up.

If I were you, I wouldn't eat it.

Have you thought of buying a new one?

If I were you, I'd redecorate it.

If I were you, I'd look for a new one.

If I were you, I wouldn't overspend.

55.8 REWRITE THE HIGHLIGHTED PHRASES, CORRECTING THE ERRORS

I'd apply

1. _____
2. _____
3. _____
4. _____
5. _____
6. _____
7. _____

To: Jake

Subject: New job

Hi Jake,

What a great opportunity! If I were you, I'll apply for the job immediately. You'll need to update your résumé. I won't worry if I were you. You have great qualifications. If you were me, I'd get a professional to look at it. And you must prepare for your interview. Have you thought practicing with a friend? If I were you, I think of some questions to ask about the company. And you'll need a new suit. If I was you, I'll buy something classic. You'll need references! How about ask Gillian to write you one?
Emily

56 Real and unreal situations

English uses conditional sentences to talk about possibilities. Use the first conditional or the second conditional depending on how likely the situation is.

⚙ **New language** First and second conditional
Aa Vocabulary Collocations for business meetings
🧩 **New skill** Talking about possibilities

⚙ **56.1 MATCH THE BEGINNINGS OF THE SENTENCES TO THE CORRECT ENDINGS**

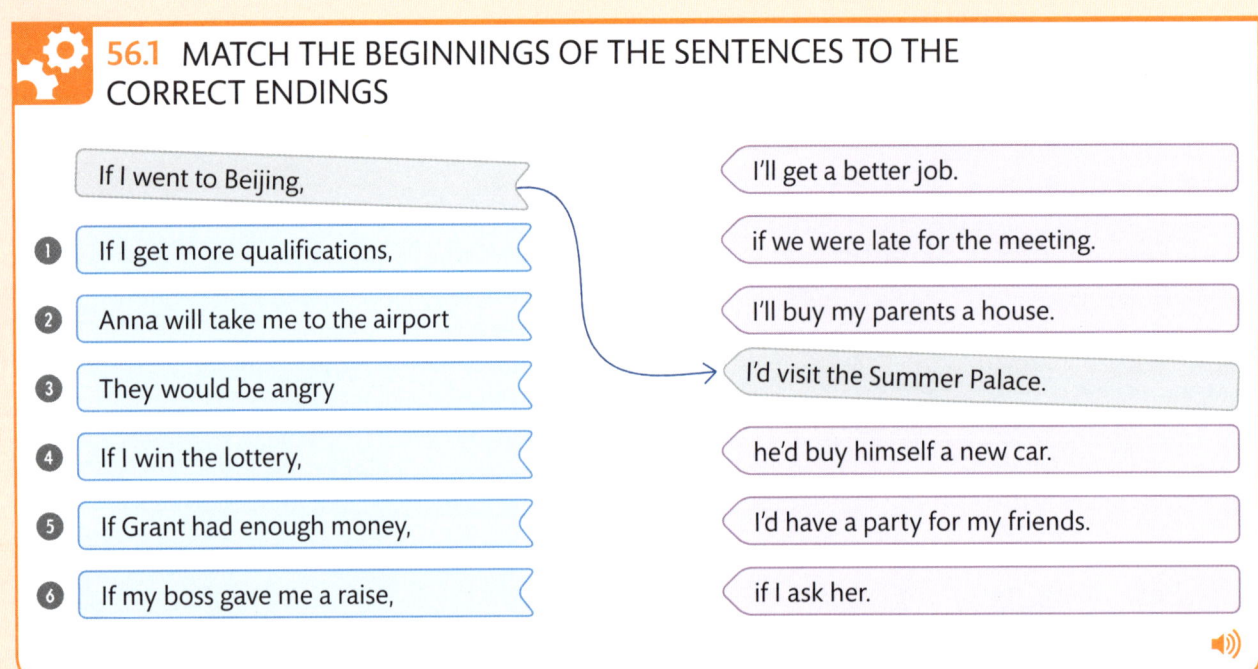

If I went to Beijing,

1 If I get more qualifications,

2 Anna will take me to the airport

3 They would be angry

4 If I win the lottery,

5 If Grant had enough money,

6 If my boss gave me a raise,

I'll get a better job.

if we were late for the meeting.

I'll buy my parents a house.

I'd visit the Summer Palace.

he'd buy himself a new car.

I'd have a party for my friends.

if I ask her.

🔊

⚙ **56.2 FILL IN THE GAPS USING THE PHRASES IN THE PANEL**

If _____ *I saw* _____ a robbery, I'd call the police immediately.

1 I _____ it if I became a famous celebrity.

2 If _____ the next train, we'll get there in time.

3 You would remember her if _____ her again.

4 Henry _____ so happy if he got that promotion.

5 If we arrive there first, _____ you a seat.

we catch   we'll save   wouldn't like   ~~I saw~~   you met   would be

🔊

162

If I miss this train, I'd get the next one. ☐
If I miss this train, I'll get the next one. ✔

1 It would be amazing if I could play the guitar. ☐
It will be amazing if I could play the guitar. ☐

2 If I have my phone with me, I'd take a photo of that. ☐
If I had my phone with me, I'd take a photo of that. ☐

3 If you wear a coat today, you won't feel cold. ☐
If you wore a coat today, you won't feel cold. ☐

4 If you vacuum the living room, I'll do the dishes. ☐
If you vacuum the living room, I'd do the dishes. ☐

5 I'd build more hospitals if I were the President. ☐
I'd build more hospitals if I am the President. ☐

6 If we will have more time, we could have lunch together. ☐
If we had more time, we could have lunch together. ☐

7 If the baby stops crying, I'll watch some TV. ☐
If the baby would stop crying, I'll watch some TV. ☐

8 If you will say anything, she won't listen. ☐
If you say anything, she won't listen. ☐

9 I'll text you if you give me your number. ☐
I'd text you if you give me your number. ☐

10 If that company will win an award, I will be surprised. ☐
If that company won an award, I'd be surprised. ☐

11 Chris will make dinner if you buy the food. ☐
Chris will make dinner if you would buy the food. ☐

12 If you asked the sales assistant, she'll help you. ☐
If you ask the sales assistant, she'll help you. ☐

13 If she will see a snake, she wouldn't be afraid. ☐
If she saw a snake, she wouldn't be afraid. ☐

56.4 LISTEN TO THE AUDIO AND ANSWER THE QUESTIONS

Carol and Alex are discussing how to reduce waste in their office by recycling.

> Alex thinks people need to recycle more.
> **True** ✓   **False** ☐   **Not given** ☐

❶ Alex wants to recycle paper and coffee cups.
True ☐   **False** ☐   **Not given** ☐

❷ Carol doesn't want to recycle plastic.
True ☐   **False** ☐   **Not given** ☐

❸ Plastic is more difficult to recycle than paper.
True ☐   **False** ☐   **Not given** ☐

❹ Alex would take bottles to the recycling center.
True ☐   **False** ☐   **Not given** ☐

❺ Carol wants to ask her boss to help.
True ☐   **False** ☐   **Not given** ☐

56.5 READ THE EMAIL AND WRITE ANSWERS TO THE QUESTIONS AS FULL SENTENCES

> What sales target has Helena set?
> _She has set a target of a 15 percent rise in profits._

❶ What do they need to give priority to?

_____

❷ What is Jackson going to do?

_____

❸ How often will the sales team hold meetings?

_____

❹ What will they do at these meetings?

_____

❺ Who will George hold talks with?

_____

❻ What does he want his team to do?

_____

✉

To: Sales Team

Subject: Synopsis of sales meeting

Hi all,
At this month's meeting, Helena, the Sales Director, set us a target of a 15 percent increase in profits by the end of the year. So now we need to give priority to online sales. Jackson is going to give some thought to this. I've asked him to submit a report at the next meeting. From next month, the sales team will hold weekly meetings to review figures and set new goals if necessary. I'll hold talks with my senior staff members on a regular basis so that they can update me. I know that my team can set a precedent for the rest of the company. It's going to be a great year. Great job, everyone!
George
Sales Manager

Lawrence ~~gave~~ / held / ~~set~~ discussions with his senior staff.

1 She **sets** / gives / holds a limit on the time we can take off.

2 Can you **hold** / give / set off on sending that report until I've checked it?

3 Melanie has just set / held / **given** some great advice to her staff.

4 Do we need to give / **hold** / set a meeting after lunch today?

5 Would you set / hold / **give** me some help with this report?

6 They decided to give / **set** / hold an easier target this month.

7 I haven't set / **given** / held much thought to that proposal yet.

8 The company has gave / held / **set** limits on staff expenses.

9 Do you know when they're going to set / **hold** / give talks?

10 Our company has **set** / given / held a precedent for excellence.

11 Rohit always gives / **sets** / holds weekly goals to motivate his team.

12 My boss is happy to set / **give** / hold help to anyone who asks him.

13 The company gave / set / **held** discussions to decide plans for the year.

14 Not enough companies **give** / hold / set priority to training.

💬 56.7 USE THE CHART TO CREATE EIGHT CORRECT SENTENCES
AND SAY THEM OUT LOUD

We held talks last week.

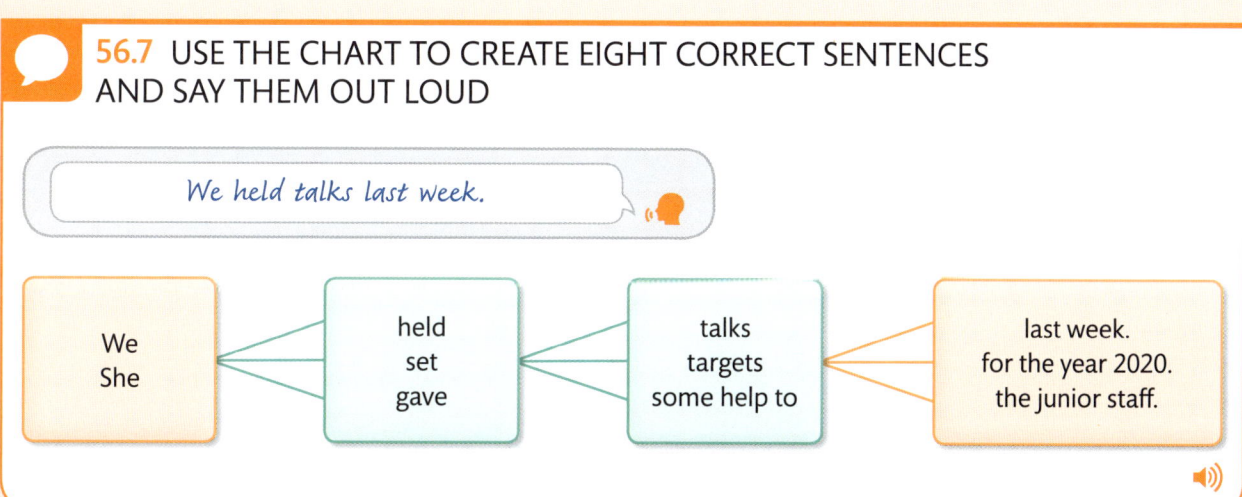

| We / She | held / set / gave | talks / targets / some help to | last week. / for the year 2020. / the junior staff. |

Being specific

A relative clause is a part of a sentence that provides more information about the subject. A defining relative clause identifies the subject we are talking about.

⚙ **New language** Defining relative clauses
Aa **Vocabulary** Personal characteristics
🧩 **New skill** Describing people and jobs

57.1 REWRITE THE SENTENCES USING DEFINING RELATIVE CLAUSES

Is that your cousin? Does he live in Los Angeles?
Is that your cousin who lives in Los Angeles?

❶ That's the woman. She got a good promotion.

_____

❷ Is that the store? Does it sell computer software?

_____

❸ Jamie has met a woman. She is cheerful and kind.

_____

❹ He's the teacher. He teaches Spanish.

_____

❺ A butcher is someone. He sells meat.

_____

❻ You should go on a diet. It should be healthy.

_____

❼ That's the apple tree. We planted it last year.

_____

❽ I'd like a job. It should be exciting and well paid.

_____

❾ We want to buy a house. The house must be near the coast.

_____

🔊

57.2 FILL IN THE GAPS USING THE PHRASES IN THE PANEL

Matthew has a great job _____*that he loves*_____ .

that I recommended
that is healthy
who has been
who can speak
~~that he loves~~
who works
that shows
who knows
that was too
who lived in Tokyo

1 I like the woman _____ at reception.

2 We bought some furniture _____ expensive.

3 They went to a restaurant _____ .

4 Jenny is going out with a man _____ you.

5 Mr. Jason has a son _____ a lawyer since 2009.

6 Lance is my friend _____ for six months.

7 It's important to have a diet _____ .

8 I'd like to meet someone _____ Italian.

9 Is that the sports channel _____ baseball?

57.3 LISTEN TO THE AUDIO, THEN NUMBER THE SENTENCES IN THE ORDER YOU HEAR THEM

A He works in a city that is cosmopolitan and busy. ☐

B She'd like to meet someone who is funny and self-confident. ☐

C I'm looking for an interesting job that I'll enjoy. 1

D The candidate must be a person who is reliable. ☐

E We met a person who works with you. ☐

F I knew someone who had a similar job to yours. ☐

G There are a lot of interesting places that you can visit. ☐

H It's important to have co-workers who you get along with. ☐

I That's the position that I'd really like to have. ☐

J Our firm needs someone who can make decisions. ☐

JOBS

VACANCIES

Preschool Teacher: Full-time Parklands Preschool

We are looking for a teacher who is caring, good-humored, and reliable to work in our busy preschool. The successful candidate will be conscientious and self-confident, and must have two years of experience. We are a happy team at Parklands Preschool and we're looking for someone who is fun-loving as well as reliable and calm.

cheerful and positive	=	*good-humored*
① someone who wants to do their job well	=	_____
② someone you can trust	=	_____
③ not excited or nervous	=	_____
④ someone who likes having fun	=	_____
⑤ someone who believes in him/herself	=	_____

Aa **57.5** READ THE CLUES AND WRITE THE ANSWERS IN THE CORRECT PLACES ON THE GRID

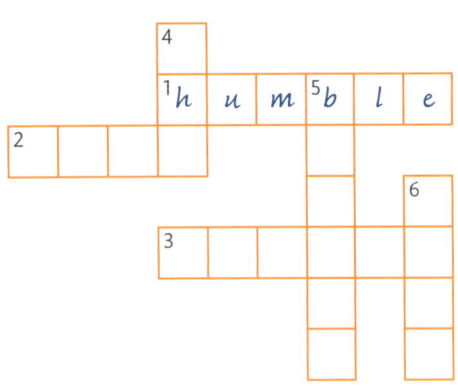

ACROSS

① not arrogant

② the opposite of hard-working

③ well-mannered

DOWN

④ not self-confident

⑤ the opposite of interesting

⑥ the opposite of generous

shy

mean

~~humble~~

boring

lazy

polite

57.6 REWRITE THE SENTENCES USING DEFINING RELATIVE CLAUSES, THEN SAY THEM OUT LOUD

Sarah is a teacher. She wants a promotion.

Sarah is a teacher who wants a promotion.

1. I know an interesting man. He plays the saxophone.

2. Eva bought a new dress. It cost a fortune!

3. We have a Chinese manager. She comes from Shanghai.

4. I have a new boss. He's good-humored and cheerful.

5. Melanie didn't like the shoes. They were on sale.

6. Joe is a student. He's studying for his accountancy exams.

7. She often goes to a café. It's near the river.

8. He's a famous author. He has sold millions of books.

9. He wants a new job. The job should be well paid and interesting.

10. I'm working on a project. It's really exciting.

58 Adding information

Like defining relative clauses, non-defining relative clauses add extra information about something. However, the information is not essential, but gives extra detail.

 New language Non-defining relative clauses
Aa Vocabulary Personal characteristics
New skill Describing people, places, and things

58.1 FILL IN THE GAPS USING THE WORDS IN THE PANEL

Our library, _which is next to the museum_, is closing down.

1. My colleagues, _____, are very funny.

2. My sister's dog, _____, doesn't have a tail.

3. His cousin Bastian, _____, is a great performer.

4. Her Italian teacher, _____, is really outgoing.

5. My friend Ed, _____, has a new job in a restaurant.

6. Their summer house, _____, is really expensive.

7. The weather today, _____, should improve later.

8. The office chair, _____, is really uncomfortable.

who sings	~~which is next to the museum~~	which is terrible
which is small and black	who comes from Naples	who's a chef
who are good friends	which is new	which is on the coast

170

58.2 MARK THE SENTENCES THAT ARE CORRECT

> Your brother Bob who is very funny, which loves playing jokes on people. ☐
> Your brother Bob, who is very funny, loves playing jokes on people. ☑

❶ My house keys, which I lost somewhere, have been found by the police. ☐
My house keys I lost somewhere, that have been found by the police. ☐

❷ Alexia's grandmother who is 84 this year plays tennis twice a week. ☐
Alexia's grandmother, who is 84 this year, plays tennis twice a week. ☐

❸ The new art gallery, who will open next year is such a beautiful building. ☐
The new art gallery, which will open next year, is such a beautiful building. ☐

❹ A friend of Dad's, which told me about this job is the CEO. ☐
A friend of Dad's, who told me about this job, is the CEO. ☐

❺ Our neighbor Giles, who you met once, is coming for dinner on Friday. ☐
Our neighbor Giles, who you met once, that is coming for dinner on Friday. ☐

58.3 REWRITE THE SENTENCES, CORRECTING THE ERRORS

> This novel, what I bought at the station is totally fascinating.
> *This novel, which I bought at the station, is totally fascinating.*

❶ The evening classes, what I'm starting next week, are now completely full.

_____

❷ Sunita, which works in marketing, is very good at her job.

_____

❸ My car what is 10 years old, is always breaking down.

_____

❹ The mail, who is usually here by 8:30am, was late this morning.

_____

❺ The blizzards in Canada, started three days ago, are now over.

_____

58.4 CROSS OUT THE INCORRECT WORD IN EACH SENTENCE

My new blender, ~~who~~ / which I bought last week, has broken already.

1. My friend Peter, what / who lives in Norway, is coming to stay.

2. The new sales assistant, who / which starts next week, is called Ivan.

3. Is the beautiful house, which / who is across from the park, for sale?

4. Linda's colleague Eva, who / what moved to Brazil, has sent us an email.

5. Alex, what / who always plays the lottery, has won it at last!

6. The gallery, who / which we visited last year, has a wonderful collection of paintings.

7. Calum, who / which went to school with me, is my oldest friend.

8. The Black Friday sales, what / which I can't stand, are starting next week.

9. Georgina, who / which works at the bank, is getting married to Tom.

58.5 LISTEN TO THE AUDIO, THEN NUMBER THE PICTURES IN THE ORDER THEY ARE DESCRIBED

A ☐

B ☐

C 1

D ☐

E ☐

F ☐

58.6 READ THE EMAIL AND ANSWER THE QUESTIONS

Sandy has just moved into a new apartment.
True ✓ False ☐ Not given ☐

To: Jacinta

Subject: We've moved in!

Hi Jacinta,

We've just moved into our new apartment and we're getting to know the neighbors. Mr. Ramirez, who lives across from us, is a teacher at the High School. He's very polite. Shannon and Eddie, who live in the apartment below us, are Australian. They're very outgoing and funny. We're so lucky because our apartment is in a great location. The park, which is across the road, is very pretty and full of trees. And the library, which is just a 10-minute walk away, has lots of great books for the children. This apartment, which isn't expensive, is just perfect!

Come and visit us soon.

Much love,

Sandy

1. Mr. Ramirez is a Spanish teacher.
True ☐ False ☐ Not given ☐

2. The man who lives across from Sandy is very rude.
True ☐ False ☐ Not given ☐

3. Shannon and Eddie are a young couple.
True ☐ False ☐ Not given ☐

4. The Australian neighbors are outgoing and funny.
True ☐ False ☐ Not given ☐

5. The park, which is across the road, is full of trees.
True ☐ False ☐ Not given ☐

6. It takes Sandy 20 minutes to walk to the library.
True ☐ False ☐ Not given ☐

7. The library has lots of great children's books.
True ☐ False ☐ Not given ☐

8. The apartment, which Sandy loves, is expensive.
True ☐ False ☐ Not given ☐

58.7 USE THE CHART TO CREATE FOUR CORRECT SENTENCES AND SAY THEM OUT LOUD

The café, which we really like, isn't expensive.

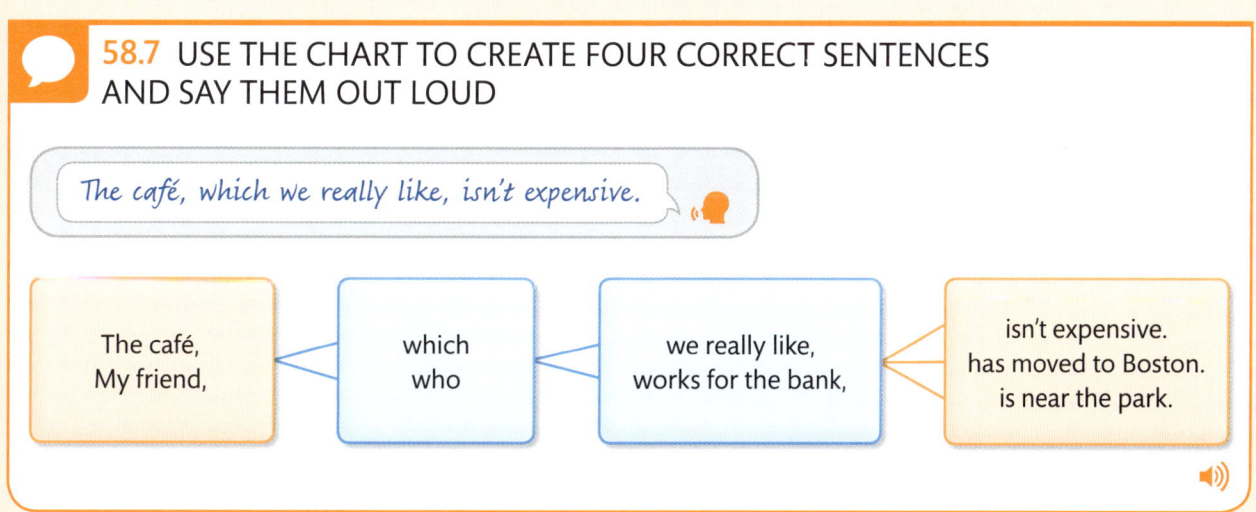

| The café,
My friend, | which
who | we really like,
works for the bank, | isn't expensive.
has moved to Boston.
is near the park. |

59 What was happening when?

To report on past events, such as a crime or accident, you often need to explain what else was happening at the time. Use the past continuous to do this.

New language Past continuous
Aa Vocabulary Verb / noun collocations
New skill Talking about events at given times

59.1 FILL IN THE GAPS USING THE PAST CONTINUOUS TENSE

The children ___were watching___ (watch) the TV program in the living room.

1 Elliot _____ (have) lunch with his friends from college.

2 This time last week we _____ (sing) in the local choir.

3 Olivia _____ (do) her homework when I called at her house.

4 They _____ (play) in the front yard yesterday morning.

Aa 59.2 MARK THE SENTENCES THAT ARE CORRECT

I've just had an interesting discovery. ☐
I've just made an interesting discovery. ☑

1 You shouldn't make advantage of people. ☐
You shouldn't take advantage of people. ☐

2 It has time to learn something new. ☐
It takes time to learn something new. ☐

3 They were having a discussion outside. ☐
They were making a discussion outside. ☐

4 I didn't make a view one way or another. ☐
I didn't take a view one way or another. ☐

5 Scientists make new discoveries every day. ☐
Scientists take new discoveries every day. ☐

6 I've never made the chance to travel. ☐
I've never had the chance to travel. ☐

7 Will you make a discussion about it? ☐
Will you have a discussion about it? ☐

8 She had the chance of a lifetime. ☐
She made the chance of a lifetime. ☐

9 I tried to take sense of the argument. ☐
I tried to make sense of the argument. ☐

59.3 SAY THE SENTENCES OUT LOUD USING THE PAST CONTINUOUS

I _____ *was having* _____ (have) dinner with my family.

1 Your father _____ (drive) to work.

2 We _____ (pick) apples in the back yard.

3 Daniela _____ (talk) to her friends.

4 You _____ (wait) at the train station.

5 The bus _____ (stop) outside the post office.

6 Terry and Ian _____ (work) late on Tuesday.

7 She _____ (walk) across the street.

8 It _____ (rain) yesterday afternoon.

9 They _____ (wash) the dishes in the kitchen.

Aa 59.4 FILL IN THE GAPS USING THE WORDS IN THE PANEL TO CREATE EIGHT MORE COLLOCATIONS

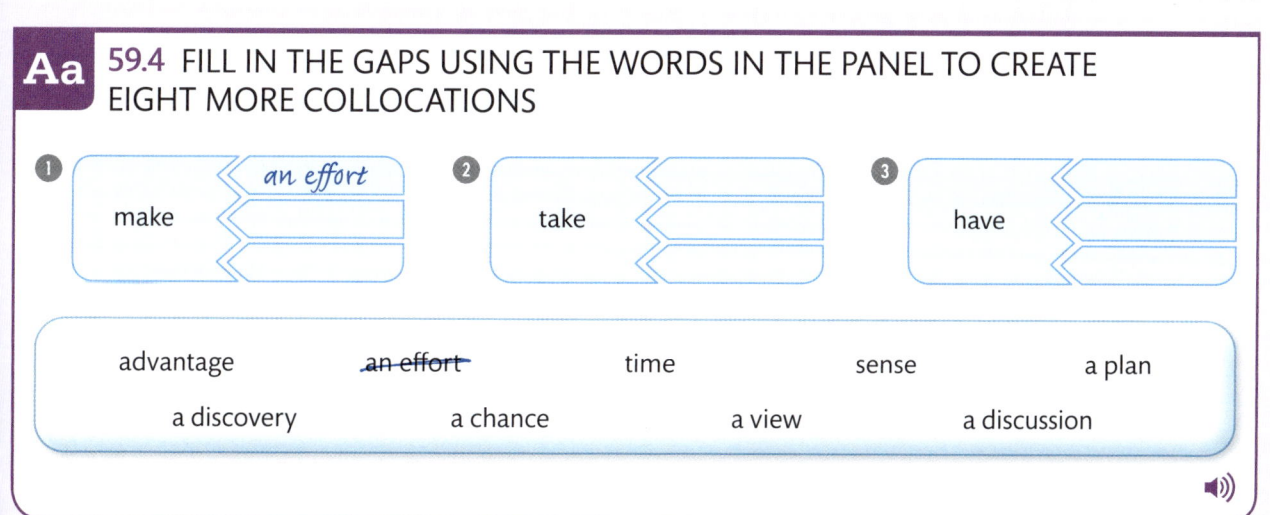

1 make — *an effort*

2 take

3 have

| advantage | an effort | time | sense | a plan |
| a discovery | a chance | a view | a discussion | |

59.5 READ THE REPORT AND ANSWER THE QUESTIONS

Mr. Robins was doing the laundry.
True ☐   False ☑

1 Two people were standing outside his house.
True ☐   False ☐

2 They were looking at a front yard across the street.
True ☐   False ☐

3 The woman was wearing a black skirt.
True ☐   False ☐

4 The man was wearing a leather jacket.
True ☐   False ☐

5 Mr. Robins heard breaking glass at 12:20pm.
True ☐   False ☐

6 The robbers were carrying two heavy bags.
True ☐   False ☐

7 The woman was shouting at the man.
True ☐   False ☐

YOUR CITY

DAYLIGHT ROBBERY

Robbers break into a home in broad daylight

Mr. Robins was washing the dishes in his kitchen when he saw two people outside his house.
It was about noon. The two people were looking at the house across the street. The woman was wearing a black skirt and a leather jacket. The man was wearing jeans and a blue shirt. At about 12:20 he heard the sound of breaking glass. He looked out of the window and he saw the same two people.

They were quickly getting into a car and they were carrying two heavy bags. The woman was talking angrily on her phone. The man was shouting at her to get into the car. As they drove away, Mr. Robins noticed the broken window of the house across the street.

Aa   59.6 FILL IN THE GAPS USING THE COLLOCATIONS IN THE PANEL

He couldn't _make sense_ of the document.

1 You have to _____ if you want to succeed.

2 It _____ to learn the truth.

3 Did the police _____ at the house?

4 They _____ about the problem.

5 She often _____ of people.

6 Did you _____ to see the movie?

7 He _____ that it was a bad decision.

| make an effort | ~~make sense~~ | took time | takes advantage |
| took the view | make a discovery | have a chance | had a discussion |

60 Vocabulary

Aa **60.1** **THE NATURAL WORLD** WRITE THE WORDS FROM THE PANEL
UNDER THE CORRECT PICTURES

Earth

1 _____

2 _____

3 _____

4 _____

5 _____

6 _____

7 _____

8 _____

9 _____

10 _____

11 _____

12 _____

13 _____

14 _____

15 _____

16 _____

17 _____

18 _____

19 _____

rhino	leaf	turtle	grass	Sun	tiger	Moon
bear	spider	whale	planet	owl	lizard	parrot
Earth	elephant	tree	monkey	star	mosquito

61 Setting the scene

To set the scene in a story, English uses the past continuous to describe the background situation, and descriptive adjectives to say what a place is like.

⚙ **New language** Past continuous
Aa **Vocabulary** Adjectives to describe places
🧩 **New skill** Setting the scene for a story

61.1 FILL IN THE GAPS BY PUTTING THE VERBS INTO THE PAST CONTINUOUS

It was a beautiful day and the sun _____*was shining*_____ (shine) brightly.

① The birds _____ (sing) in the trees in the beautiful, open countryside.

② Children _____ (play) soccer in the park.

③ The young man _____ (sit) on the beach under a starry sky.

④ It was a stormy night and the wind _____ (blow) through the trees.

⑤ Bees _____ (buzz) around the garden on this hot summer afternoon.

61.2 LISTEN TO THE AUDIO AND NUMBER THE SCENES IN THE ORDER THEY ARE DESCRIBED

Mr. Coulter's lucky escape!

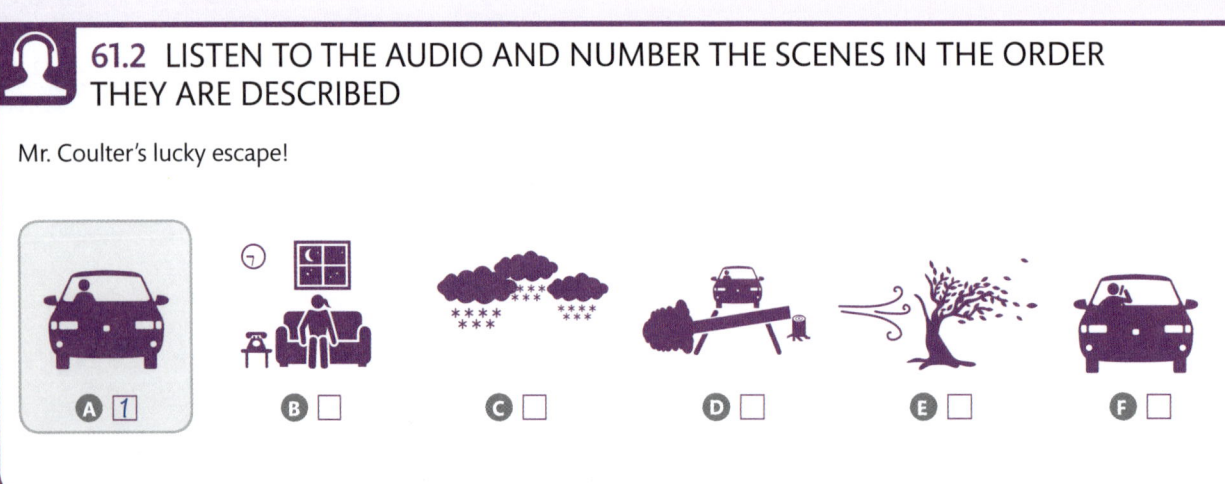

A 1   **B** ☐   **C** ☐   **D** ☐   **E** ☐   **F** ☐

61.3 READ THE STORY AND ANSWER THE QUESTIONS AS FULL SENTENCES

> What were people doing in the town?
> *People were shopping in the stores.*

1 Where were the children running?

_____

2 What was the weather like?

_____

3 What did the air smell of?

_____

4 Where was Alice Goodson sitting?

_____

5 Who was she waiting for?

_____

6 What was walking toward her?

_____

7 What was Tom Hudson doing?

_____

Unexpected Encounter

CHAPTER 1

It was a typical day in the little Canadian town. People were shopping in the stores and children were laughing and running up and down the sidewalk. The sun was shining brightly and the air was heavy with the smell of wild flowers. There wasn't a cloud in the sky. Alice Goodson was sitting on a bench across from the supermarket. She was waiting for her mother to come out of the store.

Suddenly the sound of laughter changed to screams. People started running in all directions. "It's a bear! It's a bear!" cried a little boy. And sure enough, a large black bear was slowly walking across the sidewalk toward Alice. Luckily, at that very moment, police officer Tom Hudson was driving into town…

Aa 61.4 MATCH THE DEFINITIONS TO THE CORRECT ADJECTIVES

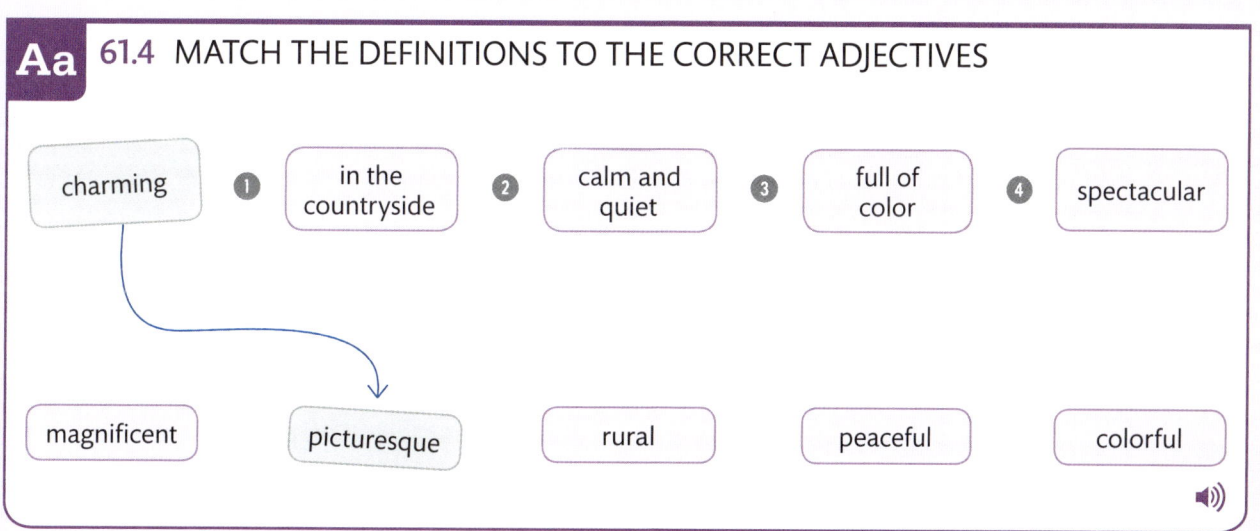

charming **1** in the countryside **2** calm and quiet **3** full of color **4** spectacular

magnificent   picturesque   rural   peaceful   colorful

62 Interrupted actions

English often uses the past continuous and the past simple together to tell stories, especially when one event interrupts another.

⚙ **New language** Past continuous and past simple
Aa **Vocabulary** Travel and leisure
🧩 **New skill** Describing interrupted actions

62.1 FILL IN THE GAPS, PUTTING THE VERBS IN THE CORRECT TENSES

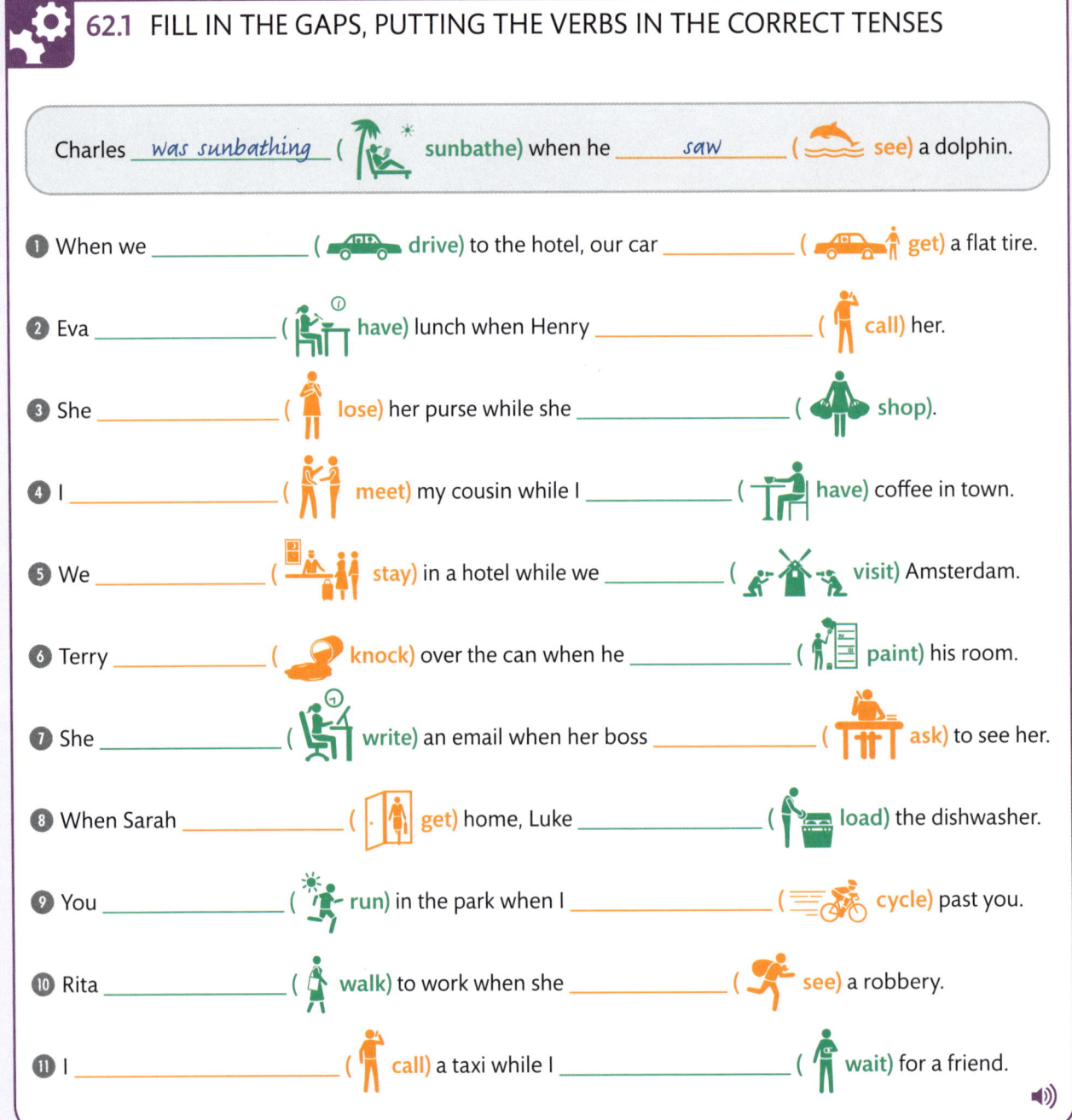

Charles ___was sunbathing___ (🏖 sunbathe) when he ___saw___ (🐬 see) a dolphin.

① When we _____ (🚖 drive) to the hotel, our car _____ (🚗 get) a flat tire.

② Eva _____ (🍽 have) lunch when Henry _____ (📱 call) her.

③ She _____ (lose) her purse while she _____ (🛍 shop).

④ I _____ (🤝 meet) my cousin while I _____ (☕ have) coffee in town.

⑤ We _____ (🏨 stay) in a hotel while we _____ (🌬 visit) Amsterdam.

⑥ Terry _____ (knock) over the can when he _____ (🎨 paint) his room.

⑦ She _____ (💻 write) an email when her boss _____ (ask) to see her.

⑧ When Sarah _____ (🚪 get) home, Luke _____ (load) the dishwasher.

⑨ You _____ (🏃 run) in the park when I _____ (🚴 cycle) past you.

⑩ Rita _____ (🚶 walk) to work when she _____ (🎒 see) a robbery.

⑪ I _____ (📞 call) a taxi while I _____ (wait) for a friend.

🔊

62.2 CROSS OUT THE INCORRECT WORDS IN EACH SENTENCE

> You ~~made~~ / **were making** dinner when the TV program **started** / ~~was starting~~.

1 Oscar **watched** / **was watching** TV when we **arrived** / **were arriving** from the airport.

2 Rose **was drying** / **dried** the dishes when she **was dropping** / **dropped** a plate.

3 I **fell** / **was falling** off my chair when I **fixed** / **was fixing** the light in the kitchen.

4 Lloyd **hurt** / **was hurting** his ankle while he **was skiing** / **skied** down the mountain.

5 They **were listening** / **listened** to the radio as they **drove** / **were driving** home.

6 Shelley **played** / **was playing** the piano when the phone **rang** / **was ringing**.

7 Lucy **was falling** / **fell** and hurt her arm when they **were hiking** / **hiked** near the hills.

8 The cat **chased** / **was chasing** a mouse when it **ran** / **was running** across the road.

9 Alex **met** / **was meeting** Sam when he **walked** / **was walking** down the street.

 62.3 MATCH THE BEGINNINGS OF THE SENTENCES TO THE CORRECT ENDINGS

I was drinking a soda		when I was walking around Paris.
1 Ben saw Rachel in the post office		when she burned her hand.
2 They were reading the menu	→	when I spilled it on the table.
3 We saw a turtle		when the waiter came to their table.
4 I was leaving the party		when it started to rain.
5 Brad was eating a hot dog		when we were swimming in the ocean.
6 They were playing outside		when everyone started to dance.
7 Maria was cooking dinner		when he was mailing a package.
8 I saw the Eiffel Tower		when he spilled ketchup on his shirt.

62.4 LISTEN TO THE AUDIO AND ANSWER THE QUESTIONS

Karl sat down while he was waiting for the bus.
True ☐ **False** ☑

1 Louisa bought some ice cream at the beach.
True ☐ **False** ☐

2 Rex crashed his skateboard into a truck.
True ☐ **False** ☐

3 Luke saw a bird while he was skiing.
True ☐ **False** ☐

4 Misaki ate a cookie while she was reading.
True ☐ **False** ☐

5 Jake was talking to Emma when he fell down.
True ☐ **False** ☐

62.5 SAY THE SENTENCES OUT LOUD, FILLING IN THE GAPS

Anita _____was baking_____ (bake) a cake when her children _____got_____ (get) home.

1 While we _____ (shop), we _____ (meet) Janey at the mall.

2 I _____ (write) an email when you _____ (text) me.

3 Francis _____ (tile) the bathroom while he _____ (stay) with us.

4 Tom _____ (look) for his phone when he _____ (find) his wallet.

5 The train _____ (arrive) while you _____ (buy) a newspaper.

6 Rita _____ (walk) in the park when she _____ (see) a squirrel.

7 We _____ (learn) Spanish while we _____ (live) in Madrid.

8 They _____ (wait) under a tree while it _____ (rain).

9 They _____ (sweep) the floor when he _____ (knock) on the door.

182

62.6 READ THE BLOG AND ANSWER THE QUESTIONS

Anna's Blog

HOME | ENTRIES | ABOUT | CONTACT

POSTED MONDAY, APRIL 3

COLORFUL LUXOR

Luxor is an ancient city, full of color and astonishing sites. While I was staying there, I visited the ancient temple of Karnak. What a fascinating place! Much of the temple is still intact.

On day two, I stayed in a small hotel near the Valley of the Kings. While I was staying there, I visited the tomb of Rameses IX. While I was traveling back to my hotel, I saw a group of children. They were playing soccer next to one of the tombs. It was a bizarre sight to see this mix of ancient and modern.

On my last day, I visited the exotic "souk" in Luxor. This is the Egyptian market. It wasn't as touristy as I expected. And while I was shopping, I stopped at a small café. I drank hibiscus tea and ate dates. It was absolutely delicious! I had a fabulous time, and would love to visit Luxor again.

Luxor is a modern city.
True ☐ False ✔

1 Anna thinks the temple of Karnak is interesting.
True ☐ False ☐

2 The temple of Karnak is completely ruined.
True ☐ False ☐

3 Anna visited the tomb of Rameses IX.
True ☐ False ☐

4 Anna saw some children inside a tomb.
True ☐ False ☐

5 The "souk" is an Egyptian temple.
True ☐ False ☐

6 Anna thought the "souk" was very touristy.
True ☐ False ☐

7 While Anna was shopping, she went to a café.
True ☐ False ☐

8 She ate dates in the hotel.
True ☐ False ☐

9 She drank jasmine tea in the café.
True ☐ False ☐

63 Events in the past

English uses the past simple passive to talk about events in the past when it is the effect of an action that is important, rather than the cause of the action.

 New language Past simple passive

Aa Vocabulary Environmental disasters

New skill Talking about important events

63.1 FILL IN THE GAPS BY PUTTING THE VERBS IN THE PAST SIMPLE PASSIVE

The steel factory _____ was damaged _____ (**damage**) in the fire.

1. Many people _____ (**injure**) in the train accident last night.

2. A man and two children _____ (**rescue**) after the boat capsized in the lake.

3. Too many trees _____ (**cut down**) last year.

4. Thankfully, people's homes _____ (**not flood**) during the storms last week.

5. The country's most beautiful river _____ (**pollute**) by industrial chemicals.

6. The old office building _____ (**not demolish**). It was restored instead.

7. The beaches _____ (**cover**) in oil when the oil tanker sank off the coast.

8. The animals _____ (**not hurt**) when there was a fire at the zoo.

9. The hotel _____ (**destroy**) by a hurricane last summer.

10. Toxic chemicals _____ (**spill**) onto the road when a truck crashed into the barrier.

11. Three men _____ (**question**) by the police after the incident.

63.2 REWRITE THE SENTENCES, CORRECTING THE ERRORS

> This building weren't build in 2002.
> *This building wasn't built in 2002.*

1 Chemicals were release into the air.

2 The factory was destroy yesterday.

3 The lake wasn't pollute with oil.

4 The drinking water were contaminate.

5 Some of the animals were kill.

6 The trees was all cut down.

7 The animals and birds was rescued.

8 Many fish was find dead.

9 All the passengers were rescue.

10 The train line wasn't damage.

11 Some people was injure.

12 The café wasn't destroy in a fire.

13 All the fields were flood.

14 Our train was delay for an hour.

15 Many dolphins were save.

🔊

63.3 LISTEN TO THE AUDIO AND MARK WHETHER THE EVENTS ARE DESCRIBED USING THE ACTIVE OR PASSIVE VOICE

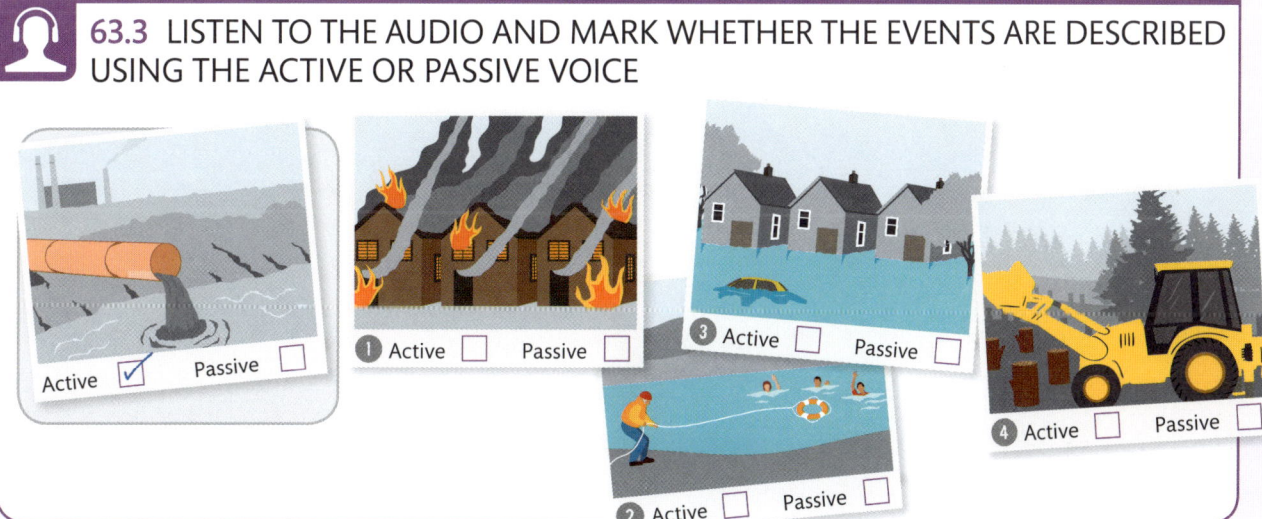

Active ✓   Passive ☐

1 Active ☐   Passive ☐

2 Active ☐   Passive ☐

3 Active ☐   Passive ☐

4 Active ☐   Passive ☐

63.4 SAY THE SENTENCES OUT LOUD USING THE PAST SIMPLE PASSIVE

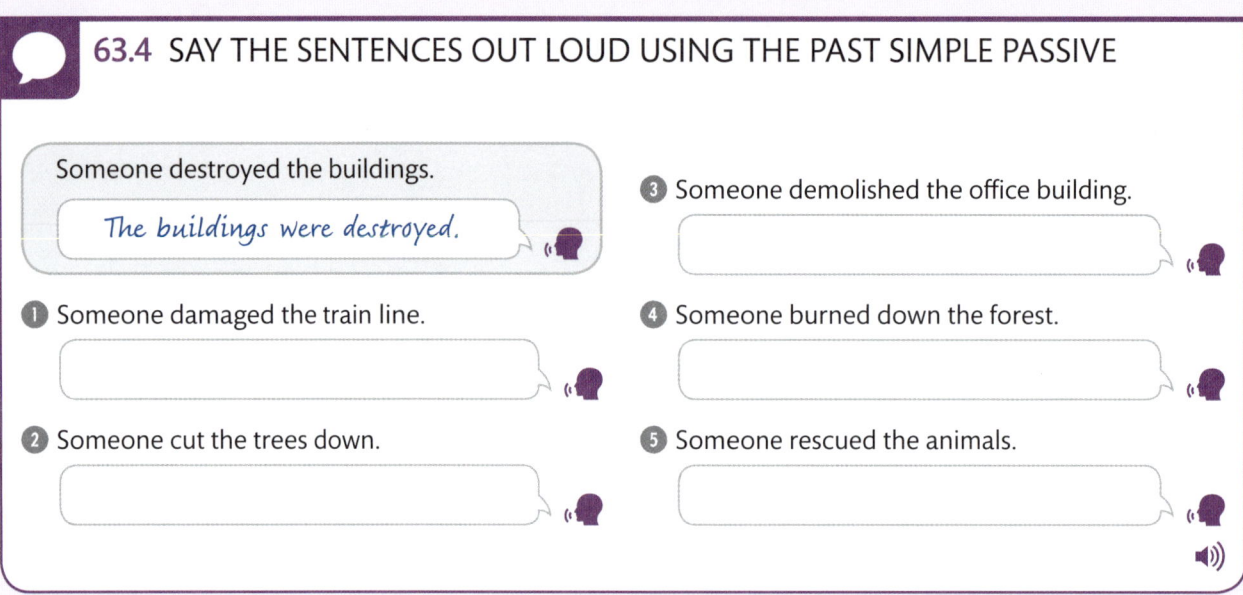

Someone destroyed the buildings.

The buildings were destroyed.

1 Someone damaged the train line.

2 Someone cut the trees down.

3 Someone demolished the office building.

4 Someone burned down the forest.

5 Someone rescued the animals.

63.5 REWRITE THE SENTENCES, PUTTING THE WORDS IN THE CORRECT ORDER

forest | The | fire. | destroyed | in | was | the

The forest was destroyed in the fire.

1 oil | beaches | were | in | covered | yesterday. | The

_____

2 weekend. | on | were | the | delayed | trains | All | the

_____

3 buildings | storm. | weren't | The | the | during | flooded

_____

4 were | fire. | people | Some | the | injured | in

_____

5 storm. | the | damaged | line | The | train | was | during

_____

Aa 63.6 FILL IN THE GAPS USING THE WORDS IN THE PANEL

Scientists say extreme weather is caused by _global climate change._

1. The _____ happened when the oil tanker sank.

2. The explosion was caused by a _____ in the factory.

3. _____ is caused when polluted air mixes with fog.

4. Droughts in some parts of the world may lead to _____ .

5. Soil erosion is sometimes caused by _____ .

6. Twelve people were rescued from the sea after the _____ .

7. The _____ happened when the river burst its banks.

shipwreck

~~global climate change~~

gas leak

famine

flood

smog

oil spill

deforestation

63.7 READ THE ARTICLE AND WRITE ANSWERS TO THE QUESTIONS AS FULL SENTENCES

What happened to the oil tanker?

It was thrown onto its side.

1. How many crew were rescued?

_____

2. Where were they taken?

_____

3. What was spilled into the ocean?

_____

4. What happened to the sea birds?

_____

5. What was found on the beach?

_____

OIL SPILL
Leakage from oil tanker wreaks havoc on marine life

An oil tanker was caught in a violent storm off the Florida coast last weekend. The oil tanker was on its way to Mexico when it was thrown onto its side by huge waves and powerful winds. Eighteen crew were rescued by the emergency services late on Saturday night and they were taken to the hospital to be checked. During the weekend thousands of gallons of oil were spilled into the ocean. On Monday morning, hundreds of birds were rescued from the beach by volunteers. The birds were covered in oil and many of them were dying. Thousands of dead fish were found in the sea and on the beach. This is an environmental disaster on a huge scale.

64 Before and after

English uses the past perfect with the past simple to talk about two or more events that happened at different times in the past.

⚙ **New language** Past perfect and past simple
Aa Vocabulary Visual arts
🧩 **New skill** Describing sequences of past events

⚙ **64.1 FILL IN THE GAPS BY PUTTING THE VERBS IN THE PAST SIMPLE AND PAST PERFECT TENSES**

She _____loved_____ (love) the present I _____had given_____ (give) her for Christmas.

1 The movie _____ (start) by the time we _____ (arrive) at the movie theater.

2 It _____ (be) the most impressive sculpture I _____ (see) for a long time.

3 They _____ (close) the road because there _____ (be) an accident.

4 Mary _____ (do) the shopping before I _____ (can) offer to help.

5 Gregory _____ (travel) around Asia before he _____ (go) to college.

6 She _____ (not see) him for years, but it _____ (be) just like old times.

◀))

⚙ **64.2 REWRITE THE SENTENCES, CORRECTING THE ERRORS**

I went to Paul's house in the morning, but he already went to work.
I went to Paul's house in the morning, but he had already gone to work.

1 The gallery call for my painting before I finish it.

_____

2 She had known she had met Peter and Sarah somewhere before.

_____

3 When I get home, I realized I forget my car key at my friend's house.

_____

4 Some people have already left when we arrived at my friend's birthday party.

_____

◀))

64.3 MATCH THE BEGINNINGS OF THE SENTENCES TO THE CORRECT ENDINGS

I called my sister,

① The thieves broke into the house

② He hadn't seen the hole in the road

③ She put on a warm coat

④ He didn't cook dinner until

⑤ They really enjoyed the meal

⑥ You didn't ask me

⑦ I couldn't remember

so he drove into it.

he had taken the dog for a walk.

where they had been on vacation.

but she had already gone to bed.

how my interview had gone.

because he had forgotten to lock the door.

we had cooked for them.

because it had started to snow.

 64.4 LISTEN TO THE AUDIO, THEN NUMBER THE PICTURES IN THE ORDER THEY ARE DESCRIBED

Ⓐ ☐

Ⓑ ☐

Ⓒ ☐

Ⓓ ☐

Ⓔ 1

Ⓕ ☐

64.5 FILL IN THE GAPS USING THE PHRASES IN THE PANEL

We offered to help, but he __*had already fixed*__ it.

1 I called the office, but everyone _____ .

2 Finn _____ again even though he had already seen it.

3 Helen was sorry that she _____ kinder.

4 Paul _____ bed after he had loaded the dishwasher.

5 He _____ before anyone else had finished theirs.

6 Liz called Jill but she _____ her phone.

7 I couldn't remember where we _____ before.

8 I'm sorry you _____ that we had already gone out.

9 He _____ after he had tried on three pairs.

10 The waiter left after he _____ our orders.

didn't know
had taken
had turned off
bought some jeans
had already left
hadn't been
finished his meal
~~had already fixed~~
watched the movie
had met
went to

64.6 SAY THE SENTENCES OUT LOUD, FILLING IN THE GAPS

When I __*arrived*__ (arrive) at work, the meeting __*had*__ already __*started*__ (start).

1 She _____ (not be) hungry because she _____ already _____ (eat).

2 Grant _____ already _____ (make) dinner when Rosa _____ (get) home.

3 Anna _____ (feel) tired because she _____ (be) shopping all day.

4 He _____ (pass) his driving test because he _____ (have) a lot of lessons.

5 Eric _____ (send) the report to his boss after he _____ (check) it.

64.7 READ THE ARTICLE AND WRITE ANSWERS TO THE QUESTIONS IN FULL SENTENCES

CURE FOR SMALLPOX

How Edward Jenner accidentally discovered the world's first vaccine

In the late 18th century, an English doctor called Edward Jenner wanted to find a cure for smallpox. Smallpox was a serious disease that killed a lot of people every year. Jenner noticed that if you had had cowpox, which was a similar but less serious disease, you didn't catch smallpox. In 1796, he did an experiment to prove his theory. He gave cowpox to a little boy by infecting a small cut on his arm. After the little boy had recovered, Jenner infected him again with smallpox. The little boy never became ill with smallpox and Jenner decided it was because the cowpox had protected him. The little boy's name was James Phipps and he had received the first vaccination in the world.

STATUE OF BRITISH PHYSICIAN EDWARD JENNER

What disease did Jenner want to find a cure for in the late 18th century?

Jenner wanted to find a cure for smallpox.

---

1 What did Jenner notice about people who had had cowpox?

---

2 What method did Jenner use to give the little boy cowpox?

---

3 What happened after Jenner had infected the little boy with cowpox?

---

4 When did Jenner infect the little boy with smallpox?

---

5 What happened after Jenner had infected the little boy with smallpox?

---

6 Why didn't the little boy get smallpox even though he was infected by Jenner?

---

65 First times

When you talk about the first time something happened, such as visiting a new place, you often use "never" or "ever" with the past perfect or present perfect.

⚙ **New language** "Never" / "ever" with past tenses
Aa **Vocabulary** Travel adjectives
🧩 **New skill** Describing new experiences

65.1 CROSS OUT THE INCORRECT WORD IN EACH SENTENCE

 That was a fantastic vacation. We had ~~ever~~ / **never** been to Bali before.

1  It was the first time we had ever / never eaten sushi. We loved it.

2  We stayed in Seville. I had ever / never seen flamenco dancing before.

3  It was the first time he had ever / never ridden a horse. He fell off twice!

4  She had ever / never been scuba diving before. She saw a beautiful turtle.

5  It was the first time she had ever / never visited Paris. She saw the Eiffel Tower.

6  He was so happy. He had ever / never had so many birthday presents.

7  We had ever / never run a marathon before. It was totally exhausting.

8  It was the first time I had ever / never seen the Great Pyramids. They were amazing.

9  He didn't know what to do. He had ever / never had a flat tire before.

10  They weren't happy. They had ever / never had such bad service before.

11  It was awesome! It was the first time I had ever / never flown in a helicopter.

65.2 MARK THE SENTENCES THAT ARE CORRECT

> I don't like sports. I had never played basketball or volleyball. ☐
> I don't like sports. I've never played basketball or volleyball. ☑

1. Eva is very excited. She had ever seen a play at the theater before. ☐
   Eva is very excited. She has never seen a play at the theater before. ☐

2. He loves it. It was the first time he had ever driven a sports car. ☐
   He loved it. It was the first time he had ever driven a sports car. ☐

3. Robin has broken his leg. It is the first time he has ever been to a hospital. ☐
   Robin has broken his leg. It is the first time he had ever been to a hospital. ☐

4. They had never visited Rio de Janeiro before. It was amazing. ☐
   They have ever visited Rio de Janeiro before. It was amazing. ☐

🔊

65.3 LISTEN TO THE AUDIO AND ANSWER THE QUESTIONS

Mike and Rachel are talking about places they have been to in Asia.

Where did Rachel go for the first time last year?
Thailand ☐
India ☑
Vietnam ☐

1. Which city did Rachel visit in Rajasthan?
   Kolkata ☐
   Delhi ☐
   Jaipur ☐

2. The most beautiful thing she had ever seen was...
   the elephant festival ☐
   the city ☐
   the colorful markets ☐

3. Has Mike ever been to India?
   Yes, he has been once. ☐
   Yes, he has been several times. ☐
   No, he hasn't. ☐

4. Which country has Rachel never been to?
   Thailand ☐
   Vietnam ☐
   Cambodia ☐

5. What did Mike see for the first time in Bangkok?
   An ancient palace ☐
   A Buddhist temple ☐
   A castle ☐

Hi Phil,

This is the first time we have _ever been_ to Spain. We've just spent the morning in the Barrio Santa Cruz in Seville. It has been _____ with tourists for years and the streets are lined with _____ old flats. It's a long way from the modern _____ apartment buildings. Then, we walked to the Alcázar, an _____ palace. We _____ seen anything so beautiful.

See you soon! Lily

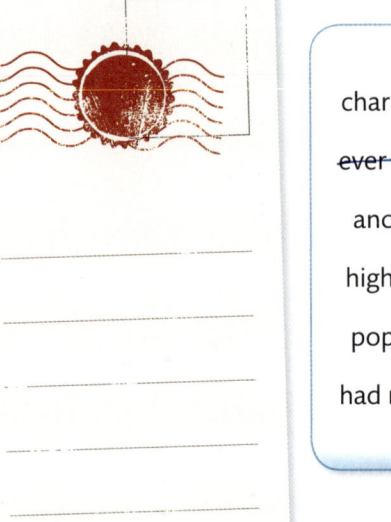

charming

~~ever been~~

ancient

high-rise

popular

had never

65.5 SAY THE SENTENCES OUT LOUD, FILLING IN THE GAPS USING PHRASES WITH "EVER" OR "NEVER"

I hadn't skied before. I skied for the first time last year.

Last year was _the first time I had ever skied._

❶ Before I learned to sail and windsurf, I hadn't tried water sports.

I _____

❷ I've never ridden a camel in the desert before.

It's the _____

❸ They hadn't been on a safari in Africa before.

It was _____

❹ We have never visited the Metropolitan Museum in New York before.

It's the _____

Aa 66.1 COMMON ENGLISH IDIOMS WRITE THE IDIOMS FROM THE PANEL UNDER THE CORRECT DEFINITIONS

Excessive or lacking restraint

over the top

7 Look after or watch carefully

_____

1 Feel unwell

_____

8 Hear information or news via gossip or rumor

_____

2 Tease or fool somebody

_____

9 Help

_____

3 Be a nuisance

_____

10 Be under time pressure to get something done

_____

4 Confront the consequences of your actions

_____

11 Have a sudden loss of confidence

_____

5 Be unwilling to commit or make a decision

_____

12 Let yourself go or relax

_____

6 Be completely and utterly in love with someone ♥

_____

13 To be kind and good-natured

_____

---

be head over heels   be against the clock   be a pain in the neck   ~~over the top~~   get cold feet

have a heart of gold   keep an eye on   sit on the fence   let your hair down   face the music

feel under the weather   lend a hand   hear something on the grapevine   pull someone's leg

67 Telling a story

The past continuous, past simple, and past perfect are often used together to describe past events in detail. This is especially helpful for telling stories.

✲° **New language** Narrative tenses
Aa Vocabulary Idioms for storytelling
New skill Using different past tenses

67.1 FILL IN THE GAPS BY PUTTING THE VERBS IN THE CORRECT TENSES

It ___*was snowing*___ (snow) heavily, so we ___*booked*___ (book) a vacation in the mountains.

1 We _____ (drive) home when a rabbit _____ (run) across the road.

2 She _____ (go) to Japan last year because she _____ (want) to go for years.

3 He _____ (buy) a house in the Caribbean after he _____ (win) the lottery.

4 Marianne _____ (live) in Lisbon when she _____ (meet) her husband.

5 I _____ (sunbathe) by the pool when a huge insect _____ (land) on my arm.

6 We _____ (walk) home one night when we _____ (see) a strange light in the sky.

7 I _____ (be) nervous because I _____ (never be) skiing before.

8 I _____ (offer) them some lunch, but they _____ (already eat).

9 When we _____ (return), someone _____ (steal) all our luggage.

10 They _____ (climb) in the Rockies when they _____ (hear) an avalanche.

11 The party _____ (already begin) by the time we _____ (arrive).

🔊

67.2 MARK THE SENTENCES THAT ARE CORRECT

People were singing and dancing when suddenly they were hearing a noise. ☐
People were singing and dancing when suddenly they heard a noise. ☑

1 The old lady had just arrived home when the doorbell rang loudly. ☐
   The old lady had just arrived home when the doorbell was ringing loudly. ☐

2 Elliot was having enough of her bad behavior and he decided to leave. ☐
   Elliot had had enough of her bad behavior and he decided to leave. ☐

3 Milly was waiting for her interview when her father sent her a text. ☐
   Milly waiting for her interview when her father sent her a text. ☐

4 I had just gone to bed when I realized I have forgotten to lock the door. ☐
   I had just gone to bed when I realized I had forgotten to lock the door. ☐

5 You couldn't read the message because you weren't putting on your glasses. ☐
   You couldn't read the message because you hadn't put on your glasses. ☐

67.3 FILL IN THE GAPS USING THE WORDS IN THE PANEL

It _____was_____ a bright summer's day and a young man _____was playing_____ his guitar.

1 A small crowd of people _____ around him to listen.

2 He stopped playing and the people _____ politely and started to walk away.

3 The man quickly put down his guitar and _____ his violin case.

4 He looked down at his small gray dog that _____ at his feet.

5 As soon as the young man _____ to play, the little dog _____.

6 It began to bark and jump around enthusiastically. The crowd _____ to watch the spectacle.

opened	had gathered	was sleeping	woke up	~~was~~
clapped		started	~~was playing~~	returned

197

67.4 MATCH THE BEGINNINGS OF THE SENTENCES TO THE CORRECT ENDINGS

The weather had been fine all day

because she had lost her teddy bear.

1. The little girl was crying

when he found a wallet on the ground.

2. I had just opened my front door

and the wind was howling in the trees.

3. Luke was walking across the street

but by the afternoon it had turned cold.

4. She had just fallen asleep

when they saw the lightning strike.

5. They were watching the storm

when a noise outside woke her up.

6. Ellie hadn't expected to marry Tim

when she broke one of her teeth.

7. Mary was eating an apple

until he proposed to her on the beach.

8. It was a cold, dark night

when I saw a large package in the hall.

 67.5 CROSS OUT THE INCORRECT WORDS IN EACH SENTENCE

The car had broken down and she was / ~~had been~~ / ~~was being~~ in the middle of nowhere.

1. They were scuba diving in the Indian Ocean when they **had seen** / **saw** / **were seeing** a pod of dolphins.

2. When Sue arrived at the party she realized that she **forgets** / **forgot** / **had forgotten** Jo's present.

3. It was the first time she **was ever** / **had ever been** / **has ever been** on vacation alone.

4. Ronnie **waited** / **had waited** / **was waiting** for his bus when he saw a young man steal a car.

5. They **had just started** / **were starting** / **started** eating their meal when the waiter fainted.

6. As he **watched** / **watches** / **had watched** the car drive away he knew he would never see her again.

7. A small group of people **stood** / **were standing** / **had stood** on the platform when they heard a scream.

8. She **had run** / **was running** / **ran** for the train when she tripped and her bag burst open.

9. Harry was looking through his telescope when he thought he **was seeing** / **saw** / **had seen** a UFO.

67.6 SAY THE SENTENCES OUT LOUD, USING THE IDIOMS IN THE PANEL

I said I'd help you.

I said I'd lend a hand.

1 Mr. Foster delayed making a decision.

2 The sales team is always alert and efficient.

3 Linda had to accept the consequences.

4 Robert's reply was absolutely correct.

5 Your little brother can be really annoying.

face the music

~~lend a hand~~

hit the nail on the head

a pain in the neck

on the ball

sat on the fence

Aa 67.7 MATCH THE PICTURES TO THE CORRECT SENTENCES

Mrs. Salter is keeping an eye on the twins this afternoon.

1

Lizzie has always been the teacher's pet.

2

Maxine heard about Jill's wedding on the grapevine.

3

Oliver is feeling under the weather so he's staying in bed.

4

Anna is very kind. She's got a heart of gold.

5

Jane and Calum are head over heels in love.

6

Dev's reaction to the news was over the top.

68 What happened when?

English uses a number of words and phrases to show the order in which past events occurred. They are often called adverbials of time, and are useful when telling a story.

 New language Time adverbs and phrases
Aa Vocabulary Storytelling devices
New skill Putting events in order

68.1 FILL IN THE GAPS USING THE PHRASES IN THE PANEL

_____ *Just as* _____ we were getting on the train, we saw her getting off.

1 She was always late for work, and _____ lost her job.

2 We got to the station at 8:50pm and left _____ .

3 Call me _____ you get home tonight.

4 _____ we got to the bar, it started to snow.

5 Sue was leaving the store _____ that we got there.

> shortly afterward
>
> at the very moment
>
> ~~just as~~
>
> consequently
>
> not long before
>
> as soon as

68.2 CROSS OUT THE INCORRECT WORDS IN EACH SENTENCE

~~Consequently~~ / **Just as** we were leaving the house, Sharon arrived.

1 **Not long before** / **Shortly afterward** I called him, he sent me an email.

2 He worked hard, and **as soon as** / **consequently** was promoted.

3 **Just as** / **Consequently** he was leaving, a parcel arrived.

4 Jack called **shortly afterward** / **just as** I got home from work.

5 I got on the Number 8 bus and saw the Number 10 bus **shortly afterward** / **just as**.

6 **Just as** / **As soon as** I heard the news, I told Phil.

7 She ate too much, and **not long before** / **consequently** felt sick.

8 **Just as** / **Shortly afterward** I was finishing my lunch, Dan walked in.

68.3 SAY THE SENTENCES OUT LOUD, FILLING IN THE GAPS USING THE WORDS IN THE PANEL

I saw Lou coming out of the store _____ *just as* _____ I was going in.

1. He drove too fast, and _____ was fined by the police.

2. I got to the party at 8pm, and Anne arrived _____ .

3. We decided to go inside _____ it started raining.

4. They had had a baby _____ they moved.

| not long before | ~~just as~~ | consequently | shortly afterward | as soon as |

68.4 REWRITE THE SENTENCES, CORRECTING THE ERRORS

As just as we were driving past the station, we saw her getting on the bus.
Just as we were driving past the station, we saw her getting on the bus.

1. She bought an expensive car shortly afters getting an exciting new job.

2. I called my parents as soon I got the results of my exams.

3. The woman slipped on the ice and subsequent fell into the water.

4. Pippa had dropped her phone in a puddle not before long it stopped working.

68.5 READ THE EMAIL AND WRITE ANSWERS TO THE QUESTIONS AS FULL SENTENCES

✉

To: Lilah S.

Subject: Henry's hiking adventure

Hi Lilah,

Did you hear about Henry's adventure last weekend? He'd arranged to go hiking in the mountains with his friend Joe. Just as he was leaving, his phone rang. It was Joe saying he couldn't come, because someone had crashed into his car not long before. As soon as they heard the news, Henry's friends said he shouldn't go. But Henry decided to go anyway.

Shortly after setting off, Henry realized he had lost his compass. He stopped at a store to buy a new one. Not long after he set off, it started to get cloudy and rain. By the time Henry had walked for two hours, he could hardly see in front of him. A few moments earlier he had been sure of the way, but now his new compass wasn't working and he was lost. Consequently, he called the mountain rescue. By the time they arrived, he was soaked and cold. They told him he'd had a lucky escape.

See you soon.

Becky x

What happened just as Henry was leaving?

His phone rang just as he was leaving.

1 Why couldn't Joe come hiking?

_____

2 What did Henry's friends say as soon as they heard the news?

_____

3 When did Henry realize that he had lost his compass?

_____

4 What happened not long after Henry set off?

_____

5 What happened by the time Henry had walked for two hours?

_____

68.6 MATCH THE PICTURES TO THE CORRECT SENTENCES

He was late getting to the station. Consequently, he missed the train.

3

She got home late and fell asleep shortly afterward.

1

As soon as the babysitter had arrived, they put on their coats.

4

Just as she blew out the candles, everyone started clapping.

2

Not long before she got home, her phone rang.

5

Just as Tom was leaving, I realized he'd left his phone on the table.

68.7 LISTEN TO THE AUDIO AND ANSWER THE QUESTIONS

 Blake is talking about his experience of moving into a new house.

Blake's phone started ringing when he was signing the papers.
True ☑ **False** ☐

1 Blake called the realtor as soon as he heard the news.
True ☐ **False** ☐

2 The buyer wanted to move later because he had gone into the hospital.
True ☐ **False** ☐

3 The movers arrived at Blake's house at the same time as Blake did.
True ☐ **False** ☐

4 Shortly after moving into his new house, Blake received flowers from the lawyer.
True ☐ **False** ☐

What other people said

We call the words that people say direct speech.
If you want to tell someone what another
person has said, it is called reported speech.

⚙ **New language** Reported speech
Aa Vocabulary Work and education
♟ **New skill** Talking about people's lives

⚙ **69.1 REWRITE THE SENTENCES USING REPORTED SPEECH**

I live in New York City with my wife and two children.
He *said that he lived in New York City with his wife and two children.*

1 I'm a police officer, and I wear a uniform to work every day.

He _____

2 I go swimming every Tuesday evening at the sports center.

She _____

3 I work in a travel agency in the southern part of a busy town.

She _____

4 Sarah and her sister like listening to jazz music and playing the piano.

You _____

5 They want to go to Mexico on vacation with their friends.

She _____

6 We usually eat sandwiches for lunch and have a hot meal in the evening.

They _____

7 Tom runs really fast, and he takes part in lots of competitions.

She _____

8 I don't like getting up in the morning, and I'm always tired at work.

He _____

9 He doesn't watch TV in the evenings because he's too busy at work.

She _____

69.2 REWRITE THE SENTENCES, PUTTING THE WORDS IN THE CORRECT ORDER

| said | was | She | that | beautiful. | house | our |

She said that our house was beautiful.

1. | liked | he | color | said | blue. | He | that | the |

2. | camping | They | year. | said | went | that | they | every |

3. | car. | bought | had | She | that | said | she | a |

4. | liked | Vancouver. | I | that | said | I | visiting |

5. | he | that | eat | didn't | said | meat. | He | red |

69.3 MATCH THE PAIRS OF SENTENCES

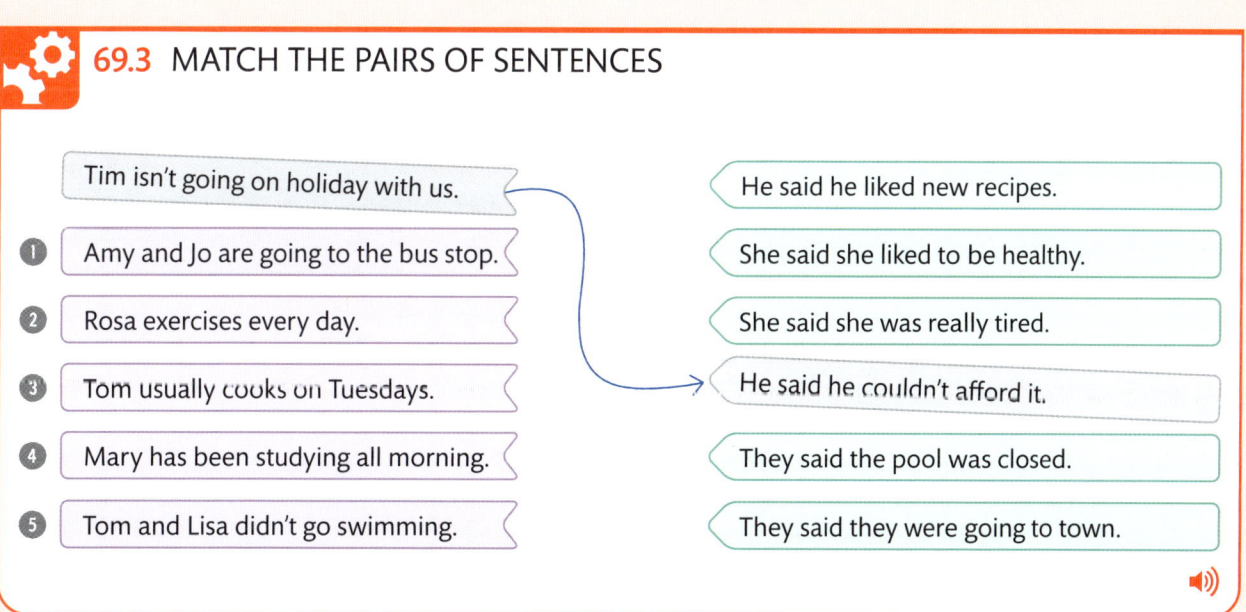

Tim isn't going on holiday with us. —→ He said he couldn't afford it.

He said he liked new recipes.

1. Amy and Jo are going to the bus stop.

She said she liked to be healthy.

2. Rosa exercises every day.

She said she was really tired.

3. Tom usually cooks on Tuesdays.

He said he couldn't afford it.

4. Mary has been studying all morning.

They said the pool was closed.

5. Tom and Lisa didn't go swimming.

They said they were going to town.

69.4 SAY THE SENTENCES OUT LOUD AS REPORTED SPEECH

I go to school in the northern part of Thailand.

He *said that he went to school in the northern part of Thailand.*

1 I work in a bookshop in a small village located near the lake.

She _____

2 We usually eat salad at lunchtimes during the week.

They _____

3 I don't like cycling downtown as it is very crowded.

He _____

4 We will probably visit our aunt in Italy to celebrate her birthday.

They _____

5 We're going to the theater on Tuesday.

She _____

6 Jane is working abroad as a teacher.

He _____

7 He's learning to play the guitar.

She _____

8 They've lived in that house for a year.

She _____

9 She's studying Japanese at the local college.

He _____

69.5 READ THE EMAIL AND WRITE ANSWERS TO THE QUESTIONS AS FULL SENTENCES

✉

To: Ben

Subject: Life in New Zealand

Hi Ben,

I'm having fun in New Zealand. It's a really amazing country. I've spent the past three weeks here in Queenstown. I'm working as a waiter in a busy restaurant. It's hard work, but the pay is good. When it's really busy, I have to help out in the kitchen.

I've made some great friends and I've been able to save some money. Queenstown is a really lively, fun city. People come here to do adventure sports, so the bars and restaurants are always full of young people. I'm going to stay here for a few more weeks, and then I'll head over to Australia to see my cousins.

Hope things are good with you.

Pete

↩ ↩↩

⫟ 🗑

Where did Pete say he was having fun?

Pete said he was having fun in New Zealand.

❶ What did he say about New Zealand?

_____

❷ How long did he say he had spent in Queenstown?

_____

❸ Where did he say he was working?

_____

❹ What did he say about the pay?

_____

❺ What did he say he had to do when it was busy?

_____

❻ What did he say he had been able to do?

_____

❼ Why did he say people came to Queenstown?

_____

❽ How long did he say he was going to stay there?

_____

❾ Who did he say he would see in Australia?

_____

70 Telling things to people

You can use both "say" and "tell" in reported speech.
The meaning is the same, but using "tell" allows you
to specify who someone was talking to.

⚙ **New language** Reported speech with "tell"
Aa Vocabulary Collocations with "say" and "tell"
🧩 **New skill** Talking about truth and lies

70.1 FILL IN THE GAPS USING "SAID" OR "TOLD"

She ___*said*___ that she loved music.

4 You _____ that you would do the dishes.

1 We _____ him that we could help.

5 I _____ him that I had to work late.

2 He _____ me that he had a sister.

6 Rob _____ that he loved his job.

3 Tina _____ that she lived in the suburbs.

7 You _____ us it was your birthday.

🔊

70.2 MARK THE SENTENCES THAT ARE CORRECT

She said she would come to the party. ☑
She said me she would come to the party. ☐

1 Henry said us that he had a new car. ☐
Henry told us that he had a new car. ☐

2 We said him that the film was boring. ☐
We told him that the film was boring. ☐

3 I told Jim to call you in the evening. ☐
I said Jim to call you in the evening. ☐

4 Maria said me that it was her bike. ☐
Maria said that it was her bike. ☐

5 They told us it would start in 10 minutes. ☐
They told it would start in 10 minutes. ☐

6 We said them the food was bad. ☐
We told them the food was bad. ☐

7 I told I wanted to leave early. ☐
I said that I wanted to leave early. ☐

8 Gina told me it was her anniversary. ☐
Gina told it was her anniversary. ☐

9 Leo said that he enjoyed dancing. ☐
Leo told that he enjoyed dancing. ☐

🔊

70.3 REWRITE THE SENTENCES AS REPORTED SPEECH

I'll meet you at the restaurant. = He said _that he'd meet me at the restaurant._

1 I want to buy a car. = She told him _____

2 I'm going to Buenos Aires on vacation. = I told them _____

3 We've really enjoyed the party. = We said _____

4 I'm going to redecorate the house. = He told her _____

5 I bought a new skirt this morning. = She said _____

6 The weather is looking bad. = He told them _____

7 We'll look after your cat. = We told you _____

8 It's your turn to make dinner. = I said _____

9 We need to buy a present for Mom. = She told us _____

10 We're going to do some gardening. = We said _____

11 We'll wait for you outside. = They told me _____

12 You can make yourselves some coffee. = She said _____

🔊

70.4 LISTEN TO THE AUDIO AND ANSWER THE QUESTIONS

Finn is talking to his friend Pete about his disastrous weekend.

Finn met his girlfriend for dinner on Saturday.
True ☐ **False** ☐ **Not given** ☑

1 Finn's girlfriend Esme arrived late for lunch.
True ☐ **False** ☐ **Not given** ☐

2 Esme said she had missed the bus.
True ☐ **False** ☐ **Not given** ☐

3 Finn thought Esme was lying.
True ☐ **False** ☐ **Not given** ☐

4 Esme got a taxi home.
True ☐ **False** ☐ **Not given** ☐

5 Finn told her not to call him.
True ☐ **False** ☐ **Not given** ☐

70.5 READ THE EMAIL AND FILL IN THE GAPS IN THE REPORTED SUMMARY

To: Mark
Subject: Working late

Hi Mark,
I'm writing from the office. I'm still here.
I'm going to be late home from work
tonight. My boss has just given me a report
to write up for tomorrow. I don't know why
he didn't give it to me earlier. I made pizza
for dinner yesterday and it's in the fridge,
so we'll have that when I get home. I'm
afraid I have to work early tomorrow, too.
Love, Janet

> Janet said she ___was___ writing from the office.

① She told Mark she _____ still in the office.

② She said she _____ late getting home.

③ She said her boss _____ her a report to write.

④ She said she _____ why he hadn't given it earlier.

⑤ She told Mark she _____ pizza the day before.

⑥ She said they _____ the pizza when she got home.

⑦ She said she _____ to work early the next day.

Aa 70.6 CROSS OUT THE INCORRECT WORD IN EACH SENTENCE

 Katy wouldn't **tell** / ~~say~~ me her secret yesterday.

①  I can't **tell** / **say** the difference between the twin brothers. They look the same!

②  When I saw them at the market I **said** / **told** hello and had a chat.

③  He said he wanted to **tell** / **say** something to me about my sister.

④  I knew John wasn't **saying** / **telling** the truth. He's such a liar!

⑤  You should **tell** / **say** someone if you're stressed at work.

⑥  Pete **told** / **said** me he had a fantastic vacation in Bali this summer.

70.7 USE THE CHART TO CREATE EIGHT CORRECT SENTENCES AND SAY THEM OUT LOUD

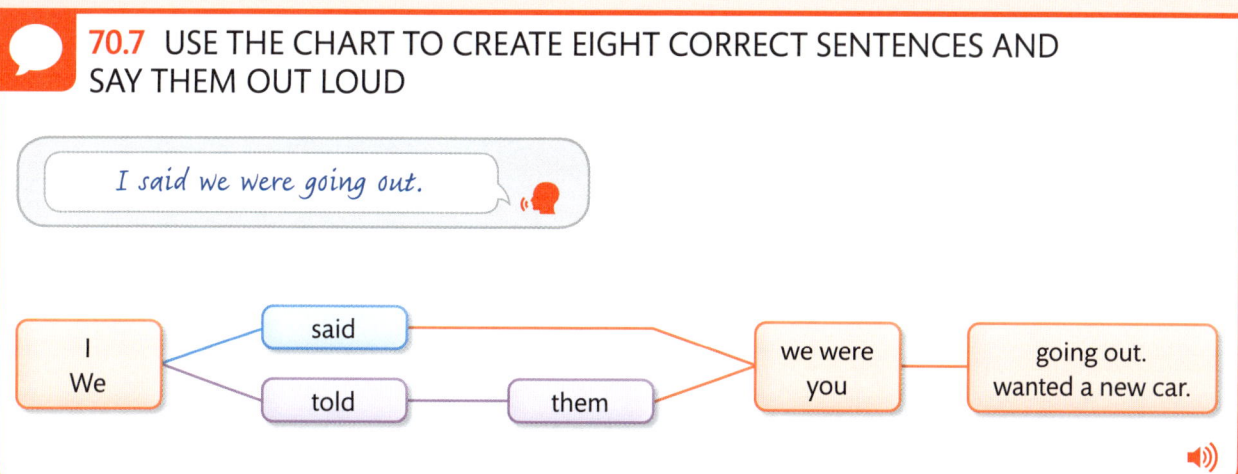

I said we were going out.

| I / We | said | | we were / you | going out. / wanted a new car. |
| told | them | | |

Aa 70.8 FILL IN THE GAPS USING "SAY" OR "TELL" IN THEIR CORRECT FORMS

When they left the house we thanked them and _____*said*_____ goodbye.

1 People won't believe you if you always _____ lies.

2 I _____ a "white lie" because I didn't want to hurt his feelings.

3 We were told that we should always _____ the truth.

4 You should _____ no if they ask you for help again. You're too busy.

5 The witness wouldn't _____ anything about the court case.

6 Let me _____ you a story about my childhood.

7 Don't believe that he's being honest just because he _____ so.

8 I asked my girlfriend to marry me, and she _____ yes.

9 Can you _____ the difference between African and Asian elephants?

10 He spoke so quietly we didn't hear him _____ hello to us.

11 It's so dark today that I can't _____ the difference between day and night.

12 Grandpa _____ us stories all the time when we were little.

13 My mother _____ me to always be polite to adults, no matter what.

14 She _____ she preferred apples to oranges any day.

Suggestions and explanations

In reported speech, you can replace "said" with a wide variety of verbs that give people more information about how someone said something.

⚙ **New language** Reporting verbs with "that"
Aa Vocabulary More reporting verbs
🧩 **New skill** Reporting explanations

Aa **71.1** READ THE CLUES AND WRITE THE REPORTING VERBS FROM THE PANEL IN THE CORRECT PLACES ON THE GRID

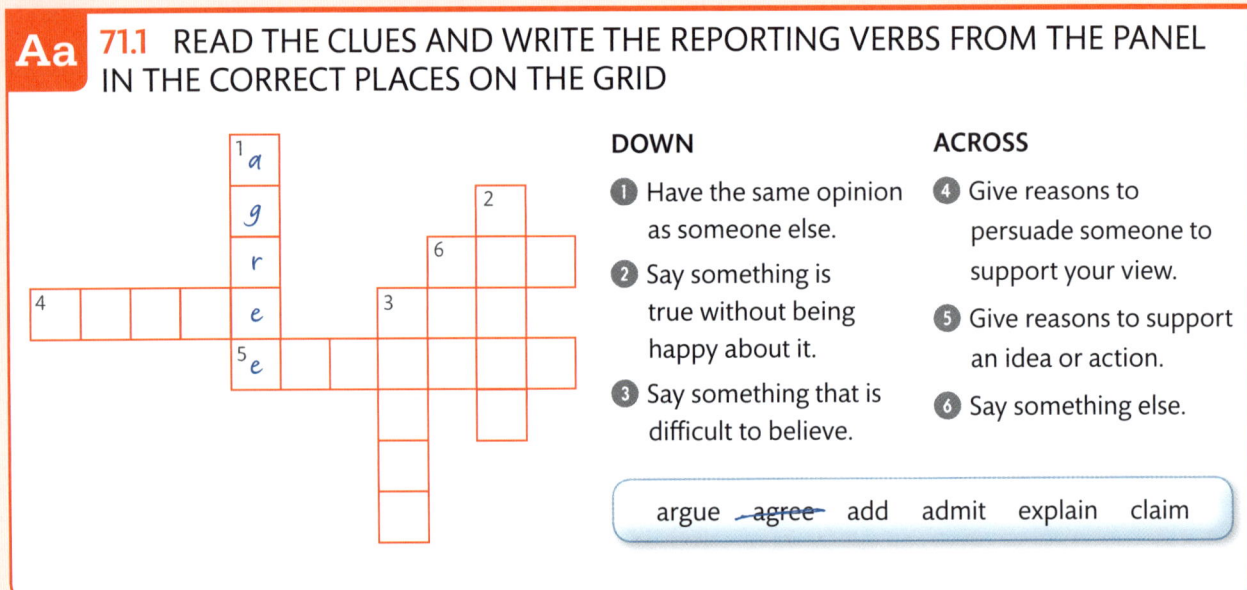

DOWN

❶ Have the same opinion as someone else.

❷ Say something is true without being happy about it.

❸ Say something that is difficult to believe.

ACROSS

❹ Give reasons to persuade someone to support your view.

❺ Give reasons to support an idea or action.

❻ Say something else.

argue ~~agree~~ add admit explain claim

71.2 REWRITE THE SENTENCES, PUTTING THE WORDS IN THE CORRECT ORDER

| explained | the | She | that | delayed. | flight | was |

She explained that the flight was delayed.

❶ change was climate He that a agreed problem. serious

_____

❷ claimed diet work. You this would that

_____

❸ he that brother couldn't admitted swim. Her

_____

🔊

71.3 REWRITE THE SENTENCES, CORRECTING THE ERRORS

> She claimed that she can drive a bus.
> *She claimed that she could drive a bus.*

1 He admitted that she is right.

_____

2 I explained him that I had lost my passport.

_____

3 We argue that the office was too hot.

_____

4 Katy agreed that his car is fantastic.

_____

5 He claimed me that he knew Alan David.

_____

6 I added that we can all have coffee.

_____

7 He admitted me that the apartment was too small.

_____

8 She claimed me that she never ate chocolate.

_____

9 I argued we that needed more vacations.

_____

10 They explained that there is a sale.

_____

11 Liz adds that it was also cheaper.

_____

12 She admitted that she doesn't know.

_____

Aa 71.4 MATCH THE PICTURES TO THE CORRECT SENTENCES

He argued that dogs were nicer than cats.

1

Mia agreed that they were ready to order their meal.

2

The assistant added that the shoes were in the sale.

3

The director admitted that the profits were down.

4

Alex claimed that he had won the lottery.

5

Peter admitted that he hated rock music.

6

She explained that the movie had already started.

71.5 SAY THE SENTENCES OUT LOUD AS REPORTED SPEECH, FILLING IN THE GAPS

You might not believe me, but I have lived in 15 different countries.

He _____ *claimed that he had lived* _____ (claim) in 15 different countries.

1 I was wrong. We don't have enough money to buy two flight tickets.

He _____ (admit) enough money to buy two flight tickets.

2 I know you don't think so, but I think the house is too small for a birthday party.

He _____ (argue) too small for a birthday party.

3 Let's get a taxi. It's late and we don't have time to wait for a bus.

She _____ (argue) time to wait for a bus.

4 You're right. This is the best Chinese restaurant in the city.

She _____ (agree) the best Chinese restaurant in the city.

5 I invested in gold, and I was rich when I was 20.

You _____ (claim) in gold and you were rich when you were 20.

6 It was a great hotel and the service was absolutely amazing.

They _____ (add) absolutely amazing.

7 We've bought new machinery, but the profits are down by 10 percent.

They _____ (admit) down by 10 percent.

8 Excuse me, but I have a terrible headache, so I have to leave early.

He _____ (explain) a terrible headache and he had to leave early.

9 I made my first million dollars before I left college.

She _____ (claim) her first million dollars before she had left college.

Mr. White and Roger are discussing the company's dismal sales figures.

Roger works for an oil company.	True ☐	False ☐	Not given ☑
❶ Roger agrees that profits were up by five percent this quarter.	True ☐	False ☐	Not given ☐
❷ Mr. White admits that he is disappointed.	True ☐	False ☐	Not given ☐
❸ The firm invested $80,000 in new machinery.	True ☐	False ☐	Not given ☐
❹ The firm bought the machinery from Germany.	True ☐	False ☐	Not given ☐
❺ Mr. White agrees that the investment will reduce costs.	True ☐	False ☐	Not given ☐
❻ Roger has not prepared an annual forecast for Mr. White.	True ☐	False ☐	Not given ☐
❼ Roger claims that profits would increase by 50 percent.	True ☐	False ☐	Not given ☐
❽ Mr. White suggests that Roger go home.	True ☐	False ☐	Not given ☐

Aa **71.7** MATCH THE BEGINNINGS OF THE SENTENCES TO THE CORRECT ENDINGS

She said → that she would see us later.

❶	Edward admitted	that we had already eaten dinner.
❷	I said	that they didn't like the hotel.
❸	They agreed	that he had forgotten the tickets.
❹	Elsa added	that it wasn't his turn to do the dishes.
❺	You suggested	that I would meet them at the café.
❻	He argued	that she also knew how to cook.
❼	We explained	that we go out for dinner.

🔊

Telling people what to do

Many reporting verbs have to take an object. English often uses these verbs to show that the speaker was giving someone orders or advice.

⚙ **New language** Verbs with object and infinitive
Aa Vocabulary Reporting verbs
🧩 **New skill** Reporting advice and instructions

72.1 MARK THE SENTENCES THAT ARE CORRECT

He encouraged me apply for the job. ☐
He encouraged me to apply for the job. ☑

1 She reminded me to buy some pizzas. ☐
She remind me to buy some pizzas. ☐

2 I asked him helped me with my project. ☐
I asked him to help me with my project. ☐

3 They encourage me to bought tickets. ☐
They encouraged me to buy tickets. ☐

4 I ordered him to drive more slowly. ☐
I ordered him drive more slowly. ☐

5 She asked me to walk the dog. ☐
She asked me walking the dog. ☐

72.2 REWRITE THE SENTENCES, PUTTING THE WORDS IN THE CORRECT ORDER

| She | him | some | groceries. | to | buy | reminded |

She reminded him to buy some groceries.

1 | encouraged | us | He | try | restaurant. | to | new | the |

2 | give | They | presentation. | asked | to | important | an | me |

3 | driving. | police | to | The | ordered | him | stop |

4 | meet | 8:30pm. | I | her | reminded | at | me | to |

72.3 REWRITE THE SENTENCES, CORRECTING THE ERRORS

> Joan ask Melanie to come over.
> *Joan asked Melanie to come over.*

1 I reminded my daughter to doing her homework.

_____

2 Lucy asked me to booking the tickets online.

_____

3 Mary encouraged to me to take some time off.

_____

4 My boss order me to complete the report.

_____

5 Joe asking me to do the dishes.

_____

6 Annie reminded me buy some bread and milk.

_____

7 I encouraged everyone try their best.

_____

🔊

72.4 READ THE ARTICLE AND PUT THE SUMMARY SENTENCES IN THE CORRECT ORDER

BUSINESS TODAY

Carla's Story

Carla worked as a secretary in a large company for two years. Then her boss, Misako, encouraged her to look at business management jobs.

"I was nervous," said Carla. "But Misako reminded me that I was good at my job, and I knew the company well."

The company asked Carla to go for an interview for a senior position, and she did really well. They offered her more training in business management, so now she has a better job and qualifications. "I'm so glad Misako encouraged me to try," said Carla.

A Misako persuaded Carla to look at business management jobs. ☐

B Carla worked as a secretary in a large company. 1

C Carla did really well at the interview for a senior position. ☐

D The company offered Carla more training in business management. ☐

E The company asked Carla to go for an interview for a senior position. ☐

F Carla was nervous, but Misako reminded her that she was good at her job. ☐

72.5 LISTEN TO THE AUDIO AND ANSWER THE QUESTIONS

Derek is telling Raj how unhappy he is in his job.

Why is Derek unhappy?

He doesn't like his lunch ☐

He doesn't like his job ☑

He hasn't got a job ☐

1 What does Derek's boss do?

Orders him to go to meetings ☐

Orders him to miss lunch ☐

Orders him to buy his lunch ☐

2 Why is Derek not happy shopping for his boss?

It's not part of his job ☐

He doesn't like shopping ☐

He doesn't have the money ☐

3 What does Raj think should Derek do?

Remind his boss that he doesn't have time ☐

Ask his boss to buy lunch ☐

Remind his boss to go shopping ☐

4 What does Raj suggest next?

Derek should look for a new job ☐

Derek should be nicer to his boss ☐

Derek should try harder at work ☐

5 What does Derek think of Raj's suggestion?

He'll probably ignore it ☐

It's a good idea ☐

It's a bad idea ☐

72.6 MATCH THE BEGINNINGS OF THE SENTENCES TO THE CORRECT ENDINGS

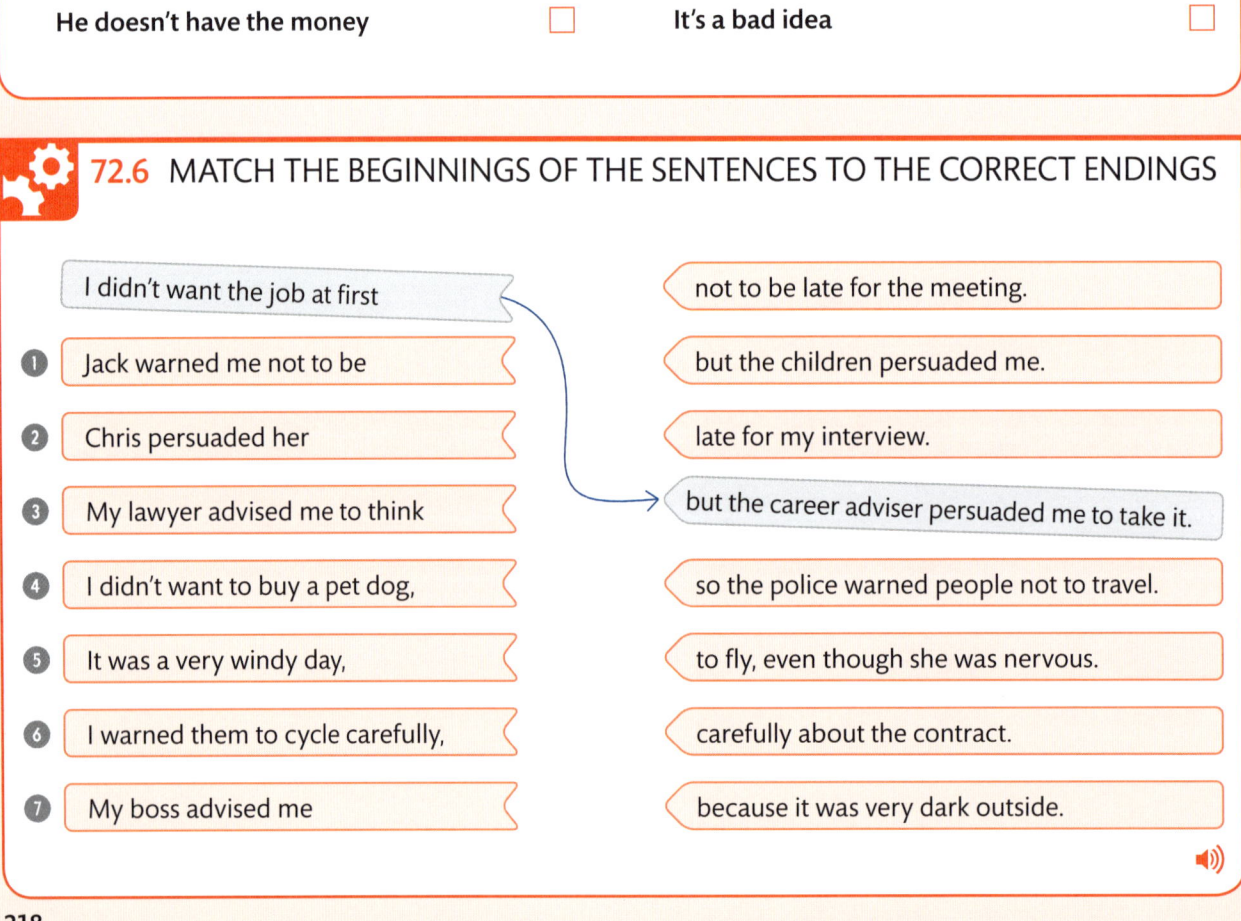

I didn't want the job at first

not to be late for the meeting.

1 Jack warned me not to be

but the children persuaded me.

2 Chris persuaded her

late for my interview.

3 My lawyer advised me to think

but the career adviser persuaded me to take it.

4 I didn't want to buy a pet dog,

so the police warned people not to travel.

5 It was a very windy day,

to fly, even though she was nervous.

6 I warned them to cycle carefully,

carefully about the contract.

7 My boss advised me

because it was very dark outside.

72.7 FILL IN THE GAPS BY PUTTING THE VERBS IN THE CORRECT FORMS

He _____*warned*_____ (warn) me _____*not to drive*_____ (not drive) too fast on the inner city roads.

❶ She _____ (order) them _____ (get out) of her office.

❷ They _____ (ask) her _____ (give) a presentation.

❸ My teacher _____ (encourage) me _____ (try) my best all the time.

❹ Her boss _____ (advise) her _____ (not forget) about the meeting.

❺ I _____ (warn) them _____ (not cycle) downtown.

❻ She _____ (remind) them _____ (take) time out for lunch.

❼ I _____ (ask) her _____ (not be) late for dinner.

❽ She _____ (ask) him _____ (clean) the kitchen.

❾ My friends _____ (advise) me _____ (look) for a new job.

❿ I _____ (encourage) Anna _____ (wear) her new jacket for the interview.

⓫ They _____ (order) everyone _____ (be) quiet.

⓬ He _____ (warn) us _____ (be) careful downtown at night.

⓭ I _____ (remind) Lucy _____ (get) new passport photos.

⓮ He _____ (ask) me _____ (not use) the computer because he needed it.

⓯ They _____ (persuade) me _____ (invest) in the company.

🔊

 72.8 USE THE CHART TO CREATE 12 CORRECT SENTENCES AND SAY THEM OUT LOUD

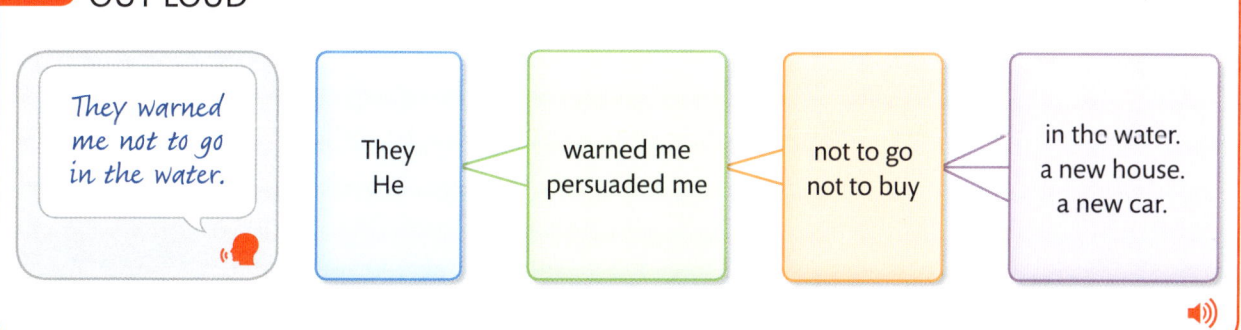

🔊

219

73 What other people asked

You can use reported questions to tell someone what someone else has asked. Direct questions and reported questions have different word orders.

⚙ **New language** Reported questions
Aa **Vocabulary** Collocations with "raise"
🧩 **New skill** Reporting direct questions

⚙ **73.1 MARK THE SENTENCES THAT ARE CORRECT**

He asked me what my name was. ☑
He asked me what was my name. ☐

1 She asked me what was I doing. ☐
She asked me what I was doing. ☐

2 He asked her what he could to help. ☐
He asked her what he could do to help. ☐

3 We asked her what time it was. ☐
We asked her what it time was. ☐

4 They asked him where was he going. ☐
They asked him where he was going. ☐

5 I asked her who was at the meeting. ☐
I asked her was who at the meeting. ☐

6 She asked me when would I worked. ☐
She asked me when I would work. ☐

7 He asked him where he could sit. ☐
He asked him where he could sat. ☐

8 I asked you what you are doing. ☐
I asked you what you were doing. ☐

9 She asked me where should she to park. ☐
She asked me where she should park. ☐

10 They asked him when he would arrive. ☐
They asked him when he will arrive. ☐

11 We asked them why are they leaving. ☐
We asked them why they were leaving. ☐

🔊

⚙ **73.2 REWRITE THE DIRECT QUESTIONS AS REPORTED QUESTIONS**

What can I do to help?
He asked me _what he could do to help_ .

1 Where will they have lunch?
She asked me _____ .

2 What time is the conference?
I asked them _____ .

3 Why can't he come to the office?
She asked him _____ .

4 Why are you leaving early?
We asked them _____ .

5 When will we start the meeting?
I asked you _____ .

🔊

73.3 REWRITE THE SENTENCES, PUTTING THE WORDS IN THE CORRECT ORDER

eat. | me | we | asked | She | when | would | to | like

She asked me when we would like to eat.

❶ were | I | you | you | late. | asked | why

___

❷ they | live. | asked | She | him | would | where

___

❸ were | to | we | you | going | We | discuss. | asked | what

___

❹ chairing | who | meeting. | I | was | asked | the | her

___

❺ me | they | help. | asked | They | to | what | do | could

🔊

73.4 LISTEN TO THE AUDIO AND MARK WHETHER EACH PICTURE SHOWS A DIRECT QUESTION OR A REPORTED QUESTION

Direct ☐ Reported ☑

❶ Direct ☐ Reported ☐

❸ Direct ☐ Reported ☐

❷ Direct ☐ Reported ☐

❹ Direct ☐ Reported ☐

left. | her | asked | He | when | train | the

He asked her when the train left.

4. she | We | what | wanted. | her | asked

_____

1. him | he | I | knew. | who | asked

_____

5. me | liked. | I | asked | who | He

_____

2. where | She | me | lived. | asked | I

_____

6. he | where | I | worked. | asked | him

_____

3. asked | we | did. | They | us | what

_____

7. arrived. | She | we | us | when | asked

_____

73.6 READ THE PASSAGE AND REWRITE THE HIGHLIGHTED QUESTIONS USING REPORTED SPEECH

Ed asked Elsa who would be at the Conference.

1. _____

2. _____

3. _____

4. _____

YOUR CITY

Environment talks

Ed Knox interviews Elsa Martinez about the Conference on Environmental Change

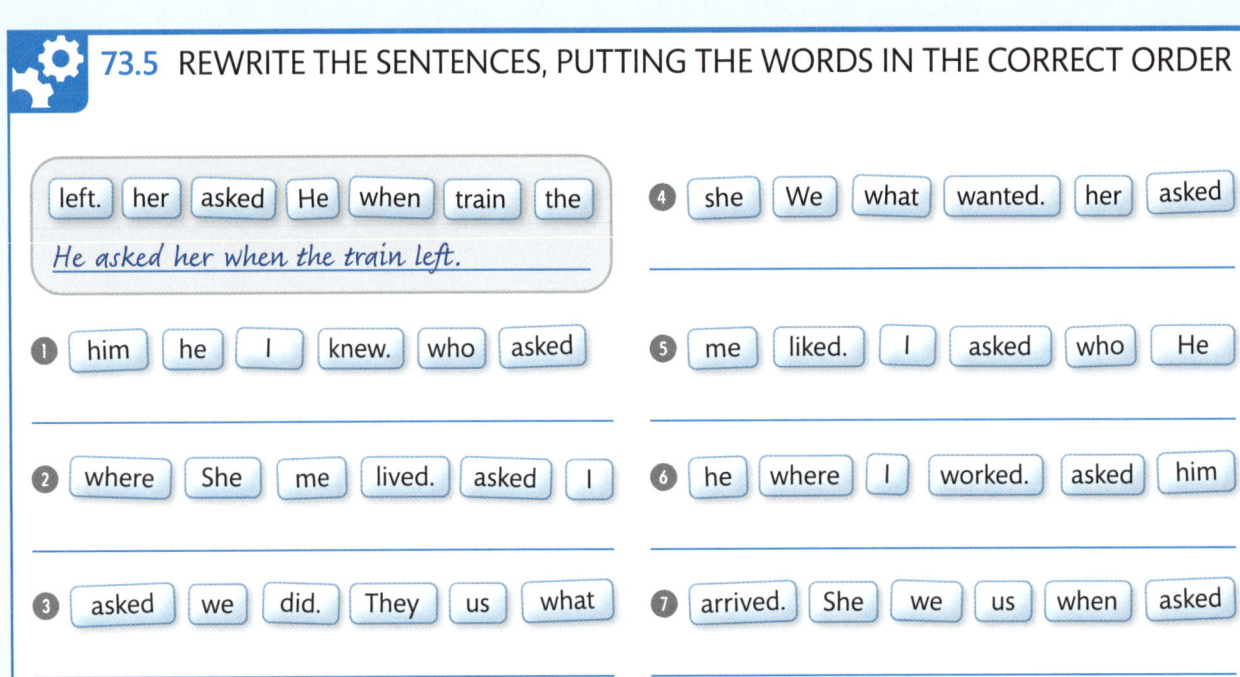

So, Elsa, who will be at the Conference?
There will be a number of world famous specialists.

When will the speakers give their speeches?
They will give speeches in the morning and there will be an open forum for questions after lunch.

What kind of topics will the speeches be about?
There will be speeches about renewable energies, conservation issues, and deforestation, to name a few.

When do tickets go on sale?
You can buy tickets now. They're already on sale.

Great. And where can people get tickets?
Please go to the website and order tickets online.

73.7 REWRITE THE DIRECT QUESTIONS AS REPORTED QUESTIONS

Who do you know here in your new neighborhood?
He asked me *who I knew in my new neighborhood.*

1 Where do you go on vacation every year?

He asked me _____

2 What time are we having lunch with Jamie tomorrow?

She asked me _____

3 Why can't we get a taxi to work instead of waiting for the bus?

She asked me _____

4 What kind of music do you usually like to listen to?

He asked me _____

5 When does the rock concert by the famous Swedish rock band finish?

She asked me _____

6 What company do you work for in southern Buenos Aires?

He asked me _____

🔊

Aa 73.8 FILL IN THE GAPS USING THE WORDS IN THE PANEL TO FORM COLLOCATIONS WITH "RAISE"

We need to raise _____*money*_____ for this environmental campaign.

1 At the meeting, Mr. Thomas raised _____ of funding.

2 We need to raise _____ about the dangers of climate change.

3 When asked to vote, nearly everyone raised their _____ .

4 The cheering was so loud, it nearly raised _____ .

5 Falling interest rates are raising _____ among investors.

| fears | ~~money~~ | the roof | the question | hands | awareness |

🔊

74 Reporting simple questions

Simple questions can be answered with "yes" and "no." English uses "if" and "whether" to report simple questions.

⚙ **New language** "If" and "whether"

Aa Vocabulary Verb + preposition collocations

🧩 **New skill** Reporting simple questions

⚙ **74.1 REWRITE THE DIRECT QUESTIONS AS REPORTED QUESTIONS, FILLING IN THE GAPS**

> Will you be at the meeting?
>
> I asked him if *he would be at the meeting.*

① Are we going to be on time?

He asked me _____

② Is that woman your boss?

He asked her _____

③ Do you have the sales figures?

She asked me _____

④ Have you brought the files?

We asked him _____

⑤ Would you like some coffee?

I asked her _____

⑥ Have you met the sales team?

I asked them _____

⑦ Was the train on time?

She asked me _____

⑧ Is Helen working late?

He asked her _____

⑨ Have you written the report?

You asked me _____

🔊

💬 **74.2 USE THE CHART TO CREATE 16 CORRECT SENTENCES AND SAY THEM OUT LOUD**

> *I asked them if they wanted to meet for coffee.*

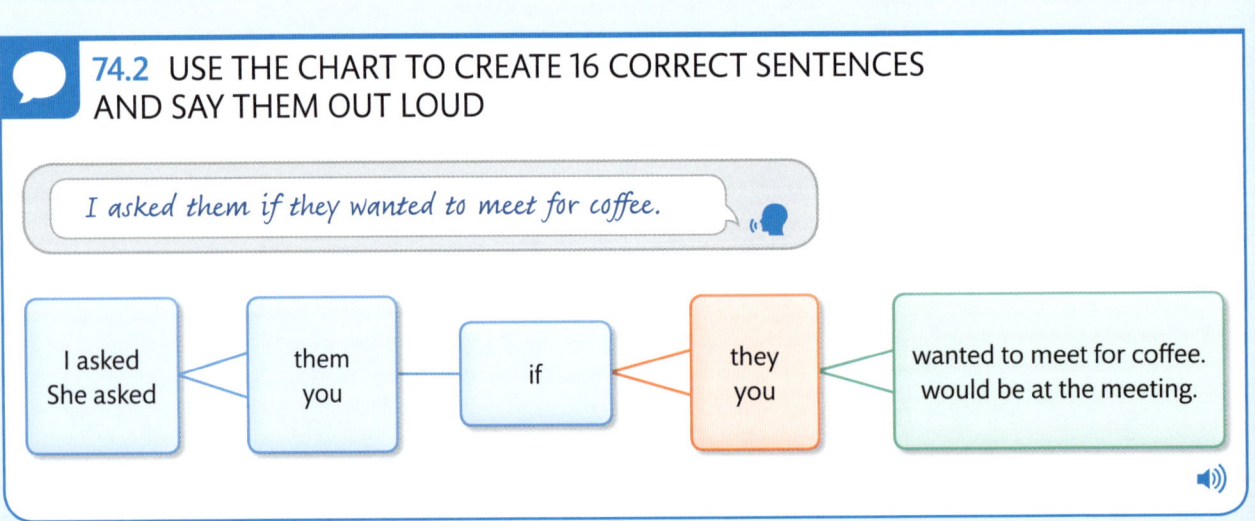

| I asked / She asked | them / you | if | they / you | wanted to meet for coffee. / would be at the meeting. |

🔊

74.3 LISTEN TO THE AUDIO AND ANSWER THE QUESTIONS

Nadia is asking David how his recent job interview went.

Nadia asked David if his interview had been today.
True ☐ **False** ✔

1 She asked him if he had given a presentation.
True ☐ **False** ☐

2 She asked him if they had been pleased.
True ☐ **False** ☐

3 She asked him if the manager was her ex-boss.
True ☐ **False** ☐

4 Nadia asked David if he liked Mr. Carter.
True ☐ **False** ☐

5 She asked him if he would accept the job.
True ☐ **False** ☐

74.4 FILL IN THE GAPS USING THE WORDS IN THE PANEL

Our manager asked us _____*whether*_____ we needed more support.

1 She asked him if he had _____ the new sales figures.

2 I asked _____ if she wanted another glass of water.

3 Mr. Salter asked them _____ they had met their targets.

4 We asked the secretary if she _____ order us a taxi.

5 He asked us if we _____ waiting for a long time.

6 Janet asked _____ if they knew when the meeting would start.

| ~~whether~~ | would | had been | whether | them | her | seen |

74.5 MATCH THE CORRECT PICTURES TO THE SENTENCES

He asked me if I spoke Italian or French.

You asked me if I wanted to be a chef or a doctor.

She asked him if he played soccer or golf.

 **3**

I asked her whether she preferred music or art.

  4

She asked me if I wanted water or fruit juice.

5

He asked whether they should go by bus or taxi.

74.6 REWRITE THE DIRECT QUESTIONS AS REPORTED QUESTIONS, FILLING IN THE GAPS

Do you want to leave?

He asked me if ___I wanted to leave.___

1 Do you like Eva or Liz?

She asked him if _____ .

2 Do you play tennis or chess?

I asked them whether _____ .

3 Do you speak Arabic or Chinese?

They asked me if _____ .

4 Would you like tea or coffee?

We asked her if _____ .

5 Do you want milk or cream?

You asked us if _____ .

6 Do you prefer books or magazines?

She asked her if _____ .

7 Should I call or text her?

He asked me if _____ .

8 Would you like cookies or cake?

They asked us if _____ .

9 Do you prefer TV or movies?

She asked me whether _____ .

10 Would you prefer to be famous or rich?

We asked them whether _____ .

11 Do you like dogs or cats?

He asked him if _____ .

Aa 74.7 REWRITE THE SENTENCES, CORRECTING THE ERRORS IN THE PREPOSITIONS

> Her company became a great success after a big fund invested money on it.
> _Her company became a great success after a big fund invested money in it._

1 I can always count in my family to support me in difficult times.

_____

2 Sheila works very hard because she wants to provide to her children.

_____

3 I work in a bank, but I dream at becoming a famous soccer star.

_____

4 The flood was terrible! Water poured onto all the houses on the street.

_____

5 The driver was accused in causing the accident by driving too quickly.

_____

6 The campaigners promised to fight with the government's decision.

_____

74.8 REWRITE THE HIGHLIGHTED PHRASES, CORRECTING THE ERRORS

> _he would come to the meeting_

1 _____

2 _____

3 _____

4 _____

5 _____

To: Bill

Subject: Friday's meeting

Hi Bill,

I asked Jamie if **he will come to the meeting** on Friday and he asked me if **I have known what time the meeting was.** Is it at 2pm? I've asked the sales team if **they could presented this month's figures.** I've also asked Mr. Rogers in accounts if **he has wanted to give a presentation.** I've asked Sara if **she could organized refreshments.** I've asked Jill in human resources if **she will like to attend** the meeting, too.

See you on Friday.

Ray

75 Polite questions

Indirect questions are more polite than direct questions. In spoken English, you might use them to ask people who you don't know very well about practical issues.

⚙ **New language** Indirect questions
Aa Vocabulary Practical issues
🧩 **New skill** Asking polite questions

75.1 REWRITE THE INDIRECT QUESTIONS, CORRECTING THE ERRORS

> Do you know where can I buy a ticket for the evening show?
> _Do you know where I can buy a ticket for the evening show?_

1 Could you tell me what time is it in the United Arab Emirates?

2 Do you know where can I buy interesting illustrated books for my children?

3 Do you know where is the new science museum for children?

4 Could you tell me how far is the station from my new neighborhood?

5 Could you tell me when leaves the next train for London?

6 Do you know why were Tom and Andrea late for the meeting yesterday?

7 Do you know how long will it take to travel from Los Angeles to Washington?

8 Do you know when starts the sales presentation for the new product?

9 Could you tell me when starts the meeting for the new members in the team?

10 Could you tell me how much will the flight to Edinburgh cost?

75.2 LISTEN TO THE AUDIO AND MARK WHAT TYPE OF QUESTION IS BEING ASKED IN EACH PICTURE

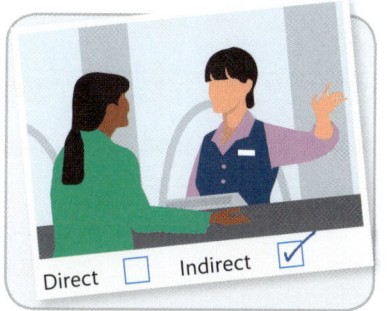

Direct ☐   Indirect ☑

1 Direct ☐   Indirect ☐

2 Direct ☐   Indirect ☐

3 Direct ☐   Indirect ☐

4 Direct ☐   Indirect ☐

5 Direct ☐   Indirect ☐

75.3 SAY THE SENTENCES OUT LOUD AS INDIRECT QUESTIONS

When do the stores open?

Do you know when the stores open?

1 Where is the museum?

2 How much is a pizza and salad?

3 How do I get to Newmarket?

4 What time should we leave?

5 Why is the train delayed?

6 How much are those shoes?

7 How far is it to the hotel?

75.4 MARK THE INDIRECT QUESTIONS THAT ARE CORRECT

Do you know why are we waiting? ☐
Do you know why we are waiting? ☑

1 Do you know why hasn't started the movie? ☐
Do you know why the movie hasn't started? ☐

2 Do you know how I can find the museum? ☐
Do you know how find I the museum? ☐

3 Could you tell me if the taxi is here yet? ☐
Could you tell me if is the taxi here yet? ☐

4 Do you know how far is it to the station? ☐
Do you know how far it is to the station? ☐

5 Do you know if Tom is at home? ☐
Do you know is Tom at home? ☐

6 Do you know how much will cost the tickets? ☐
Do you know how much the tickets will cost? ☐

7 Do you know how much fruit we need? ☐
Do you know how much fruit do we need? ☐

🔊

75.5 MATCH THE STATEMENTS WITH THE INDIRECT QUESTIONS

I'm looking for Matt.

1 There's the movie theater.

2 The sky looks cloudy.

3 I want to drive into town.

4 Joe wants to buy something.

5 I'd like to sit down.

6 I don't have any cash.

7 I'd like to buy a magazine.

8 We need coffee.

9 I want to go surfing.

10 I want to learn French.

11 I'd like to go for a walk.

Do you know whether it is raining?

Do you know where the corner shop is?

Could you tell me if this chair is occupied?

Do you know where Matt is?

Could you tell me where a nice café is?

Do you know how far it is to the beach?

Could you tell me when the movie starts?

Do you know when the stores open?

Do you know if there's a bank nearby?

Do you know where my car keys are?

Could you tell me where the park is?

Do you know if this tutor is good?

🔊

75.6 REWRITE THE SENTENCES AS INDIRECT QUESTIONS

Is there a lot of traffic on the highway near the office?
Do you know if there is a lot of traffic on the highway near the office?

1 What would you like to do in the evening after the soccer game?

_____

2 Where is the nearest restaurant to my sister's new house?

_____

3 Are those traditional dresses made of silk or cotton?

_____

4 Is the flight to Barcelona delayed or canceled?

_____

5 Has the train from Denver arrived yet?

_____

75.7 SAY THE SENTENCES OUT LOUD AS INDIRECT QUESTIONS

Can we wait here?

Do you know if we can wait here?

1 When was this house built?

2 Is this table reserved?

3 Is this Italian or Spanish cheese?

4 Why is the hotel restaurant closed?

5 Is there a gym near here?

76 Wishes and regrets

English uses the verb "wish" to talk about present and past regrets. The tense of the verb that follows "wish" affects the meaning of the sentence.

⚙ **New language** "Wish" with past tenses
Aa Vocabulary Life events
🧩 **New skill** Talking about regrets

⚙ 76.1 CROSS OUT THE INCORRECT WORDS IN EACH SENTENCE

 I wish I **could** / ~~can~~ / ~~would~~ play the electric guitar.

① I wish we **lived** / ~~live~~ / ~~will live~~ in a bigger house in a nice neighborhood.

② I wish I ~~won't~~ / ~~don't~~ / **didn't** have to drive to work today.

③ I wish we ~~eat~~ / ~~ate~~ / **would eat** Japanese food more often.

④ I wish the dog **would** / ~~will~~ / ~~does~~ stop barking at the children.

🔊

⚙ 76.2 MATCH THE SENTENCES THAT GO TOGETHER

I want to earn more money.

I wish I had a small puppy.

① I've got some travel brochures.

I wish I could speak French.

② I want to learn French.

I wish the children wouldn't fight.

③ The children are fighting.

I wish I could get a promotion.

④ I'd love a pet.

I wish I didn't have to call my boss.

⑤ I have to call my boss.

I wish I could go traveling.

🔊

USE "I WISH" AND THE PAST SIMPLE TO TALK ABOUT EACH SITUATION, SPEAKING OUT LOUD

This computer game is expensive.

I wish this computer game wasn't expensive.

1 You can't afford a new car.

2 You don't have a winter coat.

3 Your house is too cold.

4 You'd like to live on the coast.

5 A child is screaming.

6 You'd like a trumpet.

7 You can't speak Italian.

8 You don't have a cat.

9 You have to work hard.

10 You'd like to go swimming.

11 You can't afford a vacation.

12 You don't have enough time.

13 You don't like your neighbors.

14 You can't cook Chinese food.

15 You don't have long hair.

I've lost my car keys. I wish I _____*had kept*_____ (keep) them in a safe place.

① I'm late. I wish I _____ (wake up) an hour earlier.

② I've failed my driving test. I wish I _____ (have) more lessons.

③ I feel sick. I wish I _____ (not eat) so much dessert.

④ It's raining. I wish I _____ (bring) my new umbrella.

⑤ I've missed my appointment. I wish I _____ (take) a taxi and not the bus.

⑥ I don't like my bedroom. I wish I _____ (not paint) it orange.

⑦ I don't like this movie. I wish I _____ (stay) at home.

⑧ This food is terrible. I wish I _____ (choose) a different restaurant.

⑨ I've lost my bag. I wish I _____ (not bring) it with me.

⑩ I'm really tired. I wish I _____ (go) to bed earlier last night.

⑪ I've broken this vase. I wish I _____ (not drop) it on the floor.

⑫ I'm hungry. I wish I _____ (eat) some breakfast.

⑬ I've got a flat tire. I wish I _____ (not drive) to work this morning.

76.5 FILL IN THE GAPS USING THE PHRASES IN THE PANEL

I overslept again. I wish I _____ *had an alarm clock* _____ .

1 That concert was terrible. I wish _____ .

2 The wind is howling outside. I wish _____ .

3 We've missed the last bus home. I wish _____ .

4 Joe didn't get the job. I wish _____ .

5 I've never been to India. I wish _____ .

6 It's cold and rainy outside. I wish _____ .

7 That was rude. I wish _____ .

the weather was better

we hadn't gone

he had prepared better

~~had an alarm clock~~

it would stop

I had gone last year

you hadn't said that

there was a taxi

🔊

76.6 LISTEN TO THE AUDIO AND ANSWER THE QUESTIONS

Anna and Craig are talking about their future plans.

When did Craig hear from his family?
A few weeks ago ☐
A few days ago ☑
Never ☐

1 What does he wish they would do?
Call every week ☐
Visit more often ☐
Never call him ☐

2 What does Craig wish he had done?
More traveling ☐
More exercise ☐
Less walking ☐

3 Which country does he wish he had visited?
Austria ☐
Australia ☐
India ☐

4 Where does Anna wish she had lived?
Somewhere lively and busy ☐
Somewhere hot and sunny ☐
Somewhere cold ☐

5 Which language does she wish she had learned?
Spanish ☐
Italian ☐
Chinese ☐

 # Transcripts of listening exercises

UNIT 1

1.5 Danny: This is a great party, isn't it, Helena?

Helena: Yes, Danny. It's so nice of Mr. Adams to organize something for the staff and their friends.

Danny: Come and meet the boss. Mr. Adams, may I introduce my friend Helena?

Jack Adams: Pleased to meet you.

Helena: Delighted to meet you, too, Mr. Adams.

Jack Adams: Call me Jack.

Helena: OK, Jack.

Danny: Come and meet my colleagues, Rachel and Chris. We work in the same office. Rachel, Chris, this is my friend Helena.

Rachel: Hi, I'm Rachel. It's great to meet you, Helena. I've heard a lot about you.

Helena: I hope it's good!

Danny: Of course it is! I'm a good friend, aren't I? Hey, the band's good, aren't they? Do you like them, Helena?

Helena: Yes, their music's good, but it's a bit loud, isn't it?

Rachel: Yes. It's better to dance than talk. Come and dance with us, Helena.

Danny: I'm hungry. I'm going to have some of the food first. Mmm. It's delicious, isn't it?

Jack Adams: It certainly is.

UNIT 3
3.3

Interviewer: Jerry is a British student at the university. How are you finding life in Seville?

Jerry: It's great. I love living in a busy, noisy city. I'm from a small island near the south coast of England called the Isle of Wight. I love living on the coast and I'm used to being by the ocean. So, I'm glad Seville is on the Guadalquivir river. I like being near water.

Interviewer: Where are you staying?

Jerry: I'm sharing an apartment in the city center, in Barrio Santa Cruz. It's great.

Interviewer: And have you made any friends?

Jerry: Yes. Next weekend, I'm taking a tour around the Doñana National Park with two friends.

Interviewer: Where's the Doñana National Park?

Jerry: It's in the mountains. I'm really looking forward to going there.

Interviewer: Have a great time, Jerry. Seville is a beautiful city.

Jerry: Thank you.

UNIT 4
4.3

Sports commentator: And here are today's highlights from the Athletics Championship. The stadium was 90 percent full today and the audience was delighted to see America's Oscar Davis win the men's high jump with a jump of 2.38m. Kenya's David Mwange beat the world 800m record by 2.9 seconds. Canada's Owen Joslin won the 200m hurdles by 7/8 of a second. Canada now holds a third of all the medals. British athlete Gary Edwards won the long jump gold medal by 17 and a half cm.

4.4

News reporter: China's Li Mei won the women's high jump today with a fantastic jump of 2.07m. Jamaica's Lilly Cooper won the women's 100m in 9.5 seconds. That's 2/3 of a second faster than her last race. Australia's Anna Thompson set a new personal record in the women's 200m with a winning time of 20.8 seconds. The US currently holds 45 percent of the medals, while Australia holds 19 percent of the medals.

UNIT 5
5.4 ex:

M: How long have Tim and Alison been married?

F: Oh, for years. They got married on the 6th of August, 2009.

5.4.1

F: What time does your flight leave, Simon?

Simon: It leaves at ten to three. I have to be at the airport at 1:50.

5.4.2

M: Has Jamie finished his college course?

F: Yes, he graduated on the 30th of June.

5.4.3

Station announcer: Platform 3 for the 11:24 fast train to Edinburgh.

5.4.4

F: How old is your grandfather, Harry?

M: He's 80. It was his birthday on the 27th of November.

5.4.5

F: Have you been invited to Jane and Paul's wedding?

M: Yes. Have you?

F: Yes, I have. The ceremony is at 2:30. Do you want to go for lunch first? There's a good café near the church.

UNIT 6
6.1 ex: S-H-A-N-G-H-A-I

6.1.1 S-Y-D-N-E-Y

6.1.2 W-I-N-N-I-P-E-G

6.1.3 J-O-H-A-N-N-E-S-B-U-R-G

6.1.4 C-H-I-A-N-G M-A-I

6.1.5 B-U-C-H-A-R-E-S-T

6.1.6 I-L-L-I-N-O-I-S

6.1.7 P-A-S-A-D-E-N-A

6.1.8 H-O-B-A-R-T

6.1.9 M-U-M-B-A-I

6.1.10 E-D-I-N-B-U-R-G-H

6.3 ex: Oh three three eight eight eight seven oh one

6.3.1 Oh six eight nine nine six seven three two oh nine

6.3.2 Three three three four nine five two two zero one

3.3 Oh oh four four one two three eight six six
⋯e four

3.4 Five three six three six seven seven
⋯ven zero

3.5 Zero one fifty-five eighty-six thirty-two five

3.6 Oh two two nine three five eight

3.7 Oh one two nine six four oh nine nine nine

3.8 Zero sixty-one seventy-eight forty-three
⋯enty-five

3.9 Zero zero eleven forty-five twenty-nine eight

3.10 Oh five eight four three three two seven

3.11 Oh six five six forty-three twenty-one
⋯ety-three

UNIT 7

Interviewer: And so, Emily... why do you want a
⋯sition as an unpaid intern with our company?
Emily: Because I want a career in finance and this
⋯l be great work experience for me.
Interviewer: I see. This position is for six months,
⋯t it may lead to a full-time job with the
⋯mpany as a financial assistant.
Emily: I'd like that very much. In the future, will
⋯re be opportunities for promotion?
Interviewer: Yes, if you work hard and meet
⋯ur targets. In three or four years, you have the
⋯nce of being in a good position, and earning
⋯igh salary with generous vacation, and other
⋯nefits.
Emily: Will I have to work weekends as an intern?
Interviewer: Sometimes you will have to work
⋯ekends, but you won't have to work shifts.
Emily: Thank you. I'm really excited about
⋯rking here...

UNIT 8

⋯ So, how is your new job going, Lucy?
⋯cy: It's great. I love it. I'm happy to go to
⋯rk every day.
⋯ How are you finding the new systems
⋯d procedures?

Lucy: I often ask my colleagues for help, as
there is a lot I don't know.
M: What hours do you work?
Lucy: The hours are 9 to 6. I am never late.
In fact, I'm often early.
M: And what are the perks, or the good sides
of the job?
Lucy: I regularly travel abroad, which I love.
Last month I went to Dubai. It was amazing.
M: Wow! That sounds exciting.
Lucy: And I get to entertain clients. I sometimes
take them to restaurants. And it's all paid for by
work.
M: It sounds like they are treating you well.
Lucy: They are. I like to do my bit, too. I very
often take pastries into the office.
M: Well, it sounds like your new job is going great.
Lucy: It is!

UNIT 9
9.4

Jack: So, how was your weekend, Kate?
Kate: Great, thanks. I didn't do much. I met up
with friends on Friday night. We went out for
dinner and I stayed up late. Then, on Saturday,
I had lunch with my sister in the Park Café. That
was fun. What about you?
Jack: It was fine, thanks. I never wake up early on
the weekend, but I always work out. I meet up
with Karl at the gym every Saturday. Then we go
running. On Sundays we sometimes play tennis.
Kate: Cool! But when do you chill out?
Jack: Sunday evenings. That's my favorite time.
I'll have pizza for dinner, watch a movie, and
then I'm ready for bed.
Kate: That sounds fun, Jack. OK, time for work.
See you later.

UNIT 13
13.2

Commentator: And here is one of our favorite
items in this season's evening collection by
Miller Brown. Tonight, Elena is wearing a
stunning black evening dress with gold and silk
trim. This long, elegant dress has a row of tiny
gold buttons down the back and silk trim around
the neck. It really is beautiful.

Now for our casual collection... perfect for
that special summer party or barbecue. Milly
looks wonderful in a polka dot summer skirt. It's
made of pale blue cotton. To finish off this stylish

summer skirt, Milly is wearing a gorgeous silk
cardigan and suede sandals by Rosa May.

UNIT 15
15.4

Fergus: Hey Ben, where are you? We're waiting
for you. Are you coming to the game?
Ben: No, I'm not. Sorry I haven't called.
My apartment is a total mess, and I forgot
that my parents are visiting this weekend.
Fergus: That sounds bad. What are you doing?
Ben: I'm doing the laundry right now. My clothes
were all over the floor! I'm going to sweep the
floor later. The kitchen is a real mess. So I need to
clear the table and load the dishwasher. I watered
the plants last night, so that's good. And I've
folded all the towels in the bathroom so that
looks better. They were on the floor, too.
Fergus: Hmm. Do you want some help?
Ben: Thanks, Fergus, but I think I'll be OK. I haven't
made the bed yet, but that won't take long. I'm
going to do that later. I usually cook lunch for
them when they visit, but I don't have time.
I'll get a takeout.
Fergus: Good idea. OK. Good luck, Ben. I hope
you get everything done in time. See you later.
Ben: OK, thanks, Fergus. I'll see you later.

UNIT 16
16.5

M: It's great to be here, Emma. How long
have you been in your new place?
Emma: A few weeks, and I love it. There's so
much to do here. My apartment is just around the
corner from a fantastic art gallery that has different
exhibitions every month. There's always something
to see. There's a great shopping center nearby. I go
there most weekends, but if I want something
different, I can go to the theater on the edge
of town, too.
M: Where do you work?
Emma: In the bank in the city center.
M: And what's your favorite tourist attraction?
Emma: Oh, that's easy. The park is the most
interesting place. There are beautiful law courts
next to it. They're nearly 300 years old. There's a
palace near there, too, but I haven't been there
yet. Maybe we could do a tour while you're here.
M: Yes, I'd like that. Let's go to the tourist
information and book a tour.
Emma: Great idea.

UNIT 17

17.4.1 One of the trees is much bigger than the other.

17.4.2 One of the lakes is slightly wider than the other.

17.4.3 One of the trees is a bit taller than the other.

17.4.4 One of the lakes is a lot wider than the other.

17.4.5 One of the houses is much taller than the other.

17.4.6 One of the tables is much lower than the other.

17.4.7 One of the houses is much wider than the other.

UNIT 18

18.3

Anna: So, what are you doing this weekend, Ollie?

Ollie: Hi, Anna. We're going to the Three Towers Theme Park. I'm so excited. I went last year and it was amazing.

Anna: Really? I hate theme parks. I find them exhausting and annoying. And don't go on the roller coaster. I went last summer and it was way too frightening.

Ollie: Really? I heard it was amazing!

Anna: Well, it is, if you want to be frightened out of your mind. I thought Ghost Ride was better.

Ollie: No, I went on that last year and I was totally bored. I waited in line for a long time and that was annoying. And then I thought the ride was boring. I was totally depressed. I'm looking forward to going on the roller coaster. It's going to be amazing.

Anna: Well, don't blame me if you hate it.

UNIT 20

20.4

When I was little I had a favorite teddy bear called Bertie. I loved him very much. He sat in my crib with me when I went to sleep, and he sat in the high chair with me when I ate. When I was older, I took him everywhere with me. If we went to town, Bertie came, too. On my first day at school, my mom hid Bertie in my school bag. When I walked through the school gates and into class, I was miserable. I didn't like being at school and I started to cry. My teacher was kind to me but I was really upset. And then, I opened my school bag and I found Bertie! I was so happy. I stopped crying immediately because I knew everything would be OK.

UNIT 24

24.3

Steve: Hello, Karl. How was your trip?

Karl: Hi, Steve. It was fantastic, thanks. In fact, I got home last Friday.

Steve: Tell me all about it.

Karl: Well, I've been to Italy every year for three years now, so I wanted to do something different. I decided to visit Iceland.

Steve: Iceland?

Karl: Yes, it's such an amazing country. First, I cycled around the south of the country. It's very pretty and very green. I spent two weeks there. The people are the friendliest people I've ever met.

Steve: Really?

Karl: Yes. Then I traveled around the north. It's amazing. It looks like the moon. I've done all kinds of new things. I've learned how to kayak. It's so much fun! You'd love it. And two days before I left, I went whale watching.

Steve: Whale watching?

Karl: Yes, we went out in a boat. There were nine of us. We saw humpback whales and lots of dolphins, too. It was amazing.

Steve: Did you learn to speak Icelandic?

Karl: Well, not really. Most people speak English, so I only learned a few words. But I've bought a book and a CD so that I can continue to study, because I want to go back next year. It's a fabulous place.

Steve: Sounds fantastic!

UNIT 25

25.8 ex: I haven't tried hang gliding yet. I'm too scared!

25.8.1 I still haven't been skydiving, but I want to try it soon.

25.8.2 I've already been snorkeling lots of times. I really love it.

25.8.3 I haven't been on safari yet. Maybe I'll go on safari in Africa one day.

25.8.4 I still haven't tried windsurfing. It looks too difficult.

25.8.5 I've just been scuba diving in Spain. It was absolutely amazing.

UNIT 26

26.4 ex: I've been painting the bedroom since last weekend.

26.4.1 He has been putting up shelves for three and a half hours.

26.4.2 I've been tiling the kitchen since yesterday.

26.4.3 They've been fitting the carpet since 9 o'clock.

26.4.4 John has been fixing the bathtub for two days.

26.4.5 Alice has been making curtains for five hours.

UNIT 28

28.1 ex: They have been playing tennis.

28.1.1 Sue has cooked dinner and she and her family are going to eat now.

28.1.2 Simon has been watching a film all night. He's going to bed now.

28.1.3 I have drunk all the milk. I was thirsty!

28.1.4 They've been running in the park. They both very tired.

UNIT 29

29.6

Matt: Hi, James. Ah, the train service in this country is terrible. I hate getting the train to work.

James: Hi, Matt. What's so bad about the trains?

Matt: Well, they're always overcrowded, and this morning my train was 20 minutes late again!

James: That's bad, I agree. But I think buses are worse. The buses are always overcrowded and they're so slow.

Matt: Yes, that's true. But if you drive, there are always traffic jams on the freeway. People get so impatient when they have to wait. And there's usually nowhere to park near work.

James: Well it's impossible for you to cycle to work, Matt. Your office is too far away.

Matt: I wish I could buy an apartment downtown. Then I could cycle to the office!

UNIT 30

30.7.1 Alex: Look what Dan bought me for my birthday! It's a digital picture frame.

Sam: Oh wow, Alex! I'd like one of those. Then I could show my photos to my friends.

30.7.2 Sam: Oh no, Alex! My battery has run out on my digital camera.

Alex: Don't worry. I'll take photos with mine and email them to you later.

30.7.3 Alex: I want to make my mom a cake.

Sam: Do you want to borrow our food mixer, Alex? It makes making cake really easy.

Alex: Yes, please. I'll stop by for it tonight.

30.7.4 Alex: Hi, Sam. Can I borrow your compass? I'm going hiking this weekend.

Sam: Sure, Alex. I'll bring it in tomorrow.

30.7.5 Alex: I love my new tablet. I can take photos with it, email, and play games.

Sam: I don't have a tablet yet. I'm going to buy one with the money I got for my birthday.

30.7.6 Sam: My MP3 player is broken, Alex.

Alex: How long have you had it, Sam?

Sam: Only three months.

Alex: You should take it back to the store you bought it from.

30.7.7 Sam: I like your new cell phone, Sam.

Alex: It's great, isn't it? I use it to take photos, make videos, and go on the internet.

Sam: How much was it?

Alex: It was $150. It was on special offer, down from $200.

30.7.8 Sam: I overslept this morning and was late for work.

Alex: Didn't your alarm go off, Sam?

Sam: No, it's really old.

Alex: I have a loud alarm clock I don't need. It was an unwanted Christmas present.

UNIT 32
32.5

You will need eight ounces of butter and six ounces of sugar. Beat them together well. Add four eggs, one at a time, and beat well. Take four teaspoons of coffee and mix it with one tablespoon of hot water. Add this to the cake mixture and mix. Then add eight ounces of flour and stir well. Put the mixture into two baking pans and bake for 40 minutes at 350 degrees Fahrenheit. To make the cream filling: Add 1 teaspoon of instant coffee to a little cold water. Add the coffee to the cream and whisk. Spread the filling between the two cakes and decorate with four ounces of walnuts.

UNIT 33
33.6

Olivia: What's this, Sharon?

Sharon: Hi, Olivia. It's my smart-house remote control. It controls the heating in the house. And you can use it to turn on the stove when you're out, too. I can prepare my dish in the morning and put it in the oven when I go out, and then an hour before I come home I can use the remote control to turn the stove on. So my meal is ready when I come home. I use it nearly every day, but not on weekends because I'm home.

Olivia: That sounds amazing. What a great gadget! What do you think of this blender that I've just bought? I love it for making soups and smoothies, but it can also peel vegetables. And you can use it as a juicer. I love using it. I used it to make fresh tomato juice this morning.

Sharon: I'd love one of those. It looks stylish, too.

UNIT 35
35.6

Dominic Hi, I'm Dominic. I'm sports mad and I love being super-fit. I go running every morning before work, even when it's raining. I like running early in the morning before everyone is awake. So I usually get home by 6:30am and then I have a shower and breakfast. I enjoy swimming, too, and I sometimes go to the pool on weekends or after work. I love being fit, but I can't stand working out in the gym. It's so boring! I prefer doing action sports and I love doing winter sports like skiing. I'm really looking forward to my next skiing trip in December. I hope to go to Italy. I want to try snowboarding for the first time this year, too, so I think it's going to be a great trip.

UNIT 36
36.2

Claire: Hello Kai, how are you?

Kai: Great. Thanks, Claire.

Claire: Are you going to Ben's party next Saturday?

Kai: No, I can't. I'm going to a concert. I bought tickets last week. Are you going to his party?

Claire: Yes, I am. I'm going with my sister.

Kai: That sounds good. We should get together another time. Are you free on Friday?

Claire: No, I'm visiting my parents. We're going to a restaurant.

Kai: I'm going to the tennis competition tomorrow. Are you?

Claire: Yes, I am. I'm playing at 10.

Kai: Oh, I'm playing at 10:30. I'll see you there!

UNIT 39

39.4 ex: I think the weather will probably be cold and windy tomorrow.

39.4.1 I think there will be a storm this weekend.

39.4.2 I'm definitely going to go snowboarding on vacation this year.

39.4.3 I think I'll call Ann tonight and tell her about my party.

UNIT 40
40.6

Alan: Doug, where are we? I don't recognize this path. I think we might be lost.

Doug: Yes, I think you're right, Alan. I think we might have taken the wrong turn about 20 minutes ago. Let's have a look on your compass. We'll soon know where we are. »

Alan: Oh, no. Where is it? I can't find it. I think I might have dropped it. Oh, that's just great. Now what are we going to do?

Doug: Don't worry. We might be able to use the GPS on my phone. Hmm, that's no use. I can't get a signal.

Alan: Let's turn back. We might find a different way down the mountain.

Doug: OK. I think we'll need to hurry. Look at the sky. It might snow soon.

Alan: One thing's for sure. If we don't get home soon, we might be in big trouble.

Doug: Hey, look. I've got a signal! Fantastic!

UNIT 42
42.3

Doctor: I think you have a bad virus, Mr. Carlton, and this is giving you a fever and making you feel tired. You must take some time off work and go home and rest.

Mr. Carlton: But doctor, I have to go to London on business tomorrow.

Doctor: I'm sorry, Mr. Carlton, but you must not go to London. You have to stay at home and rest. You must not go outside and get cold or wet. You really must sleep as much as possible.

Mr. Carlton: Do I have to stay in bed?

Doctor: No, you don't have to stay in bed, but you must rest. So you could lie down on the sofa and sleep if you want to. You must drink lots of water and eat some good healthy food. Hot soups and fruit juices would be good.

Mr. Carlton: Do I have to take any medicine?

Doctor: No, you don't have to take any medicine. Antibiotics don't cure a virus. You just have to rest and keep warm.

UNIT 43
43.2.1
M: Doctor, I think I've broken my leg.
Doctor: Your leg could not be broken because you can walk.
M: It hurts a lot.
Doctor: You might have a sprained ankle.

43.2.2
M: Doctor, I can't stop coughing.
Doctor: You might have bronchitis. Let me listen to your breathing. Yes, I think you could have bronchitis.

43.2.3
M: Doctor, I think I've got food poisoning.
Doctor: Have you been vomiting?
M: No, I haven't.
Doctor: Then you can't have food poisoning.

43.2.4
F: Doctor, my son's wrist is sore and swollen.
Doctor: What did he do to it?
F: He fell on it when he was playing soccer.
Doctor It might be broken.

43.2.5
M: Doctor, I have a temperature and I ache all over.
Doctor: Have you got a cough and a sore throat?
M: Yes, I have.
Doctor: You might have the flu.

43.2.6
M: I've got a sore throat. I think I've got tonsillitis.
Doctor: Can you swallow?
M: Yes, I can.
Doctor: It can't be tonsillitis.

UNIT 45
45.2

I started my new job today. First of all, I met my new boss. He seems to be very popular and everyone looks up to him. My colleagues Alice and Tom are nice, too. I have a tiny desk in the corner of the office, but I can put up with it since I've only just started. Alice and Tom took me to lunch in the cafeteria and we got along really well. But our other colleague Sarah didn't want to sit with us. Apparently, she doesn't eat with people at work. After lunch, I had to come up with a presentation of the sales figures for my boss. I was printing out the figures when the printer ran out of paper! But it was OK. Alice took me to the stationery department and showed me what to do. And the presentation went well and my boss was pleased. There's going to be a sales conference at the end of the month. I'm looking forward to that. It should be interesting.

UNIT 46
46.7

Noah: Hey, Thomas. You're going out tonight, aren't you?

Thomas: Yes. I'm meeting Elsa and we're going to see the comedy show at the playhouse. You've seen it, haven't you, Noah?

Noah: No, I haven't. But Rosie has seen it. You liked it Rosie, didn't you?

Rosie: Yes, it was really funny. But it's very popular. You've booked tickets, haven't you? You won't get tickets at the door tonight.

Thomas: Oh, no! I didn't know I had to book tickets!

Rosie: What?

Thomas: I thought I'd buy them at the door, didn't I?

Rosie: Doh! What are you going to say to Elsa? She's going to be really angry, isn't she?

Thomas: Yes, she's going to be mad. Well it isn't my fault, is it? Look, I'll call her and explain. Maybe we can see a movie instead.

Noah: You'll have to do more than that! Good luck, Thomas. You'll need it!

UNIT 49
49.5

Professor: First, some stearic acid is put into a test tube. It's a solid and it looks like wax. Then a thermometer is put into the test tube. Next, the test tube is put into a beaker of water and the water is heated until it boils. It should boil gradually, not too fast. The temperature at which the acid melts is recorded. Then the mixture is allowed to cool. The temperature at which the acid starts to solidify is recorded. The results are recorded on a graph.

UNIT 50

50.8.1 If Mandy doesn't feel well, she'll stay at home.

50.8.2 If we practice every day, will we win the championship?

50.8.3 Joe will get a promotion if he works har

50.8.4 If I get the laptop, will you help me writ this report?

50.8.5 If they get there early, they'll get good seats.

50.8.6 I'll make us some coffee if you fill the kettle.

50.8.7 If Ben digs the hole, I'll plant the tree.

50.8.8 We'll go to the beach if the weather is good.

UNIT 51
51.8 ex: If you want to redecorate your room, buy some paint.

51.8.1 If you're thirsty, get a drink from the fridge.

51.8.2 If you have a headache, take some painkillers.

51.8.3 If it's raining, don't forget your umbrella.

51.8.4 If you're bored, go for a walk in the park.

UNIT 52
52.7

Well: What are you planning to do this week?
Builder: We've nearly finished the wiring. As soon as that's done, we'll plaster the walls.
OK.
Builder: And then we'll start painting the kitchen when the plaster dries.
What about the plumbing?
Builder: As soon as the paint has dried, the plumber will put in the washing machine and dishwasher.
And the shelves?
Builder: When the plumber finishes work, I'll put up the shelves and fix all the units. Then your kitchen will be ready.
Fantastic! That sounds great.

UNIT 53
53

Andy: Ellen, I really hate my job. I want to start a business.
Ellen: Really? What do you want to do?
Andy: Well, if I had $5,000, I'd open a pet store.
Ellen: But you don't have $5,000!
Andy: No, but I could borrow it.
Ellen: Do you really need to open a store? Wouldn't it be easier to just sell things online?
Andy: No, that would be boring. If I sold things online, I wouldn't be able to talk to the customers.
Ellen: What would you sell in your store?

Andy: Well, everyone loves their pets, don't they? If you had a cat or a dog, you'd want to buy it a nice bed, good food, nice toys. If I had a pet store, I'd sell all of that. I'm sure it's a great idea.
Ellen: Look, Andy. Why do you hate your job?
Andy: I'm bored. I sit in an office all day. I don't earn enough money and I can't afford nice vacations.
Ellen: If you did more training, you could get a better job. And then you wouldn't be bored. If you earned more money, you'd have better vacations. I think that's a better idea than borrowing money to start a pet store.
Andy: Oh, well. I don't know. I'll think about it.

UNIT 55
55.4 ex: If I were you, I wouldn't go running in the rain.

55.4.1 Do you think I should buy this coat?

55.4.2 If I were you, I'd ask her out.

55.4.3 If I were you, I wouldn't buy that car.

55.4.4 You've been skiing in the Alps, haven't you? Do you think I'd enjoy it?

55.4.5 If I were you, I'd apply for that job.

UNIT 56
56.4

Carol: The problem is that too many people create too much waste.
Alex: Yes, you're right, Carol. If everyone recycled more, we'd reduce a lot of waste. I mean, look at the amount of paper we waste in this office. It's crazy.
Carol: Exactly, Alex. And coffee cups, too.
Alex: Yes, right. If we recycled our paper and the paper cups, we'd save a lot of waste.
Carol: That's right. And don't forget plastic. Nobody recycles their plastic water bottles. Let's do something.
Alex: Well, I would take the plastic bottles to the recycling center if someone helped collect them.
Carol: I'll help. I'll make two collection boxes and people can put their paper and plastic in them. If we put them in the kitchen, people will see them. We'd save a lot of waste.

Alex: What about cans? I'll make a collection box for cans.
Carol: Fantastic. We're really going to make a difference.

UNIT 57
57.3.1 I'm looking for an interesting job that I'll enjoy.

57.3.2 I knew someone who had a similar job to yours.

57.3.3 It's important to have co-workers who you get along with.

57.3.4 She'd like to meet someone who is funny and self-confident.

57.3.5 Our firm needs someone who can make decisions.

57.3.6 The candidate must be a person who is reliable.

57.3.7 There are a lot of interesting places that you can visit.

57.3.8 He works in a city that is cosmopolitan and busy.

57.3.9 That's the position that I'd really like to have.

57.3.10 We met a person who works with you.

UNIT 58
58.5.1 The car, which was outside our house, was stolen yesterday.

58.5.2 Sam's party, which he had on the beach, finished at 2am.

58.5.3 Mrs. Thomas, who lives next door, found a gold watch in the street.

58.5.4 The old house, which has been empty for years, burned down last week.

58.5.5 My new tablet, which Mike bought for me, takes fantastic photos. »

58.5.6 Nicola White, who teaches science, is the best teacher in the school.

UNIT 61
61.2

It was a dark and stormy evening and Mr. Coulter was driving home, late from work. It was snowing heavily and the road was black and icy. The wind was blowing fiercely and the trees along the side of the road were bending in the wind. Mr. Coulter looked at his watch. It was 6:45 and he was late. His wife Emily was waiting for him at home. He decided to stop the car and call her. As he was dialing her number, he heard a terrible noise. One of the tallest trees was crashing onto the road in front of him. It missed his car by only 20 feet. What a lucky escape!

UNIT 62

62.4 ex: Karl sat down while he was waiting for the train.

62.4.1 Louisa bought some ice cream while she was walking on the beach.

62.4.2 Rex was skateboarding when he crashed into the wall.

62.4.3 Luke was skiing down the mountain when he saw a helicopter.

62.4.4 Misaki ate a cookie while she was reading.

62.4.5 Jake was talking to Emma when his cell phone rang.

UNIT 63

63.3 ex: An industrial plastics factory polluted the river with chemicals.

63.3.1 Over 20 buildings were destroyed in a terrible fire.

63.3.2 The emergency services rescued three people from the lake.

63.3.3 Many houses were flooded during the storms over the weekend.

63.3.4 Large areas of rainforest were cut down last year.

UNIT 64

64.4.1 Mom was in the living room but Dad had already gone to bed.

64.4.2 When we got to the hotel, our friends had already arrived.

64.4.3 His room was a mess because he hadn't cleaned it up for weeks.

64.4.4 Simon met his friends in town after he had been to the gym.

64.4.5 My cat hadn't eaten its food when I got home.

64.4.6 Joe still hadn't bought anything when she called him.

UNIT 65
65.3

Mike: Have you ever been to India, Rachel?
Rachel: Yes, I went last year with two friends. It was the first time I had ever been. We went to the city of Jaipur in Rajasthan to see the elephant festival. It was incredible. I had never seen an elephant before and there were so many of them, all in colorful costumes. It was the most beautiful thing I had ever seen.
Mike: I've never been to India. I'd love to go there one day.
Rachel: But you've been to Thailand, haven't you, Mike? I've never been there.
Mike: Yes, Thailand is beautiful. When I went to Bangkok, it was the first time I had ever seen a Buddhist temple. I've never been to Vietnam, though. I've heard that's an interesting place, too.

UNIT 68
68.7

F: Hi, Blake. How did moving into your new house go?
Blake: It was really busy. I was signing the papers at the lawyer's on Friday when my phone started ringing.
F: Who was it?

Blake: It was my wife, saying the man who wa[s] buying our house had changed his mind on the move in date.
F: Oh, no. How terrible!
Blake: As soon as I heard that, I called the realtor to ask what was happening.
F: I bet you were really upset.
Blake: I was furious. But then they told me tha[t] the man's father had gone into the hospital an[d] consequently they wanted to move next week instead of today.
F: And were you able to do that?
Blake: No, we had a movers booked. In fact they arrived at the very moment I got home from the lawyer's.
F: So did you move out last Friday?
Blake: Yes, we got into the new house. Shortly afterward some flowers came with a note from the buyer to wish us well in our new house. He also said he was sorry he had to change his pla[n]
F: That was nice of him.
Blake: Yes, it was. He's moving into our old house tomorrow.

UNIT 70
70.4

Pete: Hi, Finn. How was your weekend?
Finn: A disaster. My girlfriend Esme told me she'd meet me for lunch on Saturday, at 1 o'clock, but she turned up half an hour late. She said that she hadn't been able to find her car keys, but I didn't believe her. She's always late. So we had a huge argument.
Pete: Oh, no. That doesn't sound good.
Finn: No, it wasn't. She told me that she didn't want to see me again and I said I didn't care. She walked out of the café and told me not to call her.
Pete: What are you going to do?
Finn: I don't know. I miss her and I think I overreacted. I think I should call her.
Pete: Good idea. There are worse things than being late.

UNIT 71
71.6

Mr. White: Good morning, Roger. Please sit down. I've been looking at the sales results for this quarter and they show that profits are up by 5 percent.
Roger: Yes, that's right, Mr. White.

Mr. White: I'm disappointed. This isn't as much as I was hoping.

Roger: Well, our profits have increased by 5 percent for the previous three quarters, which makes an annual increase of 20 percent. In January we invested $50,000 in new machinery. This time next year, our production costs will be half what they are now, but we will be selling more products.

Mr. White: Yes, the new investment will reduce our production costs. What is the forecast for annual profits for this time next year?

Roger: With the reduced production costs, plus an annual profit of 20 percent, the forecast looks good. I've plotted the figures on a chart. Here they are.

Mr. White: Thank you, Roger. This looks very promising. Well done. I'll look at these now and I suggest we discuss them this afternoon.

Roger: Thank you.

UNIT 72
72.5

Raj: Hi, Derek. What's the matter?

Derek: Oh, hi, Raj. I'm really fed up. I'm not happy at work.

Raj: Hey, that's a shame. Why don't you like it?

Derek: Well, the boss orders me to do all sorts of things, like go out and buy his lunch, or go shopping for him. It isn't part of my job, but it's hard to say no.

Raj: Yes, that is hard. You should remind him that you don't have time to do things like that.

Derek: You're right.

Raj: Or maybe you should look for a new job, Derek. One with a nicer boss! You could do really well in a job you enjoy.

Derek: Thanks, Raj. Maybe I will!

UNIT 73
73.4 ex: He asked her where the supermarket was.

73.4.1 They asked her what she was cooking for dinner.

73.4.2 Are you going to Matt and Anna's party Saturday?

73.4.3 What time does the train from Oxford leave?

73.4.4 The director of sales asked me why I wanted this job.

UNIT 74
74.3

Nadia: Did your interview go well, David?

David: I'm not sure. It was really tough. They asked me a lot of difficult questions.

Nadia: Did you give a presentation?

David: Yes. I had to give a 10-minute presentation about our new online products. I talked about how we had developed the products in the last few months.

Nadia: Well, that sounds good. Were they pleased?

David: I think they were quite impressed but they didn't say much.

Nadia: Is the team manager Mr. Carter?

David: Yes, it is. He's a really good manager.

Nadia: Do you like him?

David: Yes, I do. He's very professional, and he's nice, too.

Nadia: Will you hear about the job today?

David: No, I won't hear until the end of the week.

Nadia: Good luck, David. I'm sure you'll get the job. They'd be crazy not to give it to you.

David: Thanks, Nadia. I'll let you know.

UNIT 75
75.2 ex: Could you tell me where the hotel conference center is?

75.2.1 Excuse me. Do you know what time it is?

75.2.2 Do you know how much this coat is?

75.2.3 Is the taxi waiting outside?

75.2.4 Excuse me. Is that seat free?

75.2.5 Could you tell me the way to Angel Avenue?

UNIT 76
76.6

Anna: Have you heard from your family recently, Craig?

Craig: Yes, they called a few days ago. I wish they would visit more often, but I guess they're busy.

Anna: They've just been on vacation to Brazil, haven't they?

Craig: Yes, Jill and her husband went to the carnival in Rio. I wish I'd done more traveling when I had the chance. I wish I'd gone to Australia. I've always wanted to see the world.

Anna: Yes, me, too. I wish I'd lived abroad,

Answers

01

1.1 🔊
1. Mom isn't at work today, is she?
2. You're a flamenco dancer, aren't you?
3. I'm not sitting in your chair, am I?
4. This article is very interesting, isn't it?
5. They're from Beijing, aren't they?

1.2 🔊
1. You're hungry, aren't you?
2. She is Chris's boss, isn't she?
3. They're from Florida, aren't they?
4. It's warm today, isn't it?
5. You're not tired, are you?
6. We're from the same town, aren't we?
7. They're late, aren't they?
8. Saira's sister is here, isn't she?
9. You're from the US, aren't you?

1.3 🔊
1. The music is very loud, **isn't it**?
2. You're not from here, **are you**?
3. Tim is a great dancer, **isn't he**?
4. Fiona isn't here, **is she**?
5. The venue is lovely, **isn't it**?
6. I'm not late, **am I**?
7. They are dancing, **aren't they**?
8. The band is great, **isn't it**?
9. You're having a good time, **aren't you**?
10. It isn't warm today, **is it**?
11. I'm in your class, **aren't I**?
12. He isn't 30, **is he**?
13. You aren't waiting, **are you**?
14. This film is boring, **isn't it**?
15. They're playing tennis, **aren't they**?
16. We aren't early, **are we**?
17. She's beautiful, **isn't she**?
18. You aren't from Boston, **are you**?
19. He isn't outside, **is he**?
20. They're watching TV, **aren't they**?
21. You aren't hurt, **are you**?

1.4 🔊
1. You're Sarah, **aren't you**?
2. You're Sally's friend, **aren't you**?
3. Fatima is funny, **isn't she**?
4. The food is delicious, **isn't it**?
5. Dev and Jai are twins, **aren't they**?

6. You're not leaving now, **are you**?
7. I'm not boring you, **am I**?
8. The boss isn't here, **is he/she**?
9. I'm late, **aren't I**?
10. You've just woken up, **haven't you**?
11. You can't see it, **can you**?
12. He's getting old, **isn't he**?
13. They're not studying, **are they**?

1.5
1. True 2. False 3. False 4. False
5. True 6. True 7. True

1.6 🔊
1. I'm very **well, thank you**.
2. This **is Tim**.
3. **Good morning**, Mrs. Reid. How are you?
4. Hi, Sally. How **are you doing**?
5. I'm **delighted to meet** you, Ms. Chopra.
6. May **I introduce** Frank Hill?
7. I'm very pleased **to meet you**, Diana.
8. **Great to** meet you, Holly.

1.7 🔊
1. **Hi**, Maria.
2. I'm very well, **thank you**.
3. **Great** to meet you.
4. **Fine**, thanks.
5. Paul! **Great** to see you, too.

02

2.1 🔊
1. United States of America 2. Australia
3. United Kingdom 4. Germany
5. Turkey 6. Spain 7. Pakistan
8. Argentina 9. China 10. Peru
11. South Korea 12. Kenya
13. Czech Republic 14. Brazil 15. France
16. Portugal 17. Japan 18. Vietnam
19. Mongolia 20. Bolivia 21. Greece
22. Canada 23. Mexico 24. Poland

03

3.1 🔊
1. There is a tree **to the left of** the tall building in town.
2. We stayed in a small hotel just **by** the seaside.

3. The town library is **right next to** the movie theater.
4. Tom is planning on going for a walk **in** the country today.
5. Norway and Australia are on **opposite** sides of the world.
6. The Snow Slopes Ski Resort is **in** the mountains.

3.2 🔊
1. I live in the mountains.
2. I live in the city.
3. I live on the coast.
4. I live on the river.
5. I live off the coast.
6. He lives in the mountains.
7. He lives in the city.
8. He lives on the coast.
9. He lives on the river.
10. He lives off the coast.

3.3
1. False 2. True 3. True 4. Not given
5. Not given 6. True 7. True

3.4 🔊
1. The castle is **right next to** the beach.
2. The island is just **off** the coast.
3. Visitors can take boat trips **around** the island.
4. They can eat at the restaurant **on** the island.
5. The statue is **between** the café and the church.
6. The restaurant is **directly** opposite the café.
7. The lighthouse is diagonally **opposite** the church.

3.5 🔊
1. The lighthouse is just off the coast.
2. The park is diagonally opposite the lake.
3. We stayed in a chalet in the mountains.
4. There's a café right next to the theater.
5. Henry has a house by the sea.
6. It's halfway between the airport and the hotel.

3.6
1. Pacific 2. Right next to 3. 2010
4. 100km 5. North 6. On the bay

04

4.1 🔊
1. zero point seven five
2. forty-two percent
3. one sixth
4. twelve point three
5. three quarters

4.2 🔊
1. eight point three
2. seventy-nine percent
3. two and a quarter
4. zero point four
5. fifteen percent
6. one and a third

4.3
1. Davis jumped 2.38 meters.
2. Mwange beat the record by 2.9 seconds.
3. Joslin won by seven eighths of a second.
4. Canada holds a third of all medals.
5. Edwards won by 17½ centimeters.

4.4
1. 100 2. 9.5 3. 2/3 4. 200 5. 20.8
6. 45% 7. 19%

4.5 🔊
1. **twen**ty 2. six**teen** 3. seven**teen**
4. **eigh**ty 5. **fif**ty 6. nine**teen**
7. **six**ty 8. four**teen** 9. **sev**enty
10. eigh**teen** 11. **thir**ty

4.6 🔊
1. The Jamaican sprinter lost by **four fifths** of a second.
2. Tracey Livingstone won the race by **three twelfths** of a second.
3. The Russian contestant won by an **eighth** of an inch.
4. There were a total of **forty** runners in the marathon this year.
5. The American won the 100 meters back stroke by **five sixths** of a second.
6. Maxwell Peterson came in **ninth** place out of 48 contestants.

05

5.1 🔊
1. It's ten thirty. / It's half past ten.
2. It's eleven forty-five. / It's quarter to twelve.
3. It's twelve o'clock.
4. It's two fifty. / It's fourteen fifty. / It's ten to three.
5. It's three twenty-four. / It's fifteen twenty-four. / It's twenty-four minutes past three.
6. It's five fourteen. / It's seventeen fourteen. It's fourteen minutes past five.
7. It's seven thirty-seven. / It's nineteen thirty-seven. / It's twenty-three minutes to eight.
8. It's nine forty-eight. / It's twenty-one forty-eight. / It's twelve minutes to ten.

5.2 🔊
1. The eleventh of February, two thousand and ten
2. March fourth, two thousand and twelve
3. September twenty-third, two thousand and six
4. The thirty-first of December, two thousand and fourteen
5. February fifteenth, two thousand and eight

5.3 🔊
1. My flight leaves at ten to seven in the morning.
2. The train arrived at twenty-five past nine.
3. I called you at quarter to two yesterday afternoon.
4. The bus was late. It arrived at six thirty.
5. My English class finishes at five to five.
6. I have a doctor's appointment at twenty-five past eight.
7. The show starts at half past seven.

5.4
1. 14:50 2. June 30 3. 11:24
4. November 27 5. 2:30pm

06

6.1
1. Sydney 2. Winnipeg 3. Johannesburg
4. Chiang Mai 5. Bucharest 6. Illinois
7. Pasadena 8. Hobart 9. Mumbai
10. Edinburgh

6.2 🔊
1. C-A-L-I-F-O-R-N-I-A
2. P-A-D-D-I-N-G-T-O-N
3. B-L-O-O-M-F-I-E-L-D
4. B-I-R-M-I-N-G-H-A-M
5. H-O-N-G K-O-N-G
6. C-A-M-B-R-I-D-G-E
7. S-Y-D-N-E-Y
8. N-E-W D-E-L-H-I

6.3
1. 06899673209 2. 3334952201
3. 00 44 123 86654 4. 536 367770
5. 0155 86325 6. 02229358
7. 0129640999 8. 061784325
9. 001145298 10. 05843327
11. 0656 432193

6.4 🔊
1. Queen's Walk 2. Melbourne
3. NSW 2024 4. Alice dot Watson at sunshine dot A-U 5. Zero zero six one five five zero eight eight eight four

6.5
1. Her surname is Brodie.
2. She's a sales manager.
3. She works at Trademark Printers Ltd.
4. Her phone number is 0785 9044678.
5. Her email address is rachel.brodie@trademark.com.

6.6
1. Street 2. House number 3. Title
4. Phone number 5. Zip code 6. Town
7. Email 8. First name 9. Country

07

7.1 🔊
1. plumber 2. journalist 3. architect
4. butcher 5. vet 6. firefighter
7. surgeon

7.2 🔊
1. flight attendant 2. surgeon
3. electrician 4. architect 5. travel agent
6. firefighter 7. writer 8. pilot
9. fashion designer 10. butcher

7.3
1. False 2. False 3. False 4. True
5. True 6. True 7. False

7.4 🔊

1. Annabelle starts **work** at 8:30am.
2. Joe is looking for a new **job**.
3. I've had to **work** all weekend.
4. What time do you finish **work**?
5. Sam's cousin helped him get his first **job**.
6. Laura has a well-paid **job** in finance.
7. I **work** as a freelance consultant.

7.5

1. Finance 2. Six months
3. Full-time 4. Promotion
5. High 6. Sometimes 7. Never

7.6 🔊

1. They got a pay **rise** of five percent.
2. Doctors can earn a great **salary**.
3. I'll be late home tonight. I have to work **overtime**.
4. Peter was **unemployed** for six months before he got a job.
5. This position may lead to a **full-time** job.
6. Eva might **resign** because she hates her job.
7. Henry works for himself. He is a **freelance** reporter.
8. This job has four weeks' **vacation**.

08

8.1

1. often 2. regularly 3. sometimes
4. usually 5. never 6. always 7. rarely

8.2 🔊

1. I go to the movies once a week.
2. He is never late for work.
3. They frequently eat after 7pm.
4. I nearly always cook dinner.
5. She occasionally works overseas.

8.3 🔊

1. She sometimes gets home late.
2. He almost never goes to the gym.
3. They are very often at home.
4. He hardly ever takes a bath.
5. He is always on time.
6. He rarely goes for a walk.
7. You frequently stay out late.
8. I nearly always walk to work.
9. We occasionally go out for lunch.
10. She regularly plays tennis.

11. They never go on vacation.
12. He very rarely goes to the doctor.
13. You are hardly ever late.
14. We regularly visit our uncle.
15. She often goes to the park.

8.4 🔊

1. never 2. rarely 3. occasionally
4. usually 5. regularly

8.5 🔊

1. I almost never go to the theater.
2. He nearly always gets to work early.
3. I occasionally watch a movie in the evening.
4. She is rarely late for work.
5. They sometimes have a party in December.
6. She very often has a sandwich for lunch.
7. They rarely work on the weekend.
8. You are often tired when you get to work.
9. I frequently ask my boss for help.
10. She occasionally takes the train to work.
11. I almost never have time to cook in the evening.

8.6

1. True 2. False 3. True 4. True
5. True 6. False 7. True

8.7 🔊

1. I hardly ever go to the dentist.
2. He occasionally plays hockey with Ken.
3. They usually have breakfast at 7am.
4. I almost never make the dinner.
5. She is very often at work in the evening.

8.8

1. Bobby was always tired.
2. He saw an advert for nurses in Australia.
3. He has been in Australia for six years.
4. He sometimes has to work evenings or weekends.
5. He usually finishes work at 8pm.
6. He regularly emails or video calls family and friends.
7. His family visits him once a year.

09

9.1 🔊

1. She **usually wakes up** at 6:30am.
2. Max doesn't **get up** early every day.
3. I **sometimes meet up** with my co-workers.

4. Do you **often chill out** with your friends?
5. We don't **work out** on Thursdays.
6. Mr. Wallis **checked into the hotel** on Saturday.
7. Does Laura normally **turn up** on time?

9.2 🔊

1. My brother **turns up** late for everything.
2. I **work out** at the gym twice a week.
3. Katy never **wakes up** early on Saturday mornings.
4. They sometimes **meet up** with friends on Friday.

9.3 🔊

1. We'll meet up after work.
2. He's chilling out in his room.
3. Her name never comes up.
4. They work out quite often.
5. I stay in on Friday nights.
6. The bus turned up late.
7. We ate out with our friends.
8. Jo checked into the hotel today.
9. Sam grew up in Oxford.

9.4

1. Not given 2. True 3. False
4. Not given 5. False 6. False 7. True

9.5 🔊

1. I'm **meeting up** with some of my friends from college later.
2. He likes to **chill out** in front of the TV on Friday evenings.
3. Rosa and her sister Anezka **got up** late yesterday morning.
4. I'm tired. I think I **will stay in** tonight and read my book.
5. We aren't going to **eat out** on Friday or Saturday.
6. Mr. and Mrs. Williams haven't **checked into** the hotel yet.

9.6 🔊

1. Tom **came up** in the chat.
2. Our manager **turned up** late for work.
3. Shall we **eat out** tonight?
4. Malik **grew up** in Vancouver.
5. Rob **met up** with friends yesterday.

10

10.1 🔊
① bald ② lips ③ wavy hair ④ red hair
⑤ long hair ⑥ black hair ⑦ beard
⑧ eyebrow ⑨ nose ⑩ eyelashes
⑪ ear ⑫ mouth ⑬ blond hair
⑭ pony tail ⑮ brown hair ⑯ teeth
⑰ eye ⑱ short hair ⑲ tooth

11

11.1
OPINION: **attractive**, **beautiful**
SIZE: **tall**, **thin**
SHAPE: **curly**, **straight**
AGE: **old**, **young**
COLOR: **green**, **brown**

11.2 🔊
① He has a thin brown mustache.
② Susan has gorgeous, long, thick blond hair.
③ James is a tall, thin young man.
④ She has attractive, shoulder-length, curly black hair.

11.3
① True ② Not given ③ True ④ False

11.4 🔊
① She has shoulder-length, **straight** red hair.
② He has **short** brown hair.
③ He has short **black** hair and a **beard**.
④ She has attractive, **curly** red hair.

12

12.1 🔊
① jacket ② shorts ③ dress
④ suede boots ⑤ buttons
⑥ silk scarf ⑦ leather bag
⑧ high-heels ⑨ tie ⑩ collar
⑪ belt ⑫ jeans ⑬ cardigan
⑭ checked ⑮ suit ⑯ striped
⑰ sandals ⑱ socks ⑲ t-shirt

13

13.1 🔊
① Martin is **choosing** some new boots.
② I'm **mending** my favorite wool cardigan.
③ Alison is **shopping** for some new jeans.
④ My little brother is **trying** on some pajamas.

13.2
① An evening dress ② Gold ③ A skirt
④ Pale blue ⑤ Silk

13.3 🔊
① I'm putting on a pair of new boots.
② Brian is living in a house in London.
③ She's buying a pair of casual shoes.
④ Tanya is shopping for a new dress.
⑤ I've lost a button from my cardigan.
⑥ He doesn't have a lot of expensive clothes.
⑦ They're taking a lot of photos of the city.

13.4 🔊
① She's wearing a pair of **boots**.
② He's wearing a **suit**.
③ She's wearing a pair of **sandals**.
④ He's wearing a **shirt**.
⑤ She's wearing a leather **belt**.

13.5
① True ② True ③ False ④ True ⑤ False
⑥ False ⑦ False ⑧ True ⑨ False

14

14.1 🔊
① washing machine ② bedside table
③ frying pan ④ crockery ⑤ rug ⑥ mirror
⑦ cupboard ⑧ plants ⑨ bathroom
⑩ dishwasher ⑪ living room ⑫ light
⑬ bedroom ⑭ shower ⑮ towel
⑯ kitchen ⑰ bed ⑱ lawn ⑲ saucepan

15

15.1 🔊
① Tony waters the plants every evening.
② Tom walks the dog after breakfast.
③ Katy sweeps the floor every day.
④ Mia loads the dishwasher every day.
⑤ Jamie mows the lawn every week.

15.2
Hi Harry, Emma, and Paul,
While I'm visiting your grandma this weekend, please can you do the following chores? Harry, can you **do** the laundry on Saturday and **walk** the dog twice a day? Paul, can you **do** the cooking on Saturday? Then can you **clear** the table and **load** the dishwasher? Emma, can you **make** the beds, and **fold** the towels in the bathroom, please? And don't forget to **water** the plants in the house. Thanks!

15.3 🔊
① I normally **walk** the dog in the evening, but this evening **I'm relaxing** at home.
② **We're doing** the laundry together today, but I usually **do** it myself.
③ Frank sometimes **goes** to the gym after work, but today **he's working** late.
④ Ben **is doing** the ironing today, but his dad usually **does** it.
⑤ **He's listening** to music now, but he often **watches** TV in the evening.
⑥ **I'm mowing** the lawn today, but I normally **mow** it on Saturdays.

15.4
① The laundry ② Kitchen ③ Clear the table ④ Last night ⑤ Yes ⑥ On the floor
⑦ No ⑧ Make the bed ⑨ Yes, usually

15.5 🔊
① Laura is doing the cooking tonight, but she usually does the dishes.
② I always sweep the floor before I go to bed.
③ James is walking the dog this evening, but he usually walks him every morning.
④ Salman usually waters the plants at home.
⑤ Joan is doing the laundry now, but she often gardens in the afternoon.
⑥ Jessica and Dan will clear the table after lunch.
⑦ Donald usually mows the lawn on Sunday morning.

15.6
① False ② True ③ False
④ True ⑤ False

16

16.1 🔊
1. Tony has to fill a form in for work.
2. I'm checking the train timetable out.
3. Anna will pick the shopping up.
4. They gave some leaflets out about the fair.
5. We're putting a dog show on this summer.
6. That little boy didn't pick his litter up.
7. They're going to close that store down.
8. John wants to show his cell phone off.
9. Rita is putting her coat on.

16.2 🔊
1. Can you **check** out the menu?
2. Why don't you **look** up the word online?
3. They were **giving** out free samples.
4. Did you **try** out the new cell phone?
5. I'll **pick** up the children from school.
6. They **sold** off the town parking lot.
7. He didn't **cut** down the pine tree.
8. The school is **putting** on a play.
9. Are you **taking** up hockey in college?
10. They **tore** down the old town hall.
11. What did you **find** out at the meeting?

16.3 🔊
1. I took it back.
2. They're closing it down.
3. Jess looked them up.
4. We picked it up.
5. Bob brightened it up.
6. I will look it up.
7. She tried it out yesterday.

16.4 🔊
1. She's looking it up.
2. They closed it down.
3. They're renting it out.
4. They sold it off.
5. He cleaned it up.
6. I'm checking them out.
7. They brightened it up.
8. He took it up.
9. She found them out.

16.5
1 B 2 G 3 E 4 A 5 D 6 H 7 C 8 F

16.6 🔊
1. Which paintings are in the **art gallery**?
2. Most people here are kind and **friendly**.
3. The river is **polluted** with oil.
4. It's the tallest **high-rise** building in the city.
5. The Royal Family live in the **palace**.
6. You can buy medicine at the **pharmacy**.
7. The **bustling** streets are crowded with shoppers.
8. This place isn't safe. It's **dangerous** at night.
9. The lawyer is meeting us at the **law court**.
10. His office isn't out of town. It's in the **city center**.
11. The country park is **unspoiled** and beautiful.
12. The streets are **dirty** and full of litter.
13. All the stores are in the **shopping mall**.

16.7
1. True 2. Not given 3. False
4. True 5. False

16.8
POSITIVE: **friendly, bustling, unspoiled, lively**
NEGATIVE: **dirty, crowded, dangerous, polluted**

17

17.1 🔊
1. The hospital is **a lot** taller than the church.
2. The airport is **slightly** bigger than the station.
3. The cafe is **much** smaller than the factory.
4. The tower is **slightly** taller than the tree.
5. The hotel is **a lot** smaller than the castle.

17.2 🔊
1. The school is slightly **bigger** than the church.
2. The hill is much **taller** than the tree.
3. The house is much **smaller** than the palace.
4. The car is much **faster** than the bike.
5. The door is much **wider** than the window.

17.3 🔊
1. The office is easily the tallest building in the city.
2. The Pacific is by far the biggest ocean.
3. Sudan is one of the hottest countries of all.
4. Antarctica is one of the coldest places on Earth.

17.4
1 B 2 C 3 E 4 A 5 F 6 G 7 D

17.5 🔊
1. The clock tower is much **older** than the palace.
2. This is by far the **best** book I've ever read.
3. Your house is much **bigger** than mine.
4. The tower is a bit **taller** than the lighthouse.
5. The factory is slightly **larger** than the castle.

17.6
1. The Arabian Desert is the second largest desert in the world.
2. The wettest place on Earth is in India.
3. Mawsynram is slightly wetter than Cherrapunji.
4. The Nile is by far the longest river in Africa.
5. The Nile is about 145 miles longer/slightly longer than the Amazon.
6. Mount Everest in the Himalayas is the highest place in the world.
7. The highest mountain in the world is 29,035 feet high.
8. Lake Baikal is easily the deepest lake in the world.
9. Lake Baikal is one of the largest lakes in the world.
10. Baikal is over 1,968 feet deeper than the Caspian Sea.
11. The Caspian Sea is the second deepest lake in the world.

18

18.1 🔊
1. Lily is **bored** with her piano lessons.
2. I'm **amazed** that you want to try scuba diving.
3. The class on whales and dolphins was very **interesting**.
4. Mr. Watkins was **annoyed** by all the traffic on the road.

18.2 🔊
1. Were you **surprised** when you opened your present?
2. I found this recipe for paella really **confusing**.
3. Martha wasn't **annoyed** that I was late for her party.

4 The news about the airplane accident was **shocking**.

5 Ethan is **depressed** because he failed his accounting exams.

6 I was **amazed** when I heard about your new job.

18.3

1 False **2** True **3** True **4** False
5 False **6** True **7** False

18.4

1 On a boat **2** A picnic **3** Barbecuing
4 Amazed **5** Living on a boat **6** Yes

18.5 🔊

1 Yesterday's biology class was very interesting.

2 The news of Andy and Kay's wedding wasn't surprising.

3 Are you excited about your vacation in Australia?

4 *Day of Terror* was a really frightening horror movie.

5 Losing the game was disappointing for everyone.

6 Kevin was amazed by the firework display.

7 Are they tired after their long walk in the country?

8 Chad and Dora were very relaxed after their holiday in Mauritius.

9 I think your new girlfriend is very pretty and charming.

10 Sandra was shocked when she won the lottery.

11 The article about quantum physics was a bit confusing.

18.6 🔊

1 We **quite** enjoy sailing.

2 Jane **really** loves cooking Italian food.

3 Tom **absolutely** hates wearing shorts.

4 They **really** don't like driving in traffic.

5 I **quite** like running.

6 I **really** enjoy walking my dog.

7 You **absolutely** love cycling.

8 They **really** don't like singing.

9 Alice **absolutely** hates flying.

10 We **really** love going to the cinema.

11 She **quite** likes walking in the park.

19

19.1 🔊

1 grandfather **2** father **3** uncle
4 sister **5** son **6** daughter
7 grandson **8** granddaughter

20

20.1 🔊

1 She did write a story for class.
2 John did buy her a present.
3 They did learn to read at school.
4 I did feed the cat this evening.
5 We did wait for you.

20.2 🔊 Note: The word in bold is the word which should be underlined.

1 He **did** call the babysitter.
2 Janet **did** sterilize the bottle.
3 I **did** enjoy school.
4 She **did** behave well in class.
5 He **did** bring the teacher a present.
6 They **did** work hard at school.
7 I **did** buy the baby's food.

20.3 🔊

1 baby carriage **2** stroller **3** bottle
4 diaper **5** crib **6** changing mat

20.4

1 C 2 E 3 A 4 D 5 B

20.5 🔊

1 The toy duck sank in the bath.
2 Talin drew on the wall of his bedroom.
3 He fed the baby an hour ago.
4 The children hid under the table.
5 His older sister led the way.

20.6

1 Not given **2** True **3** False **4** False
5 Not given **6** True

20.7 🔊

1 Jenny **bought** a new changing mat for her baby girl.

2 The little boy **hid** behind a tree near the playground.

3 The baby **slept** for two hours before waking up.

4 She **drew** a picture of a bird in a tree.

5 The doll **sank** in the bath rather than floating.

6 They **went** to the baby store together.

7 The baby **sat** in his high chair and played quietly.

21

21.1 🔊

1 exercise book **2** geography **3** pencil
4 ruler **5** library **6** grade **7** pencil sharpener **8** student **9** psychology
10 classroom **11** pass **12** degree **13** English
14 lecture **15** teacher **16** fail **17** science
18 text book **19** exam

22

22.1 🔊

1 I'm late and it's **unlikely** that I'll get my train in time to get home.

2 They found it too difficult to **resolve** the dispute about the best route.

3 She's so **restless** she just can't relax at all.

4 His sore back was very **painful**. It hurt every time he took a step.

5 Do you have to **rewrite** your essay? That's a shame.

6 Be **careful** when you use this product. It's toxic and can make you sick.

7 His desk is so **untidy** he can't find what he is looking for.

8 These earrings aren't gold. They're **worthless**, I'm afraid.

9 Was the little girl crying because she was **unhappy**?

22.2 🔊

1 They were hopeful for a positive result.
2 She's unlikely to play today if she's injured.
3 It is pointless to argue with your manager.
4 George wasn't able to rework his essay.
5 Her new hairstyle was really unattractive.
6 Their vacation was restful and relaxing.
7 It's careless to drive too fast.

22.3 🔊

1 Your bedroom is untidy.
2 It is painless.
3 I'm going to reapply for that job.

④ She's unlikely to be on time.
⑤ They are careless drivers.
⑥ I was hopeful for the future.
⑦ She resolved the argument.
⑧ He's unlikely to come to work.
⑨ The task was pointless.
⑩ His mustache was unattractive.
⑪ He felt powerless to argue.

23

23.1 🔊
① coach ② bus stop ③ drive a car
④ airport ⑤ pack your bags ⑥ port
⑦ get on a bus ⑧ hotel ⑨ bicycle
⑩ cruise ⑪ arrive at the airport
⑫ helicopter ⑬ train station ⑭ runway
⑮ taxi rank ⑯ reception ⑰ train ride
⑱ tram ⑲ luggage

24

24.1 🔊 Note: All answers can also use the contracted form of the present perfect.
① Stella **has written** an email to her grandparents in Boston.
② We **have had** this car for years. It's really old!
③ You **have known** Alice since you were at school together.
④ Mike **has bought** some new skis. They were really expensive.

24.2 🔊
① I **have visited** France many times in my life. I love it.
② Arabella **went** swimming at 12:30pm.
③ We **have lived** here for five years. It's our home.
④ Elsa **has been** out of the country for two months. We miss her.
⑤ Ravi **traveled** to India in March.
⑥ He **has spoken** three languages since he was a child.

24.3
① Present perfect ② Past simple
③ Present perfect ④ Past simple
⑤ Present perfect

24.4 🔊
① I've **painted** a picture for you.
② Robert **has** cycled around the park.
③ Janice has **cooked** paella lots of times.
④ I have **flown** in a helicopter.
⑤ **They've / They have** ridden a camel in Egypt.
⑥ I **have** swum in the Great Barrier Reef.
⑦ We have **brought** you a present.
⑧ I've **studied** geography and science.
⑨ The students have **left** the building.

24.5 🔊 Note: All answers can also use the contracted form of the present perfect.
① I **have learned** to speak a second language.
② We **have bought** a new house.
③ Paula and Maria **have run** a marathon.
④ You **have seen** an elephant.
⑤ David **has lived** here for six months.
⑥ Elsa **has lost** her passport again.
⑦ They **have landed** at the airport.

24.6 🔊
① **They arrived** at the hotel.
② John and Diane **ate** breakfast.
③ He **went** on vacation to Fiji.
④ **They saw** the Statue of Liberty.
⑤ Our parents **flew** to the US.
⑥ **I studied** history in college.
⑦ **They bought** some new clothes.
⑧ She **went** to Tokyo twice.
⑨ **You finished** that book.

25

25.1 🔊
① I still haven't been to China.
② She has just arrived in Egypt.
③ They haven't contacted us yet.
④ He has already packed his bags.
⑤ We have just got our passports.

25.2 🔊
① She still hasn't tried windsurfing.
② The plane has just landed.
③ I've already unpacked my bags.
④ They haven't bought their tickets yet.
⑤ He still hasn't swum in the ocean.

25.3 🔊
① I've **just** seen the mountains for the first time.
② Nick hasn't booked his flight to Nepal **yet**.
③ They've **just** bought two new backpacks for their trip to South America.

④ We've **already** learned some German on our last trip to Berlin.
⑤ Andrew has **just** missed his flight to Stockholm.
⑥ We **still** haven't tried scuba diving or snorkeling in the Indian Ocean.
⑦ Maria hasn't ordered a taxi to take her to the airport **yet**.
⑧ Joe and Paolo have **already** tried bungee jumping off a bridge.

25.4 🔊
① We've just booked the hotel and now we can book our flights.
② She has already been to Peru but she'd love to go again.
③ He still hasn't taken any photos and he's coming home tomorrow.
④ The plane has just landed and they're waiting to get off.
⑤ We haven't seen a shark yet but we've seen a dolphin.
⑥ I've already called a taxi and it will be here in 10 minutes.
⑦ She still hasn't reached the airport and now she might miss her flight.
⑧ I've just been to the bank and now I can buy some souvenirs.

25.5
① False ② False ③ True ④ Not given
⑤ False ⑥ True ⑦ True

25.6 🔊
① skydiving
② snorkeling
③ hang gliding
④ scuba diving
⑤ windsurfing

25.7 🔊
① We have **just** come back from the beach.
② They haven't tried hang gliding **yet**.
③ I **still** haven't been on safari.
④ Alexia has **already** been snorkeling before.
⑤ I haven't tried windsurfing **yet**.
⑥ We have **just** arrived at the hotel 10 minutes ago.
⑦ He's **already** been skydiving before.
⑧ Tom has **just** called us a minute ago.
⑨ They haven't done much **yet**.
⑩ I **still** haven't finished my work.
⑪ Kai has **already** booked the tour.

25.8
① No ② Yes ③ No ④ No ⑤ Yes

26

26.1 🔊 Note: All answers can also be written in contracted form.
1 Nathan **has been reading** a book in the back yard.
2 I **have been cooking** breakfast in the kitchen.
3 Mike **has been playing** tennis with his friends.
4 Ted and John **have been watching** TV all evening.
5 Mrs. Roberts **has been painting** the house this weekend.

26.2 🔊
1 He has been fishing **since** 3:30pm.
2 We've been learning Spanish **for** six weeks.
3 Ruth has been cooking **for** a long time.
4 You've been decorating **since** March 8.
5 I've been driving **since** 11:45am.
6 He's been teaching science **since** 2012.
7 She's been watching TV **for** two hours.
8 I've been learning to dance **for** two weeks.
9 Alan has been tiling the floor **since** Monday.
10 It has been snowing **for** 10 days.
11 I've been working at home **since** last April.

26.3
1 B 2 D 3 F 4 C 5 E 6 A

26.4
1 for three and a half hours
2 since yesterday
3 since 9 o'clock
4 for two days
5 for five hours

26.5 🔊
1. You've been waiting for 10 minutes.
2. You've been reading for 10 minutes.
3. You've been cooking for 10 minutes.
4. She's been waiting for 10 minutes.
5. She's been reading for 10 minutes.
6. She's been cooking for 10 minutes.
7. You've been waiting since 2 o'clock.
8. You've been reading since 2 o'clock.
9. You've been cooking since 2 o'clock.
10. She's been waiting since 2 o'clock.
11. She's been reading since 2 o'clock.
12. She's been cooking since 2 o'clock.

26.6 🔊
1 We've been **putting** up shelves all day.
2 Jane has been painting the bedroom **since** 10:30am.
3 **They've** been fixing the bathtub for six hours.
4 I've **been** tiling the kitchen since last Monday.
5 He's been fitting the carpet **since** yesterday morning.

26.7
1 shelf 2 carpet 3 bed 4 bathtub
5 tiles 6 curtains

26.8
1 for 2 helping 3 He's been 4 he's been
5 I've been 6 since 7 has been making
8 I've been cooking 9 since I got home

27

27.1 🔊
1 Has Tina been cooking lunch?
2 Have they been visiting friends?
3 Have you been studying the piano?
4 Has Dad been gardening?
5 Have they been training for a race?

27.2 🔊
1 How long have you been living there?
2 How long have you been working at the bank?
3 How long has Nina been teaching English?
4 How long have you been playing hockey?

27.3
1 Japanese 2 Since last summer 3 In high school 4 His grandma 5 Since she was five

27.4 🔊
1 How long **have you** been studying Chinese?
2 How long has he been **cooking** Indian food?
3 How long have they **been** living in Sydney?
4 How long **has** she been mountain biking?
5 How long have you **been** writing a novel?
6 How long **have you** been playing the piano?
7 How long **has** he been salsa dancing?

27.5 🔊
1 How long **has** she been **driving** that car?
2 How long **have** you been **playing** the guitar?
3 How long **has** he been **singing** in the choir?
4 How long **has** he been **cooking** dinner?
5 How long **have** you been **reading** that magazine?
6 How long **has** she been **studying** French?
7 How long **have** they been **working** in that office?
8 How long **have** you been **learning** to drive?

27.6 🔊
1 Since 2012. 2 For two years.
3 Since August. 4 Since last summer.
5 For three days. 6 For six weeks.

28

28.1
1 B 2 A 3 B 4 A

28.2 🔊
1 I've read my magazine. Now I'm going to read a book.
2 Rosa has lost her house keys. She can't get into her house.
3 He has broken the window. There's glass everywhere.
4 Monica has been cleaning the kitchen. Now she's cleaning the bathroom.
5 That little boy has been crying. His eyes are red.
6 Roger has eaten all the pretzels. The package is empty.
7 Alice and Jane have been playing tennis. They're both tired.

28.3 🔊
1 Rebecca **has been swimming**.
2 Victor and Joe **have been playing** soccer.
3 Alexia **has been sweeping** the floor.
4 Thomas **has been repairing** the car.
5 Davina **has been watching** TV.

28.4 🔊
1 I **have liked** all of his plays.
2 Dan **has been watching** TV all afternoon.
3 The movie **has started**.
4 I **have been reading** my book. I haven't finished it yet.

28.5
1 True 2 False 3 Not given
4 True 5 Not given

28.6 🔊   Note: All answers can also be written in contracted form.
1 We **have been listening** to music for hours.
2 John **has not heard** his alarm. Wake him up.
3 The waiter **has taken** our order at last.
4 It **has been raining** all day and they are bored!
5 Gillian **has had** a baby girl.

29

29.1 🔊
1 Amanda is always losing her keys. She is so **disorganized**.
2 The music is so loud it's **impossible** to hear anything.
3 It is **illegal** to smoke in many public places.
4 He **misunderstood** the traffic sign and drove the wrong way.

29.2 🔊
1 Arriving late for work is unacceptable.
2 Andy disagrees with your decision.
3 He's an irresponsible young man.
4 Maria is always impatient with people.
5 It's impossible to park in the city.

29.3 🔊
1 That was an irrational answer.
2 My son is very immature.
3 I disagree with that idea.
4 He's getting very impatient.
5 This exam question is impossible.

29.4 🔊
1 Layla has an **irrational** fear of the dark.
2 My son's friends can be quite **immature**.
3 It's **disrespectful** to laugh during a lecture.
4 Your doctor's handwriting is **impossible** to read.
5 The art exhibition was **unusual**, but interesting.

6 She **misunderstands** everything I say.
7 I **disagree** with your suggestions.
8 Jack can be **irresponsible** sometimes.
9 My boss is often **impatient** with me.
10 Our hotel room was **unacceptable**.
11 He left his room in total **disorder**.
12 It was an **unimportant** decision.
13 The chocolate cookies were **irresistible**.

29.5 🔊
1 misunderstand 2 irresponsible
3 untidy 4 impatient
5 disrespectful 6 immature

29.6
1 overcrowded 2 delayed 3 worse
4 impatient 5 cycle

29.7 🔊
1 There has also been an **accident** on freeway 25.
2 There will be long **delays** of 40–45 minutes because of the accident.
3 There are **overcrowded** trains on the eastern line because of the congestion on the roads.
4 Several trains on the western line have also been **canceled**.
5 The situation has made travel to the suburbs **impossible**.

29.8 🔊
1 It's unacceptable that the trains are so overcrowded.
2 You were very irresponsible to walk home alone after midnight.
3 There's a traffic jam and it will be impossible to get home in time.
4 The luxury chocolate cake in the shop window looked irresistible.
5 The train passengers were unimpressed with the long delays.
6 He wasn't concentrating so he misunderstood what I said.
7 It's illegal to park your vehicle in this parking lot on weekends.
8 They're always late because they're so disorganized all the time.

29.9
1 True 2 Not given 3 True
4 Not given 5 False

30

30.1 🔊
1 **The supermarket** is open on Sundays.
2 I don't like studying for **exams**.
3 **The last movie** I saw was really good.
4 It always rains during **vacations**.
5 I go to **work** by train.
6 He likes reading **the newspaper**.
7 Adam works in **the local hospital**.
8 I hate shopping for **food**.
9 **Fries** aren't good for you.
10 I like **the photo** on your desk.
11 **The boss** is happy with my work.
12 Karen has lots of **shoes**.
13 I like going to **the movie theater**.
14 **The suit** is expensive.
15 I'm going to **the bank** to get a loan.
16 Dan hates **fruit**.
17 I will spend **the money** I got from my aunt.
18 **The car** isn't working.
19 I love **dancing**.

30.2 🔊
1 Where are the keys for the shed?
2 We love playing sports.
3 The dishwasher isn't working.
4 Here's the book I borrowed.
5 The last movie I saw was terrible.
6 That woman has lots of cats.
7 When do you go back to work?
8 The person outside is my uncle.
9 Look at the tablet I bought yesterday.
10 Dentists earn a lot of money.
11 I'm going to the post office.

30.3
Hi Richard,
I've gone to **the post office** to send back **the parcel** that came **last week**. I don't want **the shoes** because they're too big for me. When I've done that, I'll go to **the supermarket** and buy **potatoes** so we can make fries for dinner. Can you check if **the cat** has eaten **the food** I left her? She wasn't feeling very well yesterday. Thanks!
Carla

30.4
1 The campsite is in the south of France.
2 She has to clean the tents.
3 She hates doing the cleaning.
4 They play games and go to the beach.
5 She buys wine from the local vineyard.

⑥ She will go back to college in the middle of September.

30.5 ◀))
① Tom **has** a dog.
② Anna and Sally **have got** a nice apartment.
③ I **have** my own bedroom.
④ She **has got**/She**'s got** a difficult job.
⑤ They **have** a new car.
⑥ I **have got**/I**'ve got** good friends.

30.6 ◀))
1. Do you have your car?
2. Do you have a car?
3. Have you got your car?
4. Have you got a car?
5. Does he have your car?
6. Does he have a car?
7. Has he got your car?
8. Has he got a car?
9. Do you have your computer?
10. Do you have a computer?
11. Have you got your computer?
12. Have you got a computer?
13. Does he have your computer?
14. Does he have a computer?
15. Has he got your computer?
16. Has he got a computer?

30.7
1 Ⓓ 2 Ⓒ 3 Ⓕ 4 Ⓐ 5 Ⓗ 6 Ⓖ 7 Ⓔ 8 Ⓑ

30.8
① True ② True ③ True ④ False
⑤ True ⑥ False ⑦ False

31

31.1 ◀))
① onion ② pasta ③ chicken
④ raspberries ⑤ ice cream ⑥ avocado
⑦ eggs ⑧ lettuce ⑨ potatoes ⑩ peach
⑪ lemonade ⑫ milk ⑬ chocolate
⑭ mango ⑮ beef ⑯ garlic ⑰ burger
⑱ cheese ⑲ tea

32

32.1 ◀))
① We've bought **ourselves** a small apartment in the town.

② The children are amusing **themselves** in the park.
③ Your little sister has fallen over and hurt **herself**.
④ You should both take photos of **yourselves** for Granny.
⑤ Dad burned **himself** while he was making dinner.

32.2 ◀))
① Help **yourself** to some more coffee, Joe.
② Did the kids enjoy **themselves** at the park?
③ The teacher told **us** to be quiet.
④ Has the computer turned **itself** off yet?
⑤ I'm helping **them** to cook lunch.
⑥ Take time off, or you'll make **yourself** sick.
⑦ Can you give **me** that book, please?
⑧ Mom cut **herself** with the bread knife.
⑨ Luckily, I didn't hurt **myself** when I fell.
⑩ I've known **him** since I was in college.
⑪ Everyone, please help **yourselves** to food.

32.3
① themselves ② ourselves
③ himself ④ itself ⑤ her
⑥ you ⑦ it ⑧ me

32.4 ◀))
Eight ounces of butter.
Six ounces of sugar.
Four eggs.
Eight ounces of flour.
Five teaspoons of instant coffee in one tablespoon of hot water.
Half a pint of cream.
Zero point three ounces of walnuts.

32.5
① No ② Yes ③ Yes ④ Yes ⑤ No

32.6
① Six ounces ② Four ③ Four teaspoons
④ One tablespoon ⑤ Eight ounces
⑥ Four ounces

32.7 ◀))
① These strawberries are delicious! So sweet and juicy.
② That soup looks tasty. Can I try some?
③ The best thing to drink on a hot day is some nice chilled orange juice.
④ Oranges can be very bitter if they're not very ripe.
⑤ Those nuts were very salty. They made me really thirsty.

⑥ I like my chilli nice and spicy, so it makes your mouth tingle.

33

33.1 ◀))
① Elsie uses that knife for **chopping** food.
② I use the remote control to **turn on** the TV.
③ My sister uses her blender for **making** soup.
④ He uses this fan to **keep** cool.
⑤ We use this machine for **washing** clothes.
⑥ She uses her laptop to **write** emails.
⑦ They use the sound system to **listen** to music.
⑧ He uses a camera for **taking** photos.
⑨ She uses this cloth to **wash** the dishes.

33.2 ◀))
① I use my phone for texting my friends.
② They use this for washing clothes.
③ She uses that knife for chopping.
④ Larry uses his laptop to send emails.
⑤ We use the refrigerator for keeping fruit.
⑥ I use the DVD player for watching movies.
⑦ She uses the sound system to play music.

33.3 ◀))
① You use it to open cans.
② You use it to dry your hair.
③ You use it to wash the dishes.
④ You use it to take photos.
⑤ You use it to cut vegetables.
⑥ You use it to keep cool.
⑦ You use it to send emails.
⑧ You use it to turn on the TV.

33.4 ◀))
① He chose that knife to cut up the carrots.
② We used the camera to take photos of the puppy.
③ She picked up her phone to text a friend.
④ I used the laptop to send you an email.
⑤ Dan went to the refrigerator to get some milk.
⑥ I turned on the DVD player to watch the movie.
⑦ Emma used the sound system to play music.
⑧ He turned on the microwave to heat up a pizza.
⑨ I used the washing machine to wash my jeans.

⑩ He turned on the sound system to listen to music.

⑪ He used the remote control to rewind the movie.

⑫ Jenny used the can opener to open a can of fruit.

33.5 🔊

① He looked for the can opener to open the can of tomatoes.

② She picked up the cloth to clean the table.

③ They opened the washing machine to put in the laundry.

④ He took the knife to cut up the fruit.

⑤ I looked for the remote control to turn on the TV.

⑥ She put the food in the refrigerator to keep it fresh.

⑦ He used his laptop to write a report.

33.6

① False ② True ③ True ④ False ⑤ True
⑥ True ⑦ True ⑧ True ⑨ False

33.7 🔊

① My phone battery is very low. Can I plug it **in** somewhere?

② There's an important email for you. Shall I print it **out**?

③ The TV is too loud. Can you turn it **down**, please?

④ There's a good movie on TV now. Let's turn it **on**.

⑤ We can't hear the radio. I'm going to turn it **up**.

⑥ I've typed the report for you, but I won't print it **out** yet.

⑦ Let's watch TV. Where's the remote control? I'll turn it **on**.

⑧ I've finished working on my laptop. I'll turn it **off** now.

33.8

① 18 inches ② Remote control
③ Red ④ Super-cool ⑤ Rotate

34

34.1 🔊

① running track ② fishing ③ boxing
④ diving ⑤ basketball ⑥ swimming pool
⑦ archery ⑧ running a marathon
⑨ skis ⑩ motor racing ⑪ judo

⑫ high jump ⑬ golf club ⑭ rugby
⑮ ice hockey ⑯ tennis racket
⑰ table tennis ⑱ baseball ⑲ cycling

35

35.1 🔊

① She can't stand **playing** tennis.

② Do you feel like **watching** a movie?

③ We missed **seeing** you at the party.

④ Andrew didn't agree **to work** on Saturday.

⑤ Joe can't stand **studying** in the evening.

⑥ Nina enjoys **swimming** in the sea.

⑦ We hoped **to pass** the exam easily.

⑧ They decided **to go** out for dinner.

⑨ I don't enjoy **scuba diving**.

⑩ Did she promise **to help** you later?

⑪ She doesn't feel like **going** shopping.

35.2 🔊

① She arranged **to send** the parcel today.

② I can't stand **listening** to jazz.

③ Todd promised **to do** his homework.

④ We missed **seeing** the grandchildren.

⑤ You don't like **riding** a bike.

⑥ Eva didn't expect **to win** a prize.

⑦ I wanted **to go** to bed early.

35.3 🔊

① She promised **to teach** us to swim.

② Edward can't stand **traveling** by bus because it's boring.

③ Alice wanted **to ski** all day with her friends.

④ Do you enjoy **working out** in the gym?

⑤ We don't like **watching** TV during the day.

⑥ I often feel like **meeting** my friends after work.

⑦ Did you decide **to go** shopping after work?

⑧ Duncan can't cope with **sitting** at a desk all day.

⑨ She's waiting **to run** in her first marathon.

35.4 🔊

1. I want to run a marathon.
2. We want to run a marathon.
3. She enjoys playing basketball.
4. She enjoys playing tennis.
5. She can't stand playing basketball.
6. She can't stand playing tennis.
7. I can't stand playing basketball.
8. I can't stand playing tennis.
9. We can't stand playing basketball.
10. We can't stand playing tennis.

35.5 🔊

① I didn't enjoy **sitting** in the stadium for hours.

② He agreed **to play** on the team with his friends.

③ They don't mind **training** three times a week.

④ Will you promise **to go** to the gym with me tomorrow?

⑤ You really love **doing** gymnastics, don't you?

⑥ Their team really didn't expect **to win** the game.

⑦ I miss **running** in the park every day now that we've moved.

⑧ Ian can't stand **watching** other people play sports.

⑨ We're waiting **to use** the squash court, but my friend is late.

35.6

① B ② C ③ F ④ D ⑤ A ⑥ E

36

36.1 🔊 Note: All answers can also be written using the long form of the present continuous.

① We**'re catching** the bus at 10:30am and going to the stadium to watch the game.

② Sarah**'s meeting** me next Sunday to go to the new exhibition at the art gallery.

③ They**'re traveling** to Italy by train. It's a long way, but it will be fun.

④ I**'m trying** a new dance class this evening. It's at the sports center at 7pm.

⑤ He**'s going** to a concert this evening, so he'll be home late.

⑥ We**'re buying** the tickets online because it's cheaper.

⑦ Clare and Hannah **are visiting** their aunt in the hospital this afternoon.

⑧ I**'m getting** up early tomorrow as I have to be at the station at 6am.

⑨ He**'s giving** a presentation to the whole company this afternoon.

⑩ We**'re flying** to Washington to meet our cousins this Christmas.

⑪ Daniel**'s taking** Rachel to the movie theater tonight to see a comedy.

36.2
1 Going to Ben's party
2 Visiting her parents
3 Playing tennis

36.3 🔊
1 She is going to France next year.
2 They are singing in a concert tonight.
3 I am catching a train at 2:20pm.
4 They are playing tennis with us this evening.
5 They are going for a run together tomorrow.

36.4 🔊
1 You should take time out for lunch or you'll get really stressed.
2 We're taking a trip to the mountains this weekend.
3 When you finish your performance, remember to take a bow.
4 If you have a pet, it's important to take good care of it.
5 Should we go to the shopping center and take a look at the new store?
6 We're taking some time off in May to do some work on the house.
7 Let's take a picture of this beautiful view.

36.5 🔊
1 She's taking a **trip** to the country next month.
2 Everyone came into the meeting and took their **seats**.
3 My sister has a dog, and she really takes **care** of it.
4 I'm going to take some time **off** and go on a trip.
5 You should take a **bow** when you finish singing.
6 Let's take a **look** at the photography exhibition.

36.6 🔊
1 Josh likes **taking photos** of old buildings.
2 Jack and Daisy always **take care** of their pet rabbit.
3 Lee finished his performance and **took a bow**.
4 Matt and Ben are **taking a look** at the paintings in the art gallery.
5 Please, **take a seat**.
6 My dad is **taking time off** work and having a vacation.

36.7 🔊
1 I need to **take time off** work next month.
2 Can you help me **take care of** the children this weekend?
3 Let's **take a look** at the new book store.
4 I'm going to **take a trip** to China. I'm really excited.
5 Let's go back onstage and **take a bow**.

37

37.1 🔊
1 Peter's going to learn to swim this year.
2 Lauren's going to train hard for the match.
3 Kate and Amy are going to run in the morning.
4 Cho is going to start a dance class.
5 Ali's going to cycle to work tomorrow.

37.2 🔊 Note: All answers can also be written in contracted form.
1 Joe **is going to walk** his dog in the park every evening after work.
2 Matt **is going to swim** for half an hour a day.
3 Liz **is going to run** four miles every day.
4 Millie and Josh **are going to ride** their bikes in the countryside more often.
5 Debbie and Shinko **are going to do** yoga every week.

37.3
1 False 2 True 3 False
4 True 5 False

37.4 🔊
1 I'm going to have a better diet because I want to be healthier.
2 Matt is going to jog to work because it's good exercise, and it's free.
3 Annie is going to start yoga because she wants to be more relaxed.
4 Lily is going to swim every day, as she wants to get really fit.
5 Si and Tom are going to join a gym because they need to lose weight.
6 I'm going to make a salad for lunch because it's low in fat and nutritious.
7 Shahid is going to stop eating burgers because they aren't healthy.
8 I'm going to join a pilates class because I want to learn something new.

37.5 🔊 Note: All answers can also be written in contracted form.
1 We **are going to go** to the theater. I've already bought the tickets.
2 I **am going to join** a local basketball team.
3 Dan **is going to train** very hard because he has a tennis competition next week.
4 Helen **is going to be** in great shape because she cycles to work every day.
5 We **are going to leave** at 11:30pm to catch the train.
6 Tomorrow evening, they **are going to train** for the game.
7 It's very hot, so it **is going to be** difficult to run today.
8 You **are going to feel** a lot healthier because you're eating better food.
9 I **am going to go** for a long run with Charlotte in the morning.
10 The other team looks very fit. It **is going to be** a difficult match.
11 Wear a coat. It **is going to snow** this afternoon.
12 Sam **is going to lose** weight because he's stopped eating burgers.
13 Jake **is going to get** fitter because he's exercising every day.

37.6 🔊
1 I'm definitely going to start tennis lessons.
2 Sally hopes she's going to lose weight.
3 Ali's certainly going to do more exercise.
4 Beth's probably going to start training for the marathon.
5 My sister thinks she's going to start dance lessons.
6 Jack doubts he's going to join a gym.
7 I'm definitely going to eat healthier foods.
8 We're probably going to cycle to work every day.

37.7 🔊
1. Pete's probably going to run a marathon.
2. Pete's probably going to eat healthier food.
3. Pete's probably going to learn to skate.
4. Pete's probably going to join a gym.
5. Pete's definitely going to run a marathon.
6. Pete's definitely going to eat healthier food.
7. Pete's definitely going to learn to skate.
8. Pete's definitely going to join a gym.
9. Pete thinks he's going to run a marathon.
10. Pete thinks he's going to eat healthier food.
11. Pete thinks he's going to learn to skate.
12. Pete thinks he's going to join a gym.
13. Pete hopes he's going to run a marathon.

14. Pete hopes he's going to eat healthier food.
15. Pete hopes he's going to learn to skate.
16. Pete hopes he's going to join a gym.

38

38.1 ◀))
❶ rainbow ❷ tornado
❸ lightning ❹ clear sky
❺ blustery ❻ hailstone
❼ flood ❽ puddle
❾ smog ❿ raindrop
⓫ snowflake ⓬ blue sky
⓭ drought ⓮ temperature
⓯ chilly ⓰ freezing
⓱ mild ⓲ hot ⓳ boiling

39

39.1 ◀))
❶ Eric and John are **going to** go to the movies on Saturday.
❷ I **will** help you do the dishes, Dad. Go and sit down.
❸ We are **going to** go skiing for our next winter vacation.
❹ He thinks it **will** rain all day today and tomorrow.
❺ I am **going to** go swimming with two friends this afternoon.
❻ Jack is **going to** take the dog for a long walk after dinner.
❼ You look hungry. I **will** make you a chicken sandwich.
❽ Jenny is **going to** study music in college when she leaves school.
❾ I think Argentina **will** win the next World Cup.
❿ Maxine is **going to** have her first baby at the end of August.
⓫ Tomorrow there **will** be heavy rain and risk of flooding.
⓬ In the year 2020, people **will** be healthier than they are now.
⓭ She is **going to** stay with her cousins in Florida next week.
⓮ Don't worry. We **will** get there in plenty of time.
⓯ They are **going to** get married on a Caribbean island in October.

❶⓰ Don't forget to put on some sun cream or you **will** get sunburned.
❶⓱ I promise we **will** be outside the theater before 8:30pm.

39.2
❶ Decision ❷ Offer
❸ Decision ❹ Prediction
❺ Promise ❻ Prediction

39.3 ◀))
❶ The weather will be rainy.
❷ The weather will be windy.
❸ The weather will be cold.
❹ The weather will be foggy.
❺ The weather will be snowy.

39.4
❶ Elena thinks there will be a storm this weekend.
❷ Elena is going to go snowboarding on vacation this year.
❸ Elena thinks she'll call Ann tonight and tell her about her party.

39.5 ◀))
❶ I know he will win the competition.
❷ I will definitely wear a warm coat if it's cold.
❸ The new office will certainly be an improvement.
❹ I doubt she will lose the tennis match.

40

40.1 ◀))
❶ I might take some photos later this afternoon.
❷ She might have gone out. She isn't in her room.
❸ I think it might rain soon. Look at those black clouds.
❹ If the traffic doesn't clear soon, we might be late.

40.2 ◀))
❶ I can't find my house keys. I might have left them at work.
❷ Samantha has a sore throat. She might have caught a cold.
❸ Look at the sky! It's black. There might be a storm soon.
❹ Where's Dan? He isn't at his desk. He might not have come to work today.

❺ These aren't my glasses. I think they might be yours.

40.3 ◀))
❶ The clouds are clearing. It **might not** snow after all.
❷ There was a robbery last night. Someone **might have seen** something.
❸ I don't want to cook tonight. I **might get** a takeout.
❹ Who is in that limousine? It **might be** someone famous.
❺ Did you hear that? I think I **might have dropped** some money.

40.4
❶ True ❷ False ❸ Not given
❹ True ❺ True

40.5 ◀))
❶ Ben might've booked a table for us.
❷ I might not've loaded the dishwasher.
❸ They might've already seen that movie.
❹ She might not've been here before.
❺ He might've caught a cold.
❻ I might not've locked the door.
❼ She might've left the theater.

40.6
1 ❸ 2 ❺ 3 ❼ 4 ❷ 5 ❹ 6 ❻ 7 ❶

41

41.1 ◀))
❶ rest
❷ test results
❸ to vomit
❹ thermometer
❺ x-ray
❻ backache
❼ recovery
❽ tonsillitis
❾ cough
❿ runny nose
⓫ medicine / medication
⓬ food poisoning
⓭ exercise
⓮ drink water
⓯ stitches
⓰ stomach ache
⓱ headache
⓲ pills / tablets
⓳ broken bone

42

42.1 🔊
1. You need to eat healthy food.
2. He can stop taking medicine.
3. It's essential she sees the doctor.
4. She must not get up.

42.2 🔊
1. You **don't have to** make an appointment at the clinic. I'll do it for you.
2. She **must** drink a lot of water. It will help her sore throat.
3. I **don't have to** take any painkillers. I don't need them because I feel better.
4. We all **must** look after ourselves and take care of our health.
5. You **must not** walk on your broken ankle. It needs time to heal.
6. It's the first day of Tanya's vacation today. She **doesn't have to** go to work.
7. Jill **has to** go to hospital for an operation, but it isn't serious.
8. I really **must** diet and do more exercise. I want to lose weight.

42.3
1. True 2. True 3. False 4. True
5. True 6. False

42.4
1. No, she doesn't have to stay in bed, but she must rest.
2. No, she must not drive for four weeks.
3. She has to take painkillers.
4. She must drink at least 1.5 liters.
5. She must call the hospital immediately.

43

43.1 🔊
1. Sam **might** go to the movie theater with Jim after work this evening.
2. Tina has red spots all over her body. She **could** have chicken pox.
3. Frank hasn't replied to my email yet. He might not **be** at work yet.
4. Harriet had a sore throat and a fever yesterday. She **might** be off sick today.
5. Dawn could **be** at the dentist's. She said she had a toothache.

6. Tom should see someone about the pain in his stomach. It might **be** appendicitis.
7. The doctor doesn't think you have broken your arm, but it **could be** a sprain.
8. That rash might not **be** serious, but you should get it checked out.
9. I don't feel very well. I've got a headache and a temperature. I **could have** the flu.
10. John isn't at work yet, which is unusual. He might **be** stuck in traffic.

43.2
1. B 2. F 3. A 4. E 5. C 6. D

43.3 🔊
1. Paula has a high temperature. She could have an infection.
2. Ryu has a stomach ache. It could be appendicitis.
3. Jo has a sore throat, but she can swallow. It might not be tonsillitis.
4. John can't stop coughing. He could have bronchitis.
5. Belinda can't lose weight. She might be eating the wrong sort of food.
6. Sam is covered in red, itchy spots. He could have chicken pox.
7. Tina has a sore wrist. It might be sprained.
8. Alan can't stop sneezing. He thinks it could be hay fever.

43.4 🔊
1. The pain in your arm could be caused by an infection.
2. My sister might not be well enough to go to work today.
3. Karim could not get out of bed because he was so ill.
4. You can't have flu because you don't have a fever.
5. It cannot be hay fever because I'm not allergic.

43.5 🔊
1. Don't worry, you **might** not be allergic to cats. It could be something else.
2. I'm afraid Jonathan's ankle is very swollen. It **could** be broken.
3. Priyanka **can't** have the flu. I saw her last night and she was fine.
4. I'm feeling a bit better today, so the doctor **might** say I can go home tomorrow.
5. My leg is so much better now that I **can** walk about on my own.
6. If someone cancels an appointment, the doctor **might** have time to see you.

43.6 🔊
1. It could be broken.
2. It couldn't be broken.
3. It might not be broken.
4. It can't be broken.
5. He could walk yesterday.
6. He couldn't walk yesterday.
7. He could get out of bed today.
8. He couldn't get out of bed today.
9. He might not get out of bed today.
10. He can get out of bed today.
11. He can't get out of bed today.
12. Her leg could be broken.
13. Her leg couldn't be broken.
14. Her leg might not be broken.
15. Her leg can't be broken.

43.7
1. True 2. False 3. Not given 4. True

44

44.1 🔊
1. Excuse me, could I ask you a question?
2. May I have a glass of water?
3. Hi Monica, can I borrow your pen?
4. Excuse me, could we sit at this table please?
5. Excuse me, may I reserve a table for tonight?
6. Could we rearrange our meeting for tomorrow?
7. May I offer you a cup of coffee?
8. Excuse me, could you move your chair?

44.2 🔊
1. No, you can't. That piece is for Avi.
2. Yes, of course.
3. I'm afraid I'm busy on Tuesday.
4. Yes, sure!
5. I'm afraid all the tickets have been sold.

44.3 🔊
1. **Sure**. Here you go.
2. No, **thank you**.
3. No, **you can't**.
4. **I'm afraid** we're fully booked.
5. Yes, **please**. Thank you.

45

45.1 🔊
1. Elaine gets along **with** her dad.
2. We're **looking** forward to seeing the movie.
3. I came **up** with a solution to the problem.
4. The players look up **to** their coach.
5. Kathy puts up **with** her husband's cooking.
6. Ollie **looks** down on most people.
7. I've run out **of** time. I'm going to be late.

45.2
1. B 2. C 3. E 4. F 5. D 6. A 7. G

45.3
1. False 2. False 3. Not given
4. True 5. False

45.4 🔊
1. We ran out of time.
2. Elena looks up to Jo.
3. Tom puts up with his job.
4. I get along with you.
5. Mark came up with an answer.
6. Sue gets along well with Ian.
7. He looks down on people.

46

46.1 🔊
1. You haven't made any coffee, have you?
2. Peter visited his parents, didn't he?
3. Jane won't wait for us, will she?
4. They've moved to Boston, haven't they?
5. He's really handsome, isn't he?
6. He hasn't met your sister, has he?
7. That wasn't your dog, was it?
8. Oh, no. We're late again, aren't we?
9. Max lived in New York, didn't he?
10. It's beautiful here, isn't it?

46.2 🔊
1. They didn't buy anything, **did** they?
2. You've seen this film, **haven't** you?
3. **We're** very happy about this, aren't we?
4. Trish hasn't been here long, **has** she?
5. Your friends know Mary, **don't** they?
6. They'll buy something, **won't** they?
7. This is a busy street, **isn't it**?
8. You haven't **found** my purse, have you?
9. They didn't look happy, **did** they?

46.3 🔊
1. They left an hour ago, **didn't they**?
2. Keith hasn't arrived yet, **has he**?
3. Sally will do the shopping, **won't she**?
4. Mark doesn't like cooking, **does he**?
5. It isn't raining today, **is it**?
6. Fred has finished painting, **hasn't he**?
7. Rebecca is in London, **isn't she**?
8. You weren't listening, **were you**?
9. We didn't see him, **did we**?

46.4
1. False 2. False 3. Not given
4. True 5. False 6. True

46.5 🔊
1. You shouldn't do that, should you?
2. Daniel would love to go, wouldn't he?
3. I could meet you later, couldn't I?
4. Sue and Aki wouldn't enjoy this, would they?
5. Callum should be here now, shouldn't he?
6. Rachel couldn't finish the exam, could she?
7. She could take the train, couldn't she?
8. They would love this film, wouldn't they?

46.6 🔊
1. We couldn't go to the party, **could we?**
2. Ivan would love to meet you, **wouldn't he?**
3. She wouldn't say anything, **would she?**
4. I could get a taxi, **couldn't I?**
5. He shouldn't be angry, **should he?**
6. You wouldn't do that, **would you?**
7. Katy couldn't make a cake, **could she?**
8. You should be happy, **shouldn't you?**
9. We could shop there, **couldn't we?**
10. Rita shouldn't worry, **should she?**
11. We would help, **wouldn't we?**

46.7
1. False 2. True 3. Not given
4. True 5. Not given 6. True
7. False 8. Not given 9. False

46.8 🔊
1. You shouldn't call now, **should you?**
2. Alice didn't call, **did she?**
3. Jake isn't tired, **is he?**
4. I could help you, **couldn't I?**
5. He wouldn't enjoy it, **would he?**
6. Sarah told you to come, **didn't she?**
7. Nick won't tell anyone, **will he?**
8. You couldn't hold this, **could you?**
9. We haven't met, **have we?**

10. It's noisy here, **isn't it?**
11. Ann would like this, **wouldn't she?**

47

47.1 🔊
1. magnet 2. to pour 3. microscope
4. safety goggles 5. electric shock
6. to float 7. thermometer 8. to repel
9. reaction 10. to freeze 11. battery
12. to sink 13. to boil 14. to mix 15. crystals
16. to melt 17. to attract 18. static electricity
19. gas

48

48.1 🔊
1. If you heat water enough, it boils.
2. When you drop an apple, it falls.
3. If you light a match, it burns.
4. When you drop a rock in water, it sinks.
5. If you put oil in water, it floats.
6. If you cool water enough, it becomes ice.
7. If you squeeze a balloon, it bursts.

48.2 🔊
1. When you **heat** chocolate, it melts.
2. When you **freeze** water, it becomes ice.
3. When you add salt to water, it **dissolves**.
4. If you **drop** an orange, it falls.
5. When you drop a glass, it **breaks**.

48.3 🔊
1. If you **put** a cork in water, it **floats**.
2. When you **heat** metal, it **expands**.
3. When you **drop** a rock, it **falls**.
4. When you **light** paper, it **burns**.

48.4 🔊
1. You make ice if you freeze water.
2. Plants don't grow if there is no sunlight.
3. You get green if you mix yellow and blue paint.
4. The grass gets wet when it rains.
5. You get smoke when you burn wood.

48.5 🔊
1. If you **light** wood, it burns.
2. When you don't water plants, they **die**.
3. If you boil water, it **makes** steam.

④ If you **rub** a balloon, it makes static electricity.
⑤ When you heat ice cream, it **melts**.
⑥ If you **cool** metal, it contracts.
⑦ If you drop a basketball, it **falls**.

48.6
① False **②** True **③** Not given **④** False
⑤ Not given **⑥** True

49

49.1 ◄))
① The water is heated until it boils.
② The thermometer is hung above the water.
③ The results are recorded on the chart.
④ After two minutes, the temperature is taken.
⑤ The water is frozen to make ice.
⑥ The mixture is allowed to cool.
⑦ Gases are released by the reaction.

49.2 ◄))
① The temperature is taken after 10 minutes.
② The oil is heated until it boils.
③ The results are recorded on the chart.
④ The liquid is boiled for 20 seconds.
⑤ The solids are compressed.
⑥ The thermometer is hung above the liquid.
⑦ The chemicals are poured into a measuring cup.
⑧ The gas is measured three times.
⑨ A thermometer is put into the jar.

49.3 ◄))
① The results **are recorded** on the chart.
② The water **is poured** into the tube.
③ The gas **is collected** in a flask.
④ The temperature **is taken** after 30 minutes.
⑤ The water **is heated** for 10 minutes until it boils.
⑥ The jars **are washed** in the laboratory.
⑦ The liquid **is boiled** in a flask for 20 minutes.
⑧ Electricity **is produced** during the experiment.
⑨ Many different calculations **are made** each day.
⑩ The solids **are compressed** for 10 minutes.
⑪ After the experiment, the data **is examined** carefully.

⑫ The thermometer **is hung** above the jar for 15 minutes.
⑬ The cells **are observed** using the latest microscope.

49.4 ◄))
① The water is heated until it boils.
② The gas is collected in a gas flask.
③ The results are recorded every 10 minutes.
④ The temperature is taken with a thermometer.
⑤ The data is examined on the computer.
⑥ The jars are washed and dried.
⑦ The liquid is stirred until the salt dissolves.
⑧ The solids are melted in a jar.
⑨ The chemicals are poured into a measuring cup.

49.5
1 **C** 2 **F** 3 **D** 4 **G**
5 **B** 6 **H** 7 **A** 8 **E**

49.6
① False **②** True **③** False **④** True **⑤** True

49.7 ◄))
① The results **are** recorded on the chart.
② The chemicals are **poured** into a measuring cup.
③ The water is **heated** until it boils.
④ The gases **are** released.
⑤ The liquid is **collected** in a jar.
⑥ The solids **are compressed** for 5 minutes.
⑦ The data is **examined** on the computer.
⑧ The thermometer **is put** into the liquid.
⑨ The temperature **is** taken after 10 minutes.

50

50.1 ◄))   Note: All answers can also use the contracted form of the future with "will."
① If I **go** on vacation, I **will bring** you back a present.
② If I **find** your keys, I **will call** you.
③ If they **visit** Paris, they **will travel** on the metro.
④ If it **doesn't rain**, we **will have** a picnic.

50.2 ◄))
① If I find my screwdriver, I'll fix the cupboard.
② If they don't hurry, they'll be late for work.
③ If we save enough money, we'll buy a new car.

④ If you don't listen to the question, you won't understand the answer.
⑤ If they work hard, they won't fail their exam.

50.3 ◄))
① If I have time, I'll read the paper.
② If you don't eat healthily, you'll be ill.
③ Will you come with me if I walk the dog?
④ If it rains, we'll stay at home.
⑤ If we go to the beach, we'll sunbathe.
⑥ If I see Martha in town, I'll say hello.
⑦ If my son falls over, he won't cry.
⑧ If she loses weight, she'll buy new clothes.
⑨ If I sweep the floor, will you do the dishes?

50.4 ◄))
① She'll move to Vancouver if she gets that job.
② I'll tell you if your wife calls.
③ You'll lose weight if you stop eating bread.
④ He'll have no money if he buys a new car.
⑤ She'll lose her job if she's late for work again.
⑥ I will make a cake if you buy some eggs.
⑦ I won't be angry if you tell me the truth.
⑧ I'll understand if he explains.
⑨ I'll be so happy if they fix the oven.

50.5 ◄))
① You won't get promoted unless you work harder.
② Unless it rains, I'll go for a walk tomorrow.
③ Unless the traffic improves, we'll miss our flight.
④ They won't help you unless you ask them.
⑤ You'll get wet unless you bring an umbrella.
⑥ I won't go to the party unless you come, too.
⑦ You'll be hungry later unless you eat breakfast.
⑧ Unless he slows down, he'll crash the car.
⑨ I'll see you tomorrow unless I have to work late.

50.6 ◄))
① They won't go sailing **unless** there's enough wind.
② **If** Mike goes to New York, he'll see the Statue of Liberty.
③ Tara won't get home on time **unless** the traffic gets better.
④ **If** I go shopping after work, I'll cook us lasagne.

⑤ **If** it snows next week, we'll go skiing.
⑥ Vicky won't be able to make the bed **unless** the sheets are clean.

50.7 ◀))
① If **he works hard**, he'll pass his exam.
② If it's sunny, **I'll wear sunglasses**.
③ If she's hungry, **she'll eat an apple**.
④ Unless **it's cold**, he won't wear a coat.
⑤ If you're sick, **I'll call the doctor**.
⑥ If **he's tired,** he won't stay up late.
⑦ If the kitchen is dirty, **he'll clean it**.
⑧ If **we're bored**, we'll watch TV.
⑨ If I'm thirsty, **I'll drink some water**.
⑩ If the cat isn't frightened, **it won't run away**.
⑪ If you listen carefully, **I'll explain**.

50.8
1 **B**   2 **C**   3 **E**   4 **D**
5 **A**   6 **H**   7 **G**   8 **F**

51

51.1 ◀))
① If you feel sick, don't go to work today.
② Go to bed if you feel tired.
③ If you want to relax, watch a movie on TV.
④ Remember to buy some milk if you go shopping.
⑤ If you're hungry, have a slice of pizza.
⑥ Don't forget your sneakers if you go to the gym.

51.2 ◀))
① If you want a new car, **buy** one.
② Don't stay up late if **you're** tired.
③ If you **see** James, tell him to call me.
④ Don't eat junk food if you want **to** lose weight.
⑤ Remember to shut the door when you **leave**.
⑥ If you like that jacket, **buy** it.
⑦ If you're hungry, **make** a sandwich.

51.3 ◀))
① If you never have any money, don't **overspend**.
② If you don't like your job, **look** for a new one.
③ Learn to relax more if you want to feel **calmer**.
④ **Turn off** your phone if you can't sleep at night.

51.4
① False   **②** True   **③** False
④ Not given   **⑤** True

51.5 ◀))
① If you don't like your job, **find** a new one.
② If you like those jeans, **buy** them.
③ If your tooth hurts, **see** the dentist.
④ If you have too many possessions, **sell** them.
⑤ If you work too hard, **take** some time off.

51.6 ◀))
① If you want to get in better shape, do some exercise.
② If you want to speak Spanish, start a class.
③ If you need some food, go shopping.
④ If you feel tired, take a vacation.

51.7 ◀))
① If you're tired in the morning, go to bed earlier.
② If you want those leather boots, buy them.
③ If you feel hungry, make yourself a cheese sandwich.
④ If you never have any money, don't overspend.
⑤ If you want to learn to swim, take some lessons.

51.8
① Solution   **②** Problem   **③** Problem
④ Solution

52

52.1 ◀))   Note: All answers can also use the contracted form of the future with "will."
① When they **arrive** at the station, I **will get** them.
② As soon as I **get** your message, I **will call** you.
③ When the bus **stops,** we **will get** off.
④ When the movie **ends,** I **will make** us some coffee.
⑤ As soon as the paint **dries,** I **will put** the curtains up.

52.2 ◀))
① When I finish breakfast, I'll go running.
② As soon as he gets home, he'll have lunch.
③ When we get to the theater, I'll buy tickets.
④ When I find a table, I'll order food.
⑤ As soon as I have the money, I'll buy a car.

52.3
① True   **②** True   **③** False
④ False   **⑤** True

52.4 ◀))
① She'll want to live here when she sees this house.
② I'll call you as soon as your cousins arrive.
③ When you see this movie, you'll laugh a lot.
④ We'll get up and dance when the music starts.
⑤ As soon as Tom buys the cheese, I'll make a pizza.
⑥ I'll order a taxi as soon as you're ready.
⑦ When the news finishes, I'll turn off the TV.
⑧ As soon as the train arrives, we'll go home.
⑨ He'll light the fire when it gets really cold.

52.5 ◀))
1. When she arrives, we'll have dinner.
2. When she arrives, I'll call you.
3. As soon as she arrives, we'll have dinner.
4. As soon as she arrives, I'll call you.
5. When I finish work, we'll have dinner.
6. When I finish work, I'll call you.
7. As soon as I finish work, we'll have dinner.
8. As soon as I finish work, I'll call you.

52.6 ◀))
① When they've called our flight number, we'll board the plane.
② As soon as they've finished tiling the kitchen, I'll put up some shelves.
③ When the baby has gone to sleep, we'll cook a nice meal.
④ As soon as we've booked our vacation, I'll buy some new clothes.

52.7
1 **D**   2 **B**   3 **E**   4 **A**   5 **C**

52.8 ◀))
① As soon as we get home, I'll call your mom.
② When she's finished work, she'll do some shopping.
③ When I've done the dishes, we'll watch that movie.
④ As soon as she sees the beach, she'll go swimming.
⑤ As soon as you've sent that email, we'll go home.

52.9 ◀))
1 I'll make soup as soon as I find the blender.
2 As soon as we're ready, we'll order our meal.
3 When he's moved to New York, he'll buy an apartment.
4 You'll love James when you meet him.
5 When you turn on the fan, we'll all feel cooler.

53

53.1 ◀))
1 If he **was** richer, he **would buy** an expensive car.
2 She **would leave** her job if she **won** the lottery.
3 If he **did** more training, he **would get** a better job.
4 If we **sold** our apartment, we **would buy** a house in Athens.
5 They **would help** you if you **asked** them.
6 We **would increase** our sales figures if we **advertised**.
7 If her job **was** easier, she **would be** happier.
8 If I **went** travelling, I **would go** to Thailand.
9 If we **had** the money, we **would start** a business.
10 He **would be** very bored if he **sat** at a desk all day.
11 If they **offered** him a raise, he **would take** it.

53.2 ◀))
1 If he had time, he'd find another job.
2 She'd call him if she knew his number.
3 If I could go anywhere, I'd go to Japan.
4 If we knew their address, we'd visit them.

53.3
1 True 2 False 3 Not given 4 True
5 True 6 True 7 Not given

53.4 ◀))
1 If I won this prize, I'd be very happy.
2 If you got promoted, you'd get a raise.
3 He'd miss his job if he changed companies.
4 They'd call us if they had time.
5 If she studied harder, she'd pass her exams.
6 If I spoke Chinese, I'd get that job.
7 You'd leave your job if you won the lottery.

53.5 ◀))
1 Did you **do** the paperwork this morning?
2 They're **making** too many mistakes.
3 Please don't **make** any more suggestions.
4 I think we should **do** business together.
5 Have you **done** the accounts yet?
6 She's just **making** a call to the manager now.
7 We've **made** an exception in your case.
8 He was able to **make** an appointment for 3pm today.

54

54.1 ◀))
1 lucky 2 surprised 3 furious
4 tired 5 distracted 6 nervous
7 jealous 8 bored 9 intrigued
10 embarrassed 11 disappointed
12 calm 13 terrified 14 relaxed
15 confused 16 stressed 17 lonely
18 irritated 19 pleased

55

55.1 ◀))
1 If I were you, I'd go trekking.
2 If I were you, I would take that job.
3 I wouldn't go to that café if I were you.
4 I would go on vacation if I were you.
5 I'd invest my money if I were you.

55.2 ◀))
1 If I were you, I'd look for a better job.
2 I wouldn't buy that suit if I were you.
3 If I were you, I'd start my own business in the city.
4 I'd go traveling around the world if I were you.

55.3 ◀))
1 If I were you, I'd **go shopping.**
2 If I were you, I'd **take an umbrella.**
3 If I were you, I'd **look for another Job.**
4 If I were you, I'd **cut my hair myself.**
5 If I were you, I'd **buy him a present.**
6 If I were you, I'd **go to the doctor.**
7 If I were you, I'd **buy a new one.**

55.4
1 Asking 2 Giving 3 Giving
4 Asking 5 Giving

55.5 ◀))
1 What about **buying a new laptop and printer for our son's birthday?**
2 Have you tried **learning how to cook healthy Indian food?**
3 What about **taking a vacation on the Italian Riviera this summer?**
4 How about **discussing the sales figures with the team after the meeting?**
5 Have you thought of **getting a new desk and chair for the office?**
6 Have you tried **applying for a new job in sales and marketing?**
7 What about **trying the new Italian restaurant for dinner tonight?**

55.6 ◀))
1 What about **going** home early?
2 How about **buying** a new car?
3 What about **visiting** us later?
4 Have you tried **talking** about it?
5 How about **organizing** a meeting?
6 Have you thought of **investing** your money?
7 Have you tried **drinking** less coffee?

55.7 ◀))
1 My car is 10 years old.
Have you thought of buying a new one?
2 I want to leave my job.
If I were you, I'd look for a new one.
3 It's cold and wet outside.
If I were you, I'd take an umbrella.
4 My home looks old-fashioned.
If I were you, I'd redecorate it.
5 It's my boss's birthday.
How about buying her a card?
6 I'm meeting an important client.
If I were you, I'd dress up.
7 I never have enough money.
If I were you, I wouldn't overspend.
8 My boyfriend and I had an argument.
Have you tried calling him?
9 This fish tastes bad.
If I were you, I wouldn't eat it.

55.8

1 I wouldn't worry 2 If I were you
3 Have you thought of practicing
4 I'd think 5 If I were you 6 I'd buy
7 How about asking

56

56.1 ◄»

1 If I get more qualifications, I'll get a better job.
2 Anna will take me to the airport if I ask her.
3 They would be angry if we were late for the meeting.
4 If I win the lottery, I'll buy my parents a house.
5 If Grant had enough money, he'd buy himself a new car.
6 If my boss gave me a raise, I'd have a party for my friends.

56.2 ◄»

1 **I wouldn't like** it if I became a famous celebrity.
2 If **we catch** the next train, we'll get there in time.
3 You would remember her if **you met** her again.
4 Henry **would be** so happy if he got that promotion.
5 If we arrive there first, **we'll save** you a seat.

56.3 ◄»

1 It would be amazing if I could play the guitar.
2 If I had my phone with me, I'd take a photo of that.
3 If you wear a coat today, you won't feel cold.
4 If you vacuum the living room, I'll do the dishes.
5 I'd build more hospitals if I were the President.
6 If we had more time, we could have lunch together.
7 If the baby stops crying, I'll watch some TV.
8 If you say anything, she won't listen.
9 I'll text you if you give me your number.
10 If that company won an award, I'd be surprised.
11 Chris will make dinner if you buy the food.
12 If you ask the sales assistant, she'll help you.
13 If she saw a snake, she wouldn't be afraid.

56.4

1 True 2 False 3 Not given
4 True 5 Not given

56.5

1 They need to give priority to online sales.
2 Jackson is going to give it some thought.
3 The sales team will hold weekly meetings.
4 They will set new goals and review figures.
5 He will hold talks with his senior staff.
6 He wants his team to set a precedent for the rest of the company.

56.6 ◄»

1 She **sets** a limit on the time we can take off.
2 Can you **hold** off on sending that report until I've checked it?
3 Melanie has just **given** some great advice to her staff.
4 Do we need to **hold** a meeting after lunch today?
5 Would you **give** me some help with this report?
6 They decided to **set** an easier target this month.
7 I haven't **given** much thought to that proposal yet.
8 The company has **set** limits on staff expenses.
9 Do you know when they're going to **hold** talks?
10 Our company has **set** a precedent for excellence.
11 Rohit always **sets** weekly goals to motivate his team.
12 My boss is happy to **give** help to anyone who asks him.
13 The company **held** discussions to decide plans for the year.
14 Not enough companies **give** priority to training.

56.7 ◄»

1. We held talks last week.
2. She held talks last week.
3. We set targets last week.
4. She set targets last week.
5. We set targets for the year 2020.
6. She set targets for the year 2020.
7. We gave some help to the junior staff.
8. She gave some help to the junior staff.

57

57.1 ◄»

1 That's the woman who got a good promotion.
2 Is that the store that sells computer software?
3 Jamie has met a woman who is cheerful and kind.
4 He's the teacher who teaches Spanish.
5 A butcher is someone who sells meat.
6 You should go on a diet that is healthy.
7 That's the apple tree that we planted last year.
8 I'd like a job that is exciting and well paid.
9 We want to buy a house that is near the coast.

57.2 ◄»

1 I like the woman **who works** at reception.
2 We bought some furniture **that was too** expensive.
3 They went to a restaurant **that I recommended**.
4 Jenny is going out with a man **who knows** you.
5 Mr. Jason has a son **who has been** a lawyer since 2009.
6 Lance is my friend **who lived in Tokyo** for six months.
7 It's important to have a diet **that is healthy**.
8 I'd like to meet someone **who can speak** Italian.
9 Is that the sports channel **that shows** baseball?

57.3

1 C 2 F 3 H 4 B 5 J 6 D
7 G 8 A 9 I 10 E

57.4 ◄»

1 conscientious 2 reliable 3 calm
4 fun-loving 5 self-confident

57.5

1 humble 2 lazy 3 polite
4 shy 5 boring 6 mean

57.6 ◄»

1 I know an interesting man who plays the saxophone.
2 Eva bought a new dress that cost a fortune!
3 We have a Chinese manager who comes from Shanghai.

4 I have a new boss who is good-humored and cheerful.

5 Melanie didn't like the shoes that were on sale.

6 Joe is a student who is studying for his accountancy exams.

7 She often goes to a café that is near the river.

8 He's a famous author who has sold millions of books.

9 He wants a new job that is well paid and interesting.

10 I'm working on a project that is really exciting.

58

58.1 🔊

1 My colleagues, **who are good friends**, are very funny.

2 My sister's dog, **which is small and black**, doesn't have a tail.

3 His cousin Bastian, **who sings**, is a great performer.

4 Her Italian teacher, **who comes from Naples**, is really outgoing.

5 My friend Ed, **who's a chef**, has a new job in a restaurant.

6 Their summer house, **which is on the coast**, is really expensive.

7 The weather today, **which is terrible**, should improve later.

8 The office chair, **which is new**, is really uncomfortable.

58.2 🔊

1 My house keys, which I lost somewhere, have been found by the police.

2 Alexia's grandmother, who is 84 this year, plays tennis twice a week.

3 The new art gallery, which will open next year, is such a beautiful building.

4 A friend of Dad's, who told me about this job, is the CEO.

5 Our neighbor Giles, who you met once, is coming for dinner on Friday.

58.3 🔊

1 The evening classes, **which** I'm starting next week, are now completely full.

2 Sunita, **who** works in marketing, is very good at her job.

3 My car, **which** is ten years old, is always breaking down.

4 The mail, **which** is usually here by 8:30am, was late this morning.

5 The blizzards in Canada, **which** started three days ago, are now over.

58.4 🔊

1 My friend Peter, **who** lives in Norway, is coming to stay.

2 The new sales assistant, **who** starts next week, is called Ivan.

3 Is the beautiful house, **which** is across from the park, for sale?

4 Linda's colleague Eva, **who** moved to Brazil, has sent us an email.

5 Alex, **who** always plays the lottery, has won it at last!

6 The gallery, **which** we visited last year, has a wonderful collection of paintings.

7 Calum, **who** went to school with me, is my oldest friend.

8 The Black Friday sales, **which** I can't stand, are starting next week.

9 Georgina, **who** works at the bank, is getting married to Tom.

58.5

1 C 2 E 3 A 4 F 5 B 6 D

58.6

1 Not given 2 False
3 Not given 4 True
5 True 6 False
7 True 8 False

58.7 🔊

1. The café, which we really like, isn't expensive.

2. The café, which we really like, is near the park.

3. My friend, who we really like, has moved to Boston.

4. My friend, who works for the bank, has moved to Boston.

59

59.1 🔊

1 Elliot **was having** lunch with his friends from college.

2 This time last week we **were singing** in the local choir.

3 Olivia **was doing** her homework when I called at her house.

4 They **were playing** in the front yard yesterday morning.

59.2 🔊

1 You shouldn't take advantage of people.

2 It takes time to learn something new.

3 They were having a discussion outside.

4 I didn't take a view one way or another.

5 Scientists make new discoveries every day.

6 I've never had the chance to travel.

7 Will you have a discussion about it?

8 She had the chance of a lifetime.

9 I tried to make sense of the argument.

59.3 🔊

1 Your father **was driving** to work.

2 We **were picking** apples in the back yard.

3 Daniela **was talking** to her friends.

4 You **were waiting** at the train station.

5 The bus **was stopping** outside the post office.

6 Terry and Ian **were working** late on Tuesday.

7 She **was walking** across the street.

8 It **was raining** yesterday afternoon.

9 They **were washing** the dishes in the kitchen.

59.4 🔊

1 make an effort, make sense, make a discovery

2 take time, take advantage, take a view

3 have a discussion, have a chance, have a plan

59.5

1 True 2 False 3 True 4 False
5 True 6 True 7 False

59.6 🔊

1 You have to **make an effort** if you want to succeed.

2 It **took time** to learn the truth.

3 Did the police **make a discovery** at the house?

4 They **had a discussion** about the problem.

5 She often **takes advantage** of people.

6 Did you **have a chance** to see the movie?

7 He **took the view** that it was a bad decision.

60

60.1 ◀)))
1. Sun
2. Moon
3. planet
4. star
5. tiger
6. leaf
7. elephant
8. bear
9. parrot
10. whale
11. mosquito
12. lizard
13. rhino
14. grass
15. monkey
16. turtle
17. spider
18. tree
19. owl

61

61.1 ◀)))
1. The birds **were singing** in the trees in the beautiful, open countryside.
2. Children **were playing** soccer in the park.
3. The young man **was sitting** on the beach under a starry sky.
4. It was a stormy night and the wind **was blowing** through the trees.
5. Bees **were buzzing** around the garden on this hot summer afternoon.

61.2
1 Ⓐ 2 Ⓒ 3 Ⓔ
4 Ⓑ 5 Ⓕ 6 Ⓓ

61.3
1. They were running along the sidewalk.
2. The sun was shining brightly.
3. The air smelled of wild flowers.
4. She was sitting on a bench across from the supermarket.
5. She was waiting for her mother.
6. A large black bear was walking toward her.
7. He was driving into town.

61.4 ◀)))
1. rural 2. peaceful
3. colorful 4. magnificent

62

62.1 ◀)))
1. When we **were driving** to the hotel, our car **got** a flat tire.
2. Eva **was having** lunch when Henry **called** her.
3. She **lost** her purse while she **was shopping**.
4. I **met** my cousin while I **was having** coffee in town.
5. We **stayed** in a hotel while we **were visiting** Amsterdam.
6. Terry **knocked** over the can when he **was painting** his room.
7. She **was writing** an email when her boss **asked** to see her.
8. When Sarah **got** home, Luke **was loading** the dishwasher.
9. You **were running** in the park when I **cycled** past you.
10. Rita **was walking** to work when she **saw** a robbery.
11. I **called** a taxi while I **was waiting** for a friend.

62.2 ◀)))
1. Oscar **was watching** TV when we **arrived** from the airport.
2. Rose **was drying** the dishes when she **dropped** a plate.
3. I **fell** off my chair when I **was fixing** the light in the kitchen.
4. Lloyd **hurt** his ankle while he **was skiing** down the mountain.
5. They **were listening** to the radio as they **drove** home.
6. Shelley **was playing** the piano when the phone **rang**.
7. Lucy **fell** and hurt her arm when they **were hiking** near the hills.
8. The cat **was chasing** a mouse when it **ran** across the road.
9. Alex **met** Sam when he **was walking** down the street.

62.3 ◀)))
1. Ben saw Rachel in the post office when he was mailing a package.
2. They were reading the menu when the waiter came to their table.
3. We saw a turtle when we were swimming in the ocean.
4. I was leaving the party when everyone started to dance.
5. Brad was eating a hot dog when he spilled ketchup on his shirt.
6. They were playing outside when it started to rain.
7. Maria was cooking dinner when she burned her hand.
8. I saw the Eiffel Tower when I was walking around Paris.

62.4
1. True 2. False 3. False 4. True 5. False

62.5 ◀)))
1. While we **were shopping**, we **met** Janey at the mall.
2. I **was writing** an email when you **texted** me.
3. Francis **tiled** the bathroom while he **was staying** with us.
4. Tom **was looking** for his phone when he **found** his wallet.
5. The train **arrived** while you **were buying** a newspaper.
6. Rita **was walking** in the park when she **saw** a squirrel.
7. We **learned** Spanish while we **were living** in Madrid.
8. They **waited** under a tree while it **was raining**.
9. They **were sweeping** the floor when he **knocked** on the door.

62.6
1. True 2. False 3. True 4. False 5. False
6. False 7. True 8. False 9. False

63

63.1 ◀))) Note: All answers with the contracted negative past simple passive can also use the long form.
1. Many people **were injured** in the train accident last night.

2 A man and two children **were rescued** after the boat capsized in the lake.

3 Too many trees **were cut down** last year.

4 Thankfully, people's homes **weren't flooded** during the storms last week.

5 The country's most beautiful river **was polluted** by industrial chemicals.

6 The old office building **wasn't demolished**. It was restored instead.

7 The beaches **were covered** in oil when the oil tanker sank off the coast.

8 The animals **weren't hurt** when there was a fire at the zoo.

9 The hotel **was destroyed** by a hurricane last summer.

10 Toxic chemicals **were spilled** onto the road when a truck crashed into the barrier.

11 Three men **were questioned** by the police after the incident.

63.2 ◀))

1 Chemicals were **released** into the air.

2 The factory was **destroyed** yesterday.

3 The lake wasn't **polluted** with oil.

4 The drinking water **was contaminated**.

5 Some of the animals were **killed**.

6 The trees **were** all cut down.

7 The animals and birds **were** rescued.

8 Many fish **were found** dead.

9 All the passengers were **rescued**.

10 The train line wasn't **damaged**.

11 Some people **were injured**.

12 The café wasn't **destroyed** in a fire.

13 All the fields were **flooded**.

14 Our train was **delayed** for an hour.

15 Many dolphins were **saved**.

63.3

1 Passive **2** Active **3** Passive **4** Passive

63.4 ◀))

1 The train line was damaged.

2 The trees were cut down.

3 The office building was demolished.

4 The forest was burned down.

5 The animals were rescued.

63.5 ◀))

1 The beaches were covered in oil yesterday.

2 All the trains were delayed on the weekend.

3 The buildings weren't flooded during the storm.

4 Some people were injured in the fire.

5 The train line was damaged during the storm.

63.6 ◀))

1 The **oil spill** happened when the oil tanker sank.

2 The explosion was caused by a **gas leak** in the factory.

3 **Smog** is caused when polluted air mixes with fog.

4 Droughts in some parts of the world may lead to **famine**.

5 Soil erosion is sometimes caused by **deforestation**.

6 Twelve people were rescued from the sea after the **shipwreck**.

7 The **flood** happened when the river burst its banks.

63.7

1 Eighteen crew were rescued.

2 They were taken to the hospital.

3 Thousands of gallons of oil were spilled into the ocean.

4 The sea birds were covered in oil.

5 Thousands of dead fish were found on the beach.

64

64.1 ◀))

1 The movie **had started** by the time we **arrived** at the movie theater.

2 It **was** the most impressive sculpture I **had seen** for a long time.

3 They **closed** the road because there **had been** an accident.

4 Mary **had done** the shopping before I **could** offer to help.

5 Gregory **had traveled** around Asia before he **went** to college.

6 She **hadn't seen** him for years, but it **was** just like old times.

64.2 ◀))

1 The gallery **called** for my painting before I **had finished** it.

2 She **knew** she had met Peter and Sarah somewhere before.

3 When I **got** home, I realized I **had forgotten** my car key at my friend's house.

4 Some people **had** already left when we arrived at my friend's birthday party.

64.3 ◀))

1 The thieves broke into the house because he had forgotten to lock the door.

2 He hadn't seen the hole in the road so he drove into it.

3 She put on a warm coat because it had started to snow.

4 He didn't cook dinner until he had taken the dog for a walk.

5 They really enjoyed the meal we had cooked for them.

6 You didn't ask me how my interview had gone.

7 I couldn't remember where they had been on vacation.

64.4

1 **E** 2 **F** 3 **B** 4 **A** 5 **C** 6 **D**

64.5 ◀))

1 I called the office, but everyone **had already left**.

2 Finn **watched the movie** again even though he had already seen it.

3 Helen was sorry that she **hadn't been** kinder.

4 Paul **went to** bed after he had loaded the dishwasher.

5 He **finished his meal** before anyone else had finished theirs.

6 Liz called Jill but she **had turned off** her phone.

7 I couldn't remember where we **had met** before.

8 I'm sorry you **didn't know** that we had already gone out.

9 He **bought some jeans** after he had tried on three pairs.

10 The waiter left after he **had taken** our orders.

64.6 ◀))

1 She **wasn't** hungry because she **had already eaten**.

2 Grant **had** already **made** dinner when Rosa **got** home.

3 Anna **felt** tired because she **had been** shopping all day.

4 He **passed** his driving test because he **had had** a lot of lessons.

5 Eric **sent** the report to his boss after he **had checked** it.

64.7

1 If they had had cowpox, they didn't catch smallpox.

2 Jenner infected a small cut on the little boy's arm.

3 The little boy recovered.

4 Jenner infected the little boy after he had recovered from cowpox.

5 The little boy didn't get smallpox.

6 He didn't get smallpox because the cowpox had protected him.

65

65.1 🔊

1 It was the first time we had **ever** eaten sushi. We loved it.

2 We stayed in Seville. I had **never** seen flamenco dancing before.

3 It was the first time he had **ever** ridden a horse. He fell off twice!

4 She had **never** been scuba diving before. She saw a beautiful turtle.

5 It was the first time she had **ever** visited Paris. She saw the Eiffel Tower.

6 He was so happy. He had **never** had so many birthday presents.

7 We had **never** run a marathon before. It was totally exhausting.

8 It was the first time I had **ever** seen the Great Pyramids. They were amazing.

9 He didn't know what to do. He had **never** had a flat tire before.

10 They weren't happy. They had **never** had such bad service before.

11 It was awesome! It was the first time I had **ever** flown in a helicopter.

65.2 🔊

1 Eva is very excited. She has never seen a play at the theater before.

2 He loved it. It was the first time he had ever driven a sports car.

3 Robin has broken his leg. It is the first time he has ever been to a hospital.

4 They had never visited Rio de Janeiro before. It was amazing.

65.3

1 Jaipur 2 the elephant festival
3 No, he hasn't. 4 Thailand
5 A Buddhist temple

65.4

Hi Phil,

This is the first time we have **ever been** to Spain. We've just spent the morning in the Barrio Santa Cruz in Seville. It has been **popular** with tourists for years and the streets are lined with **charming** old flats. It's a long way from the modern **high-rise** apartment buildings. Then, we walked to the Alcázar, an **ancient** palace. We **had never** seen anything so beautiful.

See you soon!

Lily

65.5 🔊

1 I had never tried water sports before I learned to sail and windsurf.

2 It's the first time I have ever ridden a camel in the desert.

3 It was the first time they had ever been on a safari in Africa.

4 It's the first time we have ever visited the Metropolitan Museum in New York.

66

66.1 🔊

1 feel under the weather
2 pull someone's leg
3 be a pain in the neck
4 face the music
5 sit on the fence
6 be head over heels
7 keep an eye on
8 hear something on the grapevine
9 lend a hand
10 be against the clock
11 get cold feet
12 let your hair down
13 have a heart of gold

67

67.1 🔊

1 We **were driving** home when a rabbit **ran** across the road.

2 She **went** to Japan last year because she **had wanted** to go for years.

3 He **bought** a house in the Caribbean after he **had won** the lottery.

4 Marianne **was living** in Lisbon when she **met** her husband.

5 I **was sunbathing** by the pool when a huge insect **landed** on my arm.

6 We **were walking** home one night when we **saw** a strange light in the sky.

7 I **was** nervous because I **had never been** skiing before.

8 I **offered** them some lunch, but they **had already eaten**.

9 When we **returned**, someone **had stolen** all our luggage.

10 They **were climbing** in the Rockies when they **heard** an avalanche.

11 The party **had already begun** by the time we **arrived**.

67.2 🔊

1 The old lady had just arrived home when the doorbell rang loudly.

2 Elliot had had enough of her bad behavior and he decided to leave.

3 Milly was waiting for her interview when her father sent her a text.

4 I had just gone to bed when I realized I had forgotten to lock the door.

5 You couldn't read the message because you hadn't put on your glasses.

67.3 🔊

1 A small crowd of people **had gathered** around him to listen.

2 He stopped playing and the people **clapped** politely and started to walk away.

3 The man quickly put down his guitar and **opened** his violin case.

4 He looked down at his small gray dog that **was sleeping** at his feet.

5 As soon as the young man **started** to play, the little dog **woke up**.

6 It began to bark and jump around enthusiastically. The crowd **returned** to watch the spectacle.

67.4 🔊

1 The little girl was crying because she had lost her teddy bear.

2 I had just opened my front door when I saw a large package in the hall.

3 Luke was walking across the street when he found a wallet on the ground.

4 She had just fallen asleep when a noise outside woke her up.

5 They were watching the storm when they saw the lightning strike.

6 Ellie hadn't expected to marry Tim until he proposed to her on the beach.

7 Mary was eating an apple when she broke one of her teeth.

8 It was a cold, dark night and the wind was howling in the trees.

67.5 🔊

1 They were scuba diving in the Indian Ocean when they **saw** a pod of dolphins.

2 When Sue arrived at the party she realized that she **had forgotten** Jo's present.

3 It was the first time she **had ever been** on vacation alone.

4 Ronnie **was waiting** for his bus when he saw a young man steal a car.

5 They **had just started** eating their meal when the waiter fainted.

6 As he **watched** the car drive away he knew he would never see her again.

7 A small group of people **were standing** on the platform when they heard a scream.

8 She **was running** for the train when she tripped and her bag burst open.

9 Harry was looking through his telescope when he thought he **saw** a UFO.

67.6 🔊

1 Mr. Foster sat on the fence.

2 The sales team is always on the ball.

3 Linda had to face the music.

4 Robert's reply hit the nail on the head.

5 Your little brother can be a pain in the neck.

67.7 🔊

1 Dev's reaction to the news was over the top.

2 Oliver is feeling under the weather so he's staying in bed.

3 Mrs. Salter is keeping an eye on the twins this afternoon.

4 Jane and Calum are head over heels in love.

5 Anna is very kind. She's got a heart of gold.

6 Maxine heard about Jill's wedding on the grapevine.

68

68.1 🔊

1 She was always late for work, and **consequently** lost her job.

2 We got to the station at 8:50pm and left **shortly afterward**.

3 Call me **as soon as** you get home tonight.

4 **Not long before** we got to the bar, it started to snow.

5 Sue was leaving the store **at the very moment** that we got there.

68.2 🔊

1 **Not long before** I called him, he sent me an email.

2 He worked hard, and **consequently** was promoted.

3 **Just as** he was leaving, a parcel arrived.

4 Jack called **just as** I got home from work.

5 I got on the Number 8 bus and saw the Number 10 bus **shortly afterward**.

6 **As soon as** I heard the news, I told Phil.

7 She ate too much, and **consequently** felt sick.

8 **Just as** I was finishing my lunch, Dan walked in.

68.3 🔊

1 He drove too fast, and **consequently** was fined by the police.

2 I got to the party at 8pm, and Anne arrived **shortly afterward**.

3 We decided to go inside **as soon as** it started raining.

4 They had had a baby **not long before** they moved.

68.4 🔊

1 She bought an expensive car shortly **after** getting an exciting new job.

2 I called my parents as soon **as** I got the results of my exams.

3 The woman slipped on the ice and **subsequently** fell into the water.

4 Pippa had dropped her phone in a puddle not **long before** it stopped working.

68.5

1 Joe couldn't come hiking because someone had crashed into his car not long before.

2 As soon as they heard the news, Henry's friends said he shouldn't go.

3 Shortly after setting off, Henry realized he had lost his compass.

4 Not long after he set off, it started to get cloudy and rain.

5 By the time Henry had walked for two hours, he could hardly see in front of him.

68.6 🔊

1 Not long before she got home, her phone rang.

2 He was late getting to the station. Consequently, he missed the train.

3 Just as she blew out the candles, everyone started clapping.

4 Just as Tom was leaving, I realized he'd left his phone on the table.

5 She got home late, and fell asleep shortly afterward.

68.7

1 True   2 False   3 True   4 False

69

69.1 🔊   Note: All answers can also omit "that."

1 He said that he was a police officer, and he wore a uniform to work every day.

2 She said that she went swimming every Tuesday evening at the sports center.

3 She said that she worked in a travel agency in the southern part of a busy town.

4 You said that Sarah and her sister liked listening to jazz music and playing the piano.

5 She said that they wanted to go to Mexico on vacation with their friends.

6 They said that they usually ate sandwiches for lunch and had a hot meal in the evening.

7 She said that Tom ran really fast and took part in lots of competitions.

8 He said that he didn't like getting up in the morning, and he was always tired at work.

9 She said that he didn't watch TV in the evenings because he was too busy at work.

69.2 🔊

1 He said that he liked the color blue.

2 They said that they went camping every year.

③ She said that she had bought a car.

④ I said that I liked visiting Vancouver.

⑤ He said that he didn't eat red meat.

69.3 🔊

① Amy and Jo are going to the bus stop. They said they were going to town.

② Rosa exercises every day. She said she liked to be healthy.

③ Tom usually cooks on Tuesdays. He said he liked new recipes.

④ Mary has been studying all morning. She said she was really tired.

⑤ Tom and Lisa didn't go swimming. They said the pool was closed.

69.4 🔊   Note: All answers can also omit "that."

① She said that she worked in a bookshop in a small village located near the lake.

② They said that they usually ate salad at lunchtimes during the week.

③ He said that he didn't like cycling downtown as it was very crowded.

④ They said that they would probably visit their aunt in Italy to celebrate her birthday.

⑤ She said that they were going to the theater on Tuesday.

⑥ He said that Jane was working abroad as a teacher.

⑦ She said that he was learning to play the guitar.

⑧ She said that they had lived in that house for a year.

⑨ He said that she was studying Japanese at the local college.

69.5   Note: All answers can also include "that."

① He said it was a really amazing country.

② He said he had spent three weeks in Queenstown.

③ He said he was working as a waiter in a busy restaurant.

④ He said the pay was good.

⑤ He said he had to help out in the kitchen.

⑥ He said he had been able to save some money.

⑦ He said people came to Queenstown to do adventure sports.

⑧ He said he was going to stay there for a few more weeks.

⑨ He said he would see his cousins in Australia.

70

70.1 🔊

① We **told** him that we could help.

② He **told** me that he had a sister.

③ Tina **said** that she lived in the suburbs.

④ You **said** that you would do the dishes.

⑤ I **told** him that I had to work late.

⑥ Rob **said** that he loved his job.

⑦ You **told** us it was your birthday.

70.2 🔊

① Henry told us that he had a new car.

② We told him that the film was boring.

③ I told Jim to call you in the evening.

④ Maria said that it was her bike.

⑤ They told us it would start in 10 minutes.

⑥ We told them the food was bad.

⑦ I said that I wanted to leave early.

⑧ Gina told me it was her anniversary.

⑨ Leo said that he enjoyed dancing.

70.3 🔊   Note: All answers can also omit "that."

① She told him **that she wanted to buy a car**.

② I told them **that I was going to Buenos Aires on vacation**.

③ We said **that we had really enjoyed the party**.

④ He told her **that he was going to redecorate the house**.

⑤ She said **that she bought / had bought a new skirt that morning**.

⑥ He told them **that the weather was looking bad**.

⑦ We told you **that we would look after your cat**.

⑧ I said **that it was your turn to make dinner**.

⑨ She told us **that we needed to buy a present for Mom**.

⑩ We said **that we were going to do some gardening**.

⑪ They told me **that they would wait for me outside**.

⑫ She said **that we could make ourselves some coffee**.

70.4

① True ② False ③ True

④ Not given ⑤ False

70.5 🔊

① She told Mark she **was** still in the office.

② She said she **was going to be** late getting home.

③ She said her boss **had just given** her a report to write.

④ She said she **didn't know** why he hadn't given it earlier.

⑤ She told Mark she **had made** pizza the day before.

⑥ She said they **would have** the pizza when she got home.

⑦ She said she **would have** to work early the next day.

70.6 🔊

① I can't **tell** the difference between the twin brothers. They look the same!

② When I saw them at the market I **said** hello and had a chat.

③ He said he wanted to **say** something to me about my sister.

④ I knew John wasn't **telling** the truth. He's such a liar!

⑤ You should **tell** someone if you're stressed at work.

⑥ Pete **told** me he had a fantastic vacation in Bali this summer.

70.7 🔊

1. I said we were going out.

2. We said we were going out.

3. I said you wanted a new car.

4. We said you wanted a new car.

5. I told them we were going out.

6. We told them we were going out.

7. I told them you wanted a new car.

8. We told them you wanted a new car.

70.8 🔊

① People won't believe you if you always **tell** lies.

② I **told** a "white lie" because I didn't want to hurt his feelings.

③ We were told that we should always **tell** the truth.

④ You should **say** no if they ask you for help again. You're too busy.

⑤ The witness wouldn't **say** anything about the court case.

⑥ Let me **tell** you a story about my childhood.

⑦ Don't believe that he's being honest just because he **says** so.

⑧ I asked my girlfriend to marry me, and she **said** yes.

⑨ Can you **tell** the difference between African and Asian elephants?

⑩ He spoke so quietly we didn't hear him **say** hello to us.

⑪ It's so dark today that I can't **tell** the difference between day and night.

⑫ Grandpa **told** us stories all the time when we were little.

⑬ My mother **told** me to always be polite to adults, no matter what.

⑭ She **said** she preferred apples to oranges any day.

71

71.1
① agree **②** admit **③** claim **④** argue
⑤ explain **⑥** add

71.2 🔊
① He agreed that climate change was a serious problem.

② You claimed that this diet would work.

③ Her brother admitted that he couldn't swim.

71.3 🔊
① He admitted that she **was** right.

② I **explained that** I had lost my passport.

③ We **argued** that the office was too hot.

④ Katy agreed that his car **was** fantastic.

⑤ He **claimed that** he knew Alan David.

⑥ I added that we **could** all have coffee.

⑦ He **admitted that** the apartment was too small.

⑧ She **claimed that** she never ate chocolate.

⑨ I argued **that we** needed more vacations.

⑩ They explained that there **was** a sale.

⑪ Liz **added** that it was also cheaper.

⑫ She admitted that she **didn't** know.

71.4 🔊
① The director admitted that the profits were down.

② Alex claimed that he had won the lottery.

③ He argued that dogs were nicer than cats.

④ Peter admitted that he hated rock music.

⑤ She explained that the movie had already started.

⑥ The assistant added that the shoes were in the sale.

71.5 🔊
① He **admitted that they didn't have** enough money to buy two flight tickets.

② He **argued that the house was** too small for a birthday party.

③ She **argued that they didn't have** time to wait for a bus.

④ She **agreed that this was** the best Chinese restaurant in the city.

⑤ You **claimed that you invested / claimed that you had invested** in gold and you were rich when you were 20.

⑥ They **added that the service was / added that the service had been** absolutely amazing.

⑦ They **admitted that the profits were** down by 10 percent.

⑧ He **explained that he had** a terrible headache and he had to leave early.

⑨ She **claimed that she made / claimed that she had made** her first million dollars before she had left college.

71.6
① True **②** True **③** False **④** Not given
⑤ True **⑥** False **⑦** False **⑧** False

71.7 🔊
① Edward admitted that he had forgotten the tickets.

② I said that I would meet them at the café.

③ They agreed that they didn't like the hotel.

④ Elsa added that she also knew how to cook.

⑤ You suggested that we go out for dinner.

⑥ He argued that it wasn't his turn to do the dishes.

⑦ We explained that we had already eaten dinner.

72

72.1 🔊
① She reminded me to buy some pizzas.

② I asked him to help me with my project.

③ They encouraged me to buy tickets.

④ I ordered him to drive more slowly.

⑤ She asked me to walk the dog.

72.2 🔊
① He encouraged us to try the new restaurant.

② They asked me to give an important presentation.

③ The police ordered him to stop driving.

④ I reminded her to meet me at 8:30pm.

72.3 🔊
① I reminded my daughter to **do** her homework.

② Lucy asked me to **book** the tickets online.

③ Mary **encouraged me** to take some time off.

④ My boss **ordered** me to complete the report.

⑤ Joe **asked** me to do the dishes.

⑥ Annie reminded me **to** buy some bread and milk.

⑦ I encouraged everyone **to** try their best.

72.4
1 Ⓑ **2** Ⓐ **3** Ⓕ **4** Ⓔ **5** Ⓒ **6** Ⓓ

72.5
① Orders him to buy his lunch

② It's not part of his job

③ Remind his boss that he doesn't have time

④ Derek should look for a new job

⑤ It's a good idea

72.6 🔊
① Jack warned me not to be late for my interview.

② Chris persuaded her to fly, even though she was nervous.

③ My lawyer advised me to think carefully about the contract.

④ I didn't want to buy a pet dog, but the children persuaded me.

⑤ It was a very windy day, so the police warned people not to travel.

⑥ I warned them to cycle carefully, because it was very dark outside.

⑦ My boss advised me not to be late for the meeting.

72.7 🔊
① She **ordered** them **to get out** of her office.

② They **asked** her **to give** a presentation.

③ My teacher **encouraged** me **to try** my best all the time.

④ Her boss **advised** her **not to forget** about the meeting.

⑤ I **warned** them **not to cycle** downtown.

⑥ She **reminded** them **to take** time out for lunch.

⑦ I **asked** her **not to be** late for dinner.

⑧ She **asked** him **to clean** the kitchen.

⑨ My friends **advised** me **to look** for a new job.

⑩ I **encouraged** Anna **to wear** her new jacket for the interview.

⑪ They **ordered** everyone **to be** quiet.
⑫ He **warned** us **to be** careful downtown at night.
⑬ I **reminded** Lucy **to get** new passport photos.
⑭ He **asked** me **not to use** the computer because he needed it.
⑮ They **persuaded** me **to invest** in the company.

72.8 🔊
1. They warned me not to go in the water.
2. They warned me not to buy a new house.
3. They warned me not to buy a new car.
4. He warned me not to go in the water.
5. He warned me not to buy a new house.
6. He warned me not to buy a new car.
7. They persuaded me not to go in the water.
8. They persuaded me not to buy a new house.
9. They persuaded me not to buy a new car.
10. He persuaded me not to go in the water.
11. He persuaded me not to buy a new house.
12. He persuaded me not to buy a new car.

73

73.1 🔊
① She asked me what I was doing.
② He asked her what he could do to help.
③ We asked her what time it was.
④ They asked him where he was going.
⑤ I asked her who was at the meeting.
⑥ She asked me when I would work.
⑦ He asked him where he could sit.
⑧ I asked you what you were doing.
⑨ She asked me where she should park.
⑩ They asked him when he would arrive.
⑪ We asked them why they were leaving.

73.2 🔊
① She asked me **where they would have lunch**.
② I asked them **what time the conference was**.
③ She asked him **why he couldn't come to the office**.
④ We asked them **why they were leaving early**.
⑤ I asked you **when we would start the meeting**.

73.3 🔊
① I asked you why you were late.
② She asked him where they would live.
③ We asked you what we were going to discuss.
④ I asked her who was chairing the meeting.
⑤ They asked me what they could do to help.

73.4
① Reported ② Direct
③ Direct ④ Reported

73.5 🔊
① I asked him who he knew.
② She asked me where I lived.
③ They asked us what we did.
④ We asked her what she wanted.
⑤ He asked me who I liked.
⑥ I asked him where he worked.
⑦ She asked us when we arrived.

73.6
① Ed asked Elsa / He asked her when the speakers would give their speeches.
② Ed asked Elsa / He asked her what kind of topics the speeches would be about.
③ Ed asked Elsa / He asked her when tickets went on sale.
④ Ed asked Elsa / He asked her where people could get tickets.

73.7 🔊
① He asked me **where I went on vacation every year**.
② She asked me **what time we were having lunch with Jamie the next day**.
③ She asked me **why we couldn't get a taxi to work instead of waiting for the bus**.
④ He asked me **what kind of music I usually liked to listen to**.
⑤ She asked me **when the rock concert by the famous Swedish rock band finished**.
⑥ He asked me **what company I worked for in southern Buenos Aires**.

73.8 🔊
① At the meeting, Mr. Thomas raised **the question** of funding.
② We need to raise **awareness** about the dangers of climate change.
③ When asked to vote, nearly everyone raised their **hands**.
④ The cheering was so loud, it nearly raised **the roof**.
⑤ Falling interest rates are raising **fears** among investors.

74

74.1 🔊 Note: All answers can also be written with "whether" instead of "if."
① He asked me **if we were going to be on time**.
② He asked her **if that woman was her boss**.
③ She asked me **if I had the sales figures**.
④ We asked him **if he had brought the files**.
⑤ I asked her **if she would like some coffee**.
⑥ I asked them **if they had met the sales team**.
⑦ She asked me **if the train was on time**.
⑧ He asked her **if Helen was working late**.
⑨ You asked me **if I had written the report**.

74.2 🔊
1. I asked them if they wanted to meet for coffee.
2. I asked them if they would be at the meeting.
3. I asked them if you wanted to meet for coffee.
4. I asked them if you would be at the meeting.
5. I asked you if they wanted to meet for coffee.
6. I asked you if they would be at the meeting.
7. I asked you if you wanted to meet for coffee.
8. I asked you if you would be at the meeting.
9. She asked them if they wanted to meet for coffee.
10. She asked them if they would be at the meeting.
11. She asked them if you wanted to meet for coffee.
12. She asked them if you would be at the meeting.
13. She asked you if they wanted to meet for coffee.
14. She asked you if they would be at the meeting.
15. She asked you if you wanted to meet for coffee.
16. She asked you if you would be at the meeting.

74.3
① True ② True ③ False ④ True ⑤ False

74.4 🔊
① She asked him if he had **seen** the new sales figures.

② I asked **her** if she wanted another glass of water.

③ Mr. Salter asked them **whether** they had met their targets.

④ We asked the secretary if she **would** order us a taxi.

⑤ He asked us if we **had been** waiting for a long time.

⑥ Janet asked **them** if they knew when the meeting would start.

74.5 ◀))

① She asked him if he played soccer or golf.

② He asked me if I spoke Italian or French.

③ She asked me if I wanted water or fruit juice.

④ He asked whether they should go by bus or taxi.

⑤ I asked her whether she preferred music or art.

74.6 ◀))

① She asked him if **he liked Eva or Liz.**

② I asked them whether **they played tennis or chess.**

③ They asked me if **I spoke Arabic or Chinese.**

④ We asked her if **she would like tea or coffee.**

⑤ You asked us if **we wanted milk or cream.**

⑥ She asked her if **she preferred books or magazines.**

⑦ He asked me if **he should call or text her.**

⑧ They asked us if **we would like cookies or cake.**

⑨ She asked me whether **I preferred TV or movies.**

⑩ We asked them whether **they would prefer to be famous or rich.**

⑪ He asked him if **he liked dogs or cats.**

74.7 ◀))

① I can always **count on** my family to support me in difficult times.

② Sheila works very hard because she wants to **provide for** her children.

③ I work in a bank, but I **dream of** becoming a famous soccer star.

④ The flood was terrible! Water **poured into** all the houses on the street.

⑤ The driver was **accused of** causing the accident by driving too quickly.

⑥ The campaigners promised to **fight against** the government's decision.

74.8

① I knew what time the meeting was

② they could present this month's figures

③ he wanted to give a presentation

④ she could organize refreshments

⑤ she would like to attend

75

75.1 ◀))

① Could you tell me what time it is in the United Arab Emirates?

② Do you know where I can buy interesting illustrated books for my children?

③ Do you know where the new science museum for children is?

④ Could you tell me how far the station is from my new neighborhood?

⑤ Could you tell me when the next train for London leaves?

⑥ Do you know why Tom and Andrea were late for the meeting yesterday?

⑦ Do you know how long it will take to travel from Los Angeles to Washington?

⑧ Do you know when the sales presentation for the new product starts?

⑨ Could you tell me when the meeting for the new members in the team starts?

⑩ Could you tell me how much the flight to Edinburgh will cost?

75.2

① Indirect ② Indirect ③ Direct
④ Direct ⑤ Indirect

75.3 ◀)) Note: You can replace "Do you know" with "Could you tell me" in all answers.

① Do you know where the museum is?

② Do you know how much a pizza and salad is?

③ Do you know how I get to Newmarket?

④ Do you know what time we should leave?

⑤ Do you know why the train is delayed?

⑥ Do you know how much those shoes are?

⑦ Do you know how far it is to the hotel?

75.4 ◀))

① Do you know why the movie hasn't started?

② Do you know how I can find the museum?

③ Could you tell me if the taxi is here yet?

④ Do you know how far it is to the station?

⑤ Do you know if Tom is at home?

⑥ Do you know how much the tickets will cost?

⑦ Do you know how much fruit we need?

75.5 ◀))

① There's the movie theater. Could you tell me when the movie starts?

② The sky looks cloudy. Do you know whether it is raining?

③ I want to drive into town. Do you know where my car keys are?

④ Joe wants to buy something. Do you know when the stores open?

⑤ I'd like to sit down. Could you tell me if this chair is occupied?

⑥ I don't have any cash. Do you know if there's a bank nearby?

⑦ I'd like to buy a magazine. Do you know where the corner shop is?

⑧ We need coffee. Could you tell me where a nice café is?

⑨ I want to go surfing. Do you know how far it is to the beach?

⑩ I want to learn French. Do you know if this tutor is good?

⑪ I'd like to go for a walk. Could you tell me where the park is?

75.6 ◀)) Note: You can replace "Do you know" with "Could you tell me" in all answers. You can also replace "if" with "whether."

① Do you know what you would like to do in the evening after the soccer game?

② Do you know where the nearest restaurant to my sister's new house is?

③ Do you know if those traditional dresses are made of silk or cotton?

④ Do you know if the flight to Barcelona is delayed or canceled?

⑤ Do you know if the train from Denver has arrived yet?

75.7 ◀)) Note: You can replace "Do you know" with "Could you tell me" in all answers. You can also replace "if" with "whether."

① Do you know when this house was built?

② Do you know if this table is reserved?

③ Do you know if this is Italian or Spanish cheese?

④ Do you know why the hotel restaurant is closed?

⑤ Do you know if there's a gym near here?

76.1 🔊

1. I wish we **lived** in a bigger house in a nice neighborhood.
2. I wish I **didn't** have to drive to work today.
3. I wish we **ate** Japanese food more often.
4. I wish the dog **would** stop barking at the children.

76.2 🔊

1. I've got some travel brochures. I wish I could go traveling.
2. I want to learn French. I wish I could speak French.
3. The children are fighting. I wish the children wouldn't fight.
4. I'd love a pet. I wish I had a small puppy.
5. I have to call my boss. I wish I didn't have to call my boss.

76.3 🔊

1. I wish I could afford a new car.
2. I wish I had a winter coat.
3. I wish my house wasn't so cold.
4. I wish I lived on the coast.
5. I wish that child wasn't screaming.
6. I wish I had a trumpet.
7. I wish I could speak Italian.
8. I wish I had a cat.
9. I wish I didn't have to work so hard.
10. I wish I could go swimming.
11. I wish I could afford a vacation.
12. I wish I had enough time.
13. I wish I liked my neighbors.
14. I wish I could cook Chinese food.
15. I wish I had long hair.

76.4 🔊 Note: Contracted and long forms of the past perfect are possible for all answers.

1. I'm late. I wish I **had woken up** an hour earlier.
2. I've failed my driving test. I wish I **had had** more lessons.
3. I feel sick. I wish I **hadn't eaten** so much dessert.
4. It's raining. I wish I **had brought** my new umbrella.
5. I've missed my appointment. I wish I **had taken** a taxi and not the bus.
6. I don't like my bedroom. I wish I **hadn't painted** it orange.
7. I don't like this movie. I wish I **had stayed** at home.
8. This food is terrible. I wish I **had chosen** a different restaurant.
9. I've lost my bag. I wish I **hadn't brought** it with me.
10. I'm really tired. I wish I **had gone** to bed earlier last night.
11. I've broken this vase. I wish I **hadn't dropped** it on the floor.
12. I'm hungry. I wish I **had eaten** some breakfast.
13. I've got a flat tire. I wish I **hadn't driven** to work this morning.

76.5 🔊

1. That concert was terrible. I wish **we hadn't gone**.
2. The wind is howling outside. I wish **it would stop**.
3. We've missed the last bus home. I wish **there was a taxi**.
4. Joe didn't get the job. I wish **he had prepared better**.
5. I've never been to India. I wish **I had gone last year**.
6. It's cold and rainy outside. I wish **the weather was better**.
7. That was rude. I wish **you hadn't said that**.

76.6

1. Visit more often
2. More traveling
3. Australia
4. Somewhere hot and sunny
5. Spanish

Acknowledgments

The publisher would like to thank:
Jo Kent, Trish Burrow, and Emma Watkins for additional text; Thomas Booth, Helen Fanthorpe, Helen Leech, Carrie Lewis, and Vicky Richards for editorial assistance; Stephen Bere, Sarah Hilder, Amy Child, Fiona Macdonald, and Simon Murrell for additional design work; Simon Mumford for maps and national flags; Peter Chrisp for fact checking; Penny Hands, Amanda Learmonth, and Carrie Lewis for proofreading; Elizabeth Wise for indexing; Tatiana Boyko, Rory Farrell, Clare Joyce, and Viola Wang for additional illustrations; Liz Hammond for editing audio scripts and managing audio recordings; Hannah Bowen and Scarlett O'Hara for compiling audio scripts; Jordan Killiard for mixing and mastering audio recordings; Heather Hughes, Tommy Callan, Tom Morse, Gillian Reid, and Sonia Charbonnier for creative technical support; Priyanka Kharbanda, Suefa Lee, Shramana Purkayastha, Isha Sharma, Sheryl Sadana for editorial support; Yashashvi Choudhary, Jaileen Kaur, Bhavika Mathur, Richa Verma, Anita Yadav, Apurva Agarwal for design support; Deepak Negi and Nishwan Rasool for picture research; Rohan Sinha for managerial and moral support.

All images © Dorling Kindersley Limited
For more information, please visit
www.dk.com/uk/information/contact-us